50 WIGAN LEGENDS
IN THEIR OWN WORDS

RICHARD DE LA RIVIERE

LP

League Publications Ltd
Wellington House
Briggate
Brighouse HD6 1DN
England

First published in Great Britain in 2023
by League Publications Ltd

A CIP catalogue record for this book is available
from the British Library

ISBN: 978-1-901347-42-5

Designed and Typeset by League Publications Limited
Printed by H Charlesworth & Co Ltd, Wakefield

CONTENTS

INTRODUCTION

I've been interviewing Rugby League players past and present since 2005, and here are 50 of the best I've done with those who graced the fields of Central Park and the DW Stadium.

Around a third of the interviews in this book are reproduced exactly how they went into League Express or Rugby League World magazine at the time. About a third have been updated and approximately a third have never been published before.

The first of the 50 I spoke to was Terry Newton, who was the cover star of a magazine called Thirteen I published in 2005, and I'm still scarred from the experience of trying to sell copies at Knowsley Road one evening. Unable to update the article with Terry, his biographer Phil Wilkinson kindly gave me an insight into his dealings with Terry and into the tragic events of September 2010.

The only other interviewee to have passed away since I spoke to him is the great Bill Ashurst who died in 2022. He told me some fabulous stories. I can vividly picture his mother chasing him around the house with a poker when he told her he was going to become a dad at 17, and I can still hear his laughter as he recounted the tale.

My thanks go to everybody featured in this book, and in particular to Green Vigo for providing the foreword. I'm sure Green won't mind me saying that it took about a year for me, John Gray, Graham Starkey and Roy Seddon, the scout who signed him in South Africa in 1973, to persuade him to speak to me. I'm sure you'll agree it was worth the wait. His life story is truly remarkable.

My thanks also go to Martyn Sadler, the chair of League Publications Ltd, for publishing this book and to Stephen Ibbetson for the splendid design work. Wigan Warriors have been wonderful to deal with, especially Alastair Hancock, Stewart Frodsham, Dave Swanton and Kris Radlinski. Keith Sutch, who runs the club's past players' association, set up several interviews with those who wore the cherry and white in the 1960s and 1970s, and I could not be more grateful to him for that.

RICHARD DE LA RIVIERE
JULY 2023

FOREWORD

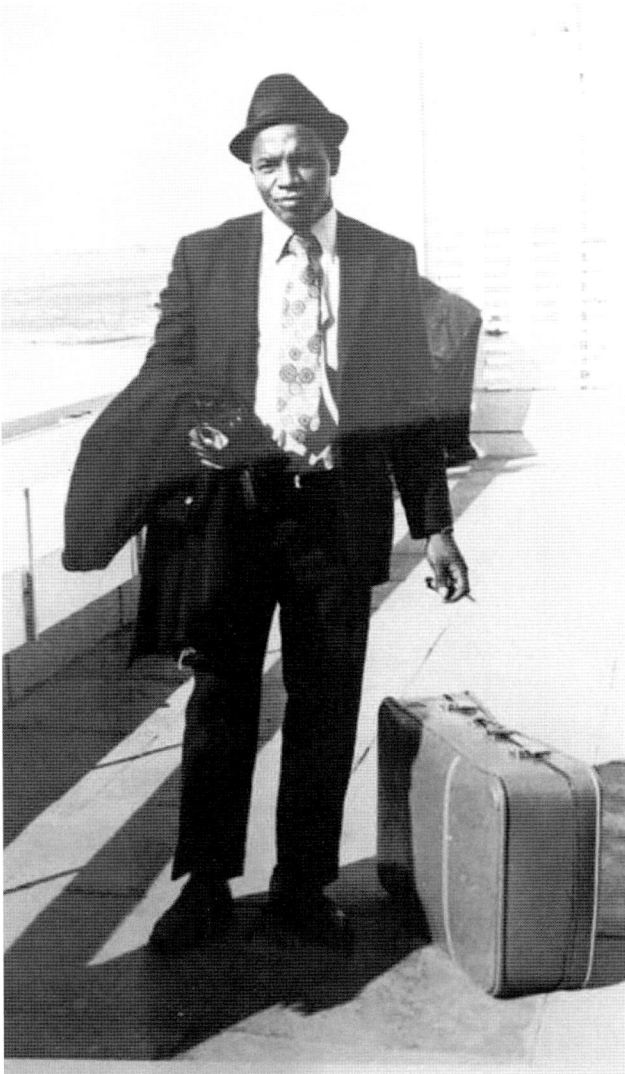

It was the biggest honour of my life to play for Wigan, and I can't quite believe that all these years later, people are still interested in my career and in what I have to say.

When I see who else is interviewed in this book, it's fantastic to appear alongside them. Many of them won far more than I did and played in better teams, but I'm still proud of what we achieved at Wigan in what were difficult times for the club.

I played at Central Park with some incredible players like my best friend Bill Ashurst, John Gray, Keiron O'Loughlin, George Fairbairn, Bill Francis, Colin Clarke and my centre David Hill. Five of them are interviewed in this book. I even played alongside the great Kurt Sorensen in the 1976-77 season, but he slipped through Wigan's net and became a superstar elsewhere.

I enjoyed people telling me they had liked reading my interview with Richard when it was published in League Express, and I'm glad it's reproduced in this book for anyone who didn't read it. At least people know I'm still alive despite various reports to the contrary!

As I explained in my interview, it wasn't all sweetness and light for me at the club, but whenever I see Wigan on the television, I smile to myself and know that I played for the biggest and best rugby club in the world.

GREEN VIGO
JULY 2023

JOE LYDON

1986-1994

One of three Wiganers in the Widnes team that beat Wigan at Wembley in 1984, Joe Lydon scored two long-range tries and won the Lance Todd Trophy. Two seasons later, he was in the cherry and white after a world-record £100,000 transfer. The wonderfully talented Lydon enjoyed a glorious eight-and-a-half years as a Wigan player, winning dozens of trophies. He excelled for Great Britain and played for Eastern Suburbs in the Winfield Cup.

WHAT better way to prepare for a Joe Lydon interview than hopping onto YouTube to relive his greatest moments? Those Wembley tries for Widnes. Finishing off that stunning length-of-the-field move against the Kiwis. His classic try against Australia against Old Trafford - "No one did that to Garry Jack," Wally Lewis once told me. The 61-yard drop goal against Warrington in 1989. They're all there.

Lydon hit the big time at the age of 11, playing at Wembley in the traditional 11-year old's curtain raiser before the 1975 Challenge Cup Final. His Wigan Schools' side lost 8-0 to Widnes before the Chemics beat Warrington 14-7 in the main event.

"What an experience at such a young age," said Lydon. "Mike Gregory sadly didn't make the game because he had a tummy bug. David Hulme played for Widnes. Both teams went down on the same coach. Staying in a hotel was new for most of us. Both sets of players were probably all too nervous to play the game as well as we could, it was an occasion to be treasured. We got to meet the Widnes Challenge Cup-winning players, and I got a picture with Mick Adams and Eric Hughes. Nine years later, I was playing alongside them at Wembley."

"I played in such a strong Wigan St Pats team. Shaun Wane, Andy Platt, Ian Gormley, Dave Woods, Kevin Eagan, Mike Gregory and I eventually turned pro, following in the footsteps of many others from the club. I'd known Mike from playing with and against each other at school - union on a Saturday and League on a Sunday. We went to sixth-form college together and were mates for life - as it turned out, not long enough by half. I'm not sure if Mike ever had a chance to play for our hometown Wigan, but he was totally committed to Warrington.

"I got a call from Mike one Sunday morning. He'd had problems with his neck and thumbs, thinking it was some sort of nerve damage. The prognosis turned out to be as bleak as it gets, telling me he had Motor Neurone Disease. I didn't know much about this terrible disease then. A lot of us were probably in denial. I didn't quite believe it would take him so young. He was so full of life, as a captain and leader at Warrington and with Great Britain. In our social circles, he was just a great person to be with. It was tough. I still think about him so often and the same old stories get told every time his many friends get together. As my best man, he met his wife Erica at our wedding as she was maid of honour. Greg was living with me at the time - not that I asked him to, he just decided he was! That was Greg.

"He'd have gone on to be a great coach. He was already proving that. Like Vince Karalius, who coached me at Widnes, Mike had an aura about him. He could bring people together, as he did with the England Academy team that beat Australia in 2002. A mark of Mike was his decision to go to Swinton as a young coach, having been assistant to Shaun McRae at St Helens. I said, 'Are you sure you want to go to Swinton? It sounds like a tough gig,' but he said, 'I need to go and learn my craft. I need to go away and be a head coach somewhere else.' A lot of people, myself included, would have stayed at St Helens or looked for another easier and more lucrative pathway. One of the sad things about his illness was he'd started to master coaching. The illness cut his dream career short as well as his life."

THE INVINCIBLES provided the opposition for Lydon's sixth start as a professional Rugby League player, having joined Widnes from Wigan St Pats. The 1982 Kangaroos would go on to win all 22 of their matches and would be regarded as one of the greatest teams ever assembled. The 18-year-old graphic-design student had already started at fullback and wing, underlining his versatility from the outset of his professional career. This was just his second start at centre.

"I had no intention of going to Wigan or anyone else, but Dougie Laughton persuaded me to go to Widnes," he said. "I remember meeting Ged Byrne in Wigan outside a sports shop one Saturday. He'd already signed for Salford from St Pats. He was a phenomenal player. He said I should sign because I'd enjoy it. Ged was a great player and as tough as teak. He once hit Ron Gibbs in a tackle in a game against Castleford one day, and I'll never forget it. Ged liked a smoke and still does. In my mind, I can see Ged putting out a cigarette with his boot just before he hit Gibbs. His timing in closing the gap on people in the tackle was an art to watch unless you were the one carrying the ball.

"I loved fullback because you could go more or less where you wanted and do what you wanted in those days. I mostly played centre or wing. I probably wouldn't have played centre at Wembley in 1984 if Tony Myler had been fit. There's another great player – probably one of the most underrated stand-offs in the game. It didn't matter to me where I was picked in the backs, but if you were fullback, you could pop up at wing or centre.

"I can remember that Widnes v Australia game clearly. I was very disappointed to lose. If we could have beaten Australia with Widnes or Wigan, it would have been one of the pinnacles of my career. It may well have been the catalyst for international victories against Australia when they had the better of us. I also remember a girl-guide band on at half-time, and we couldn't get them off the pitch. Wally Lewis just stood there looking bemused.

"I played right centre with Keiron O'Loughlin on the left. He was a fellow Wiganer. I looked up to him like he was my big brother. At a scrum, the Australia centres, Steve Rogers and Mal Meninga, doubled up on my side. "They're both on this side," I shouted over to Keiron, hoping for some help. "Good luck!" he shouted back. Thanks Keiron!

"I watched the Ashes in 1982, and I learned from it. I realised how good Australia were, but I knew I wasn't ready for it. I probably wasn't ready to play France in 1983 which was my debut [Lydon scored a try and three goals in a 20-5 win]. People say, 'If you're good enough, you're old enough', but in that era, you had to earn your respect in the team as well. You needed a bedrock of understanding as well as any natural talent."

If Lydon wasn't ready in 1983, it wasn't long before he was. In a dream 1984, he scooped the Lance Todd Trophy for two stunning Wembley tries. Five days later, he was crowned the Division One player of the year, the young player of the year and then the Greenall Whitley Man of Steel. He was just 20 years and six months.

"It was special to be recognised in such a strong field," he said. "Kevin Tamati had a phenomenal game at Wembley. He actually played in one boot and one trainer in the second half, and he was still fantastic. If I hadn't scored my second try, he'd have won the Lance Todd, and he should have done. As for player of the year, there was my roommate from the 1984 tour Garry Schofield and my Widnes teammate Tony Myler. If Tony had played at Wembley and gone on the tour, he'd probably be ranked as an all-time great.

"The coach Vince Karalius had an aura about him. He was miles ahead of his time. Andy Gregory and Keiron O'Loughlin were there. Senior players like Mick Adams, Eric Prescott and Keiron were great in their on-field coaching. They had a calmness and confidence about them. I remember Vince saying, 'If anyone waves when we come out of the tunnel, you won't start the game.' Several Wigan players waved to their families, but not us. Vince had dominated and played the game at the highest level. He was as tough as they came, but he had an understanding and empathy with players. I just had massive respect for him. He was a natural leader - charismatic and a good person. The day after the Wembley final, I hadn't been in bed long when he got me and David Hulme up. 'It's time to thank the Lord,' he said, and he took us to church."

It was inevitable that Lydon would be named on the 1984 Lions tour of Papua New Guinea, Australia and New Zealand. Great Britain were more competitive in the Ashes, but they were still whitewashed.

"I remember how naïve we were on the tour - how young we were in our attitude to performance," he said. "In one of the first training sessions, we were all in different kits, having more of a kick about in Centennial Park in Sydney than a proper pre-game session. The Australians seemed far better prepared, and the results back it up. We lost three Tests in Australia and three in New Zealand. People said we were closer to Australia than Great Britain had been in 1982, but we never really threatened them, in my opinion."

SUPERSTARS was Lydon's next project, as he emulated Keith Fielding and Des Drummond by appearing on the BBC programme, pitting his athletic prowess against the likes of rower Steve Redgrave, the four-time Olympic gold medallist. Lydon beat Redgrave to come second behind the swimmer Robin Brew. "I can't remember how it came about," said Lydon, "but it was a great experience, and it was great to meet new people. Colin Deans, the Scottish rugby union hooker, was there and so were Stuart Pearson the footballer and Phil Brown the sprinter.

The 1985 New Zealanders were a much bigger challenge, of course. They had just taken part in a colossal Trans-Tasman series, losing two games to one to Australia, but they had won the third Test 18-0. Their series with Great Britain was even tighter, ending one game each with the third - which resembled a warzone - finishing 6-all. In the first Test, Lydon finished off a stunning move to give Great Britain the lead with eight minutes left. "This is classed by Hugh McGahan as the worst forward pass in international Rugby League history," laughed Lydon, as I showed him the video of him catching Ellery Hanley's dubious pass to score. "It was a very physical series. They had a massive pack with Kurt Sorensen, Mark Graham, Hugh and the Tamatis. They were always good series."

Garry Schofield once told me a story about Lydon. Maurice Bamford was giving the Great Britain players a team talk, using a flipchart. He turned it over a few times, detailing various tactical ploys. And then he flipped it over again to reveal enormous and badly drawn genitalia. The room descended into chaos with everyone in fits of laughter as the bemused coach studied the obscenity. Lydon looked slightly sheepish as I told him the story. "Maurice was great, and I really liked him," he laughed. "If that was me, then I apologise. But I think it was actually a picture of a backside."

Within a couple of months, Lydon was a Wigan player, switching to Central Park for a record £100,000 fee. His elder brother John had been linked Wigan, but Joe was happy to put pen to paper in January 1986. Widnes coach Eric Hughes was so angry at losing his young star that he resigned. "I still remember the phone call from one of the Wigan directors, saying they wanted me," Lydon recalled. "Being a cocky sod, I said, 'They won't sell me.' He replied: "They just have." So that put me in a real position of strength. I loved my time at Widnes. They were a good team of experienced players and coaches, and I learned an awful lot about myself, the sport and what it takes to win.

"My move to Wigan came out of the blue. I was told later that Widnes needed money to redevelop the ground, so they put Tony Myler and me on the transfer list without anyone knowing. I think we were offered round a few clubs, and Wigan came in. It was Tom Rathbone, the Wigan director, who made it happen. It felt right very quickly. They had players like Shaun Edwards and Shaun Wane. They had just signed Ellery Hanley, Andy Goodway and Andy Gregory. Things started to click."

In Lydon's first full season, Wigan won the 1986-87 league title in style. Lydon scored 22 tries. Hanley touched down an incredible 59 times, although it was actually Brian Case who was the club's player of the year. What did the Kiwi Graham Lowe change after his appointment in the summer of 1986? "Graham brought a different feel to it all," said Lydon. "I had massive respect for Colin Clarke and Alan McInnes, and they were unlucky to be cut by the board, but after the 1982 Kangaroo Tour, there was a perception that Australian players and coaches were a level above and that clubs with ambition needed an overseas coach. Did he make that much of a difference? He brought technique and we prepared for games differently, but I think it was a collective effort. He and the management brought key players together. We would talk about how we would influence the game, but the key factor was that we had more time together and were more professional as a squad. One of Graham's strong points was his ability to be your friend during the week and your boss at the weekend.

"As for Brian Case, he was brilliant. Players like him and Ian Potter didn't always get the recognition they deserved.

Brian didn't do anything massively spectacular, but he was so solid. Games were won on the back of brilliance, but people like Brian were the bedrock. Every team needs ultra-dependable players like Brian and Potts."

Wigan were soon world champions. Six months after winning their first title in 27 years, Maurice Lindsay invited Australian premiers, Manly-Warringah Sea Eagles over, offering them £20,000 if they could beat Wigan. They couldn't. Wigan won a tryless match 8-2 with 36,895 spectators in attendance. Lydon was high tackled by Ron Gibbs, who was sent off, and stamped on by Dale Shearer.

"We fielded a full English team, including Richard Russell on the wing, which most people forget," said Lydon. "Dean Bell didn't play, and Graeme West was an unused sub. We knew how good Ron Gibbs was, and how tough he was, so we told Shaun Wane that Ron's reputation was that he was tough, but that he'd go soft if he got into him early. Andy Greg said, 'If you hit him in the first scrum, it'll make our day so much easier.' At half-time, Shaun was a bit bashed and bruised, and said, 'He's not as soft as you think!' 'Keep at it,' we urged him. The Australian press came in after the game to award the man of the match, and they plumped for Shaun based on how well he'd played and handled Ron Gibbs, 'the Golden Gloves champion of Australia!' I won't tell you what Shaun said, but we were howling with laughter.

"When you're with a successful team, it's really special. Wigan played Cronulla in the 2017 World Club Challenge, which was 30 years on from us beating Manly. Shaun Wane was the Wigan coach, and he invited us to present the jerseys to the Wigan team. We met up the day before the game and it was as if the Manly game had been a fortnight earlier. The conversations, the banter, the camaraderie and the nicknames were the same. It was the same with a Roosters reunion I went to recently. It's a special thing to be involved in."

Six months later, Lydon was back at Wembley, this time in a Wigan jersey. The opponents were the holders Halifax. Lydon scored a try and created another for Hanley in a thumping 32-12 win. It was the first of eight Wembley wins for the club, with Lydon also featuring in 1989, 1990, 1992 and 1993.

"Along with Keiron O'Loughlin and Andy Gregory, I'd taken some stick for being a Wiganer in the Widnes team that beat Wigan in 1984. So to go to Wembley with Wigan was special. When I made the break for Ellery, it was a set move that went slightly wrong. It should have been a switch play to Henderson Gill off the restart, but we were a little out of sync, so I just went through. There was no way I was going to score though, not with Ellery demanding the ball! Ellery was mentally and physically tough with great skill. He was just naturally gifted and so driven. His best position was loose forward because he was in the middle of everything. Opposing players often worried about him too much, so everyone else got more space which was great with many capable of exploiting it.

"The St Helens game in 1989 was massive. The atmosphere was electric. Steve Hampson had missed several cup finals with injury, and I was chuffed to give him a pass to score in the left corner, running towards the tunnel end. The team comes together in moments like that. We knew how to prepare for Wembley. We had a belief in ourselves, a desire to win and we knew how important togetherness was.

"We'd train at Central Park on the Thursday before leaving for London. One year Taffy the groundsman, Derek Jones, decided we'd had enough time because he

was preparing the pitch for the Premiership game the week after, so he started cutting the grass. We're playing at Wembley two days later, and here's the groundsman driving a tractor through the training session! It was a good place to be - not too serious and not so professional that it was daunting. They were a special group of people on and off the pitch. We had a competitive mindset and enjoyed the big occasions."

LIKE many of his Great Britain teammates, Lydon spent time in Australia's Winfield Cup. He played for Eastern Suburbs, known now as Sydney Roosters, in 1987 and 1989. "I loved it there," he said. "I had a great time. In an ideal world, I'd have stayed in Australia, but I had a contract to come back to. We were allowed to have off-seasons over there. Hugh McGahan played for them. Dean Bell was there in alternate years to me. In '87, I shared a house with Trevor Gillmeister and Brendan Hall. It was a great experience. We were coached by Arthur Beetson who was a special individual. He was similar to Vince Karalius in that he had a presence in the sport and had an aura about him. He was a good bloke who you could talk to and learn from. Looking back, I probably didn't realise how big Beatso and Vince were in the sport and how lucky I was to know and be coached by them.

"I stay in regular contact with Hugh McGahan, the former Kiwi and Roosters captain. We went from international rivals to teammates. Like Dean Bell, he was a true leader on the field and a true friend off it.

"I landed on a Thursday morning in May 1987, and we drove to Canberra on the Saturday. I was down to play reserve grade. The whole reserve team would then be substitutes for the first-team game which was straight after. Sure enough, after playing the entire reserve game, I came on in the first-grade match after five minutes because the winger David French tore his calf muscle. Throw in the post-match drinks, and I probably slept for about three days after that!"

In 1989, Martin Offiah joined Lydon at Easts and they beat Western Suburbs 12-10 at the Sydney Football Stadium. Playing for the latter were Ellery Hanley, Kelvin Skerrett and Garry Schofield. "I don't remember that game too well, but there were so many British players in Sydney in 1989. We used to get together for a Monday club - a bit like a book club for the Poms but with a slightly different twist!"

ONE character that looms large in the Joe Lydon story is Andy Gregory, with whom he played for Widnes, Wigan, Lancashire and Great Britain. I showed Lydon a clip of him scoring the only try in the 1987 Premiership Final in which Wigan beat Warrington 8-0, and it precipitated a chat about the wily halfback. Gregory chipped through on his own 20-metre line, Lydon hacked forward and beat a number of defenders including Des Drummond to score. Few scrum-halves would have done what Gregory did, but such audacity made him a legend.

"You wouldn't normally expect Greg to kick that, but he had a licence to do things like that, or at least he thought he did!" Lydon said. "The more you played with him, the more you knew he'd try things like that. If it didn't work, he'd blame you! He once took a goal-line drop out and hit his own post. It was my fault for not taking it apparently! When he was on fire, he was unstoppable, and so often he and Giz [Shaun Edwards] were the spark. If you watch the Halifax and Saints Wembley finals, it's as if they were playing the game at a different speed to everyone else and creating havoc before passing the ball onto powerhouses like Hanley, Iro and Bell. We had a team of winners and several jokers.

"When I kicked goals, one of the subs would bring on a bucket of sand. At training, prior to a home game when Ged Byrne was on the bench, Greg and I got the metal fire bucket that held the sand on the sideline, took the sand out and filled most of it with bricks and then water and placed it back in its usual place but hid the small plastic scoop which was used to bring on enough sand to take the kick. Greg said, 'First penalty on the far side, call for the sand,' so I did. Unable to find the scoop, Ged panicked,

grabbed the full bucket on the run, and his arm nearly came out of its joint. He staggered on with it, put it down, and I said, 'I've changed my mind. I'm kicking for touch.' 'Oh no you're not you ******!' as he stood there with one arm longer than the other."

Lydon and Gregory played in the 1989 Challenge Cup semi-final against Warrington when Lydon landed an astonishing 73rd-minute, 61-yard drop goal from within his own half to put Wigan a point ahead at 7-6, having just kicked a difficult penalty to level the scores. "We should have been further up the field," admitted Lydon. "For once, both Greg and Giz had run up their own backsides on the two plays before. Steve Hampson was near me, and he said, "Just hit it." So I did. If I'd thought about it for a long time, I probably wouldn't have gone for it. Mike Gregory later told me it broke Warrington because their heads dropped. It was just one point, but it gave us the lead, then Giz sealed it with a late try. They had a great pack with Boyd, Tamati, Gregory and Jackson, but we knew we had the ability if we got the ball a little bit wider."

I asked Lydon to name other stand-out moments. "There were tries that might not have been great, but they were important," he said. There was the drop goal at Halifax in the snow in 1993. I scored a try for Eastern Suburbs in the final round of 1987 that was important. I smile - and Brian Noble continues to complain - when remembering that the 1988-1995 run of cup wins started with a 2-0 win against Bradford. Nobby will try and persuade you that while others argued the toss on whether or not it was a penalty, I 'stole' five metres to be closer to the sticks to make the kick from around halfway. It's not true. It was more like ten metres!"

I was keen to know more about the Wigan dressing-room dynamic. What sort of personalities were at the club? How did they get on? And what was their collective social life like? "There were three groups," said Lydon. "Those who liked a laugh and a giggle before a game like myself, Andy Gregory and Martin Dermott. Some lads were physically sick before a game like Steve Hampson and Dean Bell. Ged Byrne couldn't eat properly before a big game! Then there were those – mainly forwards – who were ultra-aggressive. The dynamics worked and the dressing-room was a fun place to be. You were left to prepare how you wanted to prepare as long as you got yourself right.

"We had a beer on Thursdays after training. Some players travelled back to Yorkshire so maybe not them, but the nucleus of the team had a beer, and it didn't get out of hand much - maybe the bus back from Wembley was a bit lively. I remember playing Warrington in an early kick-off one day. We won and the chat was we were having a barbeque afterwards. 'Great,' I said. 'Where's the barbeque?' 'Your place!' Players from other teams might turn up too. We enjoyed each other's company. You need social time together to grow a team that can perform on the pitch.

"We still enjoy each other's company and that's the same for those I played against. I was at a Lions reunion in 2023, with so many former teammates and opponents, and there's a common bond which is special about the game of rugby. I'm looking around, looking at players I played against, and thinking, "Wow, what a player, what a character!" Someone said there were more unqualified chiropractors and dentists in that room than anywhere else given the number of broken bones and displaced teeth inflicted by some on so many across the last 60 years. Once you're in a team, once you played the sport and had the highs and the lows, you have that belonging and connection. If it's good, it lasts for life."

ANOTHER player Lydon was keen to discuss was Jonathan Davies. They barely played together - only on Great Britain's tour of New Zealand in 1990. You can see the similarities, though. The type of try Lydon was scoring in the mid-1980s was being scored by the Welshman in the 1990s.

"Jonathan was amazing," said Lydon. "I was once told the North Sydney Bears had finished their pre-match talk when the Canterbury team arrived. It was one of Jiffy's first games. They saw him and said to each other, 'Run at the little runt. He doesn't stand a chance.' Jonathan scored a try, kicked three goals and won man of the match! I saw something similar in a Test match against New Zealand in 1990. We switched sides after the toss. The Iro brothers walked past me. One of them said, 'Your mate doesn't look much like a rugby player.' They had a point. Jonathan often had his shoulders slumped and looked like he had pneumonia. Sure enough, he had a great game. At half-time, I walked past the Kiwi backs and said, 'My mate's looking pretty good now, isn't he?'

"There was a camera shop opposite our hotel on that tour. They had a huge photo of Jonathan Davies in the shop with the word 'traitor' across the top because he'd switched codes. We thought it was out of order, so we sent Kelvin Skerrett in to 'discuss' things with the owner. We watched from our rooms as the picture and headline were quickly removed."

Lydon has performed various roles in both codes since his playing days ended in 1994, starting with an assistant-coaching and management role at Wigan. "John Monie said to me as we came off at half-time one day, 'Why don't you come and sit next to me for a couple of years?' That was a sign my playing career was coming to an end! My right knee was shot at. People like Kris Radlinski, Phil Clarke, Denis Betts and Jason Robinson were coming through. I knew it was time to stop playing.

"But I don't think anyone should go from playing to coaching or management in the same club. I kind of fell into it, and I hadn't planned for it. I later became technical director at the RFL, working on the 'World Class Plan' in the late-90s. Then the RFU wanted to do something similar, and I went over to work and coach in union.

"There's a quote, 'Choice not chance determines destiny.' I think it's choice and chance. But if you can make more good choices, then you get more good chances. In coaching, you need to go away, study and determine your own plan, like Mike [Gregory] did, but don't drop into something because it rarely ends well if you've not prepared for it. If you want to coach, you need to learn your craft, and to be handed anything isn't right."

Could Lydon tell which of his teammates would be good coaches? "That's a great question," he said. "No, I don't think I ever thought about it. In hindsight, I could kid myself and say I thought Shaun Edwards or Andy Farrell would be, but I didn't think it at the time. I don't think any of us stood out as coaches. We were all different and yet the same. We learned how to win when it mattered and some of that Wigan team continue to share that knowledge and the experiences that shaped individuals into great teams."

Lydon helped organise the 1996 cross-code challenge matches between Wigan and Bath and ended up playing in the union game at Twickenham. "I have a claret jug in my office which Bath presented to me afterwards for the part I played in getting the fixtures on," said Lydon. "We were still in season, and they weren't, so I played in the union fixture because I'd played union up to signing pro. They had a great team with Andy Robinson, Jon Sleighthome, Phil de Glanville, Nigel Redman, Graham Dawe, Mike Catt, Jon Callard etc.

"We got a lot of credibility out of those games. Just watch the try that Craig Murdock scored in the second half at Twickenham. We were very good in the second half. We also won the Middlesex Sevens which was great to be a part of.

"I remember a delegation of Bath coaches and management came to see us before the first cross-code game in 1996. 'We can't do the League game,' they said. 'You're going to annihilate us.' So we sat down and agreed to take out much of our power plays if and when we gained the upper hand. At one point in the second half, I think we took two players off and didn't replace them. For the union game, they said they'd reciprocate. An early scrum at Twickenham had to be reset about three times. After it, Martin Hall came over to me and said, "What was in that arrangement of yours? I've just seen my own scrotum twice in that scrum!"

Lydon returned to Wigan in December 2007 when Ian Lenagan bought the club but left in 2010 to join the Welsh rugby union. "I was pleased that I came back to the club," he said. "They've set themselves up really well, and I hope they go from strength to strength. I still live in the town. You're attached to it whether you like it or not! The club and the game of Rugby League are a massive part of my life, and I will always be grateful for the friends made and retained."

GREEN VIGO

1973-1980

Green Vigo was widely tipped to become the first player of colour to play rugby union for the Springboks. Instead, he left Apartheid South Africa to take up a contract offer from Wigan. He was labelled the new Boston, but as Wigan fell on hard times in the 1970s, Vigo's career didn't reach the same heights as his illustrious predecessor. Nevertheless, his try-scoring exploits and his sheer flamboyancy made him one of the most iconic players of his time, and there was a place for him in the first-ever World XIII selected by Open Rugby magazine in 1978.

If you could relive one day from your career, which would it be?

The day I was presented with a player-of-the-month award by the great cricketer Freddie Trueman. Leigh's John Woods won it in the first month of the 1977-78 season, and then me in the second. It was a proud moment, and it was down to Vinnie [Wigan coach Vince Karalius] who gave me so much good advice.

I was twice named player of the year in South Africa, but I didn't get anything. For this, I got a tankard and £100! My best mate Bill Ashurst took me in his car - this old banger that would barely go up the hill. He refused to park it next to other players' cars because people would laugh at us. At the dinner, I sat next to Keith Fielding. They were so many knives and forks. I watched Keith closely because I knew he'd know how to use them. There was a photographer - if anyone has photos of that night, I'd love to see them.

Tell us about your early life in South Africa.

I'm from Saldanha Bay, which is a fishing town in Cape Province. If you look at a map, Saldanha Bay is right at the bottom. When you get there, that's it, you got to turn around because you can't go any further. On a good day, you can see Table Mountain. South Africa is massive. Everybody from around the Western Cape came looking for work because there were loads of fish. There was plenty of work. The first thing I did when I got a job on the trawlers was get my mom a radio. I came home one day, and all her friends were there, listening to it. With my next payment, I got her all the furniture we needed for the house. My brother Ronnie still lives in the house, and now it's ours because Nelson Mandela gave it to us - no more rent! It's a nice piece of land.

I remember coming home one day to a message that a white man had left a package. It was a pair of rugby boots. They used to let us train in the Army and Navy Camp in the Apartheid years. All my teammates used to live in the same street. South Africa's biggest newspaper, The Sunday Times, had a big picture of John Bevan as the Lions had just beaten the All Blacks in New Zealand. Little did I know I'd be playing against him soon in Rugby League - and when I did, he made me look a fool.

It's a beautiful place, but I'd rather be here in the UK now. In the old days, it was safe with plenty of work for everybody and you could stay out till late at night. When the ANC took over, we expected things to be good, but it isn't. Government agencies are stealing money. Everybody owns guns - even my friends - not to rob people, but to protect themselves. It's dangerous if you go to the wrong places.

What was life like in the Apartheid years for a man of colour?

I was just born into it and have to accept it. I'm not angry about it. Sometimes I watch the Springboks on TV, and I think why did I have to come to another country to play rugby?

I'm a Cape Coloured, which means I'm mixed race. Then you had the Blacks and the Whites. I hate talking about it. The Police used to come from Malmesbury. They were bad. They were looking for the Blacks for their ID. They used to stop me. Even though I'm mixed race, I look black. I saw with my own eyes them waiting at the harbour during lobster season. The police would chase Blacks, some of whom couldn't swim. They would just jump into the sea, but the police would get them out.

Across the road, my friend's mom sold illegal ale and played music at full blast, day and night. I can still remember the police kicking the door in.

But the white people treated me great because of rugby. One day during Apartheid, a friend of mine was in court. He asked me to go with him. Back then, when a black man went to court in front of a white judge, you'd had it, but the judge said, "Aren't you Green Vigo? Is this your friend?" I said yes. My friend received a fine. Outside the court, my friend started crying and acknowledged if I hadn't been there, he'd have been jailed.

I returned to Cape Town after my first year of playing Rugby League. You changed planes in Johannesburg, and I used to stay with a friend - a white guy in a white area. We went for something to eat, but the restaurant wouldn't serve me because I'm black. A black woman scrubbing the floor was frightened that I was going to cause trouble and begged me to go.

When I took my daughters, they could not believe we were not allowed where the white people lived unless you cut their grass or something. We had to be out of the town centre at 7pm or they'd find you and kick the whatever out of you.

What was South African rugby union like?

Danie Craven was the big boss. They say he hated Rugby League. That was wrong - he just believed no one should be paid to play rugby. Boy, did we make it! The whole of South Africa used to call us 'The Fishermen', and my name was on top. I've never been in a position like that. We were only playing to have fun.

When I meet my old mates in South Africa, you won't believe how much respect they give me. They keep saying I could have been the first coloured or black to play for the Boks. All the black players of the Apartheid years have now received Springbok blazers, but I don't want one because I never played for them. There's a book out with South Africa's best 100 players. I'm in it, but I don't know why as I only played club rugby.

I toured England in 1971 with the Proteas, which was the representative team for Blacks and Coloureds. It was an incredible experience. It was in November, so we never saw the sun! There was a protest at one of our games against Apartheid. I was tipped to be the first black

Springbok and people began to talk about me and my town a lot. We were amazed that people were talking about us! Wigan had a scout called Roy Seddon who lived in Pretoria, and he told them about me.

How much of an inspiration was Tom van Vollenhoven?
When I went to the movies, they would play a short newsreel first called 'African Mirror'. It often had clips of Tom van Vollenhoven scoring tries for the Boks. We used to go mad. This was during Apartheid, and we Coloureds were all hooting for him. Back then, it was the Whites and Coloureds that were into rugby, and the Blacks were mostly into football. Tom was a hero to Coloureds and Whites. When he signed for Saints, the South Africans cut him off. But it was different with me. All my Wigan games were reported in the South African papers.

What do you remember of your early days at Wigan?
I landed at Manchester Airport. There was somebody to pick me up. He took my case. "No, a white man doesn't carry a black man's stuff," I said. "This is England," he replied.
When I got to Wigan, there were so many reporters there. I could understand English, but it was hard to answer the

questions. The reporter I liked was Eric Thompson. He was in a wheelchair. He was a straight-shooting guy. "Give the lad a break - he's learning the game," he wrote in the Wigan Observer, but Norman Bibby, the chairman, didn't want to hear that. He wanted me straight in the team. I owe Graham Starkey, the coach, so much. It was Graham who put me on the wing. I remember playing Warrington in the Locker Cup friendly. Friendly? Yeah, right. They knocked all my teeth out. I remember walking to the dentist and guys working on the pavement shouted, "How do you like this game, lad?" Then you'd go to Yorkshire in the wet or the snow on a Tuesday night. God help me. Wigan sent me to college to study English - Afrikaans is my first language. When I got there, I ran away because there were no black people. The chairman went mad with me. I stayed in a hotel at first. One night, I saw a pub called the Fox and Goose. I didn't want to go in because there were no black people going in. Somebody must have known who I was and told someone inside who played for Wigan. I went in and saw a jukebox for the first time. I remember Dessie Drummond when he first came along. I liked playing against him at first, but he learned quickly, and he'd cut you in half when he tackled you! His brother Alva brought him into the game. It was Alva and Danny Wilson, Ryan Giggs's dad, who introduced me to

Manchester.

I also remember seeing the great Jim Sullivan. All he used to talk about was Van Vollenhoven.

What sort of money were you on?

I didn't know anything about money until I got to Wigan. I didn't know about signing-on fees. I'm not a clever guy. I thought people bought houses with actual cash.

Players came straight from work. They want to play because they need the cash - £30 for a win and £10 for a loss - and that's before tax. If you don't play, you get nothing.

Nobody told me anything about money or tax or how to pay bills.

Wigan got me a job with the council, picking up rocks. Somebody used to stand there, watching me work. I went to see the chairman. He sat there with his big cigar. I gave it to him. "I've come from Apartheid. I've done all the shite work over there where the white man stands there like a prison guard, and you have to ask to go for a piss." I told him I wanted to go back to South Africa. He said, "You can't play over there because you've played Rugby League." In the end, they put me on the ground staff. The directors did nothing for me. They put me in digs that sometimes I couldn't even find after training. No one looked after me. John Gray signed at the same time as me. They gave him a house, but they just dumped me in digs. They put me with an old couple. The old lady was making tea one day. The comedian Tommy Cooper was on TV. I didn't understand and turned it off. She went mad! "You don't do that to our Tommy!" As the months went by, I got used to it and I liked them all. We listened to Boer music and Jim Reeves back home. Aretha Franklin would be on Radio Mozambique. So Tommy Cooper was a bit different.

When my contract finished, I signed again because I didn't want to leave for reasons I can't really explain. I had six top clubs after me. One offered me a house and a three-year deal, but even with all the shite that had happened at Wigan, I signed for them again. I can't really tell you why I did that. Bill Ashurst couldn't believe I turned down a house to sign again with Wigan.

When I was offered a new contract, Vinnie told me to look carefully, especially under where they clipped it together because that's where they always hid the stuff they didn't want you to see. And, sure enough, he was right. Alex Murphy looked at the contract because he was interested in signing me for Salford. He said I must have been drunk when I signed it.

What are your rugby memories?

In my first season, we played Salford in the Lancashire Cup Final. Everyone wrote us off, even our washing lady, Mrs Backo. "David Watkins will beat you on his own," she and the groundsman Billy Mitchell told me. They were always telling me how good Billy Boston, Dave Bolton and Brian McTigue were. They obviously didn't rate the 1970s team. It was the same when we played Widnes. "Who's gonna stop Big Jim?" they would ask me. I had to get out of there.

We played at Leigh, my favourite ground, when I was at Wigan. I always played well there, but one day I put the ball on the 25-yard line, thinking it was the try line. That didn't go down well - if looks could kill. I remember Dennis Boyd picking the ball up, laughing.

Keith Fielding did well against me a couple of times. Next time, my centre David Willicombe and I were prepared. I stayed wider and deeper, and nothing got past me. It was like standing on a hill and looking on everything that's going on. You get the centre and wing in one go, and I stuffed both David Watkins and Fielding. David's grubbers weren't going to work, and I could get Fielding on the inside. There was no way I was moving off the wing for that whole game. I stuck to that plan for the next four years.

Vinnie said, "You're a big lad, you shouldn't be frightened of anybody." He'd done weights at Widnes, and he put me straight on to it. He told me he didn't want me to be Arnold Schwarzenegger, and he was right. I scored 29 tries in the 1977-78 season, which was only bettered by Stuart Wright because they counted his international tries. I was in such good shape.

It has been reported that you had several skirmishes with the law back then.

Yes - I wake up these days and when I open my eyes and see my ceiling, I feel good because in the past I would wake up in a police cell having been arrested for being drunk and disorderly. I did so many stupid things because of drink. It was all my fault. I can't blame anyone else. When I finished playing, I vanished from the Rugby League scene. I was just drinking. It was even reported in South African newspapers that I had died because I hadn't been seen. One day I went to the doctor because I was getting these pains. He said I would get cirrhosis if I didn't stop. It was hard for the first few days, but I've found it easy since. I thought life would be boring without drinking, but it's great. I haven't had a drink for 25 years.

Tell us about your family.

I came over as a single man, and I married a Wigan girl called Sheila. We had two daughters. I've been to South

Africa with my kids - up Table Mountain in Durban, and they loved it. My wife paid for it. She said, "Go and take the kids with you." Well, she's gone now. She died of cancer a couple of years ago. I have four grandchildren.

Was there one Wigan teammate you were particularly close to?

My best mate at Wigan was Bill Ashurst. He always had time for me. He was a great player too, and I'm so sad he died recently. He always wanted me to give my story like this, but I always told him I wasn't ready. Before he died, he was installed as one of Penrith Panthers' best players. I love you Bill. You were my best friend, and you were always there for me. I'm hurt because I didn't go to his funeral. I wasn't confident how I'd be accepted. Bill never forgot about me.

Who were the best players you came across in the British game?

The first Rugby League game I watched was Salford against Featherstone. John Newlove was stand-off for Rovers. The way he was throwing the ball around – I'd never seen anything like it. On the other side, Kenny Gill was doing the same. I'd never seen that kind of rugby. I played against the best players in English Rugby League. Every club was full of top players, not like today - I'm sorry lads. It was so tough too. Sometimes there were fights in the tunnel before a game. You'd go to Warrington to play against Alex Murphy and to stir it up with the late Dave Chisnall. What a player Dave was - he got their whole pack going. You don't see prop forwards sidestep like that now. Then you'd go to Bradford and face one of the Van Bellens and big Bill Ramsey. I used to be frightened. Roger Millward was amazing. He used to give Phil Lowe these Exocet-missile passes. Phil used to run between the centre and wing, but it all depended on Roger getting the pass right. When he did, there was no stopping Phil. Leeds had Syd Hynes, Les Dyl, John Atkinson and Alan Smith – what a team! Arthur Keegan was a brilliant fullback at Bramley. The man I hated to play against was

Jack Austin who played for various Yorkshire sides. I left him for dead once on the outside. Then, and I don't know why, I ran back into him, and he knocked me back where I'd come from. Vinnie used to go mad with me. Then there was Ken Senior at Huddersfield. He could fly. He'd run alongside and just push me into touch with a big smile on his face. I learned how to get the better of him in the end.

I've already mentioned Keith Fielding. He was faster than Offiah. Peter Smethurst went to watch Salford play Warrington a week before we played them. In the dressing room before the game, he kept warning me about Keith. Salford had the quickest and best back line with Paul Charlton, Maurice Richards, David Watkins, Chris Hesketh, Keith Fielding, Ken Gill and Peter Banner, although I think Leeds probably ran them close.

We played at Widnes one day with Geoff Aspinall, a young hooker. A scrum broke up and all of a sudden Geoff went flying through the air. Big Jim [Mills] had done him. He didn't even get sent off – they'd be calling it assault today! People were afraid of him. I'll never forget our entire Wigan team turn their backs with Big Jim just waiting for someone to take him on. Jim actually saved me from getting locked up once. I got a taxi to his nightclub but was blind drunk and didn't have the fare. Jim came out and paid it for me just as the driver was going to call the police. I was very grateful for that. These guys are so sweet off the field!

You also played for Swinton and Oldham.

Swinton was a disaster, and I don't even remember much about it. I loved playing with Alan McCurrie, Mick Morgan and Flash Flanagan at Oldham. There was Ray Ashton, Mick Worrall and Andy Goodway too, all very good players. Alan, Mick and I liked to think we invented the inside pass, but Alan would always spoil it by shouting my name so loudly that everyone knew what we were going to do! Mick still let it go one day in a game against Widnes. "Bollocks to this," I thought, "I'm gonna get killed here," so I went to the other side and Mick still let the ball go. Alan went mad. "Did you not see four of them coming for me?" I asked. I disappeared for two days, getting pissed. I didn't go to training. Oldham went mad. When Frank Myler was away, coaching the 1984 Lions Tour, the 'A' team coach was shouting and screaming and trying to show me up. If Frank or Mick or Alan shouted, I took it seriously, but not this fella. So I walked out and only went back when Frank was back from the tour and had one of my best ever seasons. In one game at Widnes, I was kicked on the knee. Joe Lydon told me to stay down. The bone was sticking out. I pushed it back in and carried on.

We played Cas in the Challenge Cup in February '85. All the football games were off due to snow, and I assumed ours would be and went to the pub the night before. Suddenly the game was switched from Watersheddings to Oldham Athletic where there was under-soil heating, but they couldn't get hold of me as I was in the pub! I had to play with a terrible hangover. It wasn't pretty. They obviously knew what I'd done, and they told me I was finished. I was going to retire at the end of the season because of my knee. I accepted their decision. It was understandable.

Anyway, all I want to say is it was great playing Rugby League against all those great players, and if wasn't for Vinnie and Frank, I wouldn't have been in the World XIII or won player-of-the-month awards. I'm so incredibly grateful for everything.

KELVIN SKERRETT

1990-1996

Kelvin Skerrett was one of the most fearsome Rugby League players in the 1980s and '90s. He had already forced his way into the Great Britain team as a Bradford Northern player when Wigan came calling in the summer of 1990. He was the cornerstone of a tremendous pack that didn't just win multiple medals, but they represented Great Britain en masse in 1992 when the Lions thrashed Australia in Melbourne. He was the first professional player to insist on having a clause in his contract that would make him a free agent when it expired, meaning his next club didn't have to pay a transfer fee - and could therefore pay him more.

SOME players were loved for their greatness, and some for their personality. With Kelvin Skerrett, it was both. He was up there with the best forwards in the world for most of his career, but he was also one of the great icons of a time that was packed with legends. His is a name that can instantly bring a smile to the faces of fans who cheered him on all those years ago.

Before I interviewed the former Great Britain and Wales international - he never actually qualified for Wales, by the way, but nobody bothered to check - I took to Twitter to ask Wigan supporters of their favourite Skerrett moments. Someone pointed to him single-handedly taking on the Saints pack in the early stages of the 1995 Challenge Cup replay and being sin-binned. Someone else shared a video of his barnstorming Wembley try in 1993 and another of his infamous leap on top of the brawlers when Wigan hosted Featherstone in a 1994 cup match. There's also the Mick Morgan commentary of the 1994 Regal Trophy Final that went viral many years later. I was interested to see how Skerrett responded to that.

A Wigan supporter Margaret Wilkinson sent me this reply, "Just loved every game he played. He was special and gave us a laugh at times. My first mentioned player when I think of my years as a supporter." Fans of other teams, most notably St Helens and Castleford, were quick to point out Skerrett's skirmishes with the disciplinary or of the instances when he was the victim of foul play like in the 1994 Premiership Final.

Kelvin's father and uncle, Ernie and Trevor, were Rugby League players. Ernie played for Bisons amateur club and then for the Great Britain amateurs. Trevor was one of the great forwards of his time. Had he not been injured, he would have captained the 1984 Lions. He played for Wakefield, Hull and Leeds.

"I watched my dad play when I was a kid," said Skerrett, "and I watched Trevor a lot when he played professionally. He was a big influence. I followed them into rugby, but if they'd played football, I'd have made a lot more money! Trevor and I never played against each other. I was at Hunslet in Division Two when he was in Division One. Then he went from Leeds to Keighley around the time I signed for Bradford Northern. It would have been frightening to play against him! As I'd seen him tackle, I'd have played on the other side of the pitch! He was a world-record signing for Hull, and he was due to captain the Great Britain tour in 1984 before he got injured, so he was clearly one of the top players."

Skerrett made his Hunslet debut on 2nd September 1984 in a 32-10 defeat at Oldham. He played the first 13 matches of the season, either in the second row or coming off the bench, but injury struck. "I broke my back in two places," he said. "I chipped two of the vertebrates in a scrum. I played the week after and it just wasn't right. Back then, you had to go to hospital on your own, so I went to A & E, told the doctor I'd played another game with it, and he couldn't believe it.

"When I signed, I could have gone to Hull. They offered me the same contract as Garry Schofield, but my uncle and dad advised me to sign for Hunslet and be a free agent after three years. I was the first player to do that. I played in a pre-season friendly for Hunslet against Halifax. Arthur Bunting came to watch me play, which resulted in Hull offering me a £36,000 contract. But I wanted to be a free agent and control my future. Hull were not interested in this as it could have opened the door for every player to want a similar contract. Hunslet were unable to match Hull's money, but I accepted a three-year deal at £2,000 a season, as long as I could be a free agent when it expired.

"So I backed myself, and after three seasons at Hunslet, it paid off, and I was able to negotiate my own contract with no transfer fee, but only after Hunslet tried to stitch me up which resulted in a tribunal. I moved to Bradford Northern and did the same again. Then it really paid off because I had performed well for Bradford and Great Britain, so when I became a free agent again, clubs went nuts they could sign a Great Britain prop with no transfer fee to pay. They just had to pay my contract, and I chose Wigan. It was a gamble. You don't know if you're going to make it, but I had belief in myself along with some sleepless nights with injuries and doubt, but what a ride! £36,000 was a lot to turn down in 1984.

"I did three seasons with Hunslet, and they ended up getting promoted. When I first signed, they had Graham King who played all his career there, even though he had other clubs after him. He was always on the fringes of Great Britain, but he probably played for the wrong club. He was a cracking scrum-half. Johnny Wolford was the loose forward. He was like Harry Pinner but slow! He was a great ball handler.

"But I was in dispute with them and missed a lot of the run-in in the promotion season [1986-87]. Hunslet wanted to re-sign me after the three years, but I was getting interest from other clubs, and Hunslet didn't want to pay as much as Bradford. I missed the back end of the season because they wouldn't pick me over the dispute, but we had a good side and they still got promoted.

"I joined Bradford in the summer of 1987. We won the Yorkshire Cup in a replay against Castleford. We also lost 2-0 to Wigan in the first round of the Challenge Cup. That was the start of their run of wins in the cup that lasted eight years. It was muddy. Wigan had a great side. Joe Lydon kicked a penalty. While everyone was arguing over the penalty, Joe nicked five or ten metres to make the kick easier. We were gutted to lose that."

In the summer of 1989, Skerrett was one of many British

players to experience a short stint in Australia's Winfield Cup. Along with Ellery Hanley and Garry Schofield, he signed for Western Suburbs, who sat near the bottom of the table. Skerrett's time with the Magpies wasn't the rosiest. He played just five games, winning on his debut against St George. There was a draw with Gold Coast Giants, close defeats to minor premiers South Sydney and Eastern Suburbs and a bigger defeat to Cronulla. Other players with a Wigan connection to feature in those matches were Hanley, Stuart Raper, Phil Blake, Joe Lydon and Martin Offiah.

"I was on the fringes of Great Britain selection and wanted to experience playing in the Australian league," Skerrett said. "John Bailey, the Wests coach, didn't seem to want me there though. Three players coming in meant three local lads going out. I was an unknown compared to Ellery and Garry, but I had a good time and made friends. Graham Mackay later came to Bradford. Brendan Tuuta came to Featherstone and Castleford.

"I didn't impress myself at Western Suburbs. My style was to play together as a pack, but I remember a fight at South Sydney one day when one of my teammates grabbed my arms and chest, and I got hit in the face! 'Shouldn't you be grabbing the opposition?' I thought. We weren't winning, and I felt like I was getting pushed out by the coach, John Bailey. I decided to leave because I wasn't playing. He asked what I would be doing when I went back. I'd hopefully have a good season and play for Great Britain, I replied. I don't think he rated my chances of that, but I saw him when I was on the Great Britain tour in 1992, and he said I'd obviously done ok. If we'd worked together, things would have been much better for both of us."

SKERRETT returned to England for the start of the 1989-90 season, which would turn out to be his last at Odsal. Within two months, he was making his Great Britain debut in an enthralling series with New Zealand. Skerrett started all three Tests and helped his country to a 2-1 series win.

"Things fell into place for me when I came back to England and I was called up by Great Britain," said Skerrett. "We lost the first Test to the Kiwis. It was so much quicker than a league game. If you got tired, you just had to keep going. The Kiwis were on form that day. We played a basic game, one-up rugby, and we didn't test them enough. Malcolm Reilly thought I'd done ok and picked me for the second Test. That's when Steve Hampson was sent off at the start for headbutting Gary Freeman. I remember Steve being so gutted at half-time. He was crying, saying how much he had let everyone down. I was so impressed by him being so honest. I never did that when I got sent off!

"We had to play 79 minutes with 12 men, but if you stick together, you can still do ok. Teams shouldn't fall apart when they have someone sent off. Central Park was the best place to play the third Test. It felt like we had a 14th man with the crowd behind us. The team got stronger through the series. We were probably shellshocked in the first Test, but the more we trained together, the better we got, and we won the series. It was a brilliant experience."

It was no surprise when Skerrett was named on the 1990 tour of Papua New Guinea and New Zealand. With Hanley, Shaun Edwards and Andy Gregory absent, Mike Gregory was the captain. Despite those absentees, Great Britain won their Test series with New Zealand. "I was injured and missed the start of the tour," said Skerrett. "I was sent to Australia for a few weeks to have a knee operation in

Sydney. I came back in for the Test series in New Zealand. I don't think I played very well though. We were getting beaten in the second Test, and I remember saying, 'We've got 'em here', and I made a break, found Garry Schofield, and Martin Offiah scored. Mike Gregory was a great captain and a great guy. I followed him like a sheep on and off the pitch! He was a good friend."

It was also in that summer that Skerrett signed for Wigan. Supporters may have wondered whether the tour manager, Maurice Lindsay, had been in his ear while he was on Test duty. Skerrett revealed he had, but not on that tour. "It was more or less sorted beforehand," he said. "I had an agreement for another deal with Bradford when I returned from Australia, but when they went back on their word over something, that gave me the chance to walk away because Wigan had made me such a good offer. Maurice had spoken to me during the 1989 series with New Zealand and said Wigan were very interested in me. They offered me extortionate money, so I was delighted when Bradford changed their minds. Who wouldn't want to go and play for Wigan, especially for a lot more money?"

In his first season at Wigan, Skerrett won a championship medal but missed out on Wembley courtesy of a delayed three-match ban after a red card at Oldham. "It took me a while to find my feet after I signed for Wigan," Skerrett said. "I struggled for six weeks or so. I couldn't get my breath. Dr Zaman wasn't at a game at home to Sheffield. The guy standing in for him was Roger Wolstenholme, a chest specialist. I came off after 20 minutes. I hadn't impressed the crowd.

"'Come and see me in the morning,' he said. He told me I had asthma. I'd never had a problem with that in my life. He tested my lungs, and I was running on a fraction of my lung capacity. I had to have ventilators at every game during my career, and I had to take them in the right order, but I don't suffer with it now. It was just when I played.

"I'd missed the 1991 semi-final through suspension and then I missed the final too," he continued. "I was due to go before the disciplinary, but the hearing was put back a couple of times. By the time my case was heard, my ban meant I missed Wembley. I thought that was unfair. I was distraught. I didn't go down to the game because they didn't need me sulking when everyone else was focusing on the game, and John Monie agreed. My first Wembley was in 1992. We were told it was just another game – 'It's just a normal rugby pitch, don't look up at the crowd.' I kept my head down and played my normal game, and we beat Castleford 28-12."

Soon after that final, and a Premiership Trophy success in which Wigan beat Leeds 74-6 and St Helens 48-16, Skerrett was one of 14 Wigan players to feature on the Lions Tour that came so close to winning the Ashes. The others were Denis Betts, Phil Clarke, Neil Cowie, Martin Dermott, Shaun Edwards, Andy Gregory, Steve Hampson, Ian Lucas, Joe Lydon, Billy McGinty, Martin Offiah, Andy Platt and David Myers who was called up mid-tour due to injuries.

"We scored more points than Australia in the 1992 series - just not in the right games!" said Skerrett. "I got a dead leg in the first game. My leg went black, but the physio Dave Fevre got me right, and I played at Melbourne. That second Test was fantastic. The full starting pack were Wigan players. We knew how to play together, and it gave us an edge. Things went right for us that night. We couldn't have played any better.

"But we lost the series and then the World Cup Final to

them at Wembley a few months later. I was upset to be on the bench for that, but you have to just do as you're told. It was so close, but it went the wrong way. You sit in the dressing-room afterwards, thinking what we should have done differently, but it's too late by then."

IN the second half of his Wigan career, Skerrett's reputation as a cross between a world-class enforcer and a bad lad with a string of disciplinary indiscretions was cemented. First came the Regal Trophy in January 1994 in which Wigan were hammered 33-2 by Castleford. Several years later, part of Castleford's in-house commentary, performed by former player Mick Morgan, went viral. "Oh, what about that!" he shouted as Skerrett flopped on Andy Hay, who had already been tackled. "Send him off! Send the dirty get off! Get him off the field. That were diabolical! Get him off the field! That's just typical of what he is. Get him walking! They don't like it! Walk him Campbell if you've got any bottle. If you've got any bottle Campbell, he should walk. That were absolute diabolical. He's given him a yellow card! I can't speyk. You bottleless get, Campbell. You dickhead!"

"Mick used to do commentaries like that for Castleford every week and they were hilarious," chuckled Skerrett. "He's a funny character. You could pick any game, and the commentary would be similar. I thought it was funny, but on the BBC version, Ray French said there wasn't much wrong with what I did and that it was just a bit late. None of the Cas players ran in upset, which is a sign they didn't think there was much wrong with it either. [Andy Hay] had said something, and we were getting beaten quite well. It

looked worse than it was!

"That defeat had been building from the start of the season," Skerrett continued. "John Dorahy had taken over from John Monie in the summer of 1993. He had some great ideas, but coaching Wigan is more about man management. Some people need picking up and some need putting down. John Monie had been exceptional at man management. John Dorahy just didn't get the players. 'Everything is going to change - forget what you've been taught,' he said when he got the job. Fair enough if it's broken, but it wasn't. He lost the dressing room. You don't get the best out of your team if they're not happy."

Five weeks after the misery of the Regal Trophy Final, Wigan entertained Featherstone Rovers in the quarter-final of the Challenge Cup. It was game number 34 of the 43 unbeaten from 1988 to 1996. Wigan won 32-14, scoring five tries. When Sam Panapa touched down for his try, a melee broke out which resulted in the sendings-off of Andy Platt and Steve Molloy. But the incident is best remembered for Skerrett running and leaping on top of the brawling players. Fans made t-shirts with the player mocked up as Superman or, in this case, Superkel, as he is still nicknamed by some supporters.

"It was quite a niggly game," Skerrett recalled. "I was taking a breather near the halfway line when the action was going on. I'd seen Andy Platt going down. I ran as fast as I could, and the adrenaline was going! I didn't hit anyone. Even when I got up, I didn't hit anyone. I meant to run into the group of players rather than over the top of them. We all got a fine for that. Then the RFL looked at it later and wanted to really punish me, but we came up with the response that if they'd already fined me, then I'd already been punished, and they couldn't punish me twice.

It worked. I never hit anyone, I just made a fool of myself!"

The next talking point that involved the Wigan prop came in the last domestic match of the 1993-94 season. Wigan avenged their Regal Trophy Final defeat to Castleford by beating them 24-20 at Old Trafford in the final of the Premiership Trophy, but Skerrett had his jaw smashed by his opposite number, Dean Sampson. It ruled him out of the wonderful win in Brisbane a week and a half later.

"Sampson took the ball in, and it was just one of those things," Skerrett mused. "If you could do that on purpose, you'd do it every week. I never moaned about it, and I told Wigan not to do anything, so I was disappointed when the club complained, because I didn't want them to. I watched the Brisbane game on the TV. It was so upsetting to miss out. I couldn't make the Australia trip because they flew the next day, but I was absolutely chuffed to see them win, especially after Brisbane had beaten us in 1992 at Central Park."

A broken thumb kept Skerrett out of the 1994 Ashes series, meaning that the last of his 16 Great Britain caps came against the Kiwis in 1993. Wigan won the league, the Challenge Cup, the Regal Trophy and the Premiership Trophy in 1994-95 which was Graeme West's first season as coach. The nearest they came to letting one of those trophies slip away was in a televised Challenge Cup match at home to St Helens. Bobbie Goulding hit an upright with a late drop-goal attempt, meaning that Wigan escaped with a 16-all draw. Many people tipped Saints to take advantage of the replay being at Knowsley Road, but Skerrett and his teammates had other ideas. Wigan ran away with a comfortable 40-24 win, after an early dust-up which saw Skerrett and Goulding sin-binned.

"We'd drawn with them at Central Park and got a bit lucky," Skerrett admitted. "We could easily have gone out of the cup. I wasn't playing well back then. The team was a bit up and down. We'd got away with it. I knew we had to get back to what we did best, and just get stuck in. The incident was just me getting beaten up by Saints players! There wasn't much wrong with the tackle.

"Those games were huge. We were in the mood that night, and we won convincingly. Our style was to do the hard work in the first 20 minutes, and then it's down to who blinks first. After 20 minutes, you find out who wants to keep coming hard."

Wigan went on to beat Batley, Widnes and Oldham to set up a second consecutive final with Leeds, which they won 30-10, having also beaten the Loiners 26-16 a year earlier. "They were quite tough games against Leeds, especially the first one when Martin Offiah went the full length of the pitch. It was great to have a player do that when you were under pressure. The 1995 final was easier, although they must have put everything into that game because we beat them 69-12 a few weeks later at Old Trafford."

SKERRETT's Great Britain career may have ended prematurely, but one last hurrah on the international stage saw him help Wales to victory in the 1995 European Championship and to the semi-finals of the World Cup later in the year. Fellow Wigan players Martin Hall, Neil Cowie and Paul Atcheson all made themselves available to play for the Welsh, who were captained by the great Jonathan Davies.

"When it was first announced that Great Britain wouldn't enter the 1995 World Cup, and it would be England and Wales instead, I was gutted because we had much more chance of winning as GB," Skerrett argued. "That's obvious to me because we'd have had players like Jonathan Davies. It was a mistake to dilute Great Britain. I didn't see the point in being part of an England team that thrashed Wales, so I spoke to Neil Cowie and Martin Hall, who I was big mates with. I said I might play for Wales, although to be perfectly honest, I'm not sure if it was my grandmother or great-grandmother who was Welsh, but nobody actually checked!* Anyway, Neil, Martin and I all made the decision to go for it. We won the European Championship in early 1995. We did well in the World Cup, although I remember being absolutely gutted after we lost to England in the semi-final at Old Trafford."

Little did he know it at the time, but Skerrett was approaching the end of his Wigan career. With the team failing to make Wembley in 1996 and with a salary cap on its way, Wigan were feeling the pinch. Skerrett left at the end of the first Super League season. "Even though I'm a Yorkshire lad, I couldn't have given any more for Wigan," he said. "I still had a season and a half to go on my contract, but Jack Robinson said the club was skint and they couldn't afford to pay me. I said I'd see the 1996 season out and then I'd leave. Warrington made an offer, and I was interested, but Alex Murphy had a managerial role there. He didn't seem to rate me based on things he'd written about me, so I thought that would be a nightmare with him there. I lived in Yorkshire still, and I signed for Halifax although that turned out to be a mistake. I wish I'd gone back to Bradford. Halifax offered less, but I felt they wanted me more. I broke my arm in my first year there and so I missed the World Club Championship with the Australian teams.

"Graeme West is a fantastic guy. He coached me in my last few seasons at Wigan. I've never been under a better coach than John Monie, but I really wanted to play for Graeme. He dragged the best out of everybody, but the style changed more to ballplaying and away from the physical side of things. Maybe they felt they didn't need me so much, but teams like that can sometimes struggle against a tough side because you still need to do the hard work first. Wigan against Sheffield at Wembley in 1998 showed that, especially in the first 20 minutes. Wigan only had one genuine prop at the start of that game.

"The best prop I played with or against was Andy Platt who was absolutely outstanding. His strength and conditioning were perfect. He was the best player to play alongside. I also loved Neil Cowie when he played for Wigan. He was similar to me - 'Get it sorted early!' Another of the greatest was Karl Fairbank at Bradford Northern. He was one of the hardest guys who never took a backward step."

The obvious question to ask Skerrett was whether or not his reputation was deserved. "No!" he said. "The reputation is built on a few videos on YouTube that people like to watch and comment on. I didn't get sent off that many times. What you have to remember is that Wigan had to get stuck in because everybody wanted to beat us. Our backs were absolutely world class, and nobody could match them, so when Wigan got beaten, it tended to be the opposition forwards who did the damage. That's why our jobs were so important. The real reason props like myself and Andy Platt were successful was the punishment we could take, not what we dished out."

*After this interview, I checked with Trevor Skerrett, and it was Kelvin's great-grandmother who was Welsh.

HENDERSON GILL

1981-1989

"And he does a bit of a boogie!" is one of the most famous lines of Rugby League commentary, as Henderson Gill celebrated his superb try for the 1988 Great Britain Lions in Sydney in his own inimitable way. The winger was Wigan's first big signing of their era of unrivalled glory. Gill went on to be one of the best players of the 1980s, scoring tries at will. He also played for Bradford Northern, Rochdale Hornets, South Sydney Rabbitohs and Bramley.

You scored two of the most famous tries of the 1980s. Is it possible to choose between Wembley 1985 and Sydney 1988 as the one which brought you the most pleasure?
I'm just happy I managed to score the tries because one was at Wembley and the other was representing my country. There's no greater honour than that, especially in Australia, when we hadn't beaten them for ten years.

Why did you go to Rochdale after starting at Bradford?
Things weren't going right for me at Bradford. I had my first bit of surgery and didn't think I was being taken seriously. I was a bit of a livewire and had problems after the op. I didn't think anyone was listening to me properly. I remember the all-conquering Kangaroos came over in 1978 when I'd just managed to break into the first team. I was really looking forward to playing against the Australian golden boy Ian Schubert and also Larry Corowa, the fastest man in Rugby League. I thought I'd done enough to make the team, but I got left out and it left a nasty taste. Rochdale was great. It was the best move I ever made. I needed nurturing and they gave me that. I was only there just over a season, but they were happy for me to move on because it would be good for me. They knew they'd get a fee for me too!

How much racist abuse did you receive in your early days, from players or spectators, and did it lessen as your career progressed?
I got a lot of racial abuse. It was due to the era. Had I encountered it from other players, there'd have been some scuffles, but it didn't really happen. Supporters were different. The Hull clubs were bad, and so were Warrington. I got a lot of stick. "Zigger, zigger zigger, Wigan's got a nigger," was one regular song. I had bananas thrown at me. I encountered it all. But these people were in a crowd of thousands, they weren't coming to say it directly. I couldn't let them put me off my game or I'd be the loser. I remember once at Hull, someone in the Threepenny Stand threw a banana. I picked it up, walked like a chimp, unpeeled it and took a bite. They were in stitches, and they applauded my tries that day. It was horrible at the time, but you had to live with it. I grew up in the streets of Huddersfield and we had to walk into town in twos or threes, because of the skinheads.

When Maurice Lindsay signed you for Wigan, the coach Maurice Bamford had wanted "a hairy-arsed forward" instead. What sort of relationship did you have with him?
I had a decent relationship because I scored tries. I scored against Barrow on my debut. He did want forwards because Wigan had just come out of the second division, but I knew wingers would score tries, and I did. I paid

them back quickly. I got my international debut after just a couple of games.

What was going through your mind as Alex Murphy delivered his infamous team talk, which ended up on TV, after defeat to Hull KR in 1983?
I was shocked that it got leaked to television. When he delivered the talk, I was glad I wasn't the focus! He had a right go at David Stephenson. But we played poor and let the crowd down. It was ok for the dressing room, it just should have stayed there. Alex was one of the greatest motivational coaches I played under, and he'd done the job as a player. I liked Alex because he said it as it was. You had to listen to him.

Were you ever on the receiving end like David was?
Not really, because a winger's job is much easier than others. I could take criticism. In the end, John Monie knew nothing about me and listened to people who told him stuff like I was missing training. But I was a team player. I did the business on the pitch. I wasn't in the papers for bad things. Me and him didn't see eye to eye, and that's how I left Wigan. I didn't like him. I was a Test player, and he didn't respect me.

When did you begin to realise Wigan were heading to the top?
I knew when I signed, Wigan were looking for significant signings. They brought in juniors like Shaun Wane, Shaun Edwards and Phil Clarke. You could tell they were building something special. The Aussies and Kiwis we brought in were big names.

Do you have a particular memory of the 1985 Wembley final?
I thought the game would never end because Hull were making a great comeback. James Leuluai, Gary Kemble, Dane O'Hara, Peter Sterling and Fred Ah Kuoi were all playing really well. But we had John 'Chika' Ferguson, who I called 'Quicksilver'. I'd had it my own way at Wigan for a while and he was good competition for me on the other side, which upped my game. We were now a threat on both sides. Then there was Brett Kenny. What a great player! Mike Ford was a very good scrum-half too. I was always comfortable in that team, and I had a good understanding with my centre David Stephenson. I always wanted early ball and he made sure I got it.

Ian Gildart has said that walking onto Central Park for the 1987 World Club Challenge was the highlight of his career. What was it like for you?
It was a very physical game. It took a lot out of us - we lost the next three games. We had to fight for every inch of ground that day. Brian Case, Shaun Wane, Ian Potter and Andy Goodway are the players people tend

to forget, but they were all superb. Ian Potter tackled anything that came near him. Brian Case made us so much ground. Shaun Wane was young and got the man-of-the-match award. Graham Lowe always said, "Let the pigs do the work!" and they did that day! At the back was the safest hands in Rugby League in Stevie Hampson. I saw Graham Eadie and Garry Jack, but Stevie is in any team I pick.

You played for South Sydney Rabbitohs in 1985.
I really enjoyed it. It was very physical, and the training shocked me. It was so tough. The lads slowed down in the first couple of sessions, so I could keep up. Craig Coleman, Mario Fenech, Tony Rampling and David Boyle were all great. I got on with them all so well. I was glad to go over and experience Australia.

You had ups and down in your Great Britain career. Did the glory of Sydney 1988 make up for not being selected in 1984?
Frank Myler was the coach in 1984 and he said that me and Ellery were overrated. I didn't take kindly to that. When we next played at Oldham, I scored and went to the bench and saluted him. I was playing well and didn't deserve to be called overrated. The only wingers doing anything in the game then were me and Des Drummond. If you check the stats, I was the top tryscorer and third top points scorer because of my goalkicking. Because he didn't pick me, he picked a stand-off in Ellery on the wing, and it was a poor tour.

Yes, 1988 made up for it. I upped my game and made sure I did the business. We were robbed in the first Test. We got it all wrong in the second Test. Then we got injuries and were written off. We all believed we could do something. The Hulme brothers did a good job. Mike Gregory was a great leader. Andy Greg was fantastic. Martin Offiah was very different that day. He was physical and bullied his opponent. He tackled like a demon!

What inspired the boogie?
I'd just done Garry Jack! I loved going around the best fullbacks. In 1985 it was Gary Kemble at Wembley. I wished I'd played against Graham Eadie at his peak and gone round him. I'd done all the top fullbacks at home, but to beat Garry in his own backyard in a Test match was the biggest thing of my career.

You always played with a smile on your face. Do you wish you saw more happy players in the game?
I loved entertaining and when the crowd sang your name, it was incredible. What more could you want? I've got a bubbly character anyway. The crowd made me the player I was. I've always said that. Without them, I'd have been a nobody. They make you or they break you. They spend their hard-earned cash, turning out in all weather. I always respected them. I signed as many autographs as I could. I don't think players spend enough time around the crowds now. People still show me photos of them as kids with me at Central Park. That makes me feel so good and I'm glad I took the time to have those photos taken.

27

SAM TOMKINS

2008-2013
2016-2018

A winner of three Grand Finals and two Challenge Cups, Sam Tomkins has enjoyed a glittering career. He won the Man of Steel twice. He was the England captain. He became the first player to score five tries on his senior debut and he scored a hat-trick in his first England international. At the age of 34, Tomkins was in his final season as a professional player in 2023 as this book was published.

EVEN the greatest need a bit of luck. Some kids don't get it and are lost to the game. If Sam Tomkins' parents had remained in Milton Keynes, or if a bunch of Academy players hadn't got into a brawl in 2005, or if Tim Smith hadn't injured his shoulder in 2009, Tomkins may have had a very different career. But things fell into place for him, and he went on to become the captain of England.

Tomkins grew up a Warrington supporter, attending games at Wilderspool with his family. He was born in Milton Keynes before his family returned to the north. "Every match seemed the same when I was young," he said. "I went with Joel, my dad and my Uncle Danny. Jonathan Davies was the first player that really caught my eye. He was electric fast and was a popular face. Then Alfie Langer came along when I had started playing rugby. I was pretty small, so seeing someone as small as him resonated with me. My last Warrington shirt had 'Langer 7' on the back."

Playing for Wigan St Pats gave the Warriors an advantage when it came to signing the young star. "I was 12 and in my first year of high school when I was asked to train with the scholarship," Tomkins recalled. "I was still an avid Warrington fan but had a chance to go with a few friends from Wigan St Pats. Training was on a Tuesday at 12pm, and I did it for years. I went through the scholarship programme, into Under-18s and Under-21s and into the first team.

"It wasn't until the second year of Academy that I was paid anything. I initially signed just before I left high school, but I didn't get offered a paid contract. It was a pay-as-you-play basis - £25 if you got selected and the team won. I wasn't getting picked, so there was no money. I had to get a job straight from high school. I wanted to go to college and get paid for rugby, but that wasn't happening, so I got a job as a greenkeeper at Ashton Golf Course.

"I did 12 months with the Academy, but Shaun Wane wouldn't pick me because I wasn't up to it. That was perfectly valid because I wasn't quite physically there, but it wasn't for the lack of trying. At the end of the first season, they said I could leave. I went back to Wigan St Pats and played in the Under-18s with my mates during the off-season - they were still playing in winter. It was a breath of fresh air to play with my friends with no pressure. It felt like that's what rugby is all about. It gave me a confidence boost. I was the best player, so it made me realise I was good enough, and it helped me kick on."

Tomkins' lucky break came in 2005 when several of his teammates, including Michael McIlorum, were suspended from an Academy Grand Final. "We had a semi-final against Widnes at Orrell," he remembered. "I was a sub and carrying the water on. We were ahead comfortably, and the hooter went. A Widnes player swung an arm in the last tackle, and a full-on 13-on-13 brawl broke out. It

was really bad, but I was happy because I figured someone would get banned! Eight players got suspended, and that meant I started the Grand Final which was at Leeds against Leeds. That was a stitch-up because we'd finished top, but Academy finals had to be played at professional stadiums, and the DW was unavailable. We beat Leeds [33-22 with Tomkins scoring a try and drop goal], and I played pretty well. After 18 months or two years, Wigan finally thought I was worth something!

"The Under-18 and Under-21 comps were so strong, and it kills me today to see no structure for kids. We were training every day. We almost took no notice of the first team because we were just focused on winning our own competitions. We were treated as professionals by Wigan. Standards were really high. There was no room for error, and that breeds good players. To have eight banned for a final and still win shows how good Wigan were.

"Thomas Coyle was probably the best player," he continued. "Lee Mossop and Chris Tuson were very good players. Stephen Roper was two years older than me, and he was a real skilful player. I'm not sure why Thomas didn't make it in Super League. He probably didn't get the right break at the right time. He had a lot of skill. He was a very good passer and kicker. He was really strong as well. A lot of halfbacks don't have the physicality, but he did. There was also a lad called Ross Bradley from Leigh. He was a 13 - a very skilful player, but he didn't quite break through. I'm still friends with guys who played in the Championship. You do need that lucky break, but it still requires a lot of hard work."

Tomkins scored 32 tries in 21 reserve matches in 2008 and couldn't have been banging on the first-team door any harder. He played one Challenge Cup match that season, scoring five tries against Whitehaven on a truly remarkable first-team debut. But it was back to the reserves for Tomkins, and he wasn't seen again in the first team until the following season when it took a bad injury to Australian stand-off Tim Smith for Tomkins to earn a run of Super League starts.

"I knew the Challenge Cup match wasn't a real game," he said. "I thought I'd get another chance in 2008, but I was 18th man pretty much all year. Brian Noble was often under pressure to play me. In the off-season, the club were organising for me to go on loan for a year to London Broncos [then called Harlequins RL], because they didn't think I'd get much game time, but it didn't happen. Then in round three, Brian told me I was on the bench for our game at Harlequins, and that was it.

"Whenever I came on, I was playing better than Tim Smith, but he was an Aussie they were paying a lot of money to, and I was a young kid on 12 grand a year. Brian felt he had to play Tim Smith. Senior players were saying I should be playing, but just being on the bench was a huge step for me because I just wanted to be involved in that environment. Tim then broke his shoulder against

Hull KR. A door closes for someone, and it was my chance. Young players can come in, play a little bit, and it might not go so well, but I had some real solid people around me. Thomas Leuluai really nurtured me as he did right through my career. He treated me so well and looked after me, and I felt confident enough to express myself.

"Going on loan can go one of two ways. Joel went on loan. Liam Farrell went to Widnes. It's not necessarily a bad thing. It depends on your position. If you're a prop and you need to play against men, it's great. But it would have been tough for me to go and lead a team because I was very young, although eventually I'd have been able to show what I could do."

When Tomkins did break into the Super League team in the early rounds of 2009, he did so at a similar time to the Academy winger Shaun Ainscough. At the time, it was hard to predict which would have the better career. "Shaun is as mad as a box of frogs - one of the funniest humans I've ever met," laughed Tomkins. "He played like he is as a bloke. He'd step back in field and have no idea where he was going to run. He's like that in life. He's a great character with loads of energy. He was a breath of fresh air. He was strong and fast - a very good winger.

"But Brian wasn't really a fan of promoting youth. He very much wanted to play a safe hand with senior players or overseas players because he had more confidence in them. That was his philosophy. He wasn't from Wigan, and he didn't understand the system as later coaches like Shaun Wane, Adrian Lam and Matty Peet did. We didn't have a bad relationship. It's just that he'd rather pick Phil Bailey over Liam Farrell and Tim Smith over me."

Tomkins quickly became a star and took in his stride the attention that came with it. "When Joel came through, I saw people wanting photos and autographs, so I had an idea it was coming, and I loved it," he said. "I was very happy to oblige. There was female attention too. As a young, skinny kid going out in Wigan as a first-teamer, the female attention was at an all-time high for me!"

TOMKINS received his first international call-up in the summer of 2009 before making a huge impression in the autumn Four Nations when he partnered fellow 20-year-old Kyle Eastmond in the halfbacks, as England beat New Zealand and gave Australia a tough first hour in the final at Elland Road.

"It's amazing that someone had confidence in two 20-year-old kids playing at six and seven against Australia," said Tomkins. "As a 33-year-old captain of England in 2022, I'd have had no confidence if someone told me they wanted to pick two 20-year-olds in the halves. It was a whirlwind time for me. There was a mid-season Test against France in Paris. I got a call from Tony Smith to say I was in the squad. I thought it was a piss take. He said I'd be 18th man, but he believed I'd go on to play a lot of international rugby, and he wanted to get me used to the environment. I couldn't believe it. It was a strange experience. I was with people I'd looked up to for years. I felt really out of place. I felt like I'd won a competition to hang around with rugby players. It made me realise I wasn't far off, but I wasn't counting on selection at the end of the year.

"I enjoyed playing with Kyle. I'd played against him for years. He was the best player in the country at our age. I knew what he could do. We roomed together from 13 or 14 at rugby camps. Kyle was a freak of a talent, a much better player than I was. He was a character who could come up with something from nothing. He could make us all look

better. I'd had so many battles with him in games between Waterhead and Wigan St Pats and then Saints and Wigan. I was sad when Kyle switched codes. He had everything to be a good Rugby League player, but also everything to be a good rugby union player. Maybe a few pound signs swayed him, but it was a massive loss to Rugby League when he left."

Tomkins' England debut came against Wales, a warm-up match ahead of the Four Nations, but nonetheless a full international. England won 48-12 with the young stand-off scoring three tries. He missed the Four Nations opener against France but played in the 26-16 defeat to Australia. He was paired with Eastmond for the first time in the 20-12 win over New Zealand which got them to the final where they lost 46-16 to Australia at Elland Road.

"The Four Nations was amazing. We were very confident against New Zealand. We'd played the Aussies at Wigan, and I played instead of Richie Myler. It was a dream come true to play in a game like that, but they were a step above us. We had a gameplan to break the Kiwis down and we delivered on that. One thing I remember that week for is getting my first boot sponsor. I'd always bought my own boots that weren't great, then my agent got a call from Nike that week wanting to sponsor me, and I wore my new boots for the first time in that game. They were the fanciest £200 boots. It was like Christmas!"

The better Tomkins played, the more unpopular he became with opposition supporters. While that might be expected, he had to contend with a level of abuse rarely seen in the British game. In games at stadia away from Wigan, including once playing for England, he received the sort of receptions Wally Lewis used to endure in Sydney. After Tomkins was booed in an England shirt at Headingley in 2011, Lewis penned an article for League Express, advising the talented playmaker to remember that "fans that abuse players have never done anything of note themselves. They're nobodies whose greatest claim to fame is abusing someone who has."

"I got shit off the fans straight away," laughed Tomkins, "but I remember booing Sean Long when Wigan played Saints, and I wasn't even a Wigan fan! We booed him because he was the best player, and I knew that. Remembering that made me realise it's not the real world when people are booing you. It's just for 80 minutes. It stood me in good stead for the tonnes more I've had since.

"The booing didn't really bother me. It was more confusion. I understood St Helens or Warrington fans booing me, but in 2011, England played The Exiles at Headingley. I jogged out onto the field with Jamie Peacock and James Graham. We went across the field, and the Leeds fans started booing. I didn't know who it was aimed at, but every time I caught the ball in the practice before the game, the fans started booing. I was in an England shirt - surely that changes things. I wasn't upset, but I was pissed off because I was playing for England. Jamie Peacock said it was a disgrace and put his arm around me. It never bothered me after that. There had been panto villains before me like Sean Long, but he didn't get booed playing for Great Britain. A few weeks later, Wigan fans started booing me ironically when I caught the ball, and that was very funny."

THE turning point for Wigan came in 2010 when the 35-year-old Michael 'Madge' Maguire replaced Brian Noble as coach. Noble had rescued the Warriors from relegation in 2006, taking them towards the right end of the table over the next three years, but when his

contract ended, the club chose not to renew it. In came Maguire, one of Melbourne Storm's assistant coaches.

"Madge came in and changed the club from day one," said Tomkins. "That's the only way to describe it. We were a semi-final team before he came, and many were content with that. From day one in pre-season, that got knocked out of us, and it was a different world to what we'd experienced before. The volume of training was outrageous. We were doing similar training, but in quantities we'd never done before. We were training the house down every day.

"There was a group of us that had come through the Shaun Wane era of the Academy. We were all hungry, young lads who wanted to do anything to win. If the group had been older or more diverse in culture, Madge might have struggled. He wasn't just doing it to the players. He changed how people worked in the offices. He was telling them how things should be done because he'd been at Melbourne Storm who had been the benchmark of Rugby League set-ups. He revolutionised the whole club."

Wigan were criticised in 2010 and 2011 for implementing wrestling tactics that the Storm had perfected under their coach Craig Bellamy. "Michael saw an opportunity to gain an advantage legally, and he took it," argued Tomkins. "Everyone was trying to replicate it, but we were doing it better than anyone else. Rugby League is a tough sport. Some tactics got highlighted, but we were doing what we were told and copying Melbourne Storm, the best team in the world. Everyone was doing it one or two years after Madge brought it to Wigan."

One event at an early army camp under Maguire that still amuses Tomkins saw the new coach cross swords with his compatriot Mark 'Piggy' Riddell, the hooker Wigan had signed from Parramatta a year earlier. "We were

used to going to Lanzarote under Brian Noble for four days training and three days sunbathing," said Tomkins. "Madge said this would be four days training. We thought it would involve a rugby ball. But no, it was a brutal four-day sleep-deprived camp. Running and running. Crazy challenges. Running through water. It was a mental test. We were so tired after four or five hours. It had never been done over here before.

"After the first day, they showed us our dorm. 'We'll wake you up at 8am for breakfast,' they said. And we believed it. But every 45 minutes, the army sergeant came in, banging pans. Then they got us up at 4am to train again. On the last morning, we all got up, and they came in screaming and shouting for us to get into our army kit. We lined up outside, but Mark Riddell had got up, taken off his camouflage gear, put on his terrible Aussie clothes, lay on his bed, put his hood up, and said, 'I'm not doing it!' 'What do you mean?' we said. 'It's not an option!'

"We all walked outside. They could see someone was missing. Who? No one would say. Madge walked into the dorm, and we could hear everything. It was schoolteacher versus naughty kid, but with lots of swearing! Riddell kept saying, 'You have a duty of care to look after us,' and we could hear Madge shouting, 'Fuck your duty of care!' We did the morning run. We finished at a pub, and all had a pint. Piggy had to walk to the pub on his own like a sad little kid, and Michael told us we'd be fined £100 if we spoke to him. So he had to stand in the corner on his own!"

Maguire was responsible not just for an upturn in Wigan's fortunes, but he changed Tomkins' career by switching him from the halves to fullback. Tomkins explained: "When I trained with Trent Barrett in 2008, he said to me, 'You'll end up at fullback.' I'd always been a halfback, and it didn't happen. When Madge arrived, he said he saw me as a fullback too. If they both thought it, I knew there was a good chance it was right, but I wasn't too keen at first.

"We played Salford and with the game won with 15 minutes left, he put me at fullback to test it. We tried it in training too, and it became more frequent. Then I started there at London away, where I'd made my Super League debut. I scored a couple of nice tries, and I was happy. The system was very attacking, playing to the backs. I knew I'd get a lot of opportunities and freedom to get more ball than in the halves. I had a licence to roam.

"Madge filled me with confidence in that role. 'How many tries will you score today?' he used to ask. 'Two,' I'd say. 'Nah, three. We'll definitely win, and you'll get man of the match.' That's how he talked to me. He pumped my tyres up before a game."

Melbourne Storm's fullback at this time was Billy Slater, sometimes regarded by Australians as the finest exponent of the position, or certainly on a par with Clive Churchill and Graeme Langlands. "We had similar styles," observed Tomkins," but there were plenty of different things about us. Madge only compared us to Melbourne players when he was assessing our fitness-test scores. He had all the scores of their players, and paired us up, so he could do comparisons. When you come into the team, people always compare you to someone. The next whoever. He just said, 'You're going to be Sam Tomkins.' He said future players would be compared to me which seemed bizarre."

Wigan's 2010 season ended perfectly, as they beat St Helens 22-10 in the Grand Final, although the match was tinged with sadness as it came six days after the suicide of the club's former hooker Terry Newton. "We felt like we'd get to the Grand Final all year," said Tomkins. "We were dominant. It would have been a disaster not to win it. That might have sounded a bold statement as Wigan hadn't won the Grand Final since 1998, but we knew we had a great coach and a great group of players. We were nervous about playing the semi-final [at Leeds] because that's the tough one - tougher than final. Once we got through, it was the dream final against St Helens. We couldn't have asked for more. It was set up for the fairy-tale ending which we got.

"It was a massive shock when the Terry Newton news came out. We had players who knew him very well like Paul Deacon and Sean O'Loughlin. They had played with him for a long time, and a lot of our players played with him at Wigan. It probably put more pressure on us because those players that knew him thought we had to do it for Terry."

Wigan failed to retain their title in 2011, but they did lift the Challenge Cup after beating Leeds at Wembley, a game which saw the Tomkins brothers, Joel and Sam, combine for a tremendous try scored by the elder sibling. Sam fielded the ball on his 10-metre line near the left-hand side of the field. He crabbed across the field, evading defenders, and found Joel near the left touchline on the 20-metre line. He beat one defender on halfway before cutting in between two more and scoring under the posts for "one of the great Wembley tries" in the words of BBC commentator Dave Woods. It opened up a 14-0 lead for Wigan en route to a 28-18 win. Sam later got fined for making a V-sign to Leeds supporters.

"We came up short in the Challenge Cup in 2010 and there was a huge focus on winning it in 2011," said Tomkins. "Leeds would be tough. They knew how to win, but we were at our best. The try that Joel scored will go

down as one of the greatest Wembley tries. As I get older, I can appreciate it more. The V-sign was the best five grand I ever spent, and you can print that. I'd do it again tomorrow."

SHAUN WANE was the next Wigan coach, taking over for the 2012 season after Maguire landed the plum South Sydney Rabbitohs job. After a trophyless first season, one which saw Tomkins win his first Man of Steel as the best player in Super League, Wane steered the team to the Challenge Cup and Super League double in 2013. The Grand Final would be the final match of Tomkins' first spell at the club, but his dream year ended in the final minute of the World Cup semi-final when a last-gasp converted try by New Zealand provided a rare moment of anguish for the young fullback.

"Shaun and Madge had a lot of similarities," said Tomkins. "They had ways of getting the best out of players. They were a great match as coach and assistant coach. Shaun added his bits to the strong foundations laid by Madge. I knew early on it would be my last year at Wigan, so you pray for the fairy-tale ending," he said. "Lee Mossop and the legend Pat Richards, an adopted Wiganer, were also leaving. It was an amazing way to finish.

"The 2013 World Cup semi-final defeat was probably worse than in 2022 because we were so dominant that day. We were the better team for 79 and a half minutes. A few dumb mistakes gave New Zealand the opportunity to pinch it at the end. It was very tough to get over, and I was off to live in New Zealand with the people who had done that to me!

"Sam Burgess was outstanding that day. Sam's a freak of a player. He's everything you want in a Rugby League player. The great players make people around them play better. That's the true sign of a great player. He was a big, strong, powerful thing, and very intelligent with it."

As John Monie, Dean Bell, Frano Botica, Andy Platt and Denis Betts had done nearly 20 years earlier, Tomkins left Wigan for Auckland, spending two seasons with New Zealand Warriors. He scored 14 tries in 37 matches, figures that were somewhat spoiled by an injury-hit second season which saw him play on 13 occasions, scoring one try. The team failed to reach the top-eight play-offs in those two seasons.

"I enjoyed living there - it's an amazing place and I grew

up a lot," said Tomkins. "I'd been firmly in my comfort zone - one mile from mum and dad, playing with my friends, no stress. I'd maybe got a little too comfortable at Wigan. I went 12,000 miles to test myself, from the best team in the UK to a mid-table NRL team. I didn't play some of my best rugby. They were tough times on the field, but I grew a lot being there. I enjoyed it massively and earned a lot of money which was a big reason for going. I nearly went to rugby union. I wanted to do something different, but I didn't know what.

"I was told about [the Wigan connection] straightaway. The club is very strong on heritage, even though they're not very old. You have a sense of where you are when you walk in, with heritage numbers and old pics everywhere. Dean Bell was part of recruitment when I was there, and he was Warrior number one because he was captain in 1995. I'd come through the Wigan Scholarship with Dean there."

Like Betts and many others in more recent times, Tomkins returned to Wigan for a second stint, but he denied that any agreement, however informal, had been in place before he went. "Sometimes there can be a first-refusal clause, but it's not worth the paper it's written on," he said. "I'd never agreed anything. I was having fun in New Zealand, but I snapped the posterior ligament in my knee. I was in a brace. My wife fell pregnant. Things weren't quite as expected. We were adapting to the idea of becoming parents, so Kris Radlinski's call was well timed. He told me about the new marquee-signing rule, saying they could pay one player what they wanted, and it wouldn't count on the salary cap. Would I be interested if the rule got passed? Yes.

"I spoke to the club for a release, but they would only release me if they could sign Roger Tuivasa-Sheck. He agreed to sign, but you have 40 or 50 days to change your mind in the NRL, so I could only sign after that. Ian Lenagan suddenly asked if I could wait another year, but I said I was going to come back in 2016 no matter what, so my agent phoned Simon Moran at Warrington. I'd have happily gone there, having supported them as a kid. He said he'd give me what I wanted, but he also predicted that Ian Lenagan would match it and I'd end up going to Wigan. But the Warrington offer was there. So for a brief period, I thought I'd go to Warrington, but Simon was right. Ian matched their offer and I went back to Wigan."

IN Tomkins' first year back, Wayne Bennett was unveiled as the new coach of England, a post he would hold from 2016 to 2019. He led Great Britain on an ill-fated and badly-planned tour of the southern hemisphere in 2019 which saw them lose to New Zealand twice, a Tonga Invitational team and Papua New Guinea. Undoubtedly the master coach in the 1990s and 2000s, Bennett was unable to change England's fortunes, and Tomkins believes the appointment was an error.

"He was a very strange character," Tomkins said. "I never expected a coach like him. He was ultra-relaxed, he didn't know names, he had no understanding of English players apart from those who played in the NRL. It was a strange set-up really. He was a different character. He leant on assistants to do a lot of the physical coaching. He was about preparing you.

"I don't think it was a good appointment. We got his experience which was great. He's had a huge effect on Rugby League in his career, but an England coach should be English. They should be homegrown and passionate about English Rugby League. That's what I believe an England coach should be. They should have come through the same system as the players. Steve McNamara did a great job. Shaun Wane has done a good job. Wayne wasn't based in England which was a problem. We used to have meetings. There'd be a big screen with him on, and it was just shit. The internet would trip out. He was blurred. It didn't feel like he was part of the group. I think the RFL knew that."

Tomkins did at least taste further glory in the cherry and white. As in his first spell, his final game for the club was a Grand Final victory at Old Trafford, although he did get off to a slow start on his return. "I'd come back in 2016 with the injury I'd sustained in New Zealand, and I made an underwhelming start," he admitted. "My return to playing wasn't as glamorous as I'd have liked. I started on the bench to help my knee recover. Once I got on the field, I was ok, and I enjoyed being back in the Wigan set-up, but after 18 months, I got the same feeling of wanting to do something else.

"Steve McNamara got the Catalans Dragons job in 2017. I'd been in touch with him since his England days. My thought turned to going there. It was a tough decision. I'd been at Wigan for so much of my career. I was reaching 29. I knew my salary was big, so I told Wigan I had the offer to go to France. Ian Lenagan said he'd come back with an offer, and I was shocked how good it was. It was a nice feeling to be wanted by Ian, Kris Radlinski and Shaun Wane, who are all friends. They offered me four years on marquee money.

"My dad's exact words were: 'That's a no-brainer, get it signed!' But I thought France might be for me. My dad was astounded. He thought I was crazy. But the Catalans offer was similar, so it didn't come down to money like when I went to New Zealand. I'd done it all at Wigan. I don't want to sound like a spoiled brat, but I wanted something else. I'd enjoyed a different culture in New Zealand, and France was pretty close to home."

The Dragons won the Challenge Cup in 2018, the season before Tomkins went there. At the time of writing, the Dragons have failed to win another major title, although Tomkins did win his second Man of Steel in 2021 as the club won the League Leaders' Shield.

With Bennett gone and Shaun Wane in charge, Tomkins captained England in the World Cup in 2022, a tournament that was delayed a year due to Covid-19. After a stunning 60-6 thumping of Samoa in Newcastle, England lost to the same opponents in golden point in the semi-final at Arsenal. Did the opening-day win over Samoa end up destabilising the campaign?

"Probably slightly," Tomkins responded, "but we didn't go into the semi-final thinking it would be the same because they'd improved significantly. We knew we were good enough if we played well, but there were uncharacteristic errors from players who don't normally make them. Samoa took their chances and got the win. I'll look back on the World Cup in 2022 as a good experience, but the overriding tone is we fell short."

Tomkins' international experiences make him no different to the majority of British players in this book. For 50 years from 1972, Great Britain and England have come close to winning a few major competitions but have been miles away on many other occasions. Tomkins, though, can console himself with the knowledge that he was arguably the dominant Super League player of the 2010s, and his deeds have elevated him into the highest echelon of Wigan Rugby League legends.

COLIN CLARKE

1963-1976
1977-1978
1984-1986 (joint coach)

Colin Clarke served Wigan for 16 years as a player, alongside legends like Billy Boston, Dave Bolton, Eric Ashton and Brian McTigue. The highlight was a Wembley win over Hunslet in 1965 which remains regarded as one of the greatest Challenge Cup finals. Along with Alan McInnes, Clarke was the joint Wigan coach for two seasons which included the classic Wembley win against Hull FC in 1985. He is the father of the Sky Sports pundit, Phil, who also excelled for Wigan.

If you could relive one day from your career, which would it be?
The 1985 Challenge Cup Final. Being joint coach and leading my hometown club into a final at Wembley was the pinnacle of everything. The last time Wigan had won the Cup was in 1965, and I had played in the final. The sheer fact it's called the greatest-ever Wembley final is further icing on the cake.

How did you come to sign for Wigan?
I signed up for three trials in November 1962. The weather was so severe I could only do one trial, which was at Blackpool, and I was a disaster. All sport ceased for about ten weeks. The end of January was deadline day for signings. I'd carried on training with the team, going to Blackpool on the sands, and I must have impressed because on 29th January 1963, Wigan signed me.

What do you remember of your debut against Castleford in April 1963?
Because so many fixtures had been postponed that winter, there was a huge backlog. Wigan played St Helens on Good Friday, Leeds on Easter Saturday and Castleford on Easter Monday, and that was my debut as a 17-year-old. For a young lad idolising Billy Boston and the others from the terraces, it was a dream, even though Billy and many of the regulars didn't play because they'd played in the previous two games. We only had three regulars in the team, and we lost.

Can you name the team?
I'll have a go. The fullback would have been John Winton. Geoff Bootle and Trevor Lake were on the wings. Trevor was quite new to the team then. Jim McCormack (Steve's dad) and Alan Davies were centres. Stan McLeod was stand-off with Frank Parr scrum-half. Jimmy Belshaw and Brian Larkin were props. I was hooker. Frank Collier and I think John Stephens were in the second row and Jack Gregory was loose forward.

All correct! Did you play many more that season?
I played two more at the end of the season – a draw at home to Cas and a defeat at Warrington. Everyone was exhausted after all the games we'd had to cram in to make up for those missing ten matches. There were so many midweek games. We were all working too. I was an apprentice at Leyland Motors where they made trucks and buses.

You won the Cup at Wembley in 1965. What are your memories?
We had contested scrums then, and Hunslet had a great hooker called Bernard Prior. There was pressure on the hooker because journalists would give out scrum figures, so everybody would judge you on those. But I managed to outhook Bernard that day, which was a great feat for me because he was a brilliant hooker.

Who were best hookers you watched?
I used to watch Bob Dagnall at St Helens because he was a great ball-getter at the scrums. I used to learn from him. Wigan had a great one in Bill Sayer. He was the Great Britain hooker on the 1962 Lions Tour.

You were suspended from the 1966 Wembley final against Saints for technical scrum offences. That sounds harsh. What were they?
The hooker was always under pressure because if the team lost and you'd lost the scrums, people blamed you, so you had to go for it. They brought a rule in - three strikes and you're out. My suspension was for foot up in the scrum - in other words striking before the ball came in because you had to anticipate just when the scrum-half would put the ball in. Laurie Gant penalised me after the first offence. Then he pulled me out and warned me. And then he sent me off. I hoped for the sympathy vote, but I got done for two games!
A while ago, I was on a sport's forum at Wigan with Michael McIlorum. He looked like I was talking in Swahili because he couldn't grasp how you could be sent off and miss Wembley for having your foot up in the scrum. It was more common than you'd think because if you kept your feet down, you'd never win the ball. Scrums in the '60s should have come with a health-and-safety warning!

How tough was the final to watch, not just because you missed out, but because Alex Murphy exploited Wigan's lack of a recognised hooker to the max.
Yes, Alex exploited the rules, and the rest is history. Wigan never seemed to have a reserve hooker, so we had to play Tommy Woosey there. He was a good lad, but he was a prop, not a hooker. St Helens had signed Bill Sayer earlier in the season to make it worse, and it was he who won most of the scrums at Wembley.
What Alex did was very clever. He kept giving away penalties when we had the ball, knowing that a scrum would be set after we had kicked to touch. You couldn't just tap it after the kick to touch like now. I hadn't seen a team do what St Helens did that day. It was a new thing. Alex found a loophole in the rules, and he exploited it. He wanted to win, and they did.

What are your memories of the 1966 tour?
I remember we went without a coach. There were just 26 players, a manager - Wilf Spavin, an assistant manager and a physio - Paddy Armour. The physio came down to

training, and we made it up as we went along. Wilf picked the team, but he was never on the training field. It seems bizarre today when you look at all the staff they have now. It was a four-and-a-half-month tour with no coach. We played about 33 games. It was a wonderful experience, and we had some great players like Alan Hardisty, Bill Burgess, Dave Robinson and Cliff Watson.

Were you disappointed not to play in the Ashes, or had you accepted you were the back-up hooker to Peter Flanagan?
I didn't class myself as the back-up hooker. I went giving myself a chance to play. I'd played against Sydney and New South Wales, so I was a bit shocked not to get picked for the Test. But the tour captain Harry Poole didn't get picked either because Dave Robinson played loose forward.
The country games were brilliant because fans out in the bush travelled miles. I enjoyed playing in New Zealand because I had a point to prove after missing the Australia Tests. I gave it every ounce of energy I had. I think I played most games in New Zealand because there were a few injuries. I played wing and then centre in one day and finished one game at stand-off against the New Zealand stand-off, Graham Kennedy.

Was it a big story that Alex didn't tour because he wasn't made captain?
No, it wasn't common knowledge at the time that that's why he pulled out.

How did you find out England had won the soccer World Cup?
I didn't know the score until I bought the Sydney Morning Herald, and there were four lines about it.
Communications weren't like they are today. To make a phone call was an event! We sent letters home instead.

After one Test against the French in 1967, you didn't play for Great Britain again until the 1973 Ashes. Why was that?
One of the problems I had was Wigan not having a back-up hooker, so I played a lot of games with injuries. I had bad knees and I needed operations at the end of most seasons - before I had my knee replacement, I'd had seven operations on it. I played in all three games of the 1973 Ashes series. There were only about 10,000 at Wembley for the first Test, which was very strange, but the Aussies wanted to play down there. I scored a try. I roomed with Ray Batten and said to him I'd do the move he did at Leeds with Bob Haigh. He was surprised I knew about it, but it worked, and I scored off it. The Aussies call it a double pump, and I came on it short and went straight through. You either scored off those or had your head taken off! Ray was a great player.

In 1971 you suffered the agony of a Championship Final defeat to Saints when they scored two late tries, including a complete fluke in the dying seconds.
The freak nature of that bounce is something I will never forget. The game was sewn up for us, and it was very hard to take when they scored those late tries. They tried a drop goal from the touchline. It was sliced and it bounced perfectly for them, and they scored in the corner. It was like the [Jack] Welsby try in 2020.
It was my childhood dream to play for Wigan alongside Billy Boston, Eric Ashton and Brian McTigue, who I

consider the greatest forward ever. We didn't win as much as we should have done. There was a more balanced league in those days. But I had a wonderful time.

Tell us more about Brian.
Brian McTigue was as tough as they ever came. He was also one of the finest gentlemen. He was a great player - a fantastic ball distributor. I was quick, so I followed Brian, knowing he'd never give me a bad ball. I had a marvellous couple of seasons with him. He taught me good habits, training wise - how to look after yourself. I roomed with him in 1965 and remember him getting me up at 6.30 to go for a walk on the golf course, and we talked about the game.

Why did you move to Salford in 1976?
I just got a call to say Salford had approached me and Wigan had agreed to let me go, so I went. I went to the Hall of Fame dinner in 2022 where David Watkins was honoured. He was an outstanding talent, and he's richly deserving of his place in the Hall of Fame. Colin Dixon played there too, and he was a fantastic player. Alex Murphy nicknamed them the Quality Street Gang. But Salford wasn't for me. They had some great players, but having been at Wigan for 13 or 14 years, I found it difficult to go to another environment, so I went back to Wigan.

You became coach at Leigh where you won the Division One Championship in 1982.
Coming towards the end of my playing career, coaching was never on my radar. I just wanted to bow out gracefully. I'd had 16 good years and thought that was it. I then had a chance meeting at a sportsman's dinner with John Stringer, the Leigh secretary, and that altered my course. I told him I was past my sell-by date, but he said they wanted an experienced player-coach for the 'A' Team because they had some good players who needed nurturing. We had further discussions, and I went to see the coach Tommy Grainey who made me player-coach of the reserves and assistant to the first team.
We made nice steady progress, but then the club told us they were bringing Alex Murphy back as general manager. To be honest, I didn't think it would work because Tommy was a proud Leigh fella, and I thought he was having authority taken away from him. Sure enough, he resigned a month later. I was promoted to first-team coach with Alex the general manager.

Who were the stand-out players?
We'd signed Eric Chisnall, Tony Cooke, Tommy Martyn, John Woods and Steve Donlan, who were all great players. Des Drummond was reaching his peak, so we had a very exciting team. I had three wonderful years at Leigh. They were a great club with great people and great fans, and I'm very glad I had that experience.

What was Des like?
He came to Leigh as a Bolton lad who didn't know a lot about the game. He played a trial and the chairman Brian Bowman paid for him to be signed. He developed into one hell of a great player. Pound for pound, they didn't come much tougher than Dessie. He was a very humble person, and he scored some wonderful tries. He was a devastating tackler. We had a brilliant attacking side with John, Steve and Dessie. It was so exciting to watch. When we had an attacking scrum, we would score two out of three because of the clinical moves they put on. Now they just get the ball and drive it in.

Do you remember the night you won the league at Whitehaven?

Of course! We took about 4,000 Leythers, and it was not a foregone conclusion because Cumbria was always a tough place to go, and we were losing at half-time. But we turned it round, and it was a great bus journey back. Most journeys back from Cumbria were on the back of a defeat, but that was a great trip back. The players had worked so hard and deserved everything.

Why did you leave Hilton Park?

I got sacked! We won the title in 1982. Murphy got head hunted by Maurice Lindsay at Wigan. On reflection, we probably overachieved in winning that Championship, but the directors thought we'd do it again, so when we were mid-table, I was replaced.

How did you end up as joint coach of Wigan with Alan McInnes?

I was out of the game for a few months and went to watch Wigan one day in 1983. Jack Robinson approached me in the bar. Maurice rang me the next day and offered me the second-team coaching job. I was also assistant to Alex Murphy with the first team, with Alan McInnes assisting with fitness. We got to Wembley in 1984 and lost to Widnes, who were too good and too strong for us in those days. During the summer of '84, Maurice and Alex had a disagreement, and he got sacked five days before the season was due to start, so they came up with the idea of Alan and me doing the job together.

How did it work?

Alan was a great organiser and planner. Every training session was planned to the finest detail. His teaching background gave him that - he was deputy head of a prestigious school in Macclesfield. It just worked. It wouldn't work for everybody, but it just did. We were completely different people. I'd just started my own business, reconditioning starting motors and alternators and other things in Standish. We just gelled. I had so much respect for Alan. We didn't go behind each other's backs. We trusted each other implicitly. We picked the team together. We never fell out. We always talked it out if we disagreed. We never seemed to have a problem picking the team.

How did it feel coaching someone like Brett Kenny?

Maurice was very ambitious and when he signed Brett, who wouldn't want him? He fitted in well, and he joined in with everything. He was different class. He had an ability to find something from nowhere when you needed it. His performance at Wembley was special. You expect it because great players like him and John Ferguson perform on the big stage.

Before the 1985 final, did Brett advise you on how to deal with Peter Sterling?

Not really. We didn't dwell too much on the opposition. We focused on ourselves and knew we had to defend well without the ball. Hull had some brilliant players. If you tried to snuff out one, you'd have problems elsewhere. We didn't have special plans for Sterling.

How tough a decision was it to fly John Ferguson back for the final for his first game since February, taking the place of regular winger Phil Ford?

In fairness to Phil Ford, it wasn't a difficult decision. John had been brilliant for us earlier in the season [September to February], so it was a no-brainer. If he was available, he would play.

How worried were you towards the end of the final as Hull roared back?

When we were well in front, I said to Alan, "I'm going to sit back and enjoy this." Then Hull scored - and scored again. It was a hectic last five minutes, knowing the quality of players they had. We were panicking at the end because one of the decisions we had was whether to bring on Nick du Toit as sub. We'd already put Danny Campbell on. Nick was fantastic with ball in hand. He was an ex-rugby union player from South Africa, but he was a bit lacking defensively. We couldn't put him on because Peter Sterling would have picked him out. I watched the highlights again a few days ago, and it still surprises me that Garry Schofield was only a substitute for Hull, but I'm glad he was!

What was behind the signing of Ellery Hanley at the start of the following season?

I really wanted it to happen and pushed for it. One of the toughest decisions was telling Phil Ford and Steve Donlan they had to go to Bradford. Steve had only been at Wigan for a few months. Along with Billy Boston, Ellery Hanley is one of the two finest players to have played for Wigan. He had a fantastic attitude to training and everything. He did everything you asked him to do.

Did the early blowing of the Halifax hooter in April 1986 cost you the league title?

Definitely! I obviously wasn't at Halifax that day, so I don't know all the facts, but it seems some sort of shenanigans went on. It isn't in doubt that the hooter went about two minutes early and it meant Featherstone didn't have a chance to kick a late drop goal when they were on top which would have handed us the title. But you can't change history.

You and Alan were sacked as joint coaches at the end of the season. What happened?

At that point, it was obvious Wigan had big ambitions. Ellery Hanley, Joe Lydon, Henderson Gill and Graeme West were on full-time contracts. We wouldn't go full time because I had my business and Alan was a deputy headmaster. We weren't going to give that up for a two-year contract, although we were never going to get that opportunity. It was still a shock, but when we were offered the job, I was realistic to know how it would end. Maurice phoned me at 10pm to sack me, and Jack Robinson phoned Alan at the same time. I was upset because we'd won four trophies - the Charity Shield, the John Player, the Lancashire Cup and the Challenge Cup - and we couldn't have come closer to winning the league. It was always on Maurice's radar to get an Antipodean coach. He thought coaching in this country was way behind. I didn't go to games immediately after, but within a few months, Phil signed for Wigan, so I went along to watch him in the second team. I've always had a what-will-be-will-be attitude, so you just get on with things, and I decided there would be no more coaching for me.

One of the highlights of Phil's career was scoring the first try in Great Britain's famous win in Melbourne in 1992. Were you there?

No, but I had all my pals around here. There were about 12 of us in the lounge, and I had a barbeque going. I remember being so elated. When my wife came home, I said, "We need to get out there!" But she couldn't get off school at short notice.

You were airborne when Phil sustained his career-ending neck injury in 1996. How do you recall that weekend?

Yes, my wife and I were going over there. I remember landing in Singapore and finding the South China Chronicle, which told me the Roosters had beaten North Queensland. We landed at Sydney airport, and a message came on the public-address system, asking us to make ourselves known. Ronnie Coote met us and told us that Phil was in hospital after an accident, but he was fine. We went to his flat and then to the hospital in North Sydney. We were too numb and in shock to be upset. But he was a clever lad, Phil. Four people were in there with broken necks. He said, "Don't panic!" He twiddled his fingers and toes which was a signal everything was working. It was a shock to see him in that condition. We were too shocked to be upset, and we had to be strong for him. After two weeks, my wife had to go back to teaching, but I stayed on for another four to look after him. He still had a big cage on his neck, but he had good people looking after him. The Roosters were magnificent, from Nick Politis down - all brilliant. The way they looked after him - and me and my wife. Phil went to Australia in 2022 for the Roosters opening their new ground, which they'd invited him to. They are a marvellous club.

NICKY KISS

1978-1989

Nicky Kiss was Wigan's hooker as they rebuilt from their 1980 relegation, right through the decade as they scooped trophy after trophy. Regular international honours eluded him, but Wigan supporters wouldn't have swapped him for anybody. Kiss was a Wigan regular for ten years and was crowned a world champion when he helped his team beat Manly in 1987.

AS a Rugby League writer, I never imagined I'd write about the Hungarian Revolution of 1956. That was until I tracked down the former Wigan and Great Britain hooker Nicky Kiss, whose parents fled Hungary separately and settled in Manchester. They met, they married, and they had five children, the oldest of which, Nicholas, was born in December 1959.

"They didn't know each other, so they came over independently," said Kiss. "My dad didn't say much about it, but my mum talked about it more. She was 16. They escaped over the mountains into Switzerland. They then went to Austria. From there, they were offered three destinations - Australia, America and England. My mum had her dad and elder sister who was living in England, so she came here.

"My grandfather had escaped Hungary years before. He was politically involved against the communists. He was outspoken and was a leader in his movement. He had to flee for his life in the end. He didn't go back to Hungary until the late 1970s because he'd have faced the death penalty, but it was eventually overturned. He was a well-thought-of person, and he hated the communists. He initially supported them because he believed in the ideology, but he soon changed his mind and fought against them.

"He'd had his own engineering firm. He was well connected because of that. In his younger days, he used to make huge iron gates for the toffs - lords and ladies etc. He was in both world wars. He lied about his age in the first world war. He was only 13 or 14, but he got in. He injured a leg, but he still fought in the second world war, although he got injured again. He always had a limp. He loved engineering because he said everything in Europe is functional and nice, but in England, it's not only functional and nice, it's also beautiful. He thought England was the best engineering place in the world.

"My parents met, got married and had me. I've got three sisters and a brother. My dad died, but my mum is still here. I've been to Hungary a few times, but I didn't go until I was 23 or 24. My siblings went lots and had a brilliant time, but it never appealed to me because I was always playing rugby and knocking about with my mates.

"My mum and dad were determined to integrate into the local community. Dad was a bespoke tailor, working by hand. People used to think we'd won the Pools because there was always a roller or a jag outside, but they belonged to his customers. My dad was a superb tailor and used good-quality material, so his customers tended to be wealthy.

"My parents faced some discrimination, but it was mainly ignorant kids. They'd hear my mum and dad speaking to us, especially my mum when we were out shopping. My dad only spoke to his customers, so his English wasn't so good, and his accent was quite thick. Mum has a lovely accent and great English, but people could still tell she was foreign, and she got some unpleasantness.

"There are a few people with the name Kiss here, but the pronunciation is different. In Hungary, the double 's' is pronounced 'sh', so it's Kish which means small or little. There were some good headlines when I played rugby like 'Kiss of Death' or Sealed with a Kiss'. I was going to write my memoirs and call them 'Kiss and Tell', but it never materialised."

The Kiss family were now based in Oldham, with Nicky playing for Saddleworth Rangers. He signed for Wigan in December 1977, aged 18, and made his first-team debut one year later in an away match at Keighley.

"I played internationally at amateur level," said Kiss. "We toured Australasia with BARLA Under-19s. I had a great time. A few had signed pro, although I hadn't. Salford fancied having a go at me. My parents asked Brian Gartland, my coach at Saddleworth Rangers, to look out for me because they knew nothing about rugby. Brian weighed up the clubs who wanted to sign me. Oldham were interested, but I didn't want to stop playing for Saddleworth. I was only about 15, but they played me in the 'A' Team as 'A N Other'. I got a fiver in a brown envelope after a game.

"Brian sussed Wigan out as the best opportunity for me to advance as a player. He said Martin Foy was going there. He said they had a great hooker in Colin Clarke, but he was getting on.

"I'm in a Whatsapp group with several ex-players of Wigan. Dave Regan set it up. There's Mick Rennox, Dave Walsh, Alan Greenall, Malcolm Swann, Steve Breheny, Colin Clarke, Mick Nanyn, Trevor Stockley, Martin Foy and Bill Francis. Amid all the jokes etc, we occasionally reminisce about our playing days. I sent a message about the night I signed my contract in one of the hospitality boxes at Central Park. It said, 'When I signed, Jack Hilton said to me, 'This is what you'll be playing on,' and he switched the floodlights on. The pitch had been freshly mowed and lined. All stands and barriers were newly painted. The window from the VIP lounge was like a black TV screen. Then, as the floodlights warmed up, the view came into brightness. That's one of the most beautiful sights I've ever seen. That was before I met you lot, and all the beautiful sights and memories come flooding back when I think of anyone of you! So thank you to you all x'"

AS Gartland predicted, Clarke didn't stay at Wigan for long after Kiss signed. The club also had Tony Karalius, who had played for Great Britain in the early-1970s. "Colin and Tony were both fantastic," said Kiss. "They were forever feeding snippets of advice. They advised me to stay off the drink despite the Monday-club [drinking] culture of the time. Tony said to me, 'Get the wind in the bank now, and it'll stand you in good stead,' meaning do loads of running now and you'll benefit as you get older. They advised me to do running before weights because you could

pull muscles and ligaments. They were both nice, but you had to be careful with first-teamers when you were a snotty-nosed kid as your relationship with them developed.

"Vince Karalius was the coach when I signed, and he instilled everything into me that I needed. He was so far ahead of his time. Wigan had a 50-metre cinder sprint track. I hadn't seen anything like it. They had their own gym. We were streets ahead of most, but there was a Monday-club attitude which distracted Wigan from being as good as they could have been.

"My first medal was the Lancashire Shield in the 'A' Team. It was ferociously contested. It was great to win that, and I started to come into my own the next season."

As Kiss was still developing, Wigan were relegated at the end of the 1979-80 season, the only campaign that Kel Coslett was coach for. The Welshman soon took over at St Helens. "Kel was unbelievable," laughed Kiss. "When he introduced himself, he said: 'Right lads, I'm Kel Coslett. I'm your coach. I've taken the job on, but really, I'm after the Saints job.' We're looking at each other, thinking, 'Did we really just hear that?' It was an amazing statement for a new Wigan coach to make!

"Relegation wasn't too big a deal for me, although the fans were distraught. I looked around me and knew we'd get promoted straightaway because we had players like John Pendlebury, Martin Foy and Mick Nanyn. I wasn't a regular first-teamer at the time, but I knew if I got my chance, they wouldn't drop me. That was the attitude of a lot of us in the 'A' Team and that's what happened when we were relegated. Division Two was perfect for a lot of the 'A' Team lads, and when we were promoted again, we were ready, and we were at the level we needed to be."

Wigan's Division Two campaign included two infamous matches. There was the defeat to Fulham in the Londoners' first-ever match, in which Kiss didn't play. Then there was a game at Fartown in March in which six players, including Kiss, were sent off. It was one of only eight games he played that season. The others to walk were Wigan's Alan Hodkinson and Les Bolton and Huddersfield's Jimmy Johnson, Glen Knight and Steve Lyons. Wigan were fined £500 with another £1,000 suspended.

"It was like rollerball," Kiss recalled with a grimace. "It was unbelievable. Alan Hodkinson was my open-side prop. He said, 'Right Kissy, the way things are going, there's going to be problems. If I end up walking, we'll struggle for ball. I'm going to take the hooker out because he's a good 'un. Keep your feet back in the next scrum, don't do anything.' I followed it to the letter. He had a go at the prop and the hooker, but mainly the hooker, and it all flared up. There was a huge melee, and I stayed right out of it. Alan and the hooker were sent off. I knew if I kept my nose clean, I'd win all the ball and we'd win.

"Then it erupted again, and I was sent off, along with one of their forwards. I was panicking all the way off the field, knowing that Alan was going to marmalize me! I stood outside the dressing-room door, listening to see if he was in the shower, so I could quickly get dressed. But he was sitting down. He looked up and went, 'Oh no, Kissy!' I said I hadn't done anything, and I'd been sent off for nowt! Even now I don't know the result [Wigan lost 9-7]. It was on the six o'clock news. Alan and I got big bans."

George Fairbairn was player-coach in Wigan's second-division campaign, but he was replaced when they were promoted by Maurice Bamford. "George was a very serious player and a great pro," said Kiss. "He was as hard as nails, but unfortunately for him, he was probably too young to have such responsibility. He was coach, captain and the leading light who everyone looked up to. I felt sorry for him. If all pros now were like George, this game would be as popular as football. He's a proper honest man.

"Maurice Bamford was a belting chap. He always had time for you. He loved the team camaraderie. He wanted us all having a crack together. He wasn't a bad tactician either, but he wouldn't change his ways. The Aussies had smashed us in 1982. The game was changing quickly, but Maurice wouldn't adapt. We probably changed too much because a lot of skills were phased out."

KISS became a regular in the side when Wigan were back in Division One, playing 32 matches in 1981-82 and 40 in 1982-83. But the following season was difficult with Kiss falling out with coach Alex Murphy who had signed the New Zealand Test hooker, Howie Tamati, and it was he who hooked at Wembley in 1984 with Kiss having walked out on the club.

"Everything positive under Alex came from [assistant coaches] Bill Ashurst, Colin Clarke and Alan McInnes. I'm not saying that to have a go at Murphy, but the game had changed so much by the time he came to Wigan, and he hadn't.

"We'd be doing something constructive in training, and then Alex would turn up. He'd scrap everything and we'd be doing donkey rides up and down the terraces instead. It was ridiculous. In the end, I said something. He knew I didn't respect him as the rugby legend he was. To invite the cameras in [in 1983] and be filmed berating the whole team was poor. I felt sorry for David Stephenson and Colin Whitfield who he really had a go at. He belittled people in front of everyone. He thought it was a positive thing to do.

"Howie Tamati came over and I spat my dummy. I wanted to keep him out of the side, but Alex was going to have him in by hook or by crook. I was told one Monday he'd be arriving on the Wednesday. Murphy said, 'It'll take him a bit to acclimatise. We're playing Leigh away and you'll be picked. If Howie's alright, I might give him part of the second half.' I said fair enough. We did all the training, and Howie had been to one session. On the day, we were near the dressing room, which was so small that Murphy only wanted the team in. Everyone else had to stay out. He read the team out. Howie was at nine. I wasn't even a sub.

"I was gutted. I took exception. At training on the Tuesday, I was in a toilet cubicle in the dressing rooms, and I shouted for a pen. One was slid into my cubicle. I wrote on some toilet paper, 'I, Nicky Kiss, want a transfer.' I signed it, dated it, and went upstairs. Murphy was there with Jack Hilton the chairman and Tom Rathbone. 'Now Nicky, what do you want?' said Jack. 'I want away from here,' I said. He was flabbergasted. 'Why do you want away?' 'Because of him,' and I pointed at Murphy who wouldn't look up.

"'Everything we do on the meadow that is constructive, he spoils the whole session. He just bursts our bubble. You're paying him, but Bill Ashurst, Colin Clarke and Alan McInnes do everything.' I threw this balled-up piece of paper down. It hit Jack on the chest and landed on his desk. I wanted to say sorry for doing that because he was a lovely man and a living legend as a player at Wigan. But all I could do was say, 'You're all at fault for bringing him here.' Jack said, 'This will be discussed in our next meeting but not now.' I left the room. Murphy hadn't looked up once. I think Wigan realised they'd made a huge mistake in employing him. I walked out of the club that night.

Nicky Kiss with Huddersfield's Hungarian player Bela Varga

"Wigan got to Wembley, and I drove down. So many Wigan fans greeted me by saying, 'You should be playing today!' I was gutted I wasn't. Keiron O'Loughlin had a great game for Widnes. His move to Widnes actually made him. He'd been a superstar at Wigan, but the local lads got overlooked and he wasn't really appreciated.

"Anyway, Murphy came back from his holiday at the start of the next season. I was still in self-exile. I went back for the annual sevens competition which Wigan won. He turned up after it had finished and demanded a bonus off Maurice Lindsay. That's when all hell broke loose, and Alex was sacked. I'd been there to speak to Maurice, but I drove home. Then Jack Robinson phoned me up and asked me to come back. I wanted paying for the previous season because what had happened wasn't my fault. They conceded, and I got some money in lieu of the season that had just gone - but not all! I also signed a new contract for the next two or three seasons."

Murphy went on to coach St Helens who played Wigan at Wembley in 1989. Wigan won 27-0. "As we came off the meadow, I was talking to Fozzy [Paul Forber] and Roy Haggerty," Kiss laughed. "I pointed at Murphy and said, 'How are you getting on with him?' They burst out laughing and said, 'Everyone calls him Smurphy behind his back.'"

Kiss and Murphy did cross paths again when the coach, now at Huddersfield, signed a Hungarian player called

Bela Varga. Needing an interpreter, Murphy contacted Kiss. "It was quite surreal," said Kiss. "He had this sprinter he wanted to sign, but he'd never played rugby before. I met the kid at a training session in Huddersfield. He was a good lad, but he couldn't speak a word of English, and he was too old to adapt to Rugby League. I told him what the game was like, and he wanted to have a go. I told him catching the ball and scoring is a bit different to just running. I said he'd get hurt and wouldn't be able to shake it off. It didn't work out for him."

Murphy was also complimentary about Kiss in the hooker's testimonial brochure in 1988. "Nicky is like a third prop forward, rough, tough and hard to put down," Murphy wrote. "I certainly wouldn't like to play against him, and I know the 100 percent effort he puts in takes its toll on opposing packs."

GREAT BRITAIN's number nine in their second Test match of 1985 was Nicky Kiss. He made his international debut alongside his club prop Shaun Wane, as they were beaten 24-16 in Perpignan by France. It was the only cap either of them would win. Another Wigan player on debut, Phil Ford, scored two tries. The hooker role, thereafter, was occupied by Hull KR's David Watkinson and Castleford's Kevin Beardmore.

"I was very proud to play for Great Britain," said Kiss. "I

played another warm-up match. Mal Reilly picked Kevin Beardmore when he took over [in 1987]. I remember a game against Halifax when I did my ankle. I was gutted because I had a real chance at that time to get back in."

Wigan were flying in the spring of 1985, which was partly down to a couple of Australians called Brett Kenny and John Ferguson, who had both signed to play for part of the 1984-85 season. "They were a breath of fresh air," said Kiss. "They were proper players. I'd originally learned from players like Bill Ashurst and Colin Clarke. Then there was a drop off when loads of players came and went.

"Kenny was incredible. He was like a ghost. He popped up from nowhere. He might be 50 yards away, then suddenly he's right next to you, screaming for the ball because he'd seen something. He had the pace, the balance and the raw power. He had incredible vision. He's an all-time great up there with Lewis, Boston, Gregory, Edwards and Hanley. Things just clicked, and there were so many great moments with Kenny and Ferguson because they could see things were on. I had the best seat in the house!

"Kenny's try at Wembley was fantastic. Ferguson's shimmy was amazing. John was like a bullet from a standing start. They could defend too. It's every players' dream to win at Wembley. I've more medals than Montgomery. I never played in a final and lost. I was like a bag of jumping beans till we got there. I remember the journey. There were roadworks, so there was a detour. There were police motorbikes to escort us. I remember going past Harrods. We went straight through like the Italian Job! I knew we were going to win even before we turned up."

Two and a half years later, Kiss played in a very different final as Wigan took on newly crowned Australian premiers, Manly-Warringah Sea Eagles in Rugby League's first - albeit unofficial - World Club Challenge. Manly boasted some wonderful players like centre Michael O'Connor, stand-off Cliff Lyons, scrum-half Des Hasler, second-rower Ron Gibbs and loose forward Paul Vautin who skippered the side. Since the 1985 Wembley final, Wigan had signed Ellery Hanley, Andy Goodway, Joe Lydon and Andy Gregory.

"I'd weighed up the team and thought, 'Who can I get to and dismantle their confidence?'" said Kiss. "I went for Vautin because he was the captain. I thought I could dismantle him from a mental point of view, and I knew I'd got through to him. I also made sure I got into his face when he played for St Helens too. He and Michael O'Connor were flown back for Wembley in 1989. I thought Vautin would tell O'Connor about me, so I got into their heads at Wembley. Henderson Gill had caught O'Connor, and I came in as well. I grabbed his hair and collar. I pulled his neck a bit and shouted, 'Let go of the ball!' And he did! I knew then we were only playing against 11 men. Those two were gone.

"Another physical game was against Castleford at Central Park. Glyn Shaw was my open side prop. Kevin Ward and I had been having a go at each other all game. Billy Thompson was ref. The final whistle went. I'd just tackled Kevin. He was stood up with the ball in front of his chest. I had hold of him. He's trying to shake me off and I wasn't letting go. Billy walked past us and just said, 'It's over.' Glyn flew past me like an Exocet missile into Kevin. He fell like a sack of spuds straight onto his back. There was a big 'Oooooh' from the crowd. Billy and the touchjudges hadn't seen it. I fell on top of Kevin. He was knocked out. I slapped him and he came around. I said, 'Don't ever do that to me again', as though I'd knocked

him out. From that day to this, I don't know if Kevin knows that I hadn't touched him!"

Another notable game that Kiss played in took place on 10th June 1989 in Milwaukee, a city in the American state of Wisconsin. Wigan played Warrington in an exhibition match in a bid to spread the game. Wigan won 12-5 with Andy Goodway scoring the only try. "We flew together and stayed in the same hotel," said Kiss. "We socialised together - it was just on the meadow there was a problem! The pitch was so small, we couldn't get out of each other's way. Les Boyd was always going to cause some damage, so I made sure I cleaned him out to create some confidence for a few others."

Little did he know it, but Kiss's career was almost at an end, as several events conspired against him. An arm injury at the start of the 1989-90 season saw new hooker Martin Dermott take his place. When Dermott was injured and Kiss fit again, new coach John Monie even selected prop Ged Staziker at hooker. The writing was on the wall. Kiss then suffered a spinal injury in a car accident in the winter. He didn't play again. His last game had been a 66-0 win against Barrow in the Lancashire Cup in October 1989 when he was 29.

"I smashed my neck and back up in the accident," he said. "I woke up in hospital and never put another pair of boots on again. Six years later, I had a brain haemorrhage. I was building my own house, and I suppose I pushed myself too far. I was very lucky. They said it was bad. I came round in theatre. I should be pushing up daisies now! There were three bleeds, and they clipped them all. I was in there nine or ten hours in all.

"I moved into coaching. I coached at Saddleworth, starting with the under-18s, then I was Waterhead's first-team coach. I was assistant to John Pendlebury in Super League with Halifax. I went back to Saddleworth and did the youth team. We emigrated to the Sunshine Coast in Australia and then came back.

"I don't go to many games now," he said. "I didn't know this for years, but ex-players are entitled to two tickets, so I'm taking that up for the first time this season [2023]. I've been to two reunions and a couple of past-players' dinners. It never occurred to me that people die, and you miss a chance to speak to them. The last dinner was at Standish. I had a good chat with Bill Ashurst who was a phenomenal player and a lovely man. Our paths crossed coaching amateur level and we always had a chat. He told me he'd just been to Australia to the Penrith Panthers. They always invited him and flew him over, but he'd had a heart attack over there. I could see he still wasn't right. A few days later, he had died. I was so glad I got the chance to have that chat with him.

"I was watching telly, aged 17 or 18. Wigan were playing Hull KR or Bradford. A scrum erupted, and Billy had taken exception to something that had gone on. He punched one prop then dropped the hooker. He virtually dropped the whole pack. He was the director of operations with the kicking and handling too, but he could also look after himself."

"I do still follow Wigan, but I do feel sorry for the players who will never experience Central Park. I adored the place. Someone sent a poem to our Whatsapp group called 'Thoughts on the Passing of Central Park' by someone called C. Storey in 1999. It's about his memories of the ground and the players that graced the field. The ending goes, 'When the site becomes a Tesco, things won't be the same, the guilty men who sold it will be in Wigan's Hall of Shame.'"

PHIL CLARKE

1989-1995

Having firmly established himself as one of the world's best back-rowers, Phil Clarke's playing career ended prematurely in 1996 when, aged 24, he broke his neck playing for Sydney Roosters. He won six league titles and five Challenge Cups at Wigan. He played 16 times for Great Britain, captaining them once, and six times for England. He was selected at loose forward in the 1993 World XIII.

If you could relive one day from your career, which would it be?

I have been a player, team manager, chief executive and commentator, but at heart I'm a fan, so I'll choose a game I once attended and sat in the crowd. I was almost 14 and travelled to Wembley on the train with friends to watch the 1985 Challenge Cup Final between Wigan and Hull FC. My dad, Colin, was the co-coach of Wigan along with Alan McInnes. I'd never experienced anything like it. I was stood high up in the ground in what felt like a modern-day Colosseum. The game contained my all-time favourite try, scored by Henderson Gill. It was an example of a team willing to attack from their own half, quite rare today with the obsession of field position. Wigan's right centre positioned himself inside the left centre, creating more attackers than defenders. The try had a combination of risk, skill and speed, with some suspense added too because you didn't know if Gary Kemble would stop Gill as he scorched down the left touchline. Hendy managed to get past him and the smile on his face at the end was the perfect way to finish it off. If I was given 30 seconds to sell the sport to someone who had never seen it, that would be the action I'd present.

Tell us about the Schoolboys' final you played in at Wembley for Wigan Under-11s against Morley.

The organisation and planning of the Wigan Schoolboys' trip to Wembley in 1982 was as good or better than any trip with Wigan or Great Britain later in my career. Teachers like Ray Unsworth, Dave Mallin, Mick Mullaney and many others made it run so smoothly. In fact, a lot of Wigan's success in the 1980s and 1990s was down to the quality of coaching in the Wigan schools and junior clubs in the decade that had preceded it. We stayed in a hotel the night before the game, and it was the first time a lot of us had stayed in a hotel before. It had a shoe-shining machine which I remember us all using! We got changed in the same big room as the brass band. That's another thing that sticks out.

Playing at Wembley was an unbelievable experience. The tunnel leading to the pitch was quite steep and you could hear the sounds before you could see the pitch or crowd. It played with your senses until you saw this magnificent arena in front of you. I ran 60 metres and dived in to score at the corner, but I had put a foot on the touchline one step short of the try line. The touchjudge raised his flag and I felt like bursting into tears! We got our medals from Stu Francis who was famous for the kids' TV programme Crackerjack, and after the match I got into the Widnes dressing room. One of our players was the nephew of a Widnes player, and he got us in. I remember the subdued atmosphere because they'd drawn. I also recall the big baths. They were those massive traditional baths. You never think that in less than ten years' time you could be back playing in the big game, but that's what happened.

As a student at Liverpool University, how were you accepted into the Wigan dressing room?

Pretty well. It was a highly competitive environment, and you were welcomed if you were willing to work hard. I am grateful to John Monie, who would organise training times around my lecture times. There was an unofficial mentoring programme that took place at Wigan. A senior player would 'adopt' a younger one. Andy Goodway looked after Denis Betts, and I was very lucky that Ged Byrne took me under his wing. In my uni holidays, I even worked with Ged, cleaning windows.

What do you remember of your time in the Alliance team?

They were my happiest days playing rugby because there wasn't the same pressure or seriousness as in the first team. I spent some memorable Friday nights with Andy Farrell, Mick Cassidy, Ged Byrne and Mike Forshaw. The best game was a Lancashire Cup Final at Central Park on a Friday against Widnes, with a crowd of almost 3,000. It was high quality and fast. If you did well in that game, you knew that you had a good chance of playing in the first team.

What are your sharpest memories, good or bad, of your Wigan career?

Getting knocked out trying to tackle Kevin Ward at Knowsley Road one day. I woke up ten minutes later, thinking that I need to improve my tackling technique. I also remember being frustrated in one game because I was determined to score more tries – I thought it was a weakness I needed to work on. We played against Leeds and Martin Offiah was scoring all these tries. I fell out with him in the match because I felt that he should have passed to me when he made a break. That was the day he scored ten tries, so I soon realised my place!

Do you have any career regrets?

Perhaps that I didn't enjoy my career more. Maybe I was too serious, and too critical of my own performances.

Ellery Hanley was ahead of you in the loose-forward pecking order. Was he a positive influence on your career?

The first time I saw him play live was at Odsal when Wigan played his Bradford team in March 1985 for a Challenge Cup quarter-final. Wigan won 7-6. Brett Kenny played for Wigan, but Ellery was by far the best player on the pitch. Everyone in the ground held their breath every time he touched the ball. When he was at Wigan, he often heaped praise onto his teammates. We sometimes forget what a huge star he was in this country. He even appeared on Wogan, which had millions of viewers, when he signed for London Monarchs. He was huge for Rugby League.

Which other players stood out for you?

Andy Gregory was the Diego Maradona of Rugby League because he was such a star on the field and a big character off it. He was the sharpest, wittiest person I've ever met. You had to have a tough skin to deal with his put downs, but he did make people laugh. Like Ellery, Shaun Edwards was very focused with a great competitive spirit. His will to win has made him successful, as he was possibly not as naturally talented as some other players. Those two set the tone for Wigan being so successful for so long. Kelvin Skerrett doesn't get many mentions, but he was a great team man, and I loved his company. Then there's Andy Farrell. Look at his incredible performance against Brisbane in 1994 when he was just a teenager. My closest friend was Denis Betts, who I am still very close to today.

You and Denis spoke in 1995 of needing a greater challenge when you left Wigan for the Winfield Cup. Was winning becoming less enjoyable?

I like a challenge and needed a new one. When the final hooter sounded at Wembley it was becoming more of a relief than an explosion of joy. The pressure and expectations had grown exponentially as each year went by. Walking up for your medal wasn't as exciting as the first time. I left because I wanted to experience the thrill of winning as an underdog again.

What are your memories of the 1990 and 1992 Lions Tours?

I loved going to Papua New Guinea and have been five times. It's a great life experience. Some Super League clubs do warm-weather training camps, but I'd suggest a trip to PNG would be a much better experience than training in a four-star hotel in Lanzarote. The first Test in Australia was amazing - the fastest game of my life. Martin Offiah had two chances to score down the left wing, but Andrew Ettingshausen just about pushed him into touch twice. In the second Test in Melbourne, I was lucky with my dummy, and I scored the first try. Scoring first is important for us because defending a lead as underdogs is easier than coming from behind. Before the third Test, I got food poisoning from a seafood restaurant and lost 10lbs, so I didn't perform as I could have. We lost 16-10, but the Aussies always seemed in control.

Why did we come up short in the 1992 and 1995 World Cup Finals?

Playing in front of 73,000 fans at Wembley in 1992, all cheering us on, was a childhood dream. Australia were the more skilful side, and their passing plays were better than ours. Andy Platt and Kevin Ward played so well, and Malcolm Reilly was outstanding in the build-up as our coach. Deryck Fox kicked brilliantly. As a halfback kicking today, he'd be right up there for accuracy and effectiveness. We had a man sin binned early in the second half. We held on for those ten minutes, but it left us a bit flat in the last quarter. In 1995, I made a mistake from a kick-off after England had gone 2-0 in front, and Rod Wishart scored a minute later. When I wake up from dreams, they're often about me making mistakes, and that one is right up there, although Wikipedia blames Andrew Farrell for the error!

When Shaun Edwards was sent off at Wembley in 1994 against Australia, did your belief that we could win waver? What did Ellery say at half-time?

Firstly, without Jonathan Davies, we don't score that try. He was a world-class player. He was small, but quick, tough and durable. People tried to hurt him, but few managed to make a dent. It was going to be hard to beat Australia with 13 men on the pitch, so with 12 it felt like Mission Impossible. I don't know if we were even that confident before the game. But Ellery's half-time speech was the best I have ever heard. I don't recall every word or sentence, but the tone and the essence were perfect. He was utterly convinced that we would win and infused that belief into us all.

What was it like to captain Great Britain in the second Test in what could have been an Ashes-winning match?

It was the best and worst memory of my career. I did let my mind wander during the week and started to imagine winning with me as captain. All my family were there. It was a huge thing, but we got hammered 38-8. It was such a crash back down to earth. Looking back, I can see how that sort of encapsulates the highs or lows of sport.

Shortly after the 1995 World Cup, you visited South Africa to coach in the townships. What was behind that?

I knew I'd been very lucky in life, so I wanted to give something back. I went out to do some voluntary coaching in Soweto and townships in the Vaal triangle. I was trying to get over the disappointment of losing in the World Cup and would encourage more players to do something like this - I know NRL players have been to places like Rwanda. Travelling is such an invaluable experience. I'll always remember going to an orphanage in Soweto - such a humbling experience. I'd been to Papua New Guinea, but I'd never been so close to the real-life conditions I experienced in the townships. I took some Roosters kit to give away and seeing the smile on the faces of those kids will stay with me forever.

You were coached at the Roosters by one of the great coaches, Phil Gould. What can you tell us about him?

He's the best orator I've ever met. He could have been a barrister and would have been brilliant defending you in court. If your coach is naturally bright and inquisitive, you have more chance of being successful. He had a fascinating personality and intelligence, and that made him someone you wanted to listen to you. Some players might not be as important as others in the team, they all have different roles, but he persuaded everyone to contribute and focus on what they needed to do well to succeed.

You played 12 games for the Roosters. Do you have a favourite?

We won at Manly in 1995 and that one game was the reason why I decided to sign for the Roosters. We were a mid-table team. They were top. You start to play sport for fun and enjoyment, but that can get lost in a professional environment. I'll always remember Phil Gould driving the bus back across Sydney Harbour Bridge after the game, windows open, singing as if we were back at school. Wonderful memories. Yes, Phil had a bus licence too!

The last game of your career came in round two of 1996 when the Roosters travelled to North Queensland. Do you remember anything of the day itself?

Yes, I was trying to buy a house in Clovelly. Houses in Sydney sell on Saturdays at street auctions. Because I was up in Townsville, I had the club solicitor bidding. I was on

the phone at midday, listening to the auction. Eventually I got the house. It was a big commitment, but by 7.35pm, I'd broken my neck and was on my way to hospital.

How did the injury happen?
It was early in the match. They kicked deep into our corner. Our fullback had been tackled two metres in from touch, with the tryline two metres behind him. Peter Jorgensen, the left winger, went to acting-half. I thought he would scoot himself, but he threw me the ball in the in-goal area. I was determined to get out, so I put my head down as the defenders approached, and my chin went down into my chest very quickly. I remember a loud cheer from the crowd, as they applauded a big tackle. I slowly got up, rolled the ball back and stood there not wanting to appear soft by leaving the field. The Roosters trainer, Ronnie Palmer, told me to come off for a minute to be assessed by the doctor.

It was unlimited interchange in Australia back then, and Phil Gould has said since that he doesn't know if he would have taken me off if subs had been limited. By the time I slowly walked off the pitch, all my neck and upper-thoracic muscles had gone into spasm to prevent me from moving my head. It's very clever the way the human body works to protect itself. Neil Halpin was the club doctor, and his experience was vital. We are so lucky that we have so many wonderful doctors within the sport. I was quickly taken to Townsville Hospital, which was a smallish regional place back then. Bizarrely, the doctor who treated me had been at Liverpool University when I was there. She just came out and said, "You've broken you neck," which was probably the best way to break the news. Straight and to the point.

What happened in the subsequent days and weeks?
I was in a lot of pain. Nick Politis, David Gyngell and a few others from the club came to visit me, and a couple of them had tears in their eyes. In the morning we flew back to Sydney and the plane had the front few rows of seats taken out, and I lay there on a stretcher. I was taken to Royal North Shore Hospital by ambulance from Sydney Airport. There were three other people in the same spinal ward. It was a very distressing scene, and I will never forget it. Sadly, they will never walk again.

There was a gap of about 15 millimetres between the C4 vertebrae and my spinal cord. The vertebrae had moved slightly, but I had a few millimetres to spare. Had the bone touched the spinal cord, it would have been profoundly serious, and I am so fortunate.

When did you know for certain your playing career was over?
We initially discussed a few options, one of which was an operation so I could play again, but when we investigated, no doctor had done that exact operation, and no one had ever played again. It didn't seem viable. So it was about four months after the injury that I knew my career was over. I had gone on a rollercoaster of thinking that I might never walk again, to believing that I could play again before finally accepting that my career was over. Ron Coote and his wife, Robyn, looked after my family and I have stayed in touch with them ever since. The club was fantastic. They have a 'who cares wins' philosophy and know that by looking after their players and staff, they will get the most out of them. It's why they're such a successful organisation.

Did you ever miss playing?
No, I'm just pleased to have made the recovery I made. The doctor told me that every morning when I throw back the bed covers, I have just won the lottery. I stayed in Australia until 1998 and the Roosters fixed it for me to work for Optus TV, covering games with former greats like Blocker Roach and Mario Fenech.

How did you get your job with Sky Sports?
In 1992, Neville Smith covered my graduation at the Philharmonic Hall in Liverpool on Boots 'n' All. It was the first time that we had really met, and we formed a connection. In 1999, Joe Lydon was doing the commentary on Academy matches and when he couldn't carry on, he recommended me - I didn't fancy coaching because I don't think I have the personality for it. I initially worked with Bill Arthur, who was very supportive, and I'm grateful to him for helping me to learn the basics. Neville was fantastic and Sky have been brilliant to work for. Working with Eddie and Stevo was a bonus as I could learn from the best. Eddie was a world-class commentator and presenter. Stevo was incredibly helpful too. His delivery was as good as anyone's. They'd been a double act for 20 years then a newcomer came along. I did feel a bit awkward at the start, but they were so welcoming, and I owe them all so much.

Have you got a favourite memory or game from your broadcasting career?
Great Britain winning against the Aussies in Sydney in 2006. No-one gave us a chance beforehand, and we got stick from the Aussie media, but I always recall Eddie telling me that we had a great chance, and I believed him. He knew that we pull off a surprise every now and then, and one was due. You do ride the game as a fan after all, and you get emotionally involved when it's your country playing, so it made it even more enjoyable.

How did you become the Great Britain team manager in 2001? Why was the GB team much improved in the early 2000s compared to the late 1990s?
I had a meeting with [coach] David Waite to improve my knowledge for my work on TV. We clicked and he later offered me a role, organising things off the field.
A lot of the improvement in the team was down to David. He put in place plans to improve British coaches as well, but I don't think they exist anymore, and that's a shame. Young coaches are just on their own with no official guidance, support or direction.

What other roles do you have in Rugby League?
I'm very proud to be a trustee of the Rugby League Benevolent Fund, helping people in both the short term and long term. My experience with a serious neck injury made me appreciate just how important help and advice can be when you most needed it.
I'm also a member of the St Helens Referees' Society. Referees and touchjudges love the game more than anybody, and they do make games possible. They also get the best view, and I can now see why they do it. They are the closest ones to the tries and get a buzz from being so involved. I'm doing what I can to help the game attract more officials because we may see a spike in new players after the World Cup [in 2022], and without enough officials, the sport could miss an opportunity to grow. It does annoy me when coaches criticise referees aggressively at the professional level because it does have a knock-on effect in the community game.

BRETT KENNY

1984-1985

One of the most naturally gifted players Rugby League has ever seen, Brett Kenny's place among the greats is firmly secure, having excelled for Parramatta Eels, New South Wales, Australia and, of course, Wigan, in a marvellous career that spanned 14 seasons from 1980 to 1993. Peter Sterling, his halfback partner for club, state and country, noted in his autobiography that, "Brett is the most naturally gifted player I have ever seen - the closest thing to poetry in motion that is possible to imagine. Some of the stuff I've seen him do over the years has been astonishing."

"OH! Beautiful ball from Kenny. It's put Stephenson in space with Gill outside him. He's only got Kemble the fullback to beat. He's got the strength. He's got the speed. And he's beaten him! Oh, as good a try as we'll see, all made for Henderson Gill by that beautiful pass from Kett Kenny. We said at the beginning about that man's silken skills..."

Commentator Ray French may have stumbled slightly on Brett Kenny's first name, but it is otherwise the perfect description of an iconic Wembley try. The scorer was Wigan's magnificent winger Henderson Gill. The creator supreme was the genius from Australia, Brett Kenny, who won the Lance Todd Trophy on that never-to-be-forgotten afternoon at Wembley in 1985.

Along with Peter Sterling, Kenny is the greatest Parramatta player of them all. It's impossible to split them. But on that day in May 1985, it was Kenny who got the better of his mate who was playing for Hull. Kenny may have only played 25 times for Wigan, but it was enough to get him into the club's Hall of Fame. After all, he delivered on the biggest stage, and many argue to this day that the 1985 Challenge Cup Final was the greatest of them all.

Kenny was elevated to Parramatta's first-grade side as a raw 19-year-old. The lanky stand-off didn't look like he'd last five minutes in the harsh environment of the Sydney competition. He debuted as a substitute on 6th July 1980 in a 28-12 defeat at Redfern Oval against South Sydney. He started the remaining games that season, all at centre.

Always the bridesmaids, the Eels hadn't won a Grand Final since their 1947 formation. In 1981, his second season, under the guidance of the great coaching guru Jack Gibson, Kenny played every match, moving to stand-off halfway through the season. His two tries against Newtown Jets in the Grand Final helped the Eels to their maiden Premiership. It had taken Parramatta 34 years to land the biggest prize of them all. It had taken Kenny just a season and a half.

"1981 was the first-ever Grand Final I played in - I didn't even play in one as a kid," Kenny revealed. "Parramatta had never won a Grand Final, and after we won, we began to realise exactly what it meant to everybody. We had to get a police escort back to the Leagues Club because our bus driver couldn't get through the crowds. Jack Gibson addressed the crowd, who were packed in like sardines, and uttered that immortal line: 'Ding dong, the witch is dead!' The next morning we discovered the fans had got a bit carried away and burned down the stadium - the Cumberland Oval! We had to play at Belmore, Canterbury's ground, for five years before our ground re-opened as Parramatta Stadium. The 1981 Grand Final is my favourite game. Playing for your country is the ultimate in one sense, but it's with guys you've sometimes only been with for a week or so. Winning a Grand Final is with guys you've

been with all year and that makes it special."

Kenny repeated those try-doubles in the next two Grand Finals - both against Manly - as the Eels chalked up three in a row. 'Bert', as he is still nicknamed, was retrospectively awarded the Clive Churchill Medal as man of the match for both of those finals. 1982 was also the year he made his State of Origin debut, the first of 17 matches he would play for the Blues. "Those early games were tough," he remembered. "I remember blowing hard after just a couple of sets, but I enjoyed them. We all wanted to play Origin, and blokes that played for Australia but not Origin were always disappointed about that. New South Wales didn't do too well at first, often losing by one game in three, but we turned it round in 1985, and I'll always remember that famous image of Steve Mortimer sinking to the turf in jubilation when we finally clinched the series. It was fantastic to finally win the State of Origin. The whole concept was great. We used to drive past the infamous Caxton Hotel en route to Lang Park when we played up in Queensland, and there would be people throwing beer cans at the bus and shouting at us. It was pretty daunting at first, but it was part of the experience, and it got us in the mood to go out and play!"

Queensland lifted the shield in State of Origin's first five years with their skipper Wally Lewis becoming a hate figure in New South Wales for his outstanding performances. There were also accusations from the media that the concept meant more to the Queensland players than it did to Kenny and his teammates. "That didn't bother me," said Kenny. "It was just a media beat-up, but the Queensland press and maybe the supporters, not the players, probably felt a bit inferior. I know Wally was annoyed with it, and probably the other players, because we were trying just as hard. I started playing against him and enjoyed the confrontation. We had to do a lot of media work together to promote State of Origin, and we became good mates. We had a lot of fun out there. There was sometimes joking when we tackled each other. It may surprise a lot of people that it wasn't always as serious as you'd imagine.

"I remember feeling sorry when watching Wally play for Australia in 1982 at the Sydney Cricket Ground because the New South Wales press were bagging him, but he deserved his spot. When we came up against each other, I really enjoyed it. We were mates and with our faces on the trophy, we had to do a lot of promotional work together for Origin. He was a tremendous footballer."

Kenny and Lewis would soon be Australia teammates, both selected on the 1982 tour of Europe. Surprisingly, it was Kenny who was selected in the stand-off jersey, as Lewis, the tour vice-captain, was axed from the starting line-up. The Kangaroos won all of their matches, a feat they repeated in 1986. "We didn't focus on going unbeaten in 1982 until the last couple of games – probably before the last club game and last Test," he said. "The club games were a worry, but not the last Test because of the neutral referee, and we were confident we wouldn't lose in France. In 1986, we didn't talk about it because we didn't want to pressure ourselves, but we knew it was a reality towards the end.

"It was a great honour to be picked in 1982, but of course I didn't really expect to get in over Wally. It was a little bit awkward to be honest, but he came over when he found out and wished me well. I managed to score in the first Test and kept my place for the next." In 1986, Kenny was selected at centre alongside Gene Miles, with Mal Meninga squeezed out. Lewis played stand-off as Australia retained the Ashes with another series whitewash. "I didn't mind centre, but if it was at club level I sometimes got a bit bored because you were further from the ruck," Kenny said. "But at Test level it was so intense, you were always involved."

BRETT KENNY was a megastar by 1984, and with English clubs now setting their sights high, he and many of his international teammates were in demand for short-term contracts. Wakefield Trinity signed Wally Lewis for ten matches in the 1983-84 season. Peter Sterling enjoyed two part-seasons at Hull FC. St Helens acquired the services of Mal Meninga in the summer of 1984. Wigan chairman Maurice Lindsay flew to Australia desperate to sign Gene Miles. He failed, although he eventually got him nearly eight years later, but he did come back with the signatures of the relatively unknown Eastern Suburbs winger John Ferguson and the Parramatta stand-off Brett Kenny. Wigan coach Alex Murphy was still unhappy, but he was sacked before the season started for having a set-to with Lindsay which allegedly involved a telephone being flung at the chairman. Colin Clarke and Alan McInnes took over as joint coaches and had the pleasure of coaching the new imports.

Parramatta lost the 1984 Grand Final, after which Kenny set off for England. He made his Wigan debut on 9th December in a 22-8 league win at Warrington with tries coming from Ian Potter, Henderson Gill and Mick Scott. The Guardian claimed Kenny "did little to inspire Wigan" but acknowledged the untidiness of the match. The stand-off played 25 matches for Wigan, scoring 19 tries in a six-month stint that would be talked about for decades by those lucky to have witnessed it.

"I didn't really think about going to England, but a few of my mates from Parramatta signed for English clubs, so I began to think about it," said Kenny. "I originally wanted to sign for the same club as one of my Parra teammates like Hull where Sterlo and John Muggleton were or Leeds who had Eric Grothe and Neil Hunt or Oldham where Paul Taylor and Chris Phelan were. But I ended up at Wigan. It couldn't have worked out better because I have so many fond memories of my time there, and every time I go back to England I'm made to feel so welcome.

"I remember my first game away at Warrington. I was told that there was a bit of local rivalry there, and with my first touch I passed back on the inside to John Ferguson and got an elbow to the back of my head. 'So this is how it's going to be,' I thought. I remember games at Central Park very well because it was a great place."

Having beaten Batley, Warrington, Bradford Northern and Hull Kingston Rovers in the Challenge Cup, Wigan were back at Wembley. They had been dismal in defeat to Widnes a year earlier, but with Kenny and Ferguson, there

was plenty of optimism even against a side as good as Hull FC who boasted not just Sterling but their four great Kiwis - Gary Kemble, Dane O'Hara, James Leuluai and Fred Ah Kuoi.

"I always watched the FA Cup Final on television, so to get to play there was a dream come true," said Kenny. "It was amazing to be on the ground a day or two before the game when the place was empty, and we did our traditional walkabout. We had a ball and chucked it around for a while before being kicked off by a couple of stewards. The day itself was fantastic and it was such a wonderful experience to play in front of so many people. The noise just hits you when you walk out. I'd never played before such a big crowd, and I didn't afterwards. It was a magical day. I got a bit of criticism for having my hands in my pockets before the game when the dignitaries were being introduced to the players, but it was never meant to be rude - it was just somewhere to put my hands. I took them out when I was introduced to them.

"The first half was fantastic for us and everything we tried seemed to come off - we scored some great tries. But they pulled us back in the second half and it got a bit nervy. I rank the game right up there with the Grand Finals I won with Parramatta - it was a great experience."

One of the big stories in the build-up was Kenny coming up against Sterling, who was magnificent in Hull's comeback, although it was Kenny who won the Lance Todd Trophy as man of the match. "He played really well," Kenny admitted. "We did it tough in the second half with Sterlo in great form. It was certainly a nervous ending for us when James Leuluai scored that try straight from our kick-off. Peter and I used to talk about the game when we were back in Australia and loads of people used to ask us what it was like to play at Wembley.

"I probably didn't appreciate the magnitude of the Lance Todd at the time. I suppose I treated it like a regular man-of-the-match award, but afterwards people explained it to me and pointed out I was the first overseas winner of it. I've got a tape of the 1985 final. I don't watch it that often, but every now and again I do. I've got great memories of playing at Wembley Stadium."

Three days later, on the Tuesday night - and this is so typical of English Rugby League - Wigan were in action again, this time in the first round of the Premiership Trophy against St Helens at Knowsley Road. At least the game had been put back 24 hours from the Monday. Wigan lost 37-14 with Kenny miles away from his Wembley form, prompting suggestions he hadn't tried because he wanted to return to Australia as soon as possible. On the Sunday, wearing number 55, Kenny lined up for Parramatta who lost 14-10 at Manly. The stand-off had played three games in eight days with a 12,000-mile flight in the middle.

"When I talk to Wigan fans even now they tell me the regard that they had for me, and I've been back several times," he said in response to the fact he had let Wigan fans down that night at Knowsley Road. "A journo over here totally misquoted me about that game and came up with a load of rubbish, and I ended up taking legal action. I had a wonderful time at Wigan, and I gave my all in every game, but you can't always be at your best, and to expect someone to is a little bit unfair."

For his efforts in both Hemispheres in 1985, Kenny was crowned the best player in the world by Open Rugby magazine. "The Golden Boot was something I didn't know too much about – I actually thought it was for goalkickers at first!" he laughed. "Two gentlemen from the Open Rugby magazine approached me and explained it was for

the best player in the world and that was fantastic to hear. I had to keep it to myself until the presentation function, which was pretty hard to do because when you win something like that you want to tell everybody about it."

KENNY returned to Australia and won the 1986 Grand Final with Parramatta against Canterbury. He had two tries disallowed in a tryless 4-2 win. He had no intention of returning to the English club scene. "I wasn't interested because I'm the sort of person who doesn't want to do something again if I was successful the first time," he said. "I won the Challenge Cup which was unexpected for me when I signed, so if I'd gone back and won nothing, it would have been a huge disappointment."

British fans saw little of Kenny after the 1986 Kangaroos Tour. He didn't play against Great Britain again. His last cap came in 1987, the same year he played his last Origin. He was still only 26. To compound his misfortune, Parramatta's last Grand Final was 1986. Their formed tailed off after that with legends like Mick Cronin, Ray Price, Steve Ella and Eric Grothe retiring one by one. Kenny and Sterling remained at the club until the early 1990s, but they commanded such hefty salaries that the Eels weren't able to adequately recruit elsewhere.

The great stand-off did have one last hurrah in him. With Sterling having retired three games into the 1992 season, Kenny assumed the captaincy. Despite a miserable Winfield Cup campaign which saw them finish 15th in a 16-team ladder, Kenny inspired his side to beat a full-strength Great Britain 22-16. At the age of 31 and facing the British captain Garry Schofield, whom he rated as

the best British player he faced, Kenny set up two of the Eels' four tries. "It's amazing what can happen when you come up against the old enemy," he said. "We were really struggling back then, and we had a lot of young blokes in the team, but I told them that it was their big chance to play against a side like Great Britain because, with no disrespect, they weren't good enough to play for Australia. It was a great night for us and although I wasn't as good as I had been, I showed I could still play a bit. We were the only club side to beat Great Britain as well which was a big deal for the club at the time.

"Garry Schofield was a great player and a real thorn in the side of anyone he came across. He could score tries from nothing when he was a young centre and then he went on to become a very good stand-off and a very good leader. Ellery Hanley was obviously pretty special, but he didn't always produce it against us at Test level. At Wigan, I thought Henderson Gill and David Stephenson were very good. In 2001 we flew over and played two legends' games against Great Britain and it was great to catch up with them all again."

To add to his Lance Todd Trophy, his Clive Churchill medals and his Golden Boot, Kenny was awarded the Australian Sports Medal in 2000 in recognition of his outstanding career. Kenny's response to being asked about it summed up his laidback approach to the game as well as anything else could. "I'd forgotten all about the Australian Sports Medal until I was cleaning out a couple of cupboards at home recently!" he laughed. "But it's on display now and it was very prestigious to win. I played the game because I loved it and to win these awards was a bonus."

RAY ASHBY

1964-1967

St Helens-born Ray Ashby made his name at Wigan where he became one of the best fullbacks in the world. He is best known for his outstanding performance at Wembley in 1965 that saw him named a joint winner of the Lance Todd Trophy along with Hunslet's Brian Gabbitas. He also played for Liverpool City and Blackpool. He won two Great Britain caps.

If you could relive one day from your career, which would it be?

The obvious one from 1965 at Wembley. I remember everything about it. When we looked around the ground on the Friday, Brian McTigue took me to the royal box and said, "Don't be like me at my first time at Wembley. As soon as you walk through the gates onto the pitch, start remembering everything. Then you'll remember it for the rest of your life." That was wonderful advice because I still remember it all.

It is still regarded as one of the truly great finals. Can you talk us through it?

I wanted Hunslet to kick off so we could enjoy some early possession, but they put it out on the full and Laurie Gilfedder kicked the penalty from halfway. That gave us all confidence. Billy Langton kicked an equalising penalty, but we never fell behind. They failed to find touch and I caught it. I was tackled on the ten-metre line and a couple of tackles later, Keith Holden scored.

I had a big part in Trevor Lake's first try. I was the dummy runner. The ball was on the Ashton-Boston side of the field. I came in on the dummy run. My Great Britain teammate Geoff Shelton should have been marking Keith, but he was taken out by my run. Keith ran behind Langton and put Lakey over. They pulled one back before half-time to make it 12-9. I missed the tackle, but I learned my lesson and saved two in the first half. I'd also stopped Geoff Gunney in the first half when it was 5-4.

I went into half-time blaming myself, but no one pointed the finger.

We'd played well and it had been a cracking game. Laurie scored another from 65 yards in the corner. With 20 minutes left, I made a break, fending off three tacklers inside our half to get up to the Hunslet 25-yard line. My dad Les, who played for Pilkington Recs, had taught me to pass the ball both ways. I ran straight at Langton, veered to the left, straightened up and then threw the perfect pass to Trevor. He could catch pigeons, so I knew he was going to score. We were 20-9 up and I think we knew it would be our day then. Hunslet got it back to 20-16, but we saw the game out.

Do you have a favourite moment?

Two. First, when I walked onto the pitch. And then when I made the break for Trevor to score, I went to the Wigan fans, and they were chanting my name. "Ashby da, da, da; Ashby, da, da, da!" It was such a wonderful feeling. I'd put those two moments up there with signing for Wigan and playing for Great Britain as the best moments of my career.

When did you find out that you and Brian had won the Lance Todd Trophy?

Cliff Morgan, the head of sport at the BBC and a Welsh rugby union international, invited me to do an interview with David Coleman, but I still didn't realise. I was celebrating with the fans, and it hadn't registered. When the penny dropped, I still didn't know Brian had won it with me. Suddenly he was stood with David Coleman, and we were going to be interviewed together. Before the interview, I asked Cliff if he smoked and when he said yes, I asked him to light me one. Fred Ward, the Hunslet skipper, was being interviewed. Then it was our turn, and I had the cig behind my back with smoke coming over my head. But it had a calming effect and I needed that! Talking of Brian and Hunslet, they have always been wonderful to me. They made me an honorary member of the Parksiders and I've got a Parksider tie. I helped beat them at Wembley, yet they've opened their arms to me, and they are so welcoming.

Going back to the start of your journey, what are your earliest Rugby League memories?

There were six in my family - I had three brothers and one sister. I went to Lowe House RC Boys School as an infant. Right the way through, there were good rugby players. I played all the way through and captained the school at rugby, football and cricket, but I fancied rugby more than the others. I was taught how to tackle properly at seven, and how not to have my head in the wrong place.

I played for the town side and the county. When I left school, there was an Under-18's league with about 12 teams. I played for Glover's Ropery. I progressed a lot and we won the league. When I was 17, Blackbrook wanted me as fullback and captain of their 18-21's team. Jack Case coached us. His son George played for us, and George's son Brian played for Wigan in the 1980s. I then had trials at Saints, but they decided I wasn't fast enough. Blackbrook's last game of the season was at Knowsley Road against Saints B team, and we beat them to win the cup, which the Saints chairman presented to me. That was quite satisfying given they'd just rejected me.

Tell us about signing with Liverpool City and your time there.

I'd played at Knotty Ash before in the under-18s and we won 55-0 with me converting all 11 tries, so I had good memories of the place. The ground was pretty primitive, and the money wasn't very good, but the guy who ran the 'A' Team at Liverpool City persuaded my dad to get me down there with some of my mates because they had so many injuries. There were six matches left in the 1954-55 season, and we won three. They'd barely won three all season.

I had to get two buses there, so it was a difficult journey. One day I was late because the buses were full, and they dropped me. I was skipper! Liverpool was a good foundation for me. I was there eight years.

One game I remember was during the big freeze of 1962-63. Barely a game was played for months, but we had a cup game against Roose, an amateur side from Barrow, at

Widnes. Widnes is a chemical town and they managed to get something from ICI to thaw the pitch. But they only put it on the middle of the field. The edges were rock hard and if you ran up the wing, your boots sounded like you were on concrete!

You earned your first Great Britain cap while you were there.

I'm not sure if I was the club's first international, but I think I was the first from the Liverpool City era to play for Great Britain. My Test debut was at Leigh against France. The floodlights may as well have been 100-watt bulbs. How I took one of the high kicks, I don't know. I had a good game and tackled well. I made a couple of breaks and got some headlines in the press. The international set-up was very different to today. There were no hotels. We made our own way to the ground and there wasn't even any training.

My second cap was also against the French, in the sludge at Swinton. That didn't suit my game. It was a tight game, but Marcel Bescos, the French skipper, got sent off. He wouldn't leave the field, so the game was held up for ten minutes.

You reached Wembley again in 1966. How do you feel about the tactics employed by Saints that day and, in particular, Alex Murphy?

I remember it all again! It was a nothing game. Colin Clarke was banned, having been sent off for premature striking at the scrum. We'd sold Bill Sayer to Saints in the summer of 1965, so in came Tommy Woosey. Joe Egan came down to teach him a few lessons, but you can't learn in three or four sessions what takes several years. It was to no avail. Alex Murphy kept giving away penalties because in those days, there'd be a scrum after you kicked for touch, and Alex knew Bill would win all the scrums against Tommy. We were starved of possession, and we lost. Many years later, I sat next to Alex at a Lance Todd dinner, and he said, "Ray, I was only bothered about going down there for the tin pot." We won two scrums all day. I don't know why the ref didn't send him off, but that just didn't happen in those days. Len Kileen kicked a goal from 65 yards that day. I couldn't believe it.

What was the rivalry like between Wigan and Saints in the 1960s?

It was really intense, but my strongest memory is that both sets of players used to share the big communal bath after a match. Both grounds had just one bath, so we'd all jump in together with bottles of ale and bottles of shampoo being passed around. Anything that had happened on the pitch was forgotten about, but we'd be able to hear the speccies walking away arguing about the game, and there we were all having a bath together!

Why did you leave Wigan?

I was looking to retire because I was in my 30s, then Blackpool kept coming to my house and persuaded me to play for them. I was pleased to go there, and they looked after me when I did my ankle ligaments.

Who was the best coach you played for?

Eric Ashton was very good, and he was there for you whether it was a rugby issue or not. He was very knowledgeable and knew the game inside out. He wasn't brash and he had a way of talking to people. He was a great man. Liverpool had a different coach every year and they all had different plans, so we never really got anywhere.

Who were the best players of your day?

The three icons were Brian Bevan, Tom van Vollenhoven and Billy Boston. I played with Brian Bevan in a charity match. I never got to play alongside Tom, only against him. Bev had the speed to veer around you and he was gone. Tommy Voll was brilliant. He was good in defence, and he had the pace to get past you on the touchline, even when you thought you had him. Billy was different. He had the speed; he could go past you or fend you. If you got him on the hips, he would knock you away. Defensively, he could pick out the centre and sort him out. As an all-round player, Billy was probably number one. I knew him the best of the three. We were roommates at Wembley, and we would chat away. You'd never know he was a rugby player because he was so modest and such a gentleman.

TERRY NEWTON

<u>2000-2005</u>

Having played for Leeds for four seasons, Terry Newton signed for Wigan at the end of 1999. He represented his hometown club for six seasons, winning the Challenge Cup at Murrayfield in 2002. He was best known for his confrontational style of play, but he was unquestionably a top-class dummy half, and he was a Great Britain regular throughout his time at Wigan. He later played for Bradford and Wakefield. His 2010 suicide, which came in the same year as a two-year ban for testing positive for an illegal substance, devastated people throughout the sport, no more so than in Wigan.

THINK of the toughest assignment you've ever been set and then compare it to this. In 2005, I went to Knowsley Road in my short-lived capacity as illegal street trader to sell copies of a Rugby League magazine called Thirteen with Terry Newton emblazoned on the cover.

After three hours of being laughed at, I'd shifted one copy. Lesson learned. Terry Newton is not popular in St Helens. And this was a few months before his final Wigan game after which he copped a huge ban for his X-rated challenges on Lee Gilmour and Sean Long, neither of whom played again that season.

I first watched Newton play for Leeds when I was a student in the city. He'd initially signed for Warrington in 1995 but changed his mind when Leeds came calling. An RFL tribunal found in favour of the Yorkshiremen. Newton played prop for their Alliance Team but was shifted to hooker by Dean Bell in 1996, a season in which he played 13 times for the first team.

Leeds signed Wayne Collins from South Queensland Crushers for the 1997 season, and he assumed the number-nine role on a full-time basis. Newton featured mainly in the back row, starting there in the last seven games of the season, five of which were at loose forward.

The Rhinos began 1998 without a hooker, with Collins retiring. Gary Hetherington had signed half the Keighley team towards the end of 1997 to help save them from bankruptcy, but it was clear that new coach Graham Murray didn't rate the hooker Phil Cantillon. I remember watching the warm-up to a pre-season match in the early months of 1998. Newton was practicing his passing off the ground for about half an hour. It didn't seem convincing that a relative novice could fill the role for an entire season in a successful side.

But he did. He was by no means the perfect hooker in 1998, but he revelled in one of the most feared packs Super League has ever seen. Newton was an 80-minute player. His dummy-half service improved through the year, and he was as physical as any of the forwards including Adrian Morley, Marc Glanville and Darren Fleary.

Leeds signed the former Great Britain hooker Lee Jackson from Newcastle Knights for the 1999 campaign. Jackson would become the first bench hooker – a tactic that every team has subsequently used. Jackson was past his mid-1990s best, but the tactic worked, particularly in the Challenge Cup semi-final when the Rhinos overturned a 10-0 deficit against Bradford with Jackson winning the BBC's man-of-the-match award.

The only downside was the lack of minutes enjoyed by Newton. With fewer substitutions permitted, Newton rarely went back on after his opening stint. He was only really playing half an hour a week, but he did at least leave Headingley with a Challenge Cup medal won at Wembley when the Rhinos crushed London Broncos 52-16. Newton

created a vital try for Brad Godden on the stroke of half-time.

"I was signed by Dean Bell at Leeds as a prop, but when I was there, he suggested I have a go at hooker, and he said I should watch Keiron Cunningham, which I did," Newton told me.

"Graham Murray is one of the best coaches I've ever played under," he said of Bell's successor. "He came in and changed the Leeds side around, and we made the Grand Final that year and then won the Challenge Cup Final the next. So my memories of Graham and that side are pretty good, with the Challenge Cup Final in 1999 being the best memory, although losing that Grand Final was hard, coming so close, but Jason Robinson denied us with a try just before half-time."

With Murray leaving Leeds after two seasons in charge, Newton also departed, transferring to the club he supported as a boy. "I'd always wanted to play for Wigan at some point in my career, but I didn't think it would come so soon," he said. "Ellery Hanley was my hero as a kid. He was the best player in the world when I was a young Wigan fan. As for Lee Jackson, that didn't really play a part. It was working. It was good for the team, and we had no complaints."

Newton soon became a key cog in a Wigan side that topped the table in 2000. Unlike at Leeds, he was a regular try scorer, and he made such an impression that one of his predecessors, Martin Dermott, labels him Wigan's greatest-ever hooker elsewhere in this book. But Newton was also a regular in front of the disciplinary committee at Red Hall. We spoke in mid-2005, a few months before that infamous final Wigan appearance, after which he was banned for several months after taking out Gilmour and Long in a 38-12 home defeat by table-topping St Helens.

"I'm an aggressive player, but I never go out to hurt anyone or give penalties away," he argued. "It's my style of play, and I'll never change it, although I may have to curb my temper a bit. If you give a few penalties away, you've just got to take it on the chin. There's a few players like Adrian Morley and Barrie McDermott who play the game on a fine line, and sometimes we overstep the mark, but our aggression is one of our attributes too."

NEWTON made his Great Britain debut in 1998 against New Zealand at Watford under Andy Goodway's coaching. The series was already lost after defeats at Huddersfield and Bolton, but Newton helped Great Britain restore some credit with a 23-all draw. Injuries meant he had to wait four years until his next cap, which came in Sydney when Great Britain, now coached by David Waite, were hammered 64-10 in a one-off Test by Australia.

Newton's first full series was in 2003 when Great Britain were whitewashed in the Ashes, with Australia snatching each game with heart-breaking late scores. His first win came in the 2004 Tri-Nations when Brian Noble's Great Britain beat New Zealand, Australia and New Zealand again, but they were annihilated 44-4 in the final by the green and golds.

Asked about his international career, Newton said, "My debut for Great Britain in 1998 in the third Test against New Zealand at Watford when Tony Smith kicked a late drop goal to draw the game was fantastic. Great Britain had lost the first two, so to come in and get a different result was a big thing. Also, the Tri-Nations game from 2004 when we beat Australia at Wigan is up there too.

"[The 64-10 defeat] was a bit of a nightmare. Travelling there and back in a week - it was a hard trip. David Waite has a lot of experience and when he came along, we started meeting earlier in the year, and he started putting things into place, so it wasn't so rushed at the end of the season. He did a great job. Brian Noble has carried on the good things, and the preparation still starts early to prepare us for New Zealand and the Australians.

"But we saved our worst performance for the final, and we let ourselves down that day with a painful loss. We saw throughout the tournament what we can do, and we've got a great chance of winning the trophy this year [2005]. Players have off days, and this time it was the biggest occasion of our careers, but we're looking to put things right."

When asked about the 2006 tour of the southern hemisphere, which was over a year away at the time of our interview, Newton said, "You want to test yourselves against the best players in their own back garden. The international stage went off for a while, but as far as the players are concerned, we want to go down under and beat them." On that tour, Newton helped the Lions beat Australia 23-12, the last time Great Britain or England have beaten them.

Newton played alongside Adrian Morley for Leeds and Great Britain and chose him as the best player he played alongside. "I've been fortunate in my career I've played with lots of great players, but I'd say Adrian Morley," he said. "My kind of player. He plays hard and never takes a backward step. He's got a great attitude to training as well."

As for the toughest opponent, Newton said, "It's hard to say having played against so many great players. There's the tough bloke like Adrian Morley and Barrie McDermott. Then there's someone like Jason Robinson who was so quick on his feet. Va'aiga Tuigamala is up there too."

Wigan were struggling when I interviewed Newton. Having lost Andy Farrell, Terry O'Connor, Adrian Lam, Gary Connolly and Mick Cassidy after 2004, coach Denis Betts was demoted and replaced by Ian Millward, who had just been sacked by St Helens. Wigan failed to make the 2005 Super League play-offs and were knocked out of the Challenge Cup, losing 75-0 at St Helens.

"Obviously it's hard replacing guys like that," said Newton, "but Denis said earlier in the year that I'm getting to the age when I've got to step up and be a bit more mature. I've probably stepped things up along with Brian Carney and Kris Radlinski in that respect to help the younger players. I just go out and play my normal game, and I'm enjoying it. I just wish we were winning more games!"

Newton picked out Harrison Hansen, Danny Tickle, Liam Colbon, Chris Ashton and James Coyle as Wigan's best prospects and predicted that Tickle would soon feature for Great Britain. "They're all learning the hard way at the

moment, and for them, it's probably for the best," he said. "We're surrounded by Academy players at the moment in the first-team squad!"

"I was surprised more than anything [with Millward's appointment]. With him being the Saints coach, it was the last thing we expected, but he is a top-class coach, and I'm just glad to be working underneath him. Not a lot has changed to be honest because he'll have more of an impact long term rather than short term.

"Coaching would be too much pressure for me! After I retire, I'd like to still be involved - maybe as a kit man at Wigan! I'd like to coach juniors I suppose, but I wouldn't be a Super League coach."

NEWTON's post-playing experiences, as we know now, were cut tragically short. Millward forced him out of Wigan at the end of the 2005 campaign, after which he spent four years at Bradford without winning a trophy. Newton's prediction that Millward would have a long-term impact at the club was woefully inaccurate, as the controversial Australian was sacked early in 2006. Wigan were bottom of Super League before they recovered under Brian Noble.

Newton, meanwhile, left the Bulls for Wakefield in 2010, but after two matches, it emerged that he had tested positive for human growth hormone (hGH). He was banned from the sport for two years.

Newton had been putting the final touches to his book along with his ghost writer Phil Wilkinson, the Wigan Observer sports editor who had also worked on the autobiographies of Adrian Morley and Kris Radlinski. The book, Coming Clean, needed a hasty rewrite and a new title before publication, and he used it to explain why he had taken the drug. He had no hesitation in admitting he had cheated.

Unable to update this interview with Newton, I called Wilkinson to ask him about his experiences of the former Wigan number nine, starting with his earliest memories. "I have friends who played against him in the amateur game," he said. "I knew of him by reputation, but I don't remember much of his time at Leeds.

"Maurice Lindsay came back to Wigan, but the signing of Terry had been done before then. A few people wondered where he would play. I took over on sport [at the Wigan Observer] in 2001. He was always alright. He was always fine to speak to even after a bad defeat. He called you out over a stupid question. When Wigan were struggling with injuries, I asked him if it was the youngest side he'd ever played in. 'No,' he said. 'My under-18's team was younger!'

"Someone told me that Terry got stabbed when he was ten, so I asked him about it. 'Who told you that?' he asked. 'It's not true. I was 12!' He had a reputation for not being the sharpest, but he was. He was a prankster too. I remember sitting on a treadmill, talking to someone and he turned it on!

"I remember one controversy in 2003. Chris Anderson, the Australia coach, wasn't happy with his tactics, and they wanted him banned. Terry was talking to [journalist] Pete Aspinwall, doing his regular newspaper column. He didn't realise Andy Wilson from The Guardian was also recording what he was saying, and he said to Pete, 'Let's see what I can get away with next week.' Andy used it in the Guardian, and the Aussies were furious.'

"Terry was more important to Wigan than many people realised. Adrian Morley and Sean O'Loughlin both told me that his strength was nullifying the best players in

the opposition. You pick out the key threats, and the big players were never as good when they played against Terry. He intimidated them and got in their faces. He played on the edge and crossed it a couple of times. He knew how to neuter the dominant forward or the superstar halfback. He nullified the threat or at least reduced it. He could also play. His passes were on the money. He was a very good support player for his size. He was obviously a really strong defender. He was more aggressive and tough than many of the middles. His biggest attribute was what Moz and Lockers said, but you might miss it if you just look at stats."

Coming Clean was published in 2010 and quickly sold out, and a softback version was printed after Newton's death. "The book idea came about in the second-floor bar of the then JJB Stadium one night" said Wilkinson. "Terry hooked me in the bar and said he was thinking of doing a book, and could I help him? It was so much fun doing it. He came to our house once, and my wife had never met him. He had this reputation, but he came to the door, took his shoes off, was dead polite and played with the kids. She said, 'I never thought he'd be like that!'"

With the book nearly completed, Newton embarked upon his time at Wakefield, but after two games, he was banned for his hGH indiscretion. "We'd pretty much finished the book, but we hadn't settled on a title," said Wilkinson. "It had a working title of 'Pulling No Punches'. We were at the proofing stage. Then the whole story came to light. It was awful to see someone go through that, making no judgement on the rights and wrongs. Human growth hormone rightfully carries a lengthy suspension. We'd spent so much time together, and it was tough.

"Once it had all calmed down, I spoke to him. He was keen to make sure the book still went ahead - thank God after all the hours I had put into it! We agreed to start and end the book with the hGH issue. I remember suggesting we remove a passage where he said he was against doping. 'Why?' he said, 'I am against it. Leave it in.' We added chapters. It's still a really good career, and his story is so eventful. He had a rough life. His sister died young. To get where he did and achieve what he did was great, and there were plenty of funny stories along the way. Brian Carney was really hands on with making sure it was spot on. He

was determined it should be perfect. His level of detail was great."

TERRY NEWTON was found hanged in the early hours of Sunday, 26th September 2010 in his family home in Orrell. The news was broken to a disbelieving public during Sky Sports' coverage of the Championship Grand Finals, although rumours had been circulating on social media.

"Andy Wilson called me and told me," Wilkinson recalled. "I was a working journo on the Wigan titles at the time. Like all deaths, you need to get everything right because there were a lot of rumours flying around, and nothing had been confirmed. It was horrible dealing with it because he was a mate as well. I remember telling Brian Carney just before he went on air. He still went out and spoke. I don't know how he did that.

"It just really hit me. I'd also been pretty close to Mike Gregory and his family, but this was different because it was so out of the blue. I got through the day, asking people for tributes, not a comfortable position to be in. I remember being in the kitchen later. My missus came in and I was just in tears. Your thoughts go to his family, but you start questioning things and second-guessing things.

"I went to his funeral at Wigan Parish Church. It was packed. There were players from all over - loads from Leeds and Bradford.

"There was one line in the book which he changed. He was putting on a brave face as he was going through the transition of not playing anymore and he had to live with the shame of the suspension. He was also pretty hands-on at his pub with his father-in-law. Matthew Johns had texted him to say, 'Strong men get up and carry on.' The book initially finished with him saying 'I'm trying,' but in the last meeting we had, he said change it to 'I have done.' Clearly, in hindsight, he hadn't. He was tormented."

Newton's death led to the formation of State of Mind, a charity which seeks to improve the mental fitness, well-being and lives of sports players, officials and communities. One of their ambassadors is Newton's former Wigan teammate, Danny Sculthorpe. You can read about Newton's legacy in Sculthorpe's interview (overleaf).

DANNY SCULTHORPE

2002-2005

Danny Sculthorpe was an immensely talented ball-playing prop forward for Rochdale, Wigan, Castleford, Wakefield, Huddersfield and Widnes. He moved to Bradford in 2009 but after sustaining a back injury, his contract was ripped up before he played a game. Without an income, Sculthorpe spiralled into depression and was close to suicide. After opening up to his family, he sought help and has recovered. When Terry Newton took his own life in September 2010, the State of Mind charity was set up, for whom Sculthorpe is an ambassador, seeking to help others with mental-health issues or addictions.

Tell us about your friendship with Terry Newton and how his passing affected you.

It's still very upsetting. I remember Danny Brough phoning me on the day of the 2010 Championship Grand Final. I was in Oldham, going to a party at my mum's. I was at Tesco, buying beer. Danny asked if I'd heard about Tez. I said, "What's he been upto now?" He said, "He's hung himself." I dropped the beers and ran to my car and broke down. We were good friends. We played together for Lancashire at 11. We drank together. We lived 100 metres apart. He used to break into my garage to nick my lawnmower or beers from my fridge. He was an animal on the field, but a really nice, shy lad off it. He didn't have much confidence, which might shock people. He was a great lad who loved his family.

How did Terry's death lead to the State of Mind charity being formed?

Malcolm Rae and Ernie Benbow from the NHS wrote into the Rugby League newspapers. Dr Phil Cooper, who had experience in drug and alcohol misuse and depression, read the letter. The three of them had a meeting, and that's how State of Mind was formed. Now we're the only sport in the world to have a round of fixtures dedicated to mental health. I was a trustee and now an ambassador. I do workshops on drugs and alcohol and coping mechanisms. I tell people it's ok not to be ok. I tell my story of losing everything when my Bradford contract was ripped up. My family noticed a big difference and made me open up. That saved my life. Talking doesn't cost anything. My doctor put me on anti-depressants, but the biggest thing was the RFL getting me to talk to a counsellor at the Sporting Chance organisation.

Hundreds of Rugby League players have sought help through Sporting Chance for things like mental health, drug and alcohol problems and gambling. Before Terry's death, the RFL had a confidential helpline, but no one ever contacted them. Terry has saved a lot of lives. We go to schools, universities, prisons, clubs and into the construction industry to do talks. It's called the Terry Newton Grassroots Project, and it's all paid for by State of Mind. At least 600 people have told us we have changed their minds on taking their lives. We did a talk recently at Workington Cricket Club, and a woman came up and said, 'It's 601 now.' Just yesterday [in April 2023], someone told us we'd saved their life. I was at the bottom of a massive hole when my career finished. I didn't think I could support my family. I thought everyone would be better off without me. Now I do this, I'm even happier than when I was playing.

If you had known then what you know now, could you have helped Terry?

Yes, absolutely. I would have noticed the signs. On the 'Super League Super Men' show he did with Sky, he was saying who he'd let down, including his wife and daughters. He was struggling. He was waving the flag on that show, crying out for help. The symptoms were there. If that happened now, I'd go for a coffee with him and if I didn't get it out of him straight away, I'd persevere. Maybe his kids would still have a dad.

There are a lot of alcohol-related stories in your autobiography. Did you drink too much as a player?

When I played, it was the thing to do. In the off-season, everyone hammered it three to four times a week. Brian Carney was the fittest, but he'd come back two stone overweight. When the season started, he was the fittest again. I did drink too much. My drinking affected my blood sugars and that drains your energy.

Ex-players have also talked about their addictions to sleeping tablets.

Sleeping tablets have been knocked on the head because there's a lot of in-house testing now. When I played, everyone was on them. When I first took one, I was crawling upstairs to bed but had the best night's sleep. I was given a box of 28, not just one, so I got used to them. When you don't have one, you can't sleep. I remember people turning up to training like they were pissed. But they weren't. They were just taking these tablets.

How does a type-1 diabetic prepare for a game of Rugby League?

You have to be really hydrated. The more hydrated a diabetic is, the better the sugar levels are. I used to take my insulin at dinnertime if we had a 3pm kick-off. I'd have a sandwich and not too much insulin. I'd test my blood three or four times in the morning, then in the changing rooms at 1.15, then before and after the warm-up. The doctor would have my testing kit and a bottle of Lucozade when I went onto the pitch. My sugar level was always high after a game, so I'd have to take insulin. But if you take too much, it would come down too quick. When I was at Wakefield, I remember a game against St Helens when I'd had a massive hypo [low glucose level] in my sleep. I was rushed into hospital and was on a drip for three or four hours. Then I discharged myself at 11am and played for an hour. My mouth was so dry it felt stuck together. I didn't tell John Kear. I just loved playing against St Helens and my brother. I love the way they played, and they looked after Paul so well. There's no way on earth I should have played, but I was desperate to.

You've had various health problems. How are you doing now?

Mentally, I'm really good, but recently, I got diagnosed with a brain tumour which involves lots of MRI scans and tests. I'm probably having it cut out soon. I'm having seizures and memory loss. I get emotional quickly - I either cry or get angry. It's a benign tumour, and it's operable. I had a funny turn in a scrum for Wigan against Limoux in 2004. I never spoke to anyone about it. I went for a run before lockdown and had the funny feeling again. My memory started going funny. I had seizures. I work with Phil Veivers, and he said I was ringing him five or six times a night to see what we were doing the next day. I didn't realise I was doing that. Some people have asked if it's connected to rugby. I don't know if it is, but I certainly wouldn't sue the game if it was. I don't agree with what these guys with the lawsuit are doing.

Did you play in the wrong era?

Yeah, I'd have been suited to the 80s or 90s. From the mid-2000s to now, props have become athletes and there's a lot less skill. Rugby clubs want props to take the ball up all day and not offload. If I put a kick in at Wigan, I'd have Adrian Lam and Andy Farrell shouting at me. But I knew I had the ability, and Terry Matterson at Castleford gave me a free reign. I was at my best there and also when I went on loan to Huddersfield - Nathan Brown was the best coach I played for. I loved Rochdale Hornets too. I could be a prop or stand-off there and did 80 minutes a game.

You were a Rochdale player when two players died during pre-season.

It was terrible. Deryck Fox was the coach. We were training the day Karl Marriott died. At the end of a session we did a 1000-metre row. The next day I woke up to hear he had died in the night. As for Roy Powell, I was running with him, and he fell headfirst into the floor. We got to him, but we couldn't try to resuscitate him because he was biting his lip. I've lost Leon Walker too and Adam Watene when I was at Wakefield. I've been through a lot of deaths and also had close friends who have taken their own lives.

Tell us about your four seasons at Wigan.

I absolutely loved playing under Stuart Raper, and I played with some outstanding players. I was unlucky to get a back injury which meant I missed the 2002 Challenge Cup Final. But I played in the 2004 final and in loads of big games like the Good Fridays against Saints. I lifted myself for those. I got on with Mike Gregory very well. He was a top bloke. You just wanted to play for him, especially when he became ill. Everyone was too emotional in the 2004 Challenge Cup Final because Greg was going through what he was going through. We had a meeting the day before, and everyone was in tears. It just drained us all.

How good a captain was Andy Farrell?

He was very tough, and we couldn't have had a better captain. Him and our kid were very similar. He was a very hard taskmaster. He turned up an hour before everyone else to run five or six miles on the treadmill. Then he'd stay longer than everyone else to do extras like kicking. You just looked up to him. I'm not surprised at how well he's done in rugby union.

Why did you leave?

Ian Millward came in, and he let me go. He told me the news ten minutes before getting on a flight to Australia. He said Paul Prescott and Bryn Hargreaves were going to be ahead of me in the pecking order. That was a shithouse trick not to do it face to face. He'd had a fallout with our kid at Saints, and he took it out on me. I remember Wigan fans were gutted, and 2006 at Castleford was probably my best year in Super League.

Was there a time when you felt you were close to winning a Great Britain cap?

Probably in 2006 when at Cas. Lots of people were saying I should be picked. I played for the England Under-21s and for England 'A' but didn't quite make the Great Britain team. But we had some decent props when I played.

What went wrong for you at Wakefield?

I didn't enjoy my rugby. I didn't rate John Kear as a coach. He treated us like schoolkids. He was a poor man-manager, and it affected the way I played. I eventually got finished over a few beers I had on a bus with Danny Brough. The bus was stacked up with beers. I paid the driver for six bottles of Budweiser. Then afterwards, John said there had been a booze ban. I was suspended for a week, along with Broughy. After the week, Danny apologised, and I didn't, so I was loaned to Huddersfield. Those six Buds were the best I ever had because Nathan Brown was a brilliant coach.

What happened at Bradford?

Huddersfield were up to the salary cap, so I signed for Bradford in October 2009. In the third week of pre-season, I was lifting weights and prolapsed a disc in my spine. I was told the op had gone well. After eight or nine days, I started getting unbelievable pain in my back. I had two massive infections including sepsis, which can kill. It was horrendous. I was on morphine and ketamine - the strongest painkillers. They fused my spine and Bradford Bulls ripped up my contract. There was a clause saying if you hadn't played in six months, they could do that, but only if the club got two independent reports. They hadn't done that. I lost my house, cars and nearly my life because of it. We settled on £40,000, but I still wasn't happy because it had led to me nearly taking my life. No money can make up for that. I hate Bradford for what they did to me. But I also thank them because it made me what I am, and I love what I'm doing now.

LIAM FARRELL

2010-present

A winner of four Grand Finals, three Challenge Cups, three League Leaders' Shields and a World Club Challenge as this book went to print, Liam Farrell has enjoyed a dream career with his beloved Wigan Warriors. He's been an England regular, he's been named in five Super League Dream Teams, he won the Harry Sunderland Trophy in 2016, and he was appointed Wigan captain at the start of the 2023 season.

IT'S 2009. I'm interviewing Brian Noble in his office at Orrell, the site of Wigan's training ground. There's a knock on the door. "Turn that off please," Noble says to me, pointing to my dictaphone. A sheepish-looking young red-headed lad walks in. Even though he hasn't yet played for the first team, I know it's Liam Farrell. Noble gives him a telling off, although I can't quite work out what he's done, and he retreats. Given the coach didn't share the 18-year-old's misdemeanour with me and, 14 years on, Farrell can't remember what he did, this may not be the best anecdote to start this piece with, but I include it because, head bowed and with muttered apologies, he didn't look like a future Wigan captain that day. But that's what he is now. He's played well over 300 games for his hometown club, and he's won a myriad of honours along the way.

Farrell was born in the summer of 1990, halfway through Great Britain's successful tour of New Zealand in which Wigan players Joe Lydon, Bobbie Goulding, Martin Dermott and Denis Betts starred, although most of the nation were far more concerned with the fortunes of England's soccer team at Italia '90. Liam's younger brother Connor also played for Wigan, and the family are distant relatives of Andy Farrell, who captained Wigan and Great Britain between 1996 and 2004.

"One of my earliest rugby memories is very vague, but I remember going to Central Park with a mate and his mum," Farrell recalled. "We went in on the side where Riley's snooker club was. The best memory I have as a supporter is [aged 11] at Murrayfield with my mum, dad and little brother and seeing Kris Rads [Radlinski] getting man of the match. I was also a ball boy in Grand Finals at Old Trafford in my early teens.

"Connor is three years younger than me. Growing up, it was a rugby-mad house. We played inside the house and outside. My dad coached us both. Weekends were packed with rugby. There were also town team games during the week. Connor was more talented than me, but he was very unfortunate with injuries. If he'd had his breaks, he'd have had a great career."

Still a year and a half away from his first-team debut, Farrell was selected to represent the England Academy in 2008 along with fellow future stars like Kallum Watkins, Paul McShane and Elliott Whitehead. They lost 68-6 and 17-10 to an Australian Combined High Schools team which included Jamal Idris, William Hopoate, Aaron Woods and Martin Taupau.

"I've got a few good memories of that tour and a couple of the lads are still playing now. It was a great tour. We had a warm-up game in Brisbane, and then we played the Schoolboys twice. We got whitewashed in the first, then we ran them close in the second. It was good to come up against some talented players like Aaron Woods. Jamal Idris shocked a lot of us with how big he was for 17.

"My chances of getting a crack at the first team were

still quite slim. I didn't have much interaction with Brian Noble, and I don't remember that bollocking, but I got my chance in 2010 when Michael Maguire had taken over. Shaun Wane was promoted to assistant coach, and he told me if I got my head down, I would have a good chance. I was 18th man and then I went on loan to Widnes."

Farrell played six matches for Widnes at the start of the 2010 season, scoring three tries, although he didn't want to go. "I couldn't think of anything worse," he said. "I just wanted to play for Wigan. I played six games, but it was the best thing I ever did. Mark Smith was there and Shane Grady. I knew a few of the players. Batley away was my first game, and that was quite an experience with the slope - running downhill in one half then climbing a mountain in the next! The Championship wasn't as fast, but it was just as physical. It gave me a chance to play against experienced players and older blokes, and that was a massive advantage to me when I went back to Wigan.

"Back at Wigan, I was 18th man for a time. I knew I was close. I was 18th again on Good Friday for the last derby at Knowsley Road, which was still a great experience even though I didn't play. Then George Carmont pulled out of the Easter Monday game against Wakefield. Phil Bailey moved to centre. Lee Mossop came in, and I went on to the bench. I was told on the Sunday which was good because I didn't have to think about the game all week. I came off the bench and got over the line. It was a special moment for me and my family. The score was a bit of a comfort blanket when I came on, but I'd have probably been terrified at the time!"

Farrell's six matches at Widnes deprive him of the one-club-man title, and I wondered if there had been any other prospects of him playing elsewhere along the way. "Not really," he said." I had offers from a few clubs before I signed for Wigan and a bit of interest from rugby union. But I only wanted to sign for Wigan. There have been a few calls about playing in the NRL but never anything concrete. I've never come close to leaving. I always signed long-term deals. Wigan is a very good club, and I've been looked after for a long time."

NOW an established first-teamer, the great moments began to roll in. The 2010 Grand Final. That last-minute Good Friday try and the Cup Final in 2011. The double in 2013. His England debut. "I'd have been happy to play just the Wakefield game in 2010," Farrell said, "but luckily the coach saw something in me, and I played 23 games and finished with a Grand Final win. It was an unbelievable experience. The club had been in transition for four or five years, so to win a Grand Final was very special. I've got loads of great memories of the year, especially sharing it with other young players like Sam Tomkins, Lee Mossop, Chris Tuson, Micky McIlorum and Darrell Goulding. Making memories with friends is the best thing about rugby.

"I'd been given a lot of chances in big games in my first season, and the 2011 World Club Challenge against St George-Illawarra was another of them. Brett Morris was a stand-out player that day. Trent Merrin was good too. They had really good players, and we learned a lot from it.

"The Good Friday game was incredible. The closest similarity in atmosphere would be the one we've just had in 2023. The crowd intensity was unbelievable. It was a back-and-forth game. Towards the end, we thought Saints were going to nick it, but we just seemed to get rolling. I can remember the last set. Harrison Hansen took in a carry, then Lee Mossop. Then we reloaded and got a bit of a shift. With Sam coming out the back and Paul Deacon at halfback, there was always a chance of a gap. It opened up from nowhere. I just had to put the ball down. 'This will be remembered for years,' people said afterwards. I thought it would die off, but it gets mentioned every Good Friday.

"We had a very strong team, having won the Grand Final in 2010, and then we brought in three players from Melbourne Storm - Ryan Hoffman, Brett Finch and Jeff Lima. We were probably favourites in the Challenge Cup Final. One of the best memories is the try from Joel [Tomkins]. Once we got in front, it didn't look like it would go any other way. I'd missed the quarter-final because Gareth Hock came back from his two-year ban, and I had to fight my way back in. I found a bit of form and played in the final."

Farrell was back in the final two years later, but it was a game that did little to excite the neutral as Wigan and Hull served up a game as far away as you could possibly get from their 1985 classic. "It doesn't matter how you win, as long as you do," said Farrell. "It was terrible weather. We just wanted to complete our sets and get into their territory. We slid over for a couple of tries. When you win at Wembley, one of the first thoughts is to back it up and win the Grand Final too. Not many teams have done it. If I remember, we didn't do well in the league, finishing fourth, but we found some good form in the play-offs. Pat Richards, Lee Mossop and Sam were leaving, and it was a bit of motivation to win it for them. And it topped off a special year for us."

A fortnight after the Grand Final, Farrell played for England against Italy at Salford in a warm-up match for the World Cup. It doesn't count as a Test cap because the sides each named several more substitutes than the usual four, but it was a proud moment for Farrell, nonetheless. The result, however, sent shockwaves throughout the sport as the Italians won 15-14. The England camp descended into further chaos that evening when a night out led to Farrell's clubmate Gareth Hock being kicked out of the squad. Farrell played against Fiji and France in the World Cup, the former being his Test debut, but he wasn't selected for the semi-final against New Zealand which England lost to a late Shaun Johnson try.

"The Italy game was one of my first real involvements with England," said Farrell. "I'd played against the Exiles, and Steve McNamara put me in the World Cup squad. There were big expectations against Italy, but we didn't perform. We took Italy for granted, and it wasn't a great start to the World Cup. It was a rude awakening, and then something happened with a night out which is always made out to be worse when you've lost. But we had a decent World Cup, and I was lucky to get my official debut off the bench against Fiji. Then I played against France. I wasn't picked for the New Zealand game. I was really disappointed, but I was quite young and was content to have been involved."

Farrell was back at Old Trafford a year later, but it was a very different outcome for Wigan. Wearing their purple alternate kit, Wigan received an early penalty after a high tackle by Mose Masoe. At the end of the ensuing set, Blake Green's high kick was allowed to bounce, and Ben Flower failed to take the ball in with the tryline at his mercy. Only 100 seconds of the game had elapsed. Lance Hohaia barged into him. Flower floored him with a right hook and then punched him again as he lay motionless on the ground. He was sent off. It was the first time a referee had brandished a card of either colour in a Super League Grand Final.

"We went into the game as favourites," Farrell remembered. "When the red card went up, I thought to myself, "This has just flipped it on its head completely." If we'd kept 13 on, you never know what would have happened. It was so disappointing. When you have a player sent off, especially that early, you know you're going to have to do a lot more work, and you'll get more tired. But you also know some of the pressure comes off you because everyone expects the other team to roll you, and we were in front at half-time. But we didn't finish our sets well in the second half, and we lost."

AFTER another Old Trafford defeat a year later, Farrell was presented with a third winner's ring for victory over Warrington in the 2016 Grand Final, and this time he won the Harry Sunderland Trophy as man of the match.

"We'd been involved in four straight Grand Finals," said Farrell, "and we'd lost in 2014 and 2015, so we wanted to put things right in 2016. It was a difficult year for me because I got an injury at the end of 2015, and I missed a large chunk of 2016. I came back with six or seven games to go and got into the Grand Final squad. We've beaten Warrington a few times in Grand Finals. Winning capped off a really good year. We had a good young team, and we saw the emergence of George Williams, Sam Powell, Dominic Crosby and Ryan Sutton that year.

"One of my greatest individual achievements is getting man of the match in a Grand Final. It's a very special memory. I heard on the pitch that I'd won it. The game wasn't yet won, but it was comfortable, and I heard it over the speakers. I tried not to think about it, even though I was ecstatic. You dream of moments like that!"

Beating Warrington set up a World Club Challenge match against Cronulla Sharks, who had just won their maiden Premiership in Australia. The game would be played 30 years after the club's first world title - won in 1987 when Wane was man of the match against Manly. The 22-6 win over the Sharks is the only win Farrell has experienced in six matches against NRL teams, but the season thereafter failed to live up to expectations.

"In the pre-season leading up to it, in any team or video meeting, Waney would talk about playing Cronulla," said Farrell. "Pre-season was aimed at that game. I probably underestimated its importance, but now I realise how special it was. The DW was packed. It was wet and cold. It was a defensive game, with two tough teams, but we were quite skilful and put some points on them."

How often did Wane tell the players he'd been man of the match against Manly? "I can't remember the exact number!" laughed Farrell.

"2017 was a struggle, coming off the high of the World Club Challenge. The season just didn't get going. Whether it was form or injuries, we couldn't put enough wins together. We crashed out of the Challenge Cup. I'm not sure if we even made the play-offs [Wigan finished sixth

after the Super 8s games and missed the top-four play-offs]. It ended up as a bad year. My most vivid memory is the meeting with Waney at end of the year. He told us our performances hadn't been good enough. It was a very brutal and honest meeting."

Wane's brutal honesty paid off as Wigan hit back in style to earn another Grand Final success. 2018 turned out to be the final season at the club for both the coach and the skipper Sam Tomkins. The club announced that Adrian Lam would take over for 2019 before Shaun Edwards returned from rugby union to coach Wigan from 2020. It was a surprising announcement, but the deal soon fell through with Edwards and Wigan blaming each other. I was keen to gauge what Farrell thought about the prospect of Edwards coaching in Super League, having been away from the sport for nearly 20 years.

"We were honest and open about what we expected from each other in 2018, and the year went pretty well," said Farrell. "Early in the year, Sam and Waney announced they would be going. I've been in seasons like that when those emotions can be used positively, and it can drive you on to success. Waney's a Wiganer, and we had to do a job for him. It was a great achievement.

"When the announcement about Shaun came about, my thoughts were he's a Wigan legend and he played the game for a long time, but you also think he's not been involved in the game for a long time. It does put some doubt in your mind. You wonder whether he's up to speed with how the game is at the moment. I just wondered how it would work. Things went on behind the scenes, and it didn't end up happening. He stayed in rugby union, and we ended up with Lammy."

ADRIAN LAM's three-year reign didn't deliver either of the two big trophies, but Wigan were incredibly unlucky to lose the 2020 Grand Final, played in an empty Hull stadium due to the Covid-19 pandemic. With extra-time looming, Saints winger Tommy Makinson attempted a long-range drop goal. The hooter sounded as the ball thudded into an upright. It bounced into the Wigan in-goal, and Jack Welsby beat the bamboozled Wigan fullback Bevan French to score.

"That Grand Final is by far the most painful loss of my career," said Farrell. "I was a much more experienced player at that point and so much has gone through my head that we could have done differently. Should we have gone for goal? Should we have kicked for touch? Should we have gone for a drop goal? It was one of those games when you think about it right through the next off-season. We'd played really well all year, and we'd won the League Leaders' Shield.

"Playing in empty stadiums was crazy, but we got used to it. We soon forgot there was no crowd when we played in an intense game, but when they started, it was so quiet, and you could hear all the voices around you. But we used it to our advantage, and we had a good year.

Lam left Wigan after a disappointing 2021 season and was replaced by Matty Peet, who guided Wigan to success in the Challenge Cup after a late try beat Huddersfield at Tottenham Hotspur's new state-of-the-art stadium. Peet didn't play professionally which is rare in modern-day coaching, so I wanted to know what he had changed and whether Farrell may have doubted his appointment as he had with that of Edwards.

"Matty's big focus was away from rugby, making sure everyone likes each other, creating a good culture, and ensuring that everyone's thought processes and actions make us a better club," explained Farrell. "He focused on a lot of off-field stuff, and he's doing an unbelievable job. It would take a Wiganer to do what he's done. I've known him for a long time. He's a few years older than me, but he's from St Pats, and I knew what kind of character he was. I wasn't involved with him in the Academy, but I knew about him.

"As for any doubts, my thoughts at the time were that I knew him as a person, and even if he hadn't played at the highest level, I knew he'd get the best out of the players. I knew he had the passion and drive to motivate players. He's so honest with us.

"We hadn't won anything for a few years, and we'd promoted players like Liam Byrne, Harry Smith and Morgan Smithies. Even Liam Marshall hadn't won anything. We didn't have a lot of big-game experience. We'd travelled well earlier in the season, and it gave the lads a great experience. It was very special to win it late on. It was the club's 20th Challenge Cup win."

Tottenham's new stadium seemed to impress everybody who went, but Farrell still prefers Old Trafford. "The Old Trafford atmosphere is right on top of you," he said. "With 75,000 people in there, it doesn't get much better. I was a ballboy there, and I just wanted to experience those rainy Saturday nights there."

FARRELL was in outstanding form in 2022, most notably in the Challenge Cup semi-final win against Saints, but injury struck late in the campaign. He missed the World Cup in which England were beaten in golden point in the semi-final by Samoa, but good news was around the corner as he was rewarded with the Wigan captaincy.

"It was medial ligaments which is roughly a ten-week injury, and the Grand Final, had we made it, was three weeks away," said Farrell. "Then there was the World Cup, which I was desperate to be part of. The surgeon said I was pushing it. I saw him a few days before the squad was announced, and he advised me not to do it as the knee was unstable. I partly enjoyed watching the World Cup, and the lads went really well, but it was a disappointing end.

"Being made Wigan captain is the proudest moment of my career. I'm proud to represent my town, my family and my teammates. I had a very good leader in Sean O'Loughlin, who was there for a long time, and with Tommy Leuluai retiring, Matty told me I was captain. It was an unbelievable feeling.

"You've got to set standards. I don't think I have to be different. I've always had good leaders around me. The best way is to lead by example. I've had to be more vocal which doesn't come natural to me, but when it comes to speaking up, and saying something uncomfortable, I don't mind if it is needed."

Farrell and I talk in May 2023 shortly after Wigan have overtaken Warrington at the top of the Super League table. I'm keen to know what a training day and a match day looks like for the modern player. "If we play on Friday, we'd be in on the Monday, and we'd arrive at 7.30am," said Farrell. "The lads sit together, socialise and have breakfast. We do our well-being markers to make sure we're ready for the day. We do 15 to 30 minutes of prep work. There's a gym session for an hour while half the team are doing skills. We have a break and then a video session. In the second half of day, there's a whole-team field session, and we work on the week's plans.

"Video sessions can vary. If we've not been performing well, we'll strip things back. We'll go back to basics and worry less on who we're playing. When we do look at the opposition, we go into a lot of detail, looking at individuals who are key threats - usually the halfbacks and the fullback.

"We have a nutritionist who is on site with us full-time. He provides all the info we need and recommends to the chef what to put on at breakfast and lunch. He recommends what supplements we take too. We're sponsored by Myprotein who provide us with everything we need, and no one takes anything else.

"There's an alcohol policy, which isn't strict, but if you're turning up training smelling of alcohol, there's a problem. Otherwise, on a free weekend, we can have a few beers.

"Matchdays are pretty chilled. The night before, I make sure I get my nutrition right. On the day itself, I'll have a stretch in the morning, take the kids to school, and watch some NRL. Things to keep your mind off the game are helpful. You don't want to play the game in your head eight hours early."

When Farrell's time as a player comes to an end, his future will lie in strength-and-conditioning coaching. In 2022, he graduated from the University of Central Lancashire with a degree in the subject, and he is now studying for a masters. I was interested to find out how he balanced student life with being a full-time rugby player.

"When I started, I got to Preston early, and did my gym work there," he explained. "I had lectures from 9am to 11, and then I came back to train with Wigan. I did that for a few years until Covid which made things easier because everything went online. It was a part-time course over five years. Going to uni as a 25-year-old was daunting. I was very nervous, so to come out with a degree was great.

"My parents were big on me getting something in place because rugby isn't a long career. It also gave me something else to think about away from the game which is good. I'm now doing a masters. My dissertation for the undergrad degree was 10,000 words and it took a lot of research and putting data together. I had to make videos and do presentations. It's quite daunting when you've been out of education for a while!"

GRAEME WEST

1982-1991
1994-1997 (coach)

The giant Kiwi Graeme West signed for Wigan in 1983 and gave the club 14 years of wonderful service as player, captain, A-Team coach and head coach. He captained the club to victory at Wembley in the classic 1985 final over Hull and returned to the Twin Towers ten years later as coach, masterminding another triumph, this time against Leeds. Under West's coaching, Wigan lost just eight times in 101 matches. He played 15 times for New Zealand between 1975 and 1985, scoring a crucial try in a 19-12 win over Australia at Lang Park in 1983.

If you could relive one day from your career, which would it be?

I'd go for the day I started to play Rugby League. I had a great uncle who was an All Black and I played rugby union from primary school until I was 16. Someone at work one day tried to convince me to switch to Rugby League. "No way," I said. "I'm not playing that game." But I was talked into going away with his team for a weekend and to have a few beers. I got on for 40 minutes, scored two tries and thought, "Jeez I love this game!"

I thought you'd go for the 1983 Lang Park Test or the 1985 Wembley final. How did the Kiwis tear up the formbook to beat such a good Australian team on that first occasion?

We'd worked real hard over a few years to get to that point. Under Cec Mountford's coaching, we improved and improved. We should have beaten Australia in 1982. We led 8-6 with five minutes to go, but they scored in the corner and won 11-8. Cec had stepped down for Graham Lowe for the 1983 games, so he got all the plaudits, but it was a brilliant performance, and it was great to finally beat them.

You captained Wigan twice at Wembley. How did you bounce back to win in 1985, after the disappointment of 1984?

Kevin Tamati and I went to watch the 1983 final between Hull and Featherstone because a few of our Kiwi mates were playing. Kevin was at Widnes and I was at Wigan. We just looked at each other and said how much we wanted to play there. A year later, we were lining up against each other, but Widnes were too good for us that day. During the 1984-85 season, we worked real well together. There were no big names in the forwards, but we did well, and the backs benefited from that. John Ferguson and Henderson Gill were great on the wings. Mike Ford and David Stephenson were good players. Brett Kenny came in as the missing link and Shaun Edwards at fullback really benefited from Kenny's ability. Wembley against Hull was just a fantastic day. It was a real team effort. The backs got the headlines, but the forwards laid the platform. The forwards had also done a real job against Hull KR in the semi-final. Shaun Wane scored the first try. My boot hit him in the knee, and he was out for the season and missed the final. I always felt bad about that!

You didn't enjoy your early days at Wigan when you were coached by Alex Murphy. Tell us the sand-bucket story.

I didn't play well in the John Player Trophy final against Leeds in 1983, and Alex hauled me off. When we were lining up a kick at goal, he sent me on with the bucket of sand. We didn't have a good relationship. The older people at Wigan always told me Murphy was one of the best players ever but, gee, as a coach, I would say he'd have to be the worst I ever had. He'd come in, yell and scream and then go home again. So, anyway, I ran back to the bench with this bucket of sand and made out I was going to throw it at him and his assistant, Bill Ashurst. They both ducked, which I found very funny. Bill said he really thought I was going to throw it. I tried to get the directors to get rid of Murphy earlier and when they eventually did, the team then took off. He got the sack after the Wigan Sevens in 1984. Colin Clarke and Alan McInnes had done all the work, and Alex just turned up for the final expecting his winning bonus. Maurice Lindsay said no, so Alex threw a telephone at him. When I next saw Maurice, he had bruises all over him.

You took over as Wigan coach in 1994 from John Dorahy. What had been happening behind the scenes?

When my first-team days ended, I was player-coach of the A-Team for five years. During that time, John Monie was great, and we had some laughs, but when Dorahy came in, everything changed. Maybe he thought I was a threat to him. He alienated the players. He was a bit arrogant. When he got the sack, they asked if I'd do the job.

In your first four games, you won a derby and two trophies. How did you prepare for that World Club Challenge win in Brisbane?

When I got the job, I spoke to the players and told them they needed to pull their socks up. Neil Cowie and Jason Robinson had been sent to the A-Team by Dorahy, which I couldn't believe - especially when he picked Inga Tuigamala on the wing for Wembley ahead of Robinson. Inga had a bit of an injury and I used that to get Jason back into the side. We beat Cas at Old Trafford in the Premiership Final, but Dean Bell and Andy Platt were off to Auckland Warriors and Kelvin Skerrett had broken his jaw against Cas. They all missed the trip to Brisbane. We got there on the Thursday, had a good run out, then I gave them two days off and said I wanted the best possible training session on Sunday. I explained to the directors that Dorahy had given the players such a hard time that they needed to unwind. Some of them went for a beer or two. At 6am on the Saturday, I went for a walk on the beach and Jack Robinson shouted over, "I've just seen Martin Hall going back to the hotel!" I thought that might be the end of my coaching career. But on the Sunday, Shaun Edwards got the players together, got their heads in the right place, and we had a superb training session. Martin Dermott was injured. Barrie-Jon Mather was playing on one leg. We only had one prop, so Billy McGinty gave it a go and he was magnificent. I was no fan of Cowie

- he was an obnoxious bastard - but he had a great game, and we came out with a win, which no one expected.

You then had a fantastic 18 months, winning two league titles and more cups.
It was such a challenge with all those competitions. The fixture pile-up was huge if you did well in the cups. In 1994-95, we only lost twice. One was at Halifax on a Wednesday night. Then we beat them by 60 points on the Sunday. I had John Pendlebury coaching the A-Team and he was great. He was as big a part of winning that Championship as anybody.

What went wrong against Salford in 1996 when Wigan eventually lost a Challenge Cup match?
When I selected the team, I picked Scott Quinnell and thought that a big forward pack would take Salford to task and the backs would then take over. We had two tries disallowed for forward passes. The penalty count was against us. We were good enough to win, but we didn't play well and that was partly my fault. We just looked at each other after the game, trying to work out what had happened.

Wigan played Bath in two cross-code games in 1996. Was there a gentleman's agreement that you wouldn't score 100 points in the Rugby League match, and why did you select yourself at the age of 42 to play at Twickenham?
There was no agreement like that, but I did take off players like Henry Paul and Andy Farrell very early, which is probably where that rumour came from. I just didn't want them getting injured. I did say to Bath at half-time that they could make as many subs as they wanted and that we would stick to just six. To be honest, we could have put 150

points past them. I know union had just gone professional, but Bath really weren't fit.
As for the return game, I'd been playing veterans' rugby union, so Joe [Lydon] and I thought we'd play. Again, we wanted to avoid injuries. But we did think we had a chance of winning if we could get the ball to our outside backs. We'd just won the Middlesex Sevens. Gary Connolly was done for a forward pass that was a poor call and we had a very good second half, running in some good tries. But their scrum was too good, and that's the main part of rugby union. After the game, my neck felt like it had had a ten-tonne rock on it!

Your time as Wigan coach ended after defeat to a 12-man St Helens team in the Challenge Cup in 1997. Were you harshly treated?
There was a bit of a shit fight happening at the top of the club. Players like Doc Murray and Paul Koloi had been signed by someone after being watched once. They were nowhere near Kiwi standard. Some of our best players had been loaned to rugby union clubs over the winter to save on wages and two came back injured. So, preparation for the Saints game was never going to be right with all that going on. Maybe I should have put my foot down further, but I did voice my concerns. After the Saints defeat, the directors didn't blame themselves for buying players who weren't good enough or for sending players to rugby union. I got the blame - probably for criticising them. I think Dave Whelan was onto them at this point, strangling the financial side of things. The team was going backwards. They actually wanted to make me football manager. Joe had done that job, but I could see he was just a puppet and didn't actually decide anything. There was no way I was doing that job, so I left.

67

MARTIN HALL

1993-1997

After playing for Oldham and Rochdale, Martin Hall was Wigan's hooker for six seasons in the mid-1990s. One hundred and forty-one appearances yielded 29 tries, of which nearly half came in the Grand Slam-winning season of 1994-95. He played for three clubs after Wigan before going into coaching.

MARTIN HALL was "the glue that holds the Wigan side together," according to Dave Hadfield, the Rugby League correspondent for the Independent. Surrounded by megastars, Hall was often lauded for his consistency and his control of the ruck area. He signed from Rochdale Hornets for £35,000 in January 1993, having started out as a teenager at Oldham.

"My dad Fred played for Oldham 198 times in the 1970s," said Hall. "That was the main reason I signed for Oldham. I was a mascot in their centenary year of 1977. I was 17 when I started in the 'A' Team. I made my debut against Widnes in October 1986. I had a couple of years there and played 10 games. Dave Topliss was a legend, and it was great to play alongside him. I remember going to a pub in Leeds after a game, and Topliss said to Frank Myler, the coach, "Hally's not an 'A' teamer, he's a first-team player." We had some top players like Mick Burke, Terry Flanagan, Des Foy, Paul Round, Mick Worrall - I could go on, there were so many.

"I moved to Rochdale in 1989. It went to a tribunal. We got promoted in my first year. We got to the semi-final of the Regal Trophy. We only won one league game, but it was a great experience to play in the top division. Rochdale had some great players like John Woods, Neil Cowie, Dean Lonergan, Logan Edwards and a lot of good young players."

Hall moved to Wigan in 1993, just before January's Challenge Cup-transfer deadline. He played just six matches in the remainder of the season, scoring two tries. "Wigan had been talked about for a while," he said. "Bradford and Featherstone also looked at me. Wigan then came in just before the Challenge Cup deadline. Martin Dermott had had one or two injuries, and Wigan were looking for cover. I took a chance, knowing I'd be second choice. I didn't go there thinking that's where I'd stay forever.

"My last Rochdale game had been on a Sunday against Carlisle. I signed for Wigan on the Monday lunchtime. That evening, Rochdale's 'A' Team played Wakefield at Spotland, and afterwards I went for a few drinks. We had a 9am session on the Tuesday morning at Robin Park where there was an indoor running track. As we were warming up, Andy Platt, whose brother Duncan I knew from Oldham, said, 'Bloody hell Hally, that Greenalls aftershave is good!'

"I'd played against most of the players, but Neil Cowie was the only one I really knew. He is larger than life and doesn't lack confidence. We were very different - I'm pretty quiet and he's very loud!"

Hall had no doubt which match was the highlight of his five years at Central Park, and it wasn't just the game that was memorable. "We won Challenge Cups, league titles and Regal Trophies, but the World Club Challenge in Brisbane was the big one," he said. "Graeme West had just taken over as coach. He was the 'A' Team coach when I was first there. He knew everyone at the club. We beat Castleford in the Premiership Final, then we flew to Australia on the Monday from Manchester via Singapore. Kelvin Skerrett had got a bad injury and Andy Platt was leaving for Auckland, so we were light on props. Billy McGinty, usually a second rower, did a great job and Neil Cowie played 80 minutes.

"The flight over was pretty entertaining. Someone mentioned this record of drinking cans of beer on a flight between the UK and Australia. The record was held by the cricketer David Boon who drank 52 cans. It was suggested we have a go at it. Nigel Wright had a go and ducked out at 20-odd cans. I'd done 38 cans by Singapore and was in reasonable fettle. Chris Butler, the conditioner, said, "Hally, you'd better stop because we're training when we get to Tweed Heads." So I stopped.

"When we got to Brisbane, Shaun Edwards did a live interview with Channel Nine. The interviewer asked him how seriously Wigan were taking the game. He said, 'Our hooker Martin Hall decided to stop drinking after his 38th can, so that shows how serious we are.' Everyone knew me then! Westy gave us a couple of days off and we had a great end-of-season trip before the Brisbane game, but we were ready when the game came round, and we beat them. In the end, the score [20-14] probably flattered Brisbane. We were well in control for most of the game, but they scored a couple of late tries.

"We were due to fly back the next day, but a few of us decided to go down to Sydney. The rest went back, and Neil Cowie broke the record with Joe Lydon acting as his counter. I tried to beat it when we flew back a week later, but I failed miserably. One of the papers rang me on my landline. I was comatose when he rang, and all he wanted to know was if I'd beaten the record. I had to say that regrettably, I'd failed!"

Hall intended to return to Australia to play club football. Along with Jason Robinson and Gary Connolly, he signed a contract with the ARL at the height of the Super League War. In the end, the trio remained with Wigan.

"Kelvin Skerrett, Andy Farrell and I were coming to the end of our contracts," said Hall. "Kelvin's was up first. We all agreed ARL deals, and we were all going to sign for Parramatta. They were central contracts, so you signed first then sorted a club later. I knew Parramatta were a big club. Then Maurice Lindsay and Super League got hold of it. Kelvin and Andy hadn't yet signed with the ARL, and they ended up signing Super League contracts and staying with Wigan. I signed with the ARL with Gary and Jason. The ARL later wanted to send me to the Gold Coast, which was an area I liked, but I didn't want to play for them. I nearly signed for Illawarra, but it didn't happen. In the end, they paid us off, and we all stayed at Wigan."

1996 saw Wigan fail to win the Challenge Cup or the Super League title, but they did play against rugby union champions Bath in two cross-code matches – under League rules at Maine Road in Manchester and union rules at Twickenham. Wigan won the former 82-6 and lost the latter 44-19. Incredibly, over a quarter of a century later, Hall is still feeling the effects of sampling life in a rugby union front row.

"I don't know how the games came about," he said. "The players had a meeting, and we were up for it. The Rugby League game was alright obviously, but the union match was horrendous. I was an old-school hooker as a kid and played when hookers used to compete for the ball, but I hadn't experienced anything like that and didn't want to again!

"The Rugby League game was very easy. We took good players off, and I ended up kicking goals with Faz and Henry off. The union game was completely different. Hookers in Rugby League are more like union scrum halves. Their props are much bigger too. Our line-up was similar in both games apart from Westy and Joe which was probably a mistake, but only one or two of the Bath forwards played in both games. They had seasoned internationals in that pack. My feet never touched the floor in any scrum at Twickenham. I got a neck injury in the training session we had against Orrell. It finished my career in 1999 and I still suffer from it now.

"I think Bath were embarrassed by what had happened at Maine Road. We took it seriously at first, but it was like tick and pass after that. They were a bit hurt by that, so they didn't hold back in the front row at Twickenham. We should have had uncontested scrums. Graham Dawe was their hooker. He was often on the bench for England. I've come by him a few times because I lived in Devon, and he was in Cornwall. He's a lovely chap. He didn't play in the League game. I had to do the lineouts as well at Twickenham. Their jumpers were all two feet taller. The other hooker stands nearby when there's a lineout. Graham was trying to intimidate me when I was throwing the ball in. I said, 'Hey pal, you get as close as you want, it'll still be a crap throw!'"

A YEAR later, Hall and his teammates returned to Australia to play in an extended version of the World Club Challenge. The competition pitted the 12 Super League clubs against their ten counterparts down under who played under the same banner - 1997 was the year of two competitions in Australia.

"At the start of that season, I'd decided not to go to the ARL," said Hall. "I got paid off, and I re-signed at Wigan. Westy got sacked after a cup defeat at St Helens. It was a very harsh call, a knee-jerk reaction by the board. Eric Hughes took over and we didn't have the best relationship. He wasn't keen on me. There was talk of me going to Halifax as a swap with Paul Rowley. Eric dropped me. I finally got into the team just before we went to Australia, and we started to put a few results together.

"Unbelievably, we were at the same hotel we'd been in when we beat Brisbane in 1994. There was a no-alcohol policy for the flight because Eric Hughes never wanted us to drink. We were business class in '94, but economy class this time. I was one of the more experienced players by now. We were given some Lucozade water bottles. Neil Cowie and I went to the duty-free shop and filled ours with Jack Daniels and got on the plane. We had two bottles of Jack Daniels each. Faz, who was the ultimate pro by this point, and Tony Smith were in front of me. I gave them both some.

"We got to Australia. We beat Canterbury in the first game which was a great performance. We were the only English team to win in Australia. We did ok against Brisbane when a few decisions didn't go our way. Neil got sent home for missing a training session which put a bad feeling in the camp. Then we got tonked at Canberra. I broke my thumb and dislocated it after ten minutes. Eric wouldn't take me off. I couldn't pass. Even my eight-year-old son at home could see there was a problem. I wasn't best pleased with Eric for not taking me off. We had a falling out in the airport, and he fined me for drinking on the flight out there!"

By this time, Hall was a Wales international, having helped the team to the semi-final of the World Cup in 1995, along with Wigan props Kelvin Skerrett and Neil Cowie and fullback Paul Atcheson. "Kelvin, Neil and I got asked to play for Wales," said Hall. "We spoke about it, and we did it. I'm very proud of that heritage and of what we achieved. We weren't a million miles away from the 1995 World Cup Final. Our first game was earlier that year against England at Ninian Park, and we beat them 18-16.

"Wigan beat Warrington on a Saturday in the Regal Trophy Final in January 1995. The Wales squad was due to meet the next day at 5pm in Cardiff. We'd been out on the Saturday night obviously. We were playing England on the Wednesday. We went down on the Sunday with Paul Atcheson who was also playing for Wales. We trained on the Monday morning which was ok. But a few players like Richard Webster weren't best pleased because their positions were under threat. No one was bothered about me though because they didn't have another hooker!

"Jiffy [Jonathan Davies] was captain. He was in the room next to me and Kel. He suggested we have a drink on the Monday night. I wasn't keen because we didn't drink 48 hours before a game, but Kel persuaded me. Jiffy is a god down there, and we ended up in this guest-house-type place, just the three of us. We got to training on the Tuesday, and Jiffy bollocked them all, saying he could feel the tension. He said we now have the best front row in world rugby, and he put them all straight."

Wales beat France and Samoa to progress to the semi-

final of the 1995 World Cup, but they were beaten 25-10 by England at Old Trafford. "I got concussed twice against Samoa," remembered Hall. "It was probably the best game I ever played in. We went drinking on the Monday night before the semi-final. Our preparation wasn't great. We had an Australian referee who did things differently which we weren't used to. We probably underachieved in the end when you look at the team we had. Man for man, I think we were better than England. There were so many Welsh fans at Old Trafford. If ever there was a time to get a Welsh team in Super League, that was it."

Hall's time at Wigan came to a conclusion at the end of the 1997 season. Having endured a rocky relationship with Eric Hughes, the next coach, the returning John Monie, brought Robbie McCormack over from Australia.

"I got fired off," he admitted. "John Monie signed Robbie McCormack, and that was it. I went to Cas, which I hated, for a month, then I went to Halifax which I enjoyed. We came third in 1998 and could have got to the Grand Final. I went to Hull in 1999 because I'd played with their coach Peter Walsh at Oldham. When I was there, I had an MRI

scan on my neck, and I was told to retire. I'd had enough anyway. I didn't want to become a journeyman.

"I got into coaching, taking over at Rochdale in 2000. I'd played there and had a lot of affinity for the place. I really enjoyed my time there. They'd come 15th out of 18 the year before, so I couldn't do much worse! I was there for three seasons, and we came third each time.

"I resigned after three years and went to Hull KR. Mal Reilly was the team manager, but I didn't really gel with Mal. My last club was Halifax, and I also coached Wales."

Hall was one of the many coaches to feature on the award-winning documentary 'Rugby League Raw', which covered the play-offs in the game's second tier for several seasons in the 2000s, but he refused to allow cameras into his team's dressing room.

"If I was watching it, I liked it," he said, "but the cameras weren't coming into my dressing room, no chance! Every club wanted them in the changing room. [Rochdale chairman] Ray Taylor, God rest his soul, tried to get me to agree, but I said no chance. The changing room is like the altar. You have to earn the right to come in!"

BILL FRANCIS

1964-1977

A Yorkshireman whose four professional clubs were west of the Pennines, Bill Francis played exactly 400 times for Wigan between 1964, when he was just 16, and 1977, scoring 159 tries in those 13 years. His Wigan side were runners-up at Wembley and in a Championship Final, but they won a Floodlit Trophy and two Lancashire Cups before he moved to St Helens. Francis also played for Wales and Great Britain, representing the latter in the 1977 World Cup Final.

What were your early rugby experiences?
I played union in the morning and League in the afternoon as a teenager. I was quite good back then, but I improved as I got older. At 15 and 16, I was playing for the Featherstone Rovers Under-17s. I was picked for Yorkshire along with Roger Millward. There was a televised Under-17's competition. Our team, Castleford and District, were a good side. Teams entered from Widnes and Wigan, and the games were on ITV on Sunday afternoons. That got me more noticed as I scored a few tries in the televised matches.

Being a Featherstone lad, how did you become a Wigan player?
Wigan saw me on TV and came to watch me play. They made an offer for me but so did Leeds, Featherstone and Castleford. I was tempted to go to Leeds, but what swayed me was the team Wigan had with all their internationals. I received £1,500 for signing. I put it in the bank as a typical Yorkshireman does! I saved it for a rainy day and ended up using it as a deposit on a house. When I was in the 'A' team, I was allowed to train with Featherstone Rovers, but when I started to get into the first team, I had to move over to Wigan. I lived with my teammate Danny Gardiner. He and his wife took me in as a lodger, and I stayed there until I got married. I got more and more accustomed to Wigan. I'd have never moved back to Yorkshire.

What do you remember of your first-team debut as a 16-year-old in a 12-0 win against Liverpool City?
I remember being very nervous. I walked into the dressing room and had never met most of them. Alan Davies was very talkative and made me feel welcome. 'What size are your feet?' he asked. 'Eleven,' I replied. 'Well, you'll not get knocked over very easily then,' he said. Billy Boston was my centre, and he only gave me the ball when he knew I had space to have a run. Ray Ashby was the Liverpool fullback. I ran down the wing, drew Ray and passed to Billy to score.

How did it feel to barely feature in the next two seasons?
Wigan had a good side, so I wasn't disappointed not to be playing. The wingmen then were very good. I was never impatient. You had to force you way into the team, and once I got in, I more or less stayed in.

Who were the best Wigan players of your time there?
Bill Ashurst was a very skilful forward. He could do anything and he was a great in-field kicker. He'd turn up for training with a hamstring problem and say he'd just need a rub down, but he turned up at the weekend and did the business. I didn't play with Eric Ashton and Billy Boston at their peak, but they were obviously great players. Dougie Laughton was a very good loose forward and Colin Clarke was an excellent hooker. George Fairbairn was one of the top fullbacks around. He was very conscientious in everything he did. He was an excellent tackler and read the game very well. Frankie Parr was one of the best scrum-halves in the game, but there were so many good players in his position that he didn't get the recognition he deserved.

What about your landlord, Danny Gardiner?
Danny was a big tough Cumbrian forward, signed from Workington Town. With his two cauliflower ears, he looked like a typical prop forward, but he was an intellectual fella. When I signed, the club asked if any of the players could take me in for a week or two, and he said yes, but it ended up being five years! He was also my boss. I was an engineer. He was a chief draughtsman then a director. We made roof supports for down the mines.

How did work pay compared to rugby?
It was very similar apart from when we lost. There was a massive difference between winning and losing pay. In my early days, it was about £16 for a win and £6.50 for a defeat.

What was Central Park like to play at?
It was superb, always with a great atmosphere. It was a pity when it was closed down, but that's another story. You could always hear the crowd because you were very close to the spectators. We were averaging 22,000 when I started, and we never had less that 12 or 13,000. But they let you know when you were playing badly!

Tell us about the 1967 Ashes series in which you played at White City.
I played for Yorkshire against Australia in 1967 when we beat them at Belle Vue. We had a good side with Roger Millward and Neil Fox. It was a competitive game, and we won 15-14. A month later, I was picked for Great Britain for the second Ashes Test. The game was at White City in London on a Friday night. It was an athletics stadium, and it was superb. I only found out I was playing on the morning of the match when I got a call at work. Gary Jordan, the winger from Featherstone, had dropped out. I'd played for Yorkshire on the left wing when we beat Australia, so I was called up. But I had to get down to London. I got my boots, and Danny drove me down. He brought me back because we had to play at Huddersfield the next day! Australia beat us 11-6. I thought I had a decent game, but Gary came back in for the third Test. I was just a replacement for that one game, and I didn't play for Great Britain again for ten years.

You gained 19 Wales caps and helped to prevent England winning the World Cup in 1975. How did you qualify?

My grandfather was Welsh, and I enjoyed my time with Wales. When we beat England at Lang Park, that was a tough match. The problem was we had to play Australia three days later, and they hadn't played for a while. It was bad timing for England too because if the games had been the other way around, they'd have probably won the World Cup. We had a tremendous pack with players like Jim Mills, Kel Coslett, John Mantle, Tony Fisher and Bobby Wanbon. In the backs, we had Eddie Cunningham, David Watkins, David Willicombe and Clive Sullivan. It was a great team.

Two years later, you came agonisingly close to winning the World Cup yourself as Great Britain lost 13-12 to Australia in the final.

We should have won that. Billy Thompson gave us a free kick when Stuart Wright was on his way through to score. There was very little between us back then. It was a very good tour. We had a good side. George Fairbairn was the fullback. Keith Fielding didn't play much, so I moved to wing from centre. We also had John Holmes, Kenny Gill, Eddie Bowman, David Ward and Steve Pritchard. We lost to Australia twice, and they were both close matches, but close isn't good enough!

What are your memories of the two big finals you lost with Wigan?

I don't think any of us will forget Colin Tyrer getting knocked out by Keith Hepworth at Wembley in 1970. It was the turning point of the match. It was a great occasion with 90-odd thousand there. The noise just hits you when you come out of the tunnel. That was very memorable. They scored just before half-time. I missed a penalty in the first half and then I was sacked because Bill Ashurst kicked after that! We played very well in the 1971 Championship

Final, and we deserved to win, but we slipped up in the last few minutes. Bill won the Harry Sunderland Trophy as man of the match. Stuart Wright let the ball bounce, and they scored, but they were miles offside.

You wore every number from one to six. What was your favourite position?

I played in all the back positions apart from scrum-half. Stand-off was my favourite position at the end, but I loved fullback.

How did your move to New Zealand come about?

Cec Mountford asked me to go to in 1973. I played for Waterside in Wellington and for the Wellington Provincial side. We lost to Auckland in the final. I played with Kevin Tamati, Kurt Sorensen and John Whitaker, a centre who later played for Warrington. When I came back from New Zealand, Graham Starkey had replaced Eric Ashton as the Wigan coach.

Why did you cross Billinge Hill for Saints?

Vince Karalius came in as Wigan coach and wanted to develop his own side. Saints came in for me, and I signed. I had a couple of good years there. We lost to Leeds in 1978 at Wembley. We should have won, but John Holmes had a good game. We missed a chance in the last few minutes when Derek Noonan dropped the ball. In 1979, we lost to Wakefield in the semi-final when David Topliss made a break in the last minute, and their winger scored. That was very painful.

Oldham and Salford were your final destinations. Tell us about those final years.

Graham Starkey came in for me in the summer of 1979 to join him at Oldham as player-coach. Graham was well ahead of his time. He was big on discipline and fitness. He was very good to work for. He was manager and I was the coach. I did 18 months. It was very difficult coaching and playing. You can't concentrate fully on either, especially on matchdays. When you're preparing to play, you should be doing the things a coach does. I then did 18 months as a player at Salford, and then I retired. I'd had enough! But I enjoyed Salford, and we had good players like Stevie Nash, Mike Coulman the prop, David Stephenson who went to Wigan afterwards, Colin Whitfield the fullback, and the wingers Keith Fielding and Maurice Richards.

Which Wigan players were you close to?

When I played, I was friends with Dougie Laughton and Bill Ashurst, but my big buddy was Peter Rowe from Wales. We were the same age and used to knock about together. There was Frankie Parr and Dave Robinson too, and Colin Tyrer used to wind everyone up by taking ages with his goalkicking! He might not have played for Wigan, but Mick Morgan was always a good friend of mine, as we went to school together, although I suppose he does have a Wigan connection what that Regal Trophy Final commentary!

Do you still follow the club?

I do. I go to a lot of games with Colin Clarke. We've been friends from me coming over in the 1960s. We go to all the home matches together, and it's great to see Wigan doing well. I enjoy watching them. They have two very good Australians in Bevan French and Jai Field. Liam Farrell has had a great career. A few players need time to gel, and maybe a couple of big forwards are still needed, but Matty Peet has done a very good job.

DENIS BETTS

1987-1995
1998-2001
2004-2005 (coach)

One of the great second-rowers of the modern era, Denis Betts played 367 matches for Wigan in two spells. He enjoyed three years with Auckland Warriors in the mid-1990s along with a handful of other Wigan greats. He was Wigan's head coach in 2004 and 2005. Betts later coached Widnes and Newcastle in Rugby League and Gloucester in rugby union.

LIKE MANY of the Wigan players of his generation, Denis Betts enjoyed a great career. He won 36 caps. He was named in the World XIII on four occasions. He won just shy of 30 winner's medals. Betts is perhaps somebody whose resolve and toughness was formed in his early life. His extraordinary teenage experiences didn't just see him become a top Rugby League player for his age without ever attending a training session. They include him becoming a dad at 14, an experience, he pointed out, which moulded him and focused him, and which ultimately paved the way for one of the most successful careers Rugby League has ever seen.

"I was 14 and she was 14," Betts recalled. "We married at 19 and had another child. That was my life. Looking back, it was good. It kept me grounded. I was loyal and determined. I loved [my partner] at the time. We'd done something stupid, and we dealt with it. I can't call it a mistake because it produced my daughter who's an outstanding human being. She's been a massive part of my life. She's 38 now, and I have two grandkids. I look pretty young for my age, and people can't believe I have a daughter who's nearly 40! It was a product of our environment and our time, but we dealt with it and went forward. It kept me on track and kept me focused."

The environment to which Betts refers is an upbringing in Salford, a dad who wasn't around and a school that in his words wasn't the best. "I was from a tough precinct," he said. "It felt like there was always something going on. Some sort of trouble. We never had anything. Everything was hand to mouth. I had good grandparents – my mum's parents kept us afloat, with things like bags of shopping. My mum's sisters were great. I was very lucky to have a family like that. My grandparents bought me my first pair of boots, and they watched me play. I wasn't going to walk away when my girlfriend became pregnant because it wasn't in my character to do so. I remember losing a lot of weight, being stressed about telling my mum. In the end, I couldn't do it, and my partner's mum came round to do it. It was a hard subject to broach!"

Brought up with football, Betts barely knew anything about Rugby League. He played at Wembley as an 11-year-old for Salford Schools and went on to excel for Leigh Miners Rangers, but he didn't actually go to training sessions. Even when he signed for Wigan, he knew little about his illustrious teammates like Ellery Hanley.

"I've spent 20-odd years coaching, putting players on pathways etc, but I was never coached as a rugby player as a kid," he said. "It's amazing, looking back. Things weren't great at home. My mum was doing two jobs. My dad wasn't around. I didn't go to a nice school or grow up in a nice area. I turned up, got picked to play for Salford Schools at Wembley and didn't play again for two years. My brother, Darren, also played in that game. He's younger than me,

but he was in the same school year. If he'd been a month younger, he'd have been in the year below and would have been the best player in his year group, so he was quite unlucky, although he did play a few first-team games for Salford in 1993.

"We were just two big lads who were naturals at sports, and we got picked, even though our school didn't have a team. We were evasive – running away from policemen and not getting beaten up helped with that! It was 1981, the year Andy Gregory played there for Widnes. We got battered by Cas.

"There wasn't much sport at school because teachers weren't doing after-school clubs, but Mr Healy and Mr Stainton got a few of us football and rugby trials. I did a trial with Lancashire Under-13s. Kevin Devine - dad of Sean who played for St Helens - was the coach. He asked me to play for Leigh Rangers. I said my dad wasn't around and my mum didn't drive. He said he'd pick me up. I told him I played football in the afternoon. He said they played mornings. So, for three years, he picked me up to play rugby and took me back afterwards. I never had one training session, I just played in the matches. I was just pretty good at it, but if it wasn't for Kevin putting himself out, I wouldn't have played.

"I also played for the England Under-16s in France without being coached. Mick Forshaw, Ian Gildart, Wayne Reid and Gary Price were in that team. I wasn't good at much apart from sport. It was an escape for me. I just caught the ball and ran as hard and fast as I could."

Betts ended up at Wigan, but it could have been Manchester United. "I was a good schoolboy footballer," he said. "I played for North West Schools and in a few finals. I grew up in Salford - my dad was a Manchester United fan, and I played football in the streets and was mad about it. Then I got a letter from Man United that they wanted to take me on as an apprentice, but I'd already been talking to Wigan. I met the board and it just happened. Looking back, I made the right choice!"

BETTS made his Wigan debut on 18th January 1987 against Workington Town at Central Park in the preliminary round of the Challenge Cup. He shared the subs' bench with Ellery Hanley who scored a hat-trick. Andy Gregory and Ian Gildart also pulled on the cherry and white for the first time, as the hosts won 68-0. Betts knew who Gildart was, but not the more illustrious Gregory.

"I scored in the corner, from a loop pass which I think came from Henderson Gill," he remembered. "Ian Gildart and I are the same age. We played for Leigh Rangers and England Schools together. I can't remember Greg making his debut that day, but I knew so little about rugby, I didn't know who all the first-teamers were. Every time I see Greg, he reminds me he made me a good player, which I can't really deny!

"When I started playing, I knew I could do it. Confidence built up, and it started to grow. It was a ruthless group, but I didn't see it as a problem. I kept my head down and avoided making eye contact with Andy Greg! Changing rooms in those days were a little bit different. Every club has an HR department now, but the world was a different place then! You kept away from senior players who could rip you to pieces if they were in the mood, but I wouldn't change it for the world.

"Graham Lowe brought Ian Roberts over from Australia when he was 21, and he told me to work with him. The game wasn't full-time, but I was at college and had a bit of spare time. Ian gave me great tips. He gave me a completely different perspective of professional sport. I also got on with Andy Goodway. He's a fantastic fella. He was so single-minded and completely focused on training full-time when no-one else was apart from maybe Ellery Hanley and Dean Bell. He was all about gym work, track work, hill work. Joe Lydon shouted at me for two years. I had to do all his defending. He'd chip over, score length-of-the-field tries and kick drop goals while I was next to him doing 40 tackles!

"We were all mates, but we weren't all drinking together. Everything was built on accountability of performance. If you didn't perform, you were told pretty quickly. Looking at the stars around you, we all knew we had to work hard to maintain the levels we were at."

The John Player Trophy Final win against Widnes in January 1989 was the game that made Betts feel accepted by his teammates. "What sticks out the most was making a half break on the right edge, and I passed to Ellery to score," he said. "He came back and jumped all over me in celebration, and that was one of the first times I felt part of the team. Before that I didn't even get changed in the senior changing room before training - you had to be invited in."

Betts' first taste of Wembley came nearly four months later when Wigan took St Helens apart, beating them 27-0. "We played them in the Premiership Trophy a week earlier, and I broke my hand," he said. "I had a big lump on it. I played, but Graham Lowe had probably intended to have me on the bench anyway. You had two subs back then, and when a change was made, that player couldn't come back on, unlike now. I went on for Nicky Kiss. Keith Mills, who did everything at the club, was trying to get him off, but Nicky wouldn't come off! I was shouting at him to come off because I wanted to play as much as possible. I didn't want to let anyone down.

"I'd been at the game against Halifax in 1988, but not in the squad - just there as a junior member of the group. I played in the 1989 final and then started in 1990 against Warrington, which we went in full of confidence, expecting to win. I remember Mike Gregory having a massive influence on that game. We won quite easily, but he was awesome. I remember more about him than I do about our performance. Joe Lydon put a massive hit on Paul Bishop. Shaun Edwards broke his cheekbone, but he stayed out there and organised things. My try wasn't great - chargedown, pick up and put down.

"I feel really fortunate. Sometimes things don't go your way, but I can only think of one time early in my career when I was dropped. I was playing on the edge against Wakefield [in September 1988], and Steve Ella ripped me apart [Wakefield won 25-20 with former Wigan player Ella scoring twice]. But I got back in the side and didn't come out again until I went to Auckland. I played under good coaches and alongside great players and had great mentors.

"Andy Goodway is still my best friend, and I speak to him often. He turned 60 recently. I said to him I'd have to reconsider our friendship, as I wasn't sure I wanted to have a 60-year-old mate! I made a lot of good friends during my career, and they're still my friends. It was the same at Gloucester. You can pick up the phone and talk to someone if you haven't spoken to them for ages. A lot of rugby lads are like that."

WIGAN played Saints again at Wembley in 1991 which was their 13th game in 45 days, having pipped Widnes to win another league title. Wigan were exhausted, but still had enough to beat Saints 13-8 with Betts winning the coveted Lance Todd Trophy as man of the match. Shaun Edwards later claimed Saints had been beaten by a bunch of cripples.

"It was a pretty tough year because we had so many games at the end," Betts said. "Everyone was pretty beaten up, and I think I was the only one to play every game [Betts did play in all 13 of those games, scoring five tries]. Saints were keen to get us back for the 27-0 scoreline in the 1989 final, and they made it tough for us, but winning was just part of our DNA. It takes a winning side to understand how to push on, and when we lost, it really hurt us which spurred us on. Shaun was probably right. Ellery had an injection in his hamstring, which no-one plays with, but he managed it, and plenty of others played injured."

By this time, Betts was a Great Britain international. He made his debut against France on March 18th 1990 and was selected to tour Papua New Guinea and New Zealand with Mal Reilly's Lions in the summer. He would go on to win 36 caps for Great Britain and England. "The 1990 tour to New Zealand was a massive part of my career," said Betts. "Lots of people pulled out of that tour, but working with Malcolm Reilly was great, because he's an iconic figure, and what he did on that tour was great. His ability to inspire people was fantastic. Going to Papua New Guinea and thinking, 'What the hell's this?' - that was the making of that team over the next couple of years. Beating Australia in 1990 at Wembley and in 1992 in Melbourne was all built on that 1990 tour and all the great things [captain] Mike Gregory and [vice-captain] Garry Schofield did. Garry was outstanding. Touring with Schoey was a real privilege. In that 1990 test series, he was brilliant. I'm glad I toured before mobile phones and social media in 1990, 1992 and 1996!"

The pinnacle of Betts' international career was captaining England in the 1995 World Cup Final. Along with Platt and Phil Clarke, he flew home at the end of his first season down under to play in the competition which celebrated Rugby League's centenary. He began as vice-captain but ended up in charge after Shaun Edwards' competition was curtailed after the opening match. "I led England out at Wembley in a World Cup Final," he said with pride. "Only Bobby Moore and I have done that. He's better remembered because he won – I'll give him that! We had some fantastic players. The final was a tight game, but we didn't play as well as we had done earlier in the tournament. It was another one we let slip. It was a great honour though, something to look back on with real pride. I've been really lucky to have played alongside some of the most unbelievable players ever to have played the game. I've had imposter syndrome!"

THE newly crowned Man of Steel, Denis Betts, left Wigan in the summer of 1995 to sample life in the Winfield Cup for three seasons with new boys Auckland Warriors. They were coached by John Monie and captained by Dean Bell. Propping for them was Andy Platt. Frano Botica kicked the goals. Betts made a barnstorming debut on 4th June 1995 with two tries in a convincing 36-12 win over Sydney Tigers – a new and temporary name for Balmain. Another ex-Wigan player, Phil Blake, was on the bench. But the Warriors missed out on the play-offs, as they also did in 1996 and 1997. The ruinous Super League War rumbled for the entire time Betts was in the Southern Hemisphere.

"I would have liked it to be simpler," he reflected, "because there was so much crap going on around the club. It was struggling to find an identity - it was New Zealand's team, then it was Auckland's team, then there were several changes in coaches and other key figures. It might have been good for future generations, but it was pretty chaotic. I can't say I loved every minute, although one of my daughters was born in Auckland. It was great for my wife and I to get away for a while. It was everything I wanted to be. I met people. I had a mid-season break in the Cook Islands, sitting on the beach. I couldn't have done that if I'd still been at Wigan!

"It would have been easier without the Super League War. I almost went to Manly. I had to choose between the two, but Dean Bell and Andy Platt were going to Auckland, and I joined them. I don't regret going. It was a fantastic part of my life. I lived in Mission Bay, an extinct volcano bay, with Rangitoto Island in the distance. It was very different to growing up on a council estate in Salford where the only piece of grass was one-metre squared with

a tree in the middle. I spent nine years without losing at Wigan, so it was a different experience, but I have 27 major trophies, so I can't have regrets. We might not have won a trophy in Auckland, but it gave me lots to talk about. Flying to Australia every other week - it was great to be part of something like that. I love New Zealand to bits. I visited the South Island and spent time with Stephen Kearney.

"I had two daughters in the UK from my first marriage, and that's what dragged me back. Maybe I should have stuck it out because their lives didn't change much just because I came back. I didn't come back because I wasn't enjoying the rugby."

DESPITE talks with St Helens, Leeds and Warrington, Betts signed again with Wigan for the 1998 season. They had missed their talismanic forward, winning only occasional silverware since his departure. "There was a feeling of vulnerability that hadn't been there when I left," said Betts. "The last game I had played in was the 69-12 Premiership win against Leeds, but when I came back it wasn't the same. However John Monie was returning, and he signed some good players, so that feeling that we could achieve anything was coming back. We got to the Challenge Cup Final but lost to Sheffield through complacency. We kept thinking it'd be okay, but then you look up at the clock and see 75 minutes have gone and think, "Oh shit." But we went on to win the Grand Final, which I missed through injury. I remember the tribute Andy Farrell paid me on the field after the final, and that was very special. I still got a winner's ring for playing the number of games I did that year."

One of the highlights of Betts' second spell at the club was the final game at Central Park - a 28-20 win over St Helens. Betts played superbly and scored the side's first try. "It's one of those games that sticks in my head as one of the most stressful games to be involved in because to lose to Saints would have been bad," he said. "Our next game was at home to Cas in the play-offs at the new JJB Stadium, and we were shot to pieces by then because of the emotion that had gone into the St Helens match. Tommy Martyn scored the final try at Central Park, even though we won. He had a great game. It was one of those days when we kept thinking, 'This bastard's going to pinch it for them!' The build-up was so draining. We just could not lose. Andy Goodway did a fantastic job in the lead-up to that game but ended up losing his job after the Cas game."

Betts played for two more seasons which yielded no further major trophies – just the League Leaders' Shield in 2000 under the coaching of Kiwi Frank Endacott. His final game was the 2001 Grand Final in which Wigan were hammered 37-6 by a Henry Paul-inspired Bradford. Wigan were coached by Stuart Raper, Betts' fourth coach in four years since his return from Auckland.

"That's just the nature of sport," Betts pointed out. "Wigan were really fortunate to have had Graham Lowe and John Monie. Everything was stable. The group was so solid with so many strong leaders. When I came back in 1998, there was still a good group of people, but the playing group didn't have the same stability. Andy Farrell was the rock everything was built around. When I became head coach and Faz left, it was a massive changing of the guard. I was head coach for only 18 months, but I was one of the longest-serving ones!"

As for Farrell, Betts is unequivocal in his praise of his former captain. "He's the best player I played with, and that's massive statement if you look at someone like Ellery. Having played with Faz for so long, he had this freakish ability. He was huge, but he could pass and kick off both sides. When he won Man of Steel for the second time, he was playing front row! The ability he had was phenomenal. If I was building a rugby player, I'd build Faz. He had it all. Leadership too. At 16, he was leading the singing on the back of the bus. 'Who does this kid think he is?' we wondered. That's why he's so successful at what he's doing now. He's so inspirational and he knows how to win."

Aged 32 when he finished playing, Betts moved into coaching, working with the club's Under-18s and -21s. He led the latter to a Grand Final win over Bradford in 2003, coaching future first-teamers Chris Melling, Shaun Briscoe, Liam Colbon, Kevin Brown, James Coyle, Bryn Hargreaves and Paul Prescott. He was soon appointed assistant to new head coach Mike Gregory in 2003. Sadly, Gregory's time as coach was curtailed by the terrible illness that would end his life all too early. His final game in charge was the Challenge Cup Final in May 2004. Betts took over. Gregory died in November 2007, aged 43.

"It was tough with Mike's illness," said Betts. "I was lucky to spend time with him in that role. I have fantastic memories of working under Mike because he was such a people person, and I can't speak highly enough of him as a player and a bloke. The injuries he had and how he came back and how he dealt with people were great. I wanted to work with him for ten years because he was a great mentor. It was so cruel. He was a fantastic father, a great human being. He'd worked so hard to get into that position, and he was a great coach. The cruelty of life

jumped on him. I helped him, although his mind was never affected. He was still as sharp as a tack. He knew what he wanted from the team and how he wanted them to play. All he wanted to do was coach.

"I don't think [the Wigan head-coach job] came too soon for me, but you need some belief from the people around you and above you. I've got two coach-of-the-month awards from then, so I couldn't have done a bad job! We were second or third in the table after Easter 2005, when we beat Saints and Hull with a team of kids, but we lost a couple of close games and panic set in at the club."

Maurice Lindsay responded by hiring Ian Millward, the hugely successful coach of St Helens, who had just lost his job for various off-field misdemeanours. Betts remained to assist Millward but believes that the Australian's appointment was an error. "Yes, I think things would have gone well if I'd stayed in charge at Wigan," he said. "Look at Nathan Brown at St George - he took over very young. I went to rugby union and reached Heineken Cup quarter-finals and Premiership finals. I've played under some of the best coaches, and what the RFU did for me was fantastic. They asked me what I needed and put me on a degree-level course that they paid for. They really try to develop their coaches. When I came back to League, people said I'd been away for too long to be a good coach again, but that was ridiculous. What it takes to organise a club, to spot talent and to build character is no different."

All these years later, like many of his old teammates, Betts knows where his heart is when it comes to Rugby League. "I'll always be a Wigan fan," he smiled. "I spent my life playing for them. My wife is from Wigan. My kids are Wigan kids - with a bit of Salford in them! It's been my home for a long time."

GEORGE FAIRBAIRN

1974-1981

One of the great fullbacks and goalkickers of the 1970s and 1980s, George Fairbairn was a Scotsman who once held England's all-time points-scoring record. He played with distinction for Wigan, where he won the Man of Steel, and Hull Kingston Rovers. He played in the 1977 World Cup Final and was one of the heroes of Odsal in 1978 when an ageing Great Britain side defeated Australia 18-14.

If you could relive one day from your career, which would it be?

Tough one – either Wembley or my first international. I'll go for my first cap. One of the reasons I switched codes was I was probably about third in the pecking order for the Scotland fullback jersey. I also qualified for England and was picked for the 1975 World Cup – I was very surprised to be called up because I'd only joined Wigan six months earlier. We toured the Southern Hemisphere, and it was a huge honour to play alongside someone like Roger Millward, who I later teamed up with at Hull KR. He was such a natural scrum-half, and I could read him from fullback. He'd turn and shout a move and suddenly pull it off.

We should have won the World Cup, but we lost to Wales at Lang Park and that proved crucial because there was no final – the World Cup went to the team that topped the group. Wales were very tough, and they had a fearsome pack.

We also played Papua New Guinea on that tour. It was the first time England or Great Britain played them, and it was certainly an eye-opening experience. We stayed in army barracks, which we were told was for our own safety. Everyone was so friendly, and they were great with us, but you still knew it wasn't wise to walk around on your own. We won 40-12, but we came off battered and bruised because they could certainly tackle, and it was boiling hot. It was clear Papua New Guinea were here to stay and they became a great addition to the international game.

Were you used to the physicality of that Wales game, having just switched codes?

People said the Wales game was dirty because of their pack, but it wasn't. We all knew each other and there was no rough stuff. One noticeable difference was there were few leg tackles in Rugby League – it was mainly upper-body stuff around the ribs and the chest. Tackling in rugby union was straight into the legs.

How strong were Wigan in 1974?

Not as strong as they went on to become! We came second in my first season, but that was as good as it got in my time there. The side was in transition, but there were some great players like Colin Clarke and Bill Francis. They were the days before contracts, so it was winning or losing pay. It was really nice to play for Wigan.

What was Green Vigo like?

He had just signed before me. He was a solid winger. He was naturally fit - very muscular. He was a real character off the field but, because of apartheid, he wasn't sure at first if he could socialise with whites off the field. It took him a bit to get used to the fact there was no segregation here. He was a very friendly guy and a great player.

You didn't win any trophies in your seven seasons at Wigan and were even relegated in 1980. What went wrong that season for the team and what did it mean for you to be named Man of Steel?

It was very hard from the start. We suddenly found ourselves sucked into a relegation battle. Four teams went down which was too many. The bottom three were never really in contention to stay up, so it was a battle between us and Workington to avoid the fourth-bottom spot. I think it was confirmed after we lost at Castleford with two games still to play. I remember the final game, at home to Leeds, which we lost 20-12. That was a depressing afternoon.

The Man of Steel certainly meant a lot to me personally. To get relegated and still win the Man of Steel is quite something. There were the normal awards like Player of the Year, Young Player of the Year, Coach of the Year, Division Two Player of the Year etc, and then they chose one of those to be Man of Steel.

With you as player-coach, Wigan were promoted at the first attempt in 1980-81, a season best remembered for Fulham beating you in their first-ever match.

Fulham had a very good squad, and it was a tough place to go to. It was strange because while it was their first game, it was our sixth game of the season. It was a big occasion. Fulham were strong and they beat us comfortably. I enjoyed the player-coach role, but it was really nerve-wracking because we were expected to go straight back up. We got back on the rails after the defeat at Craven Cottage. It was tough because we'd never been in the Second Division, and we had to work hard. We finished second and it was a big relief to be back in the top flight. But Maurice Lindsay brought in Maurice Bamford as coach, which I found disappointing because I wanted to remain player-coach, so I went to Hull Kingston Rovers.

You played in another World Cup two years later, this time with Great Britain, and lost the final 13-12 to Australia in Sydney. Do you remember your coach's post-match comments?

Ha - yes, David Watkins said they wouldn't beat us for years! I played alongside David in the 1975 World Cup, and he was also an excellent coach. When you only lose a final by a point, the optimism is understandable. I remember the Aussies beating us in Brisbane in the group game and we just weren't good enough that day. The final was closer, but they still deserved it. It was a really good game – very open and physical, but they could have won it by more.

You did beat the Australians once more – in 1978 at Odsal.

It was great to beat them at Bradford. We always felt we could win because we had a very positive mindset. They had so many excellent players, so it was a real

achievement. It levelled up the Ashes series, but unfortunately we lost the decider at Leeds.

I was initially left out of the 1979 Lions Tour but went over after a fortnight when John Woods got injured. The Aussies had just gone full time and that was probably the start of them pulling away from us. It made a big difference, and we saw it by 1982 when I played my final international. I loved my Test career - it was such an honour to play for England and Great Britain.

By this time, you'd moved to Hull KR after a record transfer fee.

When Wigan put me on the transfer list, the phone kept ringing and I signed with Rovers. Roger Millward was their coach, and they paid £72,500 for me – a world-record fee. It put pressure on me, but I had the whole of pre-season to get used to it rather than just being pitched into a game in the middle of a season. The price had nothing to do with me.

I joined a great team and played alongside John Millington, Steve Hartley, Mike Smith and Len Casey. There were some great times. We gave the 1982 Kangaroos a great game and led them at half-time. The crowd loved games like that. It was a full house with an electric atmosphere. The team was superb that day. We led at half-time and were well up for winning, but the Kangaroos came back, and you could see what a team they were. Queensland, captained by Wally Lewis, toured a year later and we were the only team to beat them. That was a great day. We had the same attitude that we were going to win, and this time we did it. We had an excellent team. It was so tight that day, and defences were well on top, but we just had enough class in the end.

How much did Wembley 1986 hurt?

It's one of those games that still haunts a bit. We lost 15-14 to Castleford but could have won it at the end. We weren't at our best, sadly. It was horrible to lose at Wembley. The missed conversion still sticks in the mind. John [Dorahy] was the regular kicker by this time, but it was just one of those things.

Did you enjoy coaching Rovers between 1991 and 1994?

I was coming to the end of my career. Roger had moved on and the club asked me if I wanted to do it. I'd enjoyed the Wigan job for that one season, so I said yes. It was hard coaching players I'd played with – on and off the pitch. Telling players what to do is one thing, but you're still wanting to go for a pint with them. I think I did ok, but there's so much to coaching with all the off-field stuff and the media commitments.

You coached Huddersfield in the 1994-95 season when you set the all-time record win, beating Blackpool Gladiators 142-4.

That game just flew past - it went at a hundred miles an hour. Greg Austin scored nine tries! It was a bit of a farce, but it was still nice to have the record - until 2018 anyway.

How did you enjoy coaching Scotland in the 1995 Emerging Nations World Cup?

That was a wonderful experience. It was difficult because there were players I'd never seen before. We beat Russia and America but lost to the Cook Islands, so we didn't qualify for the final. We'd never seen any of our opponents. The Cook Islands were a very big side and deserved to win. I coached Scotland again in 1997 and I spent time with the squad during Steve McCormack's time. The 2013 World Cup was a real highlight.

TERRY O'CONNOR

1994-2004

A model of consistency, Terry O'Connor was a mainstay in the Wigan front row for a decade, appearing for the club on 306 occasions. He experienced the tail end of the glory years, as well as the ups and downs of the first nine seasons of summer rugby. O'Connor captained Ireland in the 2000 World Cup and played 14 times for Great Britain. He was selected in the Super League Dream Team in 1996, 2000, 2001 and 2002. He has worked as a co-commentator and summariser for Sky Sports since 2007.

LIKE most of his generation, Terry O'Connor's path to the top started in the harsh world of amateur Rugby League where he played for a variety of clubs. He represented his country on an amateur tour of New Zealand before signing for Salford as a teenager. He hit the big time in 1994 with a move to Wigan, the new world champions.

"I started at Cronton which is on the outskirts at Widnes," O'Connor said. "If you were a big lad in Widnes, you were always going to be seen as a rugby player. The team moved en masse to Thatto Heath in St Helens where I went for a few years. I was in high school with a lot of players, and we went to St Maries before a load of us moved to Widnes Tigers.

"I went on a BARLA Under-19 tour where the props were Barrie McDermott, Paul Anderson, Darren Fleary and me. Back then, no one would sign pro, unless they were a worldie at 16, because everyone wanted to play for BARLA. Great players like Garry Schofield had captained BARLA's Under-19s. Only four lads from that tour didn't sign. We toured New Zealand.

"We won every fight," O'Connor laughed when I asked how they'd done. "We played against a team and one of our players was king hit. A brawl broke out, and the mayor wrote in the local paper that we were a gang of thugs on tour. Given what had happened, that wasn't really fair. Stephen Kearney was the Junior Kiwi captain, and they beat us in the two Tests. That was our first exposure to the standard we needed to be at.

"I knew Barrie before that. We'd played against each other in the North West Counties. We became close at 17 or 18. I signed for Salford just before we went. Barrie signed for Oldham when we got back. We've never clashed even when we played against each other. We've always had each other's backs on and off the pitch. There was a genuine rivalry because there were bragging rights, but our families are close. Our kids grew up together and Barrie's two daughters were bridesmaids at my daughter's wedding."

O'Connor signed for Salford on 5th August 1991. "Saints and Wigan came in for me, but my childhood hero was Steve O'Neill, and he was the assistant coach at Salford," O'Connor said. "Kevin Tamati was the coach, and he was another hero of mine at Widnes. If those two couldn't teach me anything about playing prop, I was never going to make it.

"I was a big Widnes fan when they were the original cup kings. I used to run on for the players' tie-ups even when I was 15 or 16. I remember the train stations when they went to Wembley. Widnes fans wore long white butchers' coats with messages and signatures on them. I watched them at Wembley in 1982 and 1984. They had the O'Neills, the Hulmes and the Mylers - all these brothers helped create a strong bond in the team. It was incredible how Doug Laughton sold a little chemical town to players like Martin Offiah, John Devereux, Emosi Koloto, Esene Faimalo, Kurt Sorensen, Paul Moriarty and Alan Tait."

O'Connor made three substitute appearances in 1991-92, his first season in the professional game. "The reserves was physical, but the step up to the first team was huge. It was ridiculously quick. I always say I was just a fat kid from Widnes who picked up a rugby ball and it changed my life. It gave me dreams and aspirations, and I travelled the world. I was always grateful. Everything it did and taught me was brilliant. Players and supporters constantly bag the game, but it's a brilliant product. If you line up teenagers who play football and rugby, you can tell the rugby players. They don't answer back. They're respectful.

"My first appearance was a cup game against Chorley. In my first league game, I played against Castleford, whose props were Lee Crooks and Keith England. I played with some great players at Salford. I'd watched Andy Gregory at Widnes. He was still incredible at Salford. There was also Phil Ford, Tex Evans, Matt Birkett and Peter Williams. I'm still in a Whatsapp group with them, and we still have a close bond after 33 years. Shane Hansen was one of the toughest players to play the game. Ian Blease was a class act in the back row. He ran with his elbows up and tried to offload. He kept clipping me, so I pushed him, and we had a fight. He must have thought, 'Who is this little fat kid?'"

O'Connor's breakthrough season was 1993-94 when he played 31 matches including a Regal Trophy semi-final against Wigan. Salford lost 18-12, but O'Connor was outstanding, earning a place in the League Express team of the week. Within weeks, he had signed for Wigan, although the deal was kept quiet until the summer.

"Garry Jack had taken over as coach, and he was really good," said O'Connor. "He brought a new mindset. He said to me, 'You have one job - carry the ball!' We pushed Wigan close in the Regal Trophy semi-final. I remember thinking, 'Wow, I'm up against Platt, Skerrett, Farrell, Betts and Cowie.' Wigan had a reputation for signing players that had played well against them, so I knew it was my chance, but I only had a good game because everyone else played well.

"I was on £1,500 a year plus bonuses at Salford. I was out of contract at the end of the year, and I got a call a few weeks later. Dave McKnight, my agent, did the deal to get me to Wigan. Salford got 95 grand plus Sam Panapa plus another ten grand if I played for Great Britain.

"Walking into Wigan was unbelievable, but Steve O'Neill always kept me grounded. When I told him I was going to Wigan, he shook my hand and hugged me but said if I didn't play well, they'd get rid of me. He blew my legs off with that comment! Later, when I made my Test debut, I gave him my shirt and told him he'd always been my hero. He thanked me for the shirt. Then he said, 'Do you just want to be a one-Test wonder?' He always kept me grounded."

BARRIE McDERMOTT also signed for Wigan in the summer of 1994, although his time at the club was far less rosy than O'Connor's. McDermott played 13 matches before being sold to Leeds just over a year later. 1994-95 was the last season when teams could name only two substitutes, so the pair were often competing for a place in the 15 with Kelvin Skerrett and Neil Cowie the regular starters.

"It was tough for both of us because we didn't want to see each other miss out," said O'Connor, "but there was genuine competition between us. We would shake each other's hand whoever had been picked. Baz started really strong and got picked for Great Britain a few weeks after his Wigan debut.

"Kelvin and Neil were brilliant. I loved them both. They were two tough, old-fashioned international props. Barrie and I learned a lot from them. They never made us feel uncomfortable, and they always helped. Everyone was brilliant. The best for me were Andy Farrell and Denis Betts. Andy was the best pro I've ever seen and the best player I played with by a distance. He was phenomenal on and off the pitch.

"In one of my first games, I just couldn't get the ball. If I called for the ball at Salford, I got it, but not at Wigan. Denis said, 'You're not at Salford anymore. You have to fight for it.' It was a harsh lesson. I thrived in that sort of environment and loved the competitiveness and ruthlessness. If you were cutting corners in training, the likes of Andy Farrell would absolutely hammer you. You soon learned the standards. I liked that, but I don't think Barrie did."

One of the few games the pair played together was against the touring Australia side - a match in which four substitutes per side were permitted. O'Connor and McDermott were on the bench. The latter famously elbowed Paul Sironen, an incident that is regularly watched on YouTube to this day, but O'Connor remembers his own pain.

"I carried the ball and popped my AC joint," he winced. "It was a shoulder-on-shoulder collision, running into Dean Pay. You couldn't show you were injured at Wigan. Players would say, 'If you're injured, go off, but you might not get back in.' Ian Roberts cut Mick Cassidy in two right in front of me. I remember thinking it was a different level to what we were used to. It was an eye-opener from playing at Salford."

In one game that season, O'Connor shared the two-man bench with Sean Long, who went on to earn legendary status at St Helens. In O'Connor's decade at the club, Wigan made numerous errors, but perhaps none were as glaring as letting Long slip through their fingers. "He was brilliant," admitted O'Connor. "I always thought he was unlucky at Wigan. He was phenomenal. He was tough. He was some player. He'd run at the line. He did a lot of work with Shaun Edwards. He was learning off the best. Wigan let Widnes have him in a swap for Lee Hansen. Saints wanted him, but Wigan wouldn't let them have him. It was a huge mistake, and I thought at the time it could come back to haunt us."

WIGAN swept the board in 1995, winning the Regal Trophy, the Division One championship, the Challenge Cup and the Premiership Trophy. O'Connor won a title medal but has painful memories of the first two finals. "I pulled my quad a couple of weeks before the Regal Trophy final against Warrington," he said. "With a quad, you don't know whether it's right again until you sprint. I did a fitness test before the final. I said to Graeme West, 'It should be alright.' 'Should?' he said. 'I'll make it easy for you - if you play and come off with a quad injury, you'll never play for Wigan again.' So I didn't play, and Barrie got my spot!"

"As for the Challenge Cup Final, Kelvin was banned leading up to the final, and I played really well the game before," O'Connor recalled. "But with Kelvin back, I was the 16th man. I was absolutely gutted. I didn't think I'd start but thought I might be on the bench. I always got on well with Jack Robinson. He could see I was gutted. He said he thought it was harsh and gave me a £1,000 bonus on top of my next pay packet. That blew me away."

Matchday squads increased to 17 from the summer of 1995, in time for the final winter season, meaning O'Connor was almost guaranteed to figure every week. That being the case, I wondered if he had hopes of playing in the 1995 World Cup for England and how that may have affected his future international plans.

"I got asked to play for Ireland in the Emerging Nations World Cup that was played at the same time," he said. "There were only about four or five Wigan players who didn't play in the World Cup, but I didn't want to devalue Ireland by only appearing to play for them because I hadn't got picked by England. When I came back from the 1996 Lions Tour, I then said I'd play for Ireland. Steve O'Neill being the coach was a big draw for me. If I had got picked for England, I'd have played for them, and I probably would never have played for Ireland.

"After the World Cup, we won the league again, and then I played in my first final. It was in the Regal Trophy against Saints. I'd waited a year. It was massive, and I wasn't going to let anything pass me by. Keiron Cunningham and Joey Hayes were fantastic for Saints, but we were just too good."

But Wigan certainly weren't too good six weeks later when they were beaten in the Challenge Cup for the first time since 1987. Shortly after the defeat to Salford, the Wigan Observer reported that several players had partied to excess on holiday, but O'Connor rejects the idea the players had done anything wrong.

"To be fair, we had been given time off," he argued. "There was a trip to Tenerife, but we still had a week of preparation before the Salford game. You just have to take defeat on the chin. Salford were better than us. Wigan had got to Wembley eight years in a row, and it had to come to an end sometime, but it was a really bitter pill to swallow."

The defeat to O'Connor's old club was Wigan's last game before Super League kicked off at the end of March 1996. It was 12 months earlier that Super League had hit the headlines as the game tore itself apart down under over pay-TV rights. Backed by News International, Super League offered the English clubs £87.5 million in a bid to isolate the Australian Rugby League (ARL) governing body. Players in both Hemispheres saw their earning potential rocket.

"We came in in the morning and the lads were talking about the Super League War. I didn't really know what was going on, but there was talk that Australian clubs might be interested in English players. I remember talking to Scott Quinnell and not even knowing what the ARL was. Baz came in and I told him about the APL. He said, 'Don't you mean the ARL?' That's how little I knew! We went to the offices to talk to Super League, and the whole corridor was full of players.

"I went into the room. 'We signed you on a three-year

deal,' they said. 'We want to rip it up. We'll give you a higher wage. You'll get four years and a loyalty bonus.' I was looking for the catch. I'd signed for the biggest club in the world. I didn't think it could get any better. Then I was being asked to agree to a wage increase, a longer deal, and I was walking out with a cheque for a loyalty bonus! I just asked where to sign. Neil Cowie played it the best. He went in and said, 'Give me your best offer or I'm off.' They didn't know who he'd been talking to, so he got a fortune!"

Saints pipped Wigan to the first Super League title, after which O'Connor was selected to go on the Great Britain tour of Papua New Guinea, Fiji and New Zealand. Tests with Australia were off the agenda due to the continuing Super League War. The Lions beat the Kumuls and the Bati but were whitewashed by the Kiwis. On that leg of the tour, Maurice Lindsay, the RFL chief executive, ordered 12 players home to save money on hotel bills. It was an appalling piece of public relations, but at least O'Connor avoided the cut.

"We only just got beat in the first test," said O'Connor. "We were in control until Adrian Morley was sin-binned late on. But the result put us under the pump. We lost the second Test which was also close. Then things started going wrong. I was in the Test team, and we heard rumours about lads from the midweek team being sent home. We were shocked. We moved on for the third Test, and a couple of the midweek lads came to watch. The rest got sent home. We were gobsmacked. In all honesty, it looked a bit amateurish."

THINGS also started to go wrong domestically for O'Connor. Having ended 1996 by thrashing St Helens in the Premiership Final, Wigan were knocked out of the Challenge Cup at Knowsley Road in the first match of 1997, even after O'Connor's half-cousin Bobbie Goulding was sent off. Graeme West was sacked and Shaun Edwards and Va'aiga Tuigamala left. Eric Hughes succeeded West but lasted just one season.

"1997 was a tough old year," said O'Connor. "Westy had won everything in 1995, and he was a players' favourite. Hughes came in, and I liked him. He was another of my

Widnes heroes. It was a real shock when Shaun was allowed to leave. It was a warning that it could happen to anyone. We were nowhere near Bradford in the league, but we managed to win the Premiership again. I thought Eric deserved to stay, but being a Saints legend probably counted against him, and the club wanted to bring John Monie back which they did for 1998.

"I didn't get on with John. I remember him saying when he first spoke to us that he'd been in retirement, and he'd come over here for a boat. He said it as a joke, but I didn't see eye to eye with him. He never got the best out of me. It was just one of those player-coach clashes. He probably didn't like me being a smartarse and joking around. I gave my best for Wigan in 1998, and I got on with [assistant coach] Andy Goodway. He kept my mind focused, telling me to dig in. John wanted me to go, and I'd agreed to sign with Matty Elliott at Bradford. This would have been a mid-season transfer, but as I was putting on my trainers to go and sign for Bradford, Mike Nolan, the Wigan chairman, rang to say the deal was off.

"I remember the play-off semi-final at home to Leeds. We hadn't beaten them that year. Lee Gilmour scored a wowzer of a try, and we beat them that night to reach Old Trafford. I got concussed by Daryl Powell. I got up and started threatening Jamie Mathiou. Daryl was laughing because I'd confused them. I'd have definitely failed an HIA if we'd had them then, but I went back and must have played well because Gary Connolly's missus, Kath, told me I should get knocked out every week because I had a blinder! We knew we had to go up another level to match Leeds. Their pack was horrible to play against. They weren't big like Bradford's, but they were physical, dirty and intimidating."

With O'Connor known for his sense of humour, I was keen to ask him about sledging - the subtle art of putting your opponents off with a variety of verbal offerings. I imagined he was a master of this particular dark art. "Loads of stuff went on," he said. "You'd give it to your opponents about anything - their features or anything you'd found out about them or if they made a mistake. I was good at sledging because I had a gob on me, and I always wanted the last word. I'd get at McDermott. 'He's knackered!' I'd shout. 'Run at him!' Baz always wanted to fly out of the line to leather me, so I'd tip the ball on, probably out of fear. Sometimes someone would go through, and I'd say, 'That's because of you!'

"One of the best sledges I heard was from the Saints forward Peter Shiels. He'd played with Matty Johns at Newcastle, and Matty came over to play for us. After a run-in with Andy Farrell, Shiels said, 'You were right about him, he's a ******!' Faz looked at Johnsy, and Johnsy panicked. It proper got in Faz's head that Matty had spoken to him. I recycled that one a few times! Nothing ever shut me up though. Opponents would sledge me about my rugby ability, or they'd call me fat, but I knew I was fat, and I knew I wasn't the best player, so nothing ever bothered me."

Some of O'Connor's best sledging was reserved for Gorden Tallis with the pair having a memorable fight in the 1997 World Club Championship in Brisbane. "We're really good friends now which surprises a few people," said O'Connor. "He came over in October 2022 and we had a few dinners together with his wife Gemma. It was lovely. We always laugh about what happened. Eric Hughes was our coach, and he told us about Tallis. He said he was the player to stop. Eric wanted me and Neil Cowie to knock him off his game. Nothing was working and Gorden was keeping it together. Eric got the message out again to sort him out. I was calling him every name under the sun to no avail. Then I spotted him, went back at him, and he dropped me on my head. No penalty was given. I got up and was about to sledge him. He got five of the quickest punches in. I didn't see them. But I got a belter in over the top. Then I got him again and split his nose across his face. We both got sin-binned. I got into him again as we went off. We didn't clash again when we went back on. We weren't avoiding each other though, we just didn't happen to cross paths. After the game, he said, 'Good blue, that!' Thankfully, he didn't play in the return game!

"The next day, my quote, 'My wife hits harder,' was everywhere. The fight was bigger news than the game. There was a pic of our lass in the paper because Mary Sharkey at Wigan had sent over a wedding photo. They'd superimposed boxing gloves on her! Gorden said he got hammered over that! He's a lovely fella, and I always have a laugh with him."

JOHN MONIE was sacked during 1999. His replacement was Andy Goodway who was then relieved of his duties after defeat to Castleford in the 1999 play-offs. "I really liked Andy because he was straight," said O'Connor. "He'd picked me for Great Britain in 1998, so he obviously rated me. I really enjoyed that series, and I was made up when he got the Wigan job. The club wasn't particularly stable at the time though. There were a lot of rumours behind the scenes. The ground was being sold. We were moving to the JJB stadium. No one knew Maurice Lindsay was coming back at that point. We wondered if Dave Whelan was taking over. It's not an excuse, but it didn't help.

"I don't think Andy had the money at his disposal to build the team he wanted. The last game at Central Park against Saints was one of the most pressured games I ever played. It was unthinkable to lose. Andy managed to navigate us through that. What I loved about him was he'd tell you in front of everyone if something was unacceptable. I really liked that. I've seen players who couldn't take his brutality, but I loved his honesty.

"Frank Endacott came in next, and he had a great personality. He had a good squad and a new stadium, and he probably thought it doesn't get much better. He was just what we needed. John was a technical coach. Andy was technical and a straight talker who could blow your legs off. Frank wanted to be everyone's mate, and it genuinely worked. We got to the Grand Final against St Helens in 2001. There were a couple of key moments when we lost it, but I think we were the best team in the comp that year."

Soon after the disappointment of that Grand Final came one of the highlights of O'Connor's career as he led Ireland into the 2000 World Cup. They reached the quarter-finals where they lost 26-16 to England at Headingley. "I grew up dreaming of playing for Great Britain," he said, "but my most enjoyable time came playing for Ireland. The coach was my childhood hero, Steve O'Neill. He brought in Andy Kelly who is one of my best mates now, and I was playing alongside Barrie McDermott.

"We were in the group of death with Samoa, New Zealand Maoris and Scotland. When we beat Samoa in the first game, interest in the team really took off. We had to beat the Maoris to play England. We had this unity that I've never experienced before.

"We all wanted to be there. We didn't get much money.

Ireland had to beg, borrow and steal to get kit. We all enjoyed each other's company. A few of us from that camp still go to Ireland every year. None of the Great Britain teams I played with have reunions - well, unless they don't invite me!

"We should have beaten England in the quarter-final. There were two key moments in that game - a brilliant tackle by Stuart Fielden on Kevin Campion who had broken up the middle of the field and a kick from Tommy Martyn which would have created a try for Michael Eagar had it not bounced horribly.

"That Ireland camp was much more enjoyable than the Great Britain ones I experienced. I retired from GB in 2002 when I was 31 because I wasn't really enjoying it. We'd train in the day and then watch videos of us training in the evening. There wasn't as much camaraderie, although there were no fall-outs.

"If Great Britain could have replicated what Ireland had, they would have been more successful. International rugby is not just about tactics. You get picked because you're the best in your position, so why be coached to death? In 2000, we focused on bonding and spending time with each other, not just going back to your room and watching telly. It just didn't seem to be as much fun as Ireland. Great Britain probably put too much pressure on themselves to beat Australia and New Zealand, whereas all Ireland had to do was turn up, play and then have a party."

O'Connor's other representative team was Lancashire after the War of the Roses concept was revived in 2001, under 'The Origin Game' banner. It only lasted three years with Lancashire winning in the first two years before Yorkshire hit back in style in 2003. O'Connor, who won the player-of-the-series medal in 2002, named after the former Great Britain forward Roy Powell, was a fan of the idea.

"You come through all the age groups playing for Lancashire, and there's a genuine rivalry," he said. "We loved it and it was good for the game because you had squads of 21, which meant 42 players going into camp, battling for places in the Great Britain team at the end of the season. Compare that to England playing The Exiles when you only have 17 on the field who are eligible. I don't know why they cancelled it. People who said it didn't work had no idea and had clearly never played in them. Lancashire v Yorkshire was miles better than the Exiles. It was a good stepping-stone for Great Britain."

WIGAN's next coach was Stuart Raper in 2001 after Maurice Lindsay fired Endacott. Raper was Wigan's sixth coach in their sixth season of Super League. He would become the only one to last for two years before he was unceremoniously dumped in 2003 and replaced by Mike Gregory with Denis Betts his assistant.

"I loved Stuart," O'Connor enthused. "He was direct. He got the job after success at Cas. They'd beaten us in the first game at the JJB in the 1999 play-offs. I really liked him, but he didn't get on well with all the players, probably because he was a straight talker. Technically, he was very good. He was very positive. He got us to Murrayfield, and we lifted the Challenge Cup. He was really good for me. I played some of my best stuff under him.

"A few players were outspoken on Stuart. I wasn't one of them and it's not up to a player to do that. The coach's job hangs on the results. Stuart had put up a motto in the dressing room that a couple of players ripped down when

he left, which I thought was disrespectful to someone who had just lost his job. If the chairman wants to sack a coach, that's up to him, but it shouldn't be down to the players.

"Mike was a lovely bloke and a very popular choice along with Denis Betts. I knew Denis from Salford. He would come to watch the 'A' Team because his brother Darren played for us. When Denis watched us play, you'd think Kylie Minogue had turned up such was the excitement. Mike and Denis complemented each other well. Both had captained their country. Both were winners. It's about managing people and not overcoaching them, and they both got the balance right. Mike was the players' choice, and he was brilliant. It was always going to be a successful partnership. We won eight games to get to the Grand Final after not performing well all year. When he got the job, there was a feel-good factor that came through.

"The semi-final win at Headingley was unbelievable. I'd had a crash that day. Some lads ran in front of the car and flipped over the bonnet. I was really worried about them, and I thought I'd miss the game. My head was all over the place, hoping the lad was ok. It was probably Brian Carney's best game for Wigan with the two tries he scored."

Just as Wigan thought they'd found the perfect coach, the worst of news began to filter through. Gregory was unwell, and he would be heading to America for treatment after the 2004 Challenge Cup Final at Cardiff's Millennium Stadium. He had progressive muscular atrophy, a form of motor neurone disease. He didn't return to his post and died in 2007.

"We went to Old Trafford a few days before the Grand Final and Mike fainted," O'Connor recalled. "He still hadn't been given the permanent job then - he didn't get that until the off-season. We were all joking, 'Give him the job - he wants it that bad, he's fainting!' We had no idea what was wrong with him, but it started to become apparent something was wrong in early 2004. He sat us

all down and said Cardiff would be his last game. I don't know if there was pressure from the club. It was proper heartbreaking when he spoke to us all. It was a pretty emotional room. It still wasn't confirmed how serious it was. We hoped it was Lyme disease at that stage, but obviously it was much more serious.

"A couple of weeks before the final, I got an elbow in the sternum, and I had to have it jabbed up to play in the final. In the first collision, it went, and I was in agony for the whole game. I'd already signed for Widnes and didn't want to miss it as my chances of getting to a final with Widnes were pretty slim."

However painful that sternum injury sounds, it wasn't the worst that O'Connor suffered in his 15-year professional career. "I snapped my planta fascia [a foot muscle] in 2002 when Great Britain played Australia," he said. "I was just pushing off it and I felt a snap. I was in agony. I couldn't walk. I was on crutches. The Wigan physio didn't pick it up. We played Cas the following week. When you've been on the back of a hiding [GB lost 64-10], you just want to put it right, so I played at Cas. My whole foot was injected. There must have been 15 injections in my foot to play. Each time the needle was put in, it was twisted round to squirt painkiller into the muscle. I played for four or five weeks like that. As a result, I partially ruptured the Achilles on my other leg because everything had been load-bearing on one side. I couldn't get to the bottom of it. My Achilles looked like a continuation of my calf because it was that big, and I kept getting deep sores in it.

"I played for Great Britain against New Zealand with it, and it was the nearest I came to packing the game in. I had to come down the stairs on my backside because I was in so much pain. I got to the off-season, and I was all over the place because it still hadn't been diagnosed properly. I phoned a couple of physios I knew, and I went to Manchester City to see them. Peter Schmeichel was in

the room, talking about how much he liked rugby. The problem was diagnosed straightaway. Very few people understand what players go through. They should be paid much more than they are."

O'CONNOR's next club was Widnes, his hometown. He was coached by Frank Endacott, and in his two seasons there, he played alongside former teammates Gary Connolly, Mick Cassidy and Barrie McDermott. "It was like getting a pop group back together," he laughed. "I'd agreed it in early 2004. Saints had offered me more money in 1998 and 2000. I also had talks with Darryl van der Velde at Warrington, but I wanted to stay at Wigan because I was so happy there and I had a goal of playing 300 games for them, which I eventually managed.

"Whatever money you get, the taxman will take a load of it anyway, but no one could take away my 300 games. I see lads leaving Lancashire for an extra 20 grand in Hull, and it doesn't occur to them that they have to pay eight of that in tax then they only have 12 left for relocating or travelling costs. Being a Widnes lad, I only wanted to join them after Wigan.

"We had a decent team, and I think I did ok. I really loved it. Wigan was majorly professional, but I didn't get how Widnes players wanted to go on the beer after a loss. I fell out with a few of them over that. Mick Cassidy and Gary Connolly were brilliant, and there were lots of good lads like Simon Finnegan and Shane Millard, but unfortunately not everyone had the right aspirations, and it wound me up. I remember an early worrying sign in pre-season when we were running up hills, and I was catching up with the two groups who had set off before ours. Some of them were backs. I told them they should have been embarrassed at a 34-year-old prop overtaking backs who had started earlier.

"But I enjoyed it because it was my hometown club. The only other chance I had to play for them was in 2001 when I had just signed a new deal with Wigan. They never came in for me when I was a kid."

O'Connor retired in 2006, having played 426 matches for Salford, Wigan, Widnes, Great Britain, Ireland and Lancashire. He ran three London Marathons - "I didn't believe I'd hit a wall until 20 miles. It's like someone hits you in the face with a spade. Then someone in fancy dress overtakes you and it totally demoralises you, but it's such a great feeling when it's over."

O'Connor and Barrie McDermott were then employed by Sky Sports to join Eddie Hemmings, Mike Stephenson and Phil Clarke in commentating on and summarising Super League matches. "I started with Sky in 2007," said O'Connor. "We were initially bit parts, doing the Championship or being guests on Super League games. There was Boots 'n' All too. I think we got the jobs because we had always been happy to do interviews with Angela Powers and Bill Arthur. The majority of players would say, 'I'm not doing it', but we would. We always had a good relationship with Angela, Bill, Eddie and Stevo. We'd chat to them in the bar after a game. We got the opportunity just because we did things for them. We didn't put in an application. I wouldn't even know how to write a CV!"

Along with McDermott and Brian Carney, O'Connor was on Sky duties on Sunday 26th September 2010 when the awful news broke that Terry Newton had taken his own life. Hemmings revealed the news to a stunned audience while Carney and McDermott poignantly shared their thoughts. Hemmings explained that O'Connor was too upset to join them.

"I remember it very clearly," he recalled. "It was the Championship Finals day at Warrington. In the break between the games, I noticed a couple of missed calls off Dave Allen. I thought I'd call him back after work. Nev Smith [Sky Sports producer] then told us the news. He was panicking that it would get out because it was going to be all over social media. I just couldn't speak. I couldn't get in the studio - not a cat in hell's chance.

"I'd spoken to Tez the day before. He was having a fundraiser at his pub that night. He was running around, getting bits sorted. If he knew what he'd left behind, he'd have never done it. He was probably one of the most loyal mates you could have. When he crossed the white line, he was horrible, and people judged him on that. But on the other side of the line, he was amazing. His wit was unbelievable. I had so many good times sharing a room with him with Great Britain. You didn't want to cross him though! He was an unbelievable player too. When Sky gave out Tissot watches for man of the match, he always seemed to get them at Wigan. He was like Stevo's lovechild!

"When he got done for human-growth hormones, I was in a hotel at Tenerife, looking out to the beach. He phoned me. He was quiet. I could tell he was serious. He said he'd been done for performance-enhancing drugs. Why, I asked. Only crap players take those, but he did it because he wasn't getting over injuries.

"He had a scrapper mentality when he wouldn't let anyone stand over him. We see his mum and dad every year on the anniversary – that's myself, Baz, Brian and Adrian Morley.

"I don't read autobiographies and was never interested in doing one, but I read Tez's book in two sittings, probably because he had just passed away. It was hilarious. I was laughing my head off all the way through it."

O'CONNOR's latest role in the game is that of parent. His son Jarrod played for Leeds in the 2022 Grand Final, before which Terry brought the trophy onto the field. Jarrod is a highly-rated hooker. Two days before I speak to Terry, Jarrod scores a second-half try as the Rhinos mount an incredible comeback at home to Catalans Dragons in a match televised by Channel Four. O'Connor senior is shown in the crowd with other family members. On Terry's Instagram, he has a video of him setting up a try at Odsal and then Jarrod doing the same, over 20 years on, on virtually the same patch of grass.

"The best thing Jarrod did was start in the scholarship at Widnes," O'Connor reflected. "It taught all the kids about hard work. It can be too easy for kids at the bigger clubs, but it was tough at Widnes. You get a t-shirt and a pair of shorts, and you just train as hard as you can. He's always had a work ethic. He used to box Mondays, Wednesdays and Fridays with rugby training on Tuesdays, Thursdays and Saturdays with a game on Sunday.

"He's always been very competitive. He never cut corners. He was disciplined as a young kid and took the coach's advice on board at an early age. He signed for Widnes, got the Academy player of the year in his first season, then the club went into administration, and he signed for Leeds. He loves it there. He lives there. He's settled. I doubt he'll ever come back to Lancashire. Rohan Smith's been out of this world with him. I've never heard of some of the stuff they do. All I got from coaches was, 'Get the ball and run as hard as you can!'"

JOHN BURKE

1977

Forty years ago, John Burke was paralysed, having suffered a serious neck injury playing for Workington Town against Leeds. The accident happened the day after his 21st birthday. Burke was a prodigiously talented fullback or stand-off, who had captained the England Schoolboys' team. He played for Wigan before Workington and was in line for his international debut before injury struck. Town and the Rugby League public raised enough money for Burke to have a bungalow built and in the last decade he has received significant help from the Rugby League Benevolent Fund.

What do you recall of the day of your accident?

I was excited about playing Leeds at home. Workington could beat anyone on their day, home or away. There was a decent crowd. The game started, and it was tough. As I've been told, the ball came across, but it wasn't meant for me. I jumped and caught it but landed in a sitting position, not tackled. A few players dived on top of me and that's how the injury occurred. I was on my back. Billy Thompson was the referee. He asked if I was ok. I looked at him but couldn't talk. I was carried off on a stretcher, but you wouldn't do that today. There'd be a neck brace put on you. I remember seeing John Short, the physio. I was told I had movement. I went in the ambulance to Hensingham Hospital, but it took ages to see a doctor. I only went to the spinal unit the day after, but it should have been within four hours to stop the swelling. That gives you a much better chance, but I didn't get there quick enough. My father and wife were in the hospital with me I think.

What happened over the next few days?

When you get an injury like that, it's a life-changing event. One moment you're fit and standing, the next you're not. I had to come to terms with that quickly and I did. I had to grow up quickly. I had just turned 21. I asked my father why I couldn't move my legs. He said I'd damaged my neck. I didn't understand how that affected my legs. It was tough. I was in traction for 12 weeks and couldn't move anything. My wife and daughter lived in a caravan in Hexham for 12 weeks. My mum, dad and sister came to see me each week, which was a big help. After traction, rehabilitation was a long and difficult process. I was moved from Hexham back home for a week, then to Southport Spinal Injuries for a year. I was quite near home and came home for weekends. I lived in a new semi-d etached house, but it wasn't suitable for my needs.

What did Workington Town do to help?

A lot of people from Workington raised a lot of money. Tom Mitchell was amazing, as were the players, directors and fans. With the money raised in the John Burke Trust Fund, I decided the best thing to do was build a bungalow and it's where I'm still at today. It's been a big help in my life. I've a lot of time and respect for people like George Graham, Jack Atkinson, Rene Anderson and Dick Viney - without their help I'd have really struggled. I still keep in touch with Marjorie Mitchell, Tom's daughter.

How long did it take for you to come to terms with your new life?

The sooner you come to terms with it the better. You can't dwell. And I did come to terms with it quickly as I had a daughter and a wife. It wasn't easy. I had a nice house which made things easier. I lived a full and active life and still do.

What have the Rugby League Benevolent Fund done for you?

There was no Benevolent Fund when I was injured. When it started, Dave Phillips was the manager. He came to see me and introduced himself and explained about the Benevolent Fund. He asked if there was anything I'd like. I said jokingly I'd have a new wheelchair, and they got me one! I got pally with Dave and we're still friends. Steve Ball is now the manager. If I want anything, I phone and ask if I'm ok to apply for whatever it is. They've funded a new wet room for me and a new kitchen, which has been adapted for my needs. They maintain my garden. They got me an electric bed. Most of it is to help keep me independent. I'm eternally grateful because it's made a huge difference to my life. Both Dave and Steve are fantastic people, who will help me any way they can. I'm also grateful to the Benevolent Fund. Tim Adams is a great chairman, who understands the needs of disabled people. Phil Clarke, Emma Rosewarne, Dave Hinchliffe and Geoff Burrow understand people need help from time to time. Apologies if I've missed anyone. And I'm sure everyone who has been helped will agree with me.

Do you follow Rugby League today?

I do. It's a different game to when I was playing. Most ex-players would agree with that. When I was playing, it was contested scrums. Getting rid of them was a big mistake. A contested scrum would open the game up to what it should be. Rugby League has become a bit predictable. That's the one thing I would change if I could!

Which team do you support?

I follow Leigh, Wigan and Workington! I'm a Leyther, after all. Workington are in my heart because they are a fantastic club. I'm still in contact with Mark Southward, Ike's son. And Wigan of course, I root for them too. I've been a few times but not so much now. They are my three clubs. All of them look after me when I go and see them play. I hope Cumbria can get back to where it was because it has so much to offer in Rugby League. There's a fanbase there which the RFL have to tap into and develop it. That's how you expand the game.

How did you get into Rugby League?

I excelled at school in Leigh and we had a good team. We won the England Schools competition twice. A few of us later turned professional. Then I progressed to Lancashire and then England Schools. We toured France. I played Colts instead of BARLA. I then went to Warrington under Alex Murphy and enjoyed my time there. I went to Leigh and toured with the Great Britain Colts. When I came back from the tour, a whole host of clubs were after my signature – Leigh, Rochdale, Salford, Warrington and Wigan. I chatted with them all. Wigan were the last club

I visited, and I was amazed by Central Park - the stadium, the set-up and the history. The contract was a little bigger as well, so I signed for Wigan. I didn't know if I'd done the right thing in not signing for Leigh, but I enjoyed my time there.

You captained the England Schoolboys team when the first Australian Combined High Schools team toured in 1972-73. They scored 108 tries in 12 matches and conceded just one.

That's right. I think it was the winger John Crossley who scored against them in the last game in Middlesex. That Australian team were older than us by a year. A year in a schoolboy makes a big difference. You're stronger and more developed. They were clever too. They brought over a brand of rugby we'd never witnessed and that progressed to the full international team. Les Boyd, Craig Young and Ian Schubert went on to have great careers.

You left Wigan for Workington halfway through the 1977-78 season.

I liked Peter Smethurst, one of the coaches at Wigan, very much. Vinty Karalius was alright. It was the Challenge Cup deadline for signing players. I was put on the transfer list at £12,000, which was a lot of money then. Workington came in and did the deal. It may have beaten Ike Southward's transfer record - I'm not sure. Workington excelled in the Lancashire Cup back then, so I knew I was joining a very good team.

You scored the only try of the game as Town beat Wigan 14-2 in the Lancashire Cup, just a fortnight before your injury.

Yes, I remember that. We had a very good team. Paul Charlton was at fullback, Ian Wright and John Risman were the centres. Bill Pattinson and the Gorley brothers were the back row. There were Eddie Bowman, Ralph Calvin and Alan Banks too. It was a good team. I mainly played fullback for Wigan but in the Colts I was a stand-off and that's where I played for Workington. I could play other positions in the backs, but I wasn't fast enough for the wing. I liked stand-off.

What sort of player were you?

I had a good sidestep and a good swerve. I think I had a good rugby brain. I could finish and make tries. I was a decent goalkicker as well. I could tackle. I was a good all-rounder. I scored some decent tries. I was probably what you would call a utility player.

You received an international call-up in 1978.

Yes, Tom Mitchell came to me after the Wigan game and said you're down to play a Test match, and I said "really?". He said the selectors had put pen to paper. I went home and was ecstatic. I told my parents, and they were delighted, but then I got injured - and that was that.

KRIS RADLINSKI

1993-2006
2009-present (general manager, chief executive)

Having signed for Wigan on Academy terms after trialling with St Helens, Kris Radlinski made his first-team debut in October 1993. Two years later, he was the England fullback in a World Cup. His 13-year Wigan career saw the club endure some lean times, but he still won three league titles, three Premiership Trophies and a Challenge Cup. He is one of the few players to have won both the Harry Sunderland and Lance Todd Trophies. At the time of publication, he is the Wigan Warriors chief executive.

KRIS RADLINSKI, the ultimate one-club man. Supporter, apprentice, boot cleaner, Academy player, reserve-teamer, first-teamer, Harry Sunderland Trophy winner, Lance Todd Trophy winner, international, general manager and chief executive. He has pretty much done the lot in a 30-year association with his beloved club.

He played fullback throughout the 1995 World Cup, despite barely having played there before. He helped England win the competition opener against Australia at Wembley. He earned 30 international caps. He won several winner's medals and is respected throughout the game. He turned down a mega-bucks rugby union offer and he could have gone to the NRL. He came out of retirement to steer Wigan away from relegation in 2006. He was appointed MBE a year later. He released his autobiography in 2009, the same year he began his second career with the club as general manager.

Radlinski's love affair with the club began as a young boy. "I was a home and awayer with my mum, dad and sister - every Sunday afternoon," he said. "The community game was ridiculously popular then. I'd play on a Sunday morning, then we'd jump in the car and be on the M62. I went to all the Wembleys, starting with 1985 when I was nine. There were a lot more people in Wembley then and you could stand up. I remember the journeys down there and how packed the service stations were. The build-up in the town all week was probably more substantial than it is now.

"As for heroes, Ellery [Hanley] was the superstar of the sport. Every kid in the town looked up to him. He epitomised what was possible. He seemed to have come from a different planet. Joe Lydon was a big hero of mine too. I loved everything he did on the field. And then there's Hampo [Steve Hampson]. I'd say they were my three heroes."

Radlinski's status as a one-club man came under threat on a couple of occasions, the first being before he signed for Wigan. He had a fortnight's trial with St Helens and had things turned out differently, it could have been him scoring the much-vaunted Wide to West try.

"It is realistic that I could have played with them," he admitted. "I did two weeks training with them, but I was still pretty young. I'm a realist, and I know I'm not the most talented, but I was a gutsy lad. I trained as hard as I could, and I think I impressed them with my fitness. But two weeks later, a couple of guys from Wigan came to my house. There was no money on the table.

"The Academy was all about trying to gain a professional contract. I had some incredible bonds with players like Sean Long and Simon Haughton. We were a group of mates on this great journey together. We were apprentices - cleaning boots and changing rooms. It was pretty hands on. So many bonds were created. The next level was earning a pro contract. Wigan had something like 20 internationals, so there'd be two or three thousand turning up to watch the Alliance because someone like Joe Lydon, coming to the end of his career, might be playing.

"Back then it was 13 players and two subs, and the two subs were those who had played well for the Alliance. You'd come off after 40 mins and you'd get the nod from the coach that you'd be on the bench for the first team. It was a competitive league because you wanted to be in the first team on Sunday. It was pretty hardcore. It's moved to a different level now, but the player of 20 or 30 years ago was more durable because there were no recovery protocols, and you had to play injured. Players queued up for surgery at the end of seasons. It was brutal."

While Radlinski enjoyed a great career with Wigan, Sean Long was released by the club in 1997. He dropped down a division for a short stint with Widnes, with Lee Hansen moving the other way. He then signed for St Helens where he enjoyed a stellar career.

"He is one of my favourite-ever Super League players," said Radlinski, "but you have to understand there are reasons people leave clubs. If someone is doing everything perfectly, you have to look for other reasons. Sean was at a stage when he was growing up, going out, and he had an enjoyable life. You have to make a choice as a club how you want to move things forward, but none of us doubted how good he was. He was performing in a very talented squad and holding his own."

SUNDAY 31st October 1993 saw Wigan hammered 46-0 at Castleford. They were forced to field a weakened team as Great Britain had played New Zealand the day before, beating them 29-10 at Central Park with Gary Connolly, Martin Offiah, Shaun Edwards and Phil Clarke in the side. Radlinski was named on the bench, and he made his senior debut, his only first-team game of the season.

"Some of us knew we might get the nod, and I got a call at 8pm the night before to say I was in the squad," Radlinski remembered. "I hadn't even met all the first-teamers. Every player has a seat on the bus. You sit in the wrong seat, and you get daggers! I got about 10 minutes in the game. It was a brilliant experience because it came from nowhere in my development.

"I took my son to Castleford the other week [in 2023], and I told him about it. The ground hasn't changed. It generated a great atmosphere, and you're very close to the crowd. You could hear everything they were saying. I'm a big advocate in advancing stadiums but playing in the old grounds was character building. At Watersheddings, you had to walk through the fans to get to the pitch. And it wasn't just the grounds - you should have tried catching an old Mitre Multiplex ball with no grip in the rain! Skill levels were very good because you were playing with a bar of soap."

Radlinski played 21 of Wigan's 45 matches in the 1994-95 season, deputising when one of the three-quarters - Jason Robinson, Va'aiga Tuigamala, Gary Connolly and Martin Offiah - were unavailable. He scored 18 tries, three of which came at Old Trafford as Leeds were annihilated 69-12 in the Premiership Final. He won the Harry Sunderland Trophy.

"Va'aiga Tuigamala, God rest his soul, had to go home because a family member had died," said Radlinski. "I jumped into the centre, and I was marking Kevin Iro. Everything we did came off. In the last ten minutes, I moved to fullback and that was the first time I'd ever played there in my life. I fielded a couple of kicks. After the game, I received the news England were looking at me as a fullback. By the World Cup, I'd still played fewer than five games there.

"Playing against Australia at Wembley on my Test debut in a position I didn't have a clue about was mad. There was a huge crowd, but the fearlessness of youth takes you through it. Looking back, I wonder how I did it, but you get through it. The coach had faith in me.

"The World Cup felt like such a big event. Diana Ross was paraded before the first game. A few weeks later, we played in the World Cup Final. I had laryngitis and couldn't speak – that's not ideal if you're a fullback! Just think what could have been if we'd won it. We did them in that first game, but they regathered. It's six weeks of my life I look back on very fondly. We played Fiji at Central Park which was a dream for me. And we beat Wales at Old Trafford in the semi-final."

I was keen to know whether Radlinski knew whether Kelvin Skerrett, one of his opponents in that semi-final, didn't actually qualify for Wales. "I didn't have a clue about that," he said. "I'm not entirely surprised though! I do a series of interviews with past players at Robin Park. I ask fans to fill in slips to see who they want me to interview next, and Kelvin is the overwhelming choice. He is an absolute cult hero. Kelvin was good to me. He was protective. I tended to gravitate to people I never thought I would. On a night out, the glamour boys would do their thing, and I'd be in a corner with Kelvin, Neil Cowie and Martin Hall.

"After the World Cup, Paul Atcheson was coming to the end of his Wigan career. Henry Paul played a few games there, but he wanted to play six, so I became the first-choice fullback."

The timing of the positional switch couldn't have been better as 1996 was a momentous year for Wigan. They relinquished their grip on the Challenge Cup and league title, but they won the Middlesex Sevens and Premiership Trophy and they played Bath in a two-legged cross-code challenge.

"There was loads going on in 1996," said Radlinski. "Those games with Bath at Maine Road and Twickenham were great events. We had to prepare for Rugby League games while also learning union rules, but we had players with union experience like Scott Quinnell, Inga, Joe Lydon and Shem Tatupu. Our weeks were split between training for both games. We wanted to be a part of it. It showed the power of the Wigan brand. I'm not sure it would ever happen again though. We wouldn't be able to convince our fan base and the Super League competition now, but it was a special time. I look back at it with fond memories. We had some warm-up games against Orrell, which we opened to fans to come and watch. There are many iconic moments in the history of this club, and those games are right up there."

AFTER a Challenge Cup defeat to a 12-man St Helens team, coach Graeme West was sacked. Saints legend Eric Hughes took over. He only lasted a year, as did John Monie, Andy Goodway and Frank Endacott.

"If you speak to people in the town, everyone adores Graeme West," said Radlinski. "In essence, he wasn't coaching, he was managing superstars. Big personalities needed dealing with. If things don't go well, people want to point a finger. It was a sad day for all of us. He was instrumental in my journey, coaching me in the reserve grade. I spent time with him in the lotto office, learning about the finances of the club. When bad things happen to good people, it leaves a bad taste.

"Now I'm involved in the selection of coaches, you think, 'What do the next three to five years look like?' It

stems from your original conversation with that coach. Coaches back then might have the remit to win a trophy in their first season, but now we're willing to invest more in other parts of the club. There's more structure now and more of a long-term vision. You can't be sacking a coach every year."

Monie took over for the 1998 season, taking the club back to Wembley where they surprisingly lost to Sheffield Eagles, but they reacted well and beat Leeds in Super League's first Grand Final.

"I always think about Martin Offiah's try at Wembley in 1994," said Radlinski. "It will be talked about every year as long as the competition goes on, and it makes me think [Leeds fullback] Alan Tait must hate it! The Sheffield game is the same. It will always be talked about. The Challenge

Cup has been an amazing part of my life. Sheffield were massive underdogs, and it was a harsh thing I will never forget. It is something I regret being part of. We took it for granted. We didn't give it the respect it deserved. It's still the biggest cup shock of all time.

"The first Grand Final at Old Trafford was a real positive for us. The game needed a new direction and vision. It's become one of the most iconic nights of the British sporting calendar. It's a real jewel in the crown of the sport. Jason Robinson was doing wonderful things. Andy Farrell is arguably one of the greatest Wigan players of all time. He was the best leader I played with. And Gary Connolly is one of the classiest centres the game has ever produced.

"We had a great rivalry with Leeds. Everyone remembers

97

Mick Cassidy leaving the floor and leading with his elbow on Adrian Morley at Central Park. Some of those games were brutal. Moz was fearless. There were a lot of cheap shots, and with fewer cameras around, players got away with more. Games then were as tough as they come. I understand why we have to change to move forward, but you can't help but look back at those games and enjoy them."

Wigan lost their stand-off Henry Paul and hooker Robbie McCormack after that Old Trafford success and failed to replace them adequately. Subsequently, they slumped in 1999, which was also the year they changed stadiums.

"I didn't enjoy the period when we left Central Park," Radlinski reflected. "It was a sad time because it was such an iconic stadium and such an integral part of the town. Selling it to a supermarket and moving into a football stadium didn't seem to give out the strongest message, but a lot of investment was needed at Central Park. As a player, you don't understand the politics and the rationale. You don't get consulted. That was a difficult time for the club.

"I wasn't across all the finances then. I don't know the state of the sport back then. We'd spent so hard building on the back of players like Shaun Edwards, Andy Farrell and Denis Betts. These people drove the club and demanded standards. Cheaper options were sometimes taken afterwards. We were the only professional club at one point, but other clubs started to get their businesses in order, and we were being challenged. It felt very transitional at times."

RUGBY UNION came calling in 2001, leaving Radlinski with the biggest decision of his career.

"I had some NRL interest as well," said Radlinski. "Peter Mulholland, who died recently, tried to get me to Canberra Raiders. There was no prospect of me moving to another Super League club, but the main interest was from rugby union. On one occasion, I visited every union club in London and met all the coaches. Another time, I met Clive Woodward at Manchester Airport. He wanted me to be part of the [2003] World Cup campaign.

"It came down to a Sunday-night talk with my mum and dad. When it came to it, I was number one at Wigan, playing in a very historic jersey, and I was happy there. Like mums do, she said, 'Why would you change that?' Dads are different. He said, 'What about the money and the opportunities and broadening your horizons?' In the end, I stayed."

The biggest event in 2002 for Radlinski was the Challenge Cup Final at Murrayfield, in which Wigan were expected to be beaten by Ian Millward's St Helens. The fullback spent the week in hospital with a foot infection, but after some early-morning surgery in their Edinburgh hotel, he was declared fit. He went on to win the Lance Todd Trophy after making several try-saving tackles. The game is often referred to as 'The Radlinski Final'.

"That name's a bit cringeworthy to be honest!" he said. "I'm aware the sport is about stories, build-ups and narratives. Because of my injury, there was a lot of spotlight on me. We were clear underdogs to Saints, so it was almost a free hit for us because we were expected to lose. I'm extremely grateful it happened. There were a few moments when things couldn't have gone better for me, but part of me getting the Lance Todd Trophy was the story and the build-up. It was a magical day, especially with it being against Saints."

Two years later, Wigan played the same opposition in the final in Cardiff but lost. This proved to be Mike Gregory's last game as coach before he went to America for medical treatment.

"You won't meet a more passionate Wiganer, even though he'd had a great career at Warrington," said Radlinski. "He was such a great guy, adored by so many, including all the community clubs in the area. We all knew what the job meant to him. He was just a good guy. He was honest to your face. He'd been there and done it and understood what players were going through. When his illness started to unfold, it wasn't pretty to watch. His voice was going. Things were unfolding very quickly. It wasn't a great experience. The club as a whole got some criticism for how they handled it - before the current ownership. Wigan could have looked after him differently.

"The final was emotional, but as professional sportsmen, you need to block it out. I've never looked back at that day and thought emotions lost it for us. We had enough quality to put up a better performance than we did."

Gregory's departure precipitated a chaotic few years for Wigan. His assistant and club legend Denis Betts took over and did well in 2004, but it was somewhat typical of Maurice Lindsay to demote Betts after a difficult start to 2005, despite several great players having left.

In came Ian Millward, recently discarded by St Helens. His tenure took the club to the bottom of the table. Brian Noble was appointed in 2006 to sort out the mess, during which time Radlinski played his final games for the club, coming out of retirement towards the end of the season. In his 2009 autobiography, Radlinski was critical of attitudes at the club, particularly when Millward was in charge.

"Culture is something everyone talks about now," said Radlinski. "People speak about it without understanding it or defining it. Culture for me is doing the right thing all the time. Culture is live, as I say to Matty Peet, so if you think you've got it right, you have to be prepared for it to come and bite you on the ass. What's a great professional? It's not just what they do between 9 and 3. It's what happens from 3.30pm to 9 o'clock the next morning when you're having to make decisions yourself.

"It was a time when I'd just come through an era of standards and perfection with Faz, Denis and Shaun Edwards. We'd go weeks without dropping the ball at training. If you did, Shaun would bollock you. I felt by 2005, players didn't think it mattered if someone dropped the ball. The little things were no longer so important. I'm a big believer in everyone wearing the same kit and cleaning your plates away, but we'd gone away from what had made us great.

"We lost so many great players after 2004. We didn't replace them. When things started to go wrong and you're looking for shining lights, there were none. The threat of relegation had become very real in 2006. I didn't come out and say I'd play for free when I came back. Maurice said that. I got expenses, but it wasn't much. I'd had some meetings with Brian Noble. I knew confidence was low. When that happens, bad things can happen. Look at Warrington in 2022.

"I have too much respect for the sport to think I could come in and make a difference on the field. I was past it, but I knew I could make a difference in the changing room, and I could invoke some sort of passion that would reignite something. I did six games. I was a good voice in the changing room and on the training field, but I didn't score a try. I made a few tackles, but I didn't do anything to justify playing for Wigan."

Kris Radlinski with Shaun Wane

"I AM now prouder of this job than I am of my playing days," Radlinski told me as we chatted about his time as general manager, executive director and now chief executive of Wigan.

It's quite a statement when you consider everything Radlinski achieved, yet he is prouder of his time behind a desk. How can that be? He answered that by firstly discussing how the club are bouncing back from the Covid-19 pandemic that could have bankrupted the game.

"The whole sport is still recovering," he said. "People are aware that Rugby League wasn't in a strong position before the pandemic. When it happened, I was on calls with many clubs, and they were dark times. The pressure was extreme. Across all players and personnel, we have about 150 employees. The majority were on furlough and there were five people left to run the whole business. We were in till ten every night, wondering how the hell we were going to recover.

"If it wasn't for the club benefactors and government support, the sport wouldn't be here. We weren't winning many games in 2021, and people were complaining about that, but that wasn't a priority for me because the off-field situation was so crucial. People were pointing fingers, and I got a fair amount of stick which comes with the pressure of the job. We wanted to drop the walls and let people come and see us. In my 25-year involvement with the club, things are more transparent than ever. Fans can come and buy something at Robin Park and bump into players. In a difficult financial climate, the retail business is performing better than it's ever done."

There has also been a marked improvement on the field with the team winning the 2022 Challenge Cup and finishing second in Super League. Radlinski is quick to praise the coaching team, headed up by Matty Peet.

"People were sceptical," Radlinski said. "A lot of them hadn't heard of Matty Peet. Some thought it was a cheap option. We got stick for re-signing Tommy Leuluai for one more year. We went into 2022 with so many people unsure, but we were clear with what we wanted to do.

"Crowds came back towards the end of the season. The Cup Final was amazing for the club. So many people loved the Tottenham experience, and it helped a lot of our fans regain the faith. We were disappointed with how the season ended and the way we went out in the semi was a shame. We wanted to test ourselves against St Helens because the score between us in the season was two each. Saints have done an incredible job and they've made us better.

"I knew Matt could do it. I've spoken to him every day for ten years. I know his work ethic. He learns so much about the sport and other sports. It was a brave decision but putting Shaun Wane alongside him was a big step. Shaun's here two days a week and offers him support. Matty runs things by him, and they have a great chemistry.

"Sean O'Loughlin has managed the transition from player to coach better than anyone I've ever seen. The long hours and attention to detail - he's got there quicker than I thought. He has a great aura and real humility.

"Lee Briers came in too. We interviewed him in a quiet pub because I didn't want anyone to see us. He was getting up, moving chairs and tables around to show lines of running. I don't think he thought he'd enjoy it as much as he did. He, his partner and his dad literally fell in love with the club. He found it difficult to tell us he had a new opportunity elsewhere, but I have no doubt he'll be back at the club one day. Jack Phillips came from Warrington with

Lee and did analysis work. We'll miss Lee's enthusiasm and bubbly character, but we get Tommy. He is obsessed with the sport. He's quiet but when he speaks, he's bang on the money."

Wigan were heavily criticised for their style of play in 2021 under Adrian Lam's coaching but put that right under Peet. "Style of play is important because we're in the entertainment industry," Radlinski acknowledges. "Jai [Field] and Bevan [French] were doing things that I've not seen for a long time, maybe since Jason, Martin and Ellery in the '90s. I have to say there's part of me that feels sorry for Adrian Lam because he lost Jai and Bevan in 2021 when they snapped their hamstrings. He must think what if.

"I'm really pleased he's done great things with Leigh because he had some harsh press at the time. You know how the salary cap works. They were on good salaries, and you can't just replace them. Fingers were pointed at Adrian unnecessarily. He initially signed for one year before Shaun Edwards changed his mind, but he ended up staying longer.

"I always enjoyed talking Rugby League with Adrian. He was the best player I ever played with. We had a chemistry with him at scrum-half and me at fullback. I played my best rugby when he was here."

Radlinski started working as Wigan's general manager in late 2009, three years after his playing days ended, and is now executive director. He has completed 13 years to add his 13 as a player. Perhaps the saddest day came within a year when his former teammate Terry Newton took his own life a week before the 2010 Grand Final.

"He was a loveable rogue," said Radlinski. "He played tough, but he was talented. I played behind him, Adrian Lam and Matty Johns, and I played some of my best stuff with those three who laid so much on a plate for me. We all loved him. He was a character. He was like Kelvin Skerrett, an iconic figure. When he passed, it was awful. We were building up to the Grand Final with Michael Maguire. Brian Carney phoned me to say he'd heard something and could I check it out. I hadn't heard, so I phoned some people and found out he'd killed himself.

"I'm still very close to his dad, Tony, and his mum, Val. It was a devastating loss, but it did start the State of Mind movement which has never looked back. If there's any comfort to his parents, it's that other people will be looked after sooner. In the weeks after, I read through texts that Terry and I had sent each other, looking for signs. There were none. I do remember one throwaway comment which was, "I don't know what I'll do when I finish rugby, I'll probably turn to crime." He said it as a joke, but he was unsure and scared of life after sport beginning. It was clearly something that was troubling him."

"MICHAEL MAGUIRE recruited me because he wanted to concentrate on the Rugby League and needed someone else to concentrate on things like contracts," Radlinski recalled. "He ran the team, and everything else fell to me.

"Over time, I've been given more responsibility, and only about ten percent of my time is devoted to the team. The rest is on the business. I work with communications, marketing, retail and youth development. They all report to me, and I report to the chairman. I check in with Matty every morning. He talks me through issues, then I go to the other side of the room and do other things."

As well as Covid, there have been other turbulent times in the last decade with which Radlinski has had to deal - namely Ben Flower's red card in the 2014 Grand Final for the punches he threw at St Helens' Lance Hohaia, and the more recent club rebranding.

"Ben was a situation that no-one expected, and we just had to deal with it," Radlinski recalled with a grimace. "When it happened, I went straight to the changing room. Five minutes later, he was in a car heading back to Wigan. That's actually a Manchester United policy - they have a car waiting to take a sent-off player home. We met him later that night. The lads were getting off the coach, having just lost the game. Ben was greeting them. He was deeply upset, but the lads were unbelievable with him.

"Nothing could have prepared us for it. It went viral. Piers Morgan was tweeting about it. The impact was incredible. I had to go to the disciplinary to try and defend it. They showed the clip and said, "Over to you." We could just defend his character. He is a good father and good husband, but it was just the moment that got to him.

"Ben understood everything. It was such a high-profile incident. We were concerned about Lance too. We reached out to Saints to make sure everything was ok. It was difficult for everyone.

"The rebranding and new badge was tough, but I stand by it, and it's proven to be a success because I know what people are buying in the shop. I played with the old badge on my shirt, but you have to move forward. Phil Clarke once said to me Rugby League will never die because too many people love it, but unfortunately these same people will never let the game grow.

"Mandy and Mary work in my office and they've been here for years. I knew it was a tough period because every morning there was a little treat from them on my desk! I understand people want to say things though.

"The key word in it all is education. For example when we signed Jake Wardle, we let a player go in the other direction. Many don't know how recruitment and the salary cap work, so we need to educate more to get people to understand these things.

"Social media gives us constant rumour and speculation. Someone in Wigan can make something up, and it's in Sydney in two seconds. Changes in society are things we're continually having to fight. The key thing is understanding that we do things that are right for the club. If everyone has the info I have, they'd make the same decisions, but not everyone can see my cards. I can't say I'm letting a player go because he has a terrible attitude and he drinks too much, because no one would sign him, but if people don't get it, it's down to us for not communicating things better."

One evening in 2022, Radlinski arranged a training session for every player from all 11 Wigan teams - the First Team, Reserves, Academy, Scholarship, Women, Women's Academy, PDRL (physical disability), LDRL (learning disability), Wheelchair, Touch and College teams.

"I said to Matty, 'You need to trust me on this. The players might not get much from it, but for the brand and the club, it will be the right thing to do.' I stood and watched. There were 150 players, some in wheelchairs, and I quickly realised I was wrong to say they'd get nothing out of it. I watched Tommy Leuluai practising passing with a kid with one arm. It was such a feel-good night. I don't want it to be a token thing.

"Rugby League players are in a privileged position. Some take that for granted, and I don't want our players to do that. Our players work in soup kitchens and volunteer to help the homeless. If you do things right and don't take things for granted, you'll have the best 15 years of your life."

SIR GRAHAM LOWE

1986-1989 (coach)

Graham Lowe became New Zealand coach in 1983, instantly transforming their fortunes as they tore up the formbook by beating Australia at Lang Park. They beat Great Britain in all three Tests a year later, and in 1985, they took part in two titanic series against Australia and Great Britain. Lowe coached Wigan between 1986 and 1989, landing their first league title in 27 years, the World Club Challenge and two Challenge Cups. He coached Queensland in the State of Origin in 1991 and 1992. He was knighted in 2019 for services to youth and education.

If you could relive one day from your career, which would it be?
There are too many for me to choose one. There were Test matches, Wembleys and Origins. With Wigan, we seemed to have big matches every few weeks. I never forgot where I came from or what it meant to me. I read Rugby League books as a kid in the 1950s and early 1960s. I remember one with colour photos of Wigan playing at Wembley. Coaching there was a dream I thought would never come true.

How did your coaching journey begin?
I played for my local club, Otahuhu Leopards. I had injuries and when I started a business, I knew I couldn't keep playing. It wasn't on the radar to start coaching, but they approached me to coach a junior team. I restructured how they trained and convinced them to do more. We had great success in those three years. I then coached premier grade [open age], and we won everything. Two weeks after Cronulla played Manly in the 1978 Grand Final, they came over to play us, and we beat them. I got an offer from Norths in Brisbane. The Queensland competition was very strong, so I accepted. They had just come last, and their Leagues Club was broke, but we won the Premiership in my second year. Then I got asked to coach the Kiwis.

You transformed the Kiwis, and your win at Lang Park in 1983 is an all-time great New Zealand victory. How did altering the clock in the changing room help you win that match?
Physically and skill wise, I knew we were in with a big chance. But emotionally and mentally, Australia was a big hurdle to clear as far as we were concerned, and Great Britain were in the same boat, so I tried to address some of that. I put the clock back ten minutes and said to the team, "These guys think they're so special, they'll try to get us out before we're ready." Sure enough, there was a loud knock on the changing room door for us to come out which the players would have thought was ten minutes early. It stirred everyone up. Instead of everyone going out as a team, I sent the players out one at a time, knowing the crowd would boo. Booing 15 players one at a time was a lot of effort, so they stopped and that was a little victory to us. Kurt and Dane Sorensen were back in the side. Mark Graham had hurt his knee playing for North Sydney, but we had Graeme West and Gary Prohm, who was really underrated as a loose forward. We had Howie Tamati at hooker and Mark Broadhurst at prop. We were given no chance, but we came up with plans to draw in the defence, and each time we did it, we scored.

Were you surprised how uncompetitive the Lions were in 1984?
I'd been over to Australia to watch them and couldn't believe they picked Ellery Hanley on the wing. I'd seen him play in England and knew he was too good for that. He just wasn't getting enough ball in that Great Britain team. They did move him to centre in the third Test, and he just about beat us. Little did I know, I'd coach him one day at Wigan.

You coached Oceania against Europe in France in 1984.
That was a very different experience. We had Papua New Guinean players, along with Kiwis and Australians. We prepared as hard as we could, but the promotion of the game was probably the worst I have ever seen. The Europe side hadn't prepared at all. It looked like they'd just met one another. It was a very strange game with a rock-hard pitch. They had Rocky-type music when the players came out, but there was no crowd, and we won 54-4.

The Kiwis were involved in two of the greatest Test series of all time in 1985. You lost two Tests to Australia on the hooter and drew a series with Great Britain. Nearly 37 years on, how do you look back at these six Tests?
They were very tough matches and a last glimpse of how Test football used to look. I look back on them all with pride because when Australia beat us in Auckland in the second Test, they knew they had been very lucky. They were good enough to win, but we deserved to win. That's just the way it goes. And then we beat them 18-0.
In England, Mark Graham broke his ankle and cheekbone in the first Test, and he was crucial to us. It was just a matter of hours before the third Test that we got him fit, but it was disruptive. It was an aggressive game at Elland Road. Lee Crooks kicked that great goal from the sideline to earn a series draw. He probably couldn't have kicked another of those from 100 attempts!

You referred to Graham as the best player in the world. What made him such a special player?
At that stage, I hadn't coached Ellery or Wally Lewis. Now I have, I can't separate the three of them. They are the three best players the game has seen. They were all so tough, they had ability on their own to win a match, they were unselfish and determined to help every player give their best because they were such great leaders.

Olsen Filipaina, who was playing for the Eastern Suburbs reserves, famously got the better of Lewis in 1985. Had you identified any weaknesses in Lewis?
I don't think Wally had any weaknesses. You just have to limit their opportunities. Olsen had been playing with Balmain and Easts, but he had been brainwashed into being a robotic-type player. All I did was take that away and let him play his natural game. I knew how he wanted

to play, and I knew it would surprise Wally because Wally hadn't seen that type of player. Olsen was so powerful in the hips and so quick over 10 or 15 metres. We aimed to minimise Wally's chances with the ball and then throw everything at him when we had the ball. Olsen was the ideal player for that. Rugby League only saw the best of Olsen a few times because he was so constrained. Great Britain has also fallen in love with this robotic style from Australia. It takes the flair away from the player. It is over-coaching, and Olsen is a great example of it.

That first Trans-Tasman Test also saw the infamous Tamati-Dowling fight. Is it a shame that the fight overshadowed a great series?
Yes, you don't want that sort of thing to happen, but it's not a game of marbles either. A Test match is a test of everything. In earlier days, Test matches were even more rugged, but television brought the game into people's living rooms, and the behaviour of players had to change.

Under your coaching, the Kiwis were far more entertaining and skilful than the All Blacks. How frustrating was it to know you could never match them for popularity?
I'm 75 now, and I've been involved in Rugby League since I was five. Rugby union gets such a huge advantage that you would never believe. It's changed a lot because of the players who bond together no matter which code they are playing, so old attitudes towards Rugby League have improved, but we were always treated badly even when we were the best team in the country.

Tell us about the Rainbow Warrior incident which overshadowed the French leg of your tour in 1985.
The French bombed a Greenpeace ship called the Rainbow Warrior in the Port of Auckland in July 1985, just before we left. It was on its way to protest against a planned nuclear test by the French. New Zealand is isolated and free, and we don't expect terrorist incidents. We only read about them in Europe or America, so everyone was horrified. The feeling towards the French wasn't too good, but we had to

treat that leg of the tour with respect. The media hounded us for opinions about it and we just kept saying, "No comment!" We won all the games there, but the standard of refereeing was pretty ordinary. With 20 minutes left in the last match, I sent a message to the players, saying, "Remember the Rainbow Warrior," and it gave them the chance to get rid of some frustrations!

Wigan beat the Kiwis in 1985, but you had obviously impressed Maurice Lindsay who made you their coach a year later.
I knew it would be the toughest game we would face outside the Tests, and much of the blame can be laid squarely on me. We had some young guys on tour, and I needed to see what they could do in England against hardened professionals. We played a couple of players at Wigan that probably wasn't fair on them. I knew Ellery would find them out straightaway. Ellery beat us that day, not Wigan.

Dean Bell was one of your first Wigan signings. You'd initially used him on the wing for the Kiwis.
I knew him really well because I'd seen him play so much in Auckland. He was a centre all day long with a big career in front of him at centre. Dean was so tough he wouldn't shy away from anything, but I played him on the wing in those early days for New Zealand to edge him in, and he scored a great try at Lang Park against Australia.

You signed Wally Lewis in 1986, but he didn't fulfil the contract with Lindsay accusing him of double-crossing Wigan. What happened?
We signed him, and he was keen to come, but he had a chronic shoulder injury, and he didn't pass a medical in Australia to let him go, which I found out in later years. There was no more to it than that.

You went on to win nearly everything with Wigan, but does the name Paddy Kirwan still give you nightmares?
Oldham? Well, I still remember that night! I didn't understand the importance of the Challenge Cup. Maurice said to me they hadn't won the championship in 27 years. Coming from this part of the world, that was the ultimate goal. There are no knock-out competitions here, so I didn't put the emphasis on it I should have done. I was so angry because we didn't play well, and I soon saw the despair and the effect the defeat had on people. I knew then we had to win it.

Why did you move Hanley to loose forward and how did he take it?
From the very first time I saw him play, I thought he'd be a loose forward if I coached him. He wasn't at his peak then because he wasn't getting the opportunities. No player has ever achieved what Ellery did, in moving from the backs to the forwards without it reducing the impact he had on games. His workrate increased tenfold. He was doing 30-odd tackles every week which he didn't do in the backs, and he was still a matchwinner. To make that move, do the workload and still have a huge impact on the game is incredible, and I don't think we'll ever see it again. He just accepted it when I told him I wanted to do it. He practiced how to be a loose forward more than anyone would understand. For those of us close to what he was doing, it was no surprise that he continued to dominate games and score tries.

When Wigan won the league championship in 1987, what did you think of Lindsay's idea to invite Manly over for a World Club Challenge?

I thought it was a great idea. My then-wife Karen and I were having a drink with Maurice at the Bull's Head, and we were excited about winning the championship. He asked how we would go against the top Australian sides, and I said we'd beat any of them. The Great Britain mentality was to think everything with an Australian accent was automatically great, but I believed in the British game, probably more than many in the Great Britain set-up. Maurice had Ken Arthurson's number, and we called him on the spot. Maurice had the deal done in ten minutes. It was unbelievable. It was one of the game's greatest examples of two statesmen coming up with a great idea and putting it into place with minimum fuss. The administrators of today are too self-centred to pull something like that off. They are too focused on their own little patch, but Maurice and Ken both had a global vision. The game was like a State of Origin. I was so proud of not just the players but the Wigan town. The British game had been hammered from pillar to post because Great Britain

couldn't win anything, so it put a spring in everyone's step. Wigan's team was all British that night as well, and I was really proud of that.

Relations between Hanley and the club broke down between January and March 1988 with the player staying away and finding himself transfer listed. What happened?

I take full responsibility. It was between Ellery and me, not the club. I prided myself on understanding players and getting in their heads, but I totally misread Ellery, and I will always apologise until the day I die. I put him and the club through a tough time that shouldn't have happened. But we had a chat, patched it up and never spoke about it again. A coach always learns, and that was one of the greatest learning curves of my career. I should have handled it far better.

What are your memories of the 1988 Challenge Cup Final when Wigan beat Halifax?

I couldn't believe 80 minutes could go that quick. I was totally confident in our preparation and knew we would

win. Andy Gregory was a master at the peak of his powers. Has the game ever seen a better combination than Andy, Ellery and Shaun Edwards in those positions? They all got the opportunity to do what they needed to do.

You also had disputes with Andy and Shaun.

The three of them will tell you I wouldn't compromise. That carries an incredible risk. The philosophy of the average player in the UK was different to what I was used to, but those three were world class and wanted to win as much as I did. I had my disagreements, but I loved them dearly like they were my own family because I knew what they had done for me.

You beat Saints 27-0 in the 1989 Challenge Cup Final, gaining revenge for their Wembley wins over Wigan in the 1960s.

I was absolutely confident again, although I didn't know what the score would be. I'd seen them prepare and there was so much honesty in the team. My mantra was the same after every win: "We won it with class, and we won it with style."

Do you have any other memories of Wigan?

One of Maurice's masterstrokes was bringing Jeff Hurst in to help me. He was a headteacher of a St Helens primary school. I needed help understanding the players' accents for one thing! He'd been involved with amateur football, and he became my right-hand man. He was important during the disputes with Ellery, Andy and Shaun. I could bounce things off him and I couldn't have done it without him.

Why did you leave Wigan?

I went for three years, but Maurice offered me the job for life towards the end of my third year which excited me. Even if I stopped coaching, he said they'd give me another job. I left in 1989 because I got a call from my ex-wife who asked me to go back and help one of my daughters who needed help with issues at school. It all happened very quickly. As soon as it became public, I got so many offers. I went to Manly because I was close to Ken. He was very similar to Maurice. "Forget about these other offers, you're coming here," he said. I'd still be at Wigan today otherwise. I loved Wigan more than anywhere else I've coached. I had a 20-30 year plan in my mind. We'd built a new house there. There wasn't a possibility of me leaving, but one of my children needed me, and that was it.

You coached Manly for two years.

It was great there but very different to Wigan. It is a fantastic club with a great environment in a great part of the world. They hadn't re-signed eight current internationals because they'd come tenth so that caused disruption and ill-feeling. I had to manage my way through that, and I introduced a lot of young players who went on to play for Australia. We made the semi-finals twice. We were rebuilding the team, but my health started to have a massive impact. I had a number of heart attacks, a stroke and a brain haemorrhage. I should have stopped in 1990 and had some time off, but I kept going and had to stop in 1992. I knew my health was having an impact on what I was doing. These weren't minor health issues. Karen was told by surgeons I couldn't possibly survive it at various times, so I knew I had to stop.

You coached Queensland to success in 1991 in Wally Lewis's last year. Had he become bigger than Origin itself?

He was Origin. He has his statue at Suncorp and it's not there for no reason. No player has had an influence on Origin football like him, and it was a thrill to coach him and for him to buy into my way. Mal struggled to kick goals in that series, so the games were all close. Michael O'Connor kicked an amazing goal from the sideline in the teeming rain to win the second match for the Blues. He was my Manly captain at the time. I just stood there and thought, "You bastard!"

How did you enjoy coaching Western Samoa in the 1995 World Cup?

I loved it. Even though we were unlucky against Wales, I was quietly pleased for them because it was in Wales, and it meant so much to them. But we went well with limited preparation and some knocks.

How did you end up at the North Queensland Cowboys in 1996?

I'd been retired from the club game for a couple of years, but they had sacked their coach and had a deal with Tim Sheens for 1997. They needed someone for 1996. It ended up being a very enjoyable year. Having come last in 1995, we moved up three places on a minimal budget, so we did alright.

Your last professional involvement was at Bradford Bulls. What happened?

Andrew Chalmers, a friend of mine, said they were going to go out of existence. We love the game and didn't want that to happen to such a famous club. We thought we'd do what we could to keep it going. Andrew did all the negotiating, and I came up, but the whole thing was a shambles. We started to work our way through it, but I had another heart attack. I was too far away from the people who had been looking after my health and I wanted to go back. I sold my half and had to get myself right again.

How many heart attacks have you had?

I don't know. Quite a few - I've got stents, I've had open-heart surgery twice, I've had a number of strokes. The brain haemorrhage sent a lot of that stuff off. I haven't had a heart attack for a couple of years, but I don't wait for them. I'm busier than ever before and have no intention of retiring. If the right opportunity came up now, I'd take up coaching again in a heartbeat. People say the game has changed, but I have kept as close to it as possible. The more it's changed, the more it's the same. The way the game is played now provides more opportunity to excite the fans because I'm all about attack. The defensive side is the easy side of it. The skilful side needs characters, and the game is guilty of allowing itself to be overcoached. People say I don't understand because coaching is a science. They are wrong. Coaching is an art. Science backs it up, but coaching is an art. Some coaches can get players to perform but another can't. You see it in Super League and in the NRL. They have the role, but they don't have the art of coaching.

The funny thing is, even at 75, I honestly believe I could do it all again tomorrow. I'm busier than ever at the moment. I designed a learning system for disadvantaged kids and received a knighthood for it. I'm now Sir Graham Lowe. The fire has never gone out, and I could get straight back into it tomorrow.

MARTIN OFFIAH

1992-1996

It's incredible to think that Martin Offiah only played for Wigan for four and a half years given the sheer number of tries he scored. He crossed for 30 in his first half season after joining in a world-record fee in January 1992 from Widnes. His final tally for the club was 186 in 159 matches, the most famous of which came at Wembley against Leeds in the 1994 Challenge Cup Final. With 501 career tries, Offiah is the highest-scoring Englishman in the sport's history.

TO say Martin Offiah has crammed a hell of a lot into his life would be something of an understatement.

He scored over 500 tries in a glittering Rugby League career after switching codes in 1987. He won 33 Great Britain caps and a further five for England, as well as collecting four Challenge Cups, seven league titles, six Premiership trophies, two World Club titles, three Regal Trophies, two Lancashire Cups and three Charity Shields. He was also the star of the show as Wigan won the World Sevens in Australia in 1992, when his four tries demolished Brisbane Broncos in the final.

Individually, he won the Man of Steel, the Lance Todd Trophy twice, he has an MBE, he is one of the five players on the Wembley statue, and he is a member of the Rugby League Hall of Fame.

He dabbled in other sports, representing his school at fencing and, as an Essex second-XI cricketer, his claim to fame is that he bowled out Graham Gooch in the nets. And, of course, he also played rugby union, setting alight the sevens circuit in 1987 which alerted the Rugby League scouts.

He appeared as himself in an episode of Emmerdale, settling the argument once and for all about the pronunciation of his surname (it's Off-yer). He was also in Hollyoaks and he was a contestant in the first series of the BBC's Strictly Come Dancing.

He is arguably Rugby League's most famous name. Even 20 years after his retirement, the man known as Chariots is better known to the general public than many of the leading players from the Super League era - something that says as much about his try-scoring heroics and charisma as it does about the sport's unfortunate inability to promote its leading players to the wider world. "When I finished playing, I didn't really want to get into coaching," said Offiah, "but I had some media interests. The market for jobs for ex-players isn't vast, and a lot of players are lost to the game, but I didn't want that to happen to me."

Offiah attended Woolverstone Hall, a Suffolk-based comprehensive school where pupils could board. "My brother was already there," he said, "so I didn't get homesick. It's where I discovered the sport of rugby for the first time." His sporting prowess led to a rugby union career. He went on to impress Widnes scouts with some excellent displays in the 1987 Hong Kong Sevens - when he played for the Penguins against the All Blacks alongside future League players Frano Botica, Mark Brooke-Cowden and Emosi Koloto - and in the Middlesex Sevens.

"Ray French has told the story of a try I scored against Waterloo in the Middlesex Sevens," said Offiah, "The try started with me running across my own line, before I turned left and beat a couple of his ex-pupils to score. They told him about me, and he told Saints, but one of their directors said I was an uncoordinated buffoon, so Ray told Dougie Laughton, the coach of Widnes, about me instead.

"Rugby League was viewed from afar as a great spectacle. The big games were attractive to anyone, and that was definitely the case with that 1985 Cup Final. That would be the first game that I remember sitting down and watching. I can still see Henderson Gill scoring that try and grinning like he did afterwards."

Offiah posted 42 tries in 35 matches in his debut Rugby League season, helping the Naughton Park outfit to the 1987-88 League Championship. He was crowned Man of Steel in the process. He was the first division's leading tryscorer, a feat he achieved on a further five occasions - including each of the four seasons he played for Widnes. After just eight games (and eight tries) in 1987, he was called up to the representative scene, pulling on the Lancashire jersey as the Red Rose county drew 22-all with the touring Papua New Guineans.

He made his Great Britain debut in Avignon in February 1988, just half a season into his League career, and typically marked the occasion with a try courtesy of a superb chip and chase from Shaun Edwards, who would go on to create countless tries for Offiah.

"If it wasn't for Shaun, there'd be no statue of me at Wembley," Offiah admitted. "Playing with him was a real highlight of my career. He went on to be my coach at Wasps which was pretty weird given we'd been roomies on the 1988 Lions Tour. Getting to play with him for Wigan was great. I dislocated my shoulder in 1993, and he was there for me. He was our coach on the pitch, and he gave me pep talks when things weren't going well.

"I got selected to play for Great Britain against France in 1987, and I think only Billy Boston got capped in fewer games than I did. I remember scoring my first Test try out there, but I obviously did something wrong because I didn't play against the French in the return match against them a couple of weeks later." But Offiah impressed sufficiently in the black and white of Widnes to earn a place on the Lions' tour of Papua New Guinea, Australia and New Zealand - Malcolm Reilly's first tour as coach. "I didn't know too much about Malcolm, but he was a firm guy, and he had the respect of every single player," said Offiah. "We didn't quite make it over the hump in terms of winning an Ashes series, but they were still real halcyon days.

"1988 was a tough tour and we lost a lot of players to injury. We struggled to get a team together for the last game when we had that fantastic win," said Offiah of Great Britain's against-the-odds 26-12 win at Sydney, their first win against the old enemy since 1978.

The closest Offiah came to winning the Ashes was two years later when a magnificent 20-12 win at Wembley, in which he scored, was followed by a heart-breaking 14-10 loss at Old Trafford, courtesy of a last-gasp, long-range try scored by the fearsome Mal Meninga when Offiah was off the field injured. "Carl Gibson went on to the wing and there was no way they'd have gone the length of the field if I'd been out there," Offiah pointed out with slight immodesty, but probable truth. "I watched the try unfold on a monitor in the Old Trafford dressing room as I was lying on the treatment table."

Great Britain went on to push Australia all the way in the 1992 and 1995 World Cups, as well as the 1994 Ashes series, and they whitewashed New Zealand in 1993, but Offiah never did get his hands on silverware against the green and golds.

THE tries kept coming for Offiah in the black and white of Widnes. In four full seasons, he scored 181 tries in 145 matches, as they won the league championship in 1988 and 1989 – the latter when they beat Wigan in a winner-takes-all finale at Naughton Park. "The highlights of my time at Widnes were scoring hat-tricks in my first two seasons to effectively win the championship," he said. "We beat St Helens 16-6 in 1988 when they were our nearest challengers. Then we beat Wigan in 1989. Widnes fans tell me I scored my greatest try that day, and Maurice Lindsay said it was the try that made them want to sign me. The other big Widnes highlight was winning the World Club Challenge at Old Trafford against Canberra Raiders."

Offiah was so good that it was a sad inevitability that abuse would come his way from opposition supporters. Much of it was racist. "I moved to Widnes and lived in the town and scored tries straightaway," said Offiah, "so I had no problems with them. There were lots of insults from away crowds, but I put a positive spin on it by wanting to score tries to shut the people up who were abusing me. On a wet Wednesday evening in Batley or Oldham, it wasn't always easy, and you needed something to fire you up. The opposition fans' taunts did the trick."

As well as running in the tries for Widnes and Great Britain, Offiah had three spells in the Winfield Cup - with Eastern Suburbs in 1989 and 1993 and with St George in 1991. "I loved my time in Australia," he said. "I used to watch Winfield Cup highlights on the Micron videos. I loved the sun and the big crowds. I remember Brisbane Broncos coming in, and they were massive. I loved Graeme Hughes' commentary. I just wanted to play in Australia to hear the commentators say my name! I scored a try with my first touch for Easts against Western Suburbs, who had Ellery Hanley, Garry Schofield and Kelvin Skerrett in their team - Joe Lydon also played for Easts. There was a lot of hype about that game because of the five British players. I was meant to go back in '91, but they cancelled the contract, so I signed for St George and was keen to have a good game against Easts. I scored a hat-trick against them at the Sydney Football Stadium. I went back in '93, but I dislocated my shoulder in my first game at Penrith."

Offiah's final game for Widnes was the Premiership Final against Hull at Old Trafford. He scored the only try in a 14-4 defeat. He asked to go on the transfer list before jetting to Australia to play for St George. It took over seven months for the situation to be sorted. Offiah refused to play for Widnes, who wouldn't sell him. Stalemate.

Maurice Lindsay kept chipping away at the Widnes chairman Jim Mills and eventually got his man in January 1992. The transfer fee was £440,000, easily a Rugby League record. On the same day, Wigan also signed a 16-year-old called Andrew Farrell from Orrell St James.

"It was a pretty low time," reflected Offiah. "Widnes didn't want to pay me what I was worth but still didn't want to let me go. Maurice moved heaven and earth to get me to Wigan. Leeds also came in with Dougie and offered more money than Wigan, but I wanted to go to Central Park.

"The time I moved to Wigan coincided with the BBC filming a documentary about the club," said Offiah. "That just showed that Wigan captured the national interest back then, and sadly it's something that Rugby League has lost for some reason. Rugby union becoming professional has played its part I suppose because you don't have guys like Jonathan Davies coming over anymore, and that hasn't happened in the Super League era. Players have gone the other way. Lots of other sports have strengthened and produced more and more well-known athletes."

As for his Wigan career, which yielded an avalanche of tries and trophies, I asked Offiah to pick three highlights from his time in the cherry and white. "Only three - well, I'll give it a go, but that's not easy!" he laughed. "Scoring that try against Leeds in the 1994 Challenge Cup Final is definitely one. Scoring ten tries in one game, also against Leeds, has to be another. And also going to Australia and winning the World Club Challenge in Brisbane's backyard."

THE beginning of Offiah's Central Park career was nothing short of phenomenal as, having not played for several months, he scorched in for 30 tries in 16 games in the second half of the 1991-92 season. Many of them were created by his centre partner, the great Queenslander Gene Miles, who only played for Wigan that season. "Gene was incredible," said Offiah. "He's in the top three centres I played with, alongside Darren Wright and Gary Connolly. I didn't play with Barrie-Jon Mather for long enough, but he was also good. I'd been the league's top tryscorer in each of my four seasons at Widnes, and I had this idea in my head that I could do it again in just half a season. I gave it a good go [Offiah finished ten behind Shaun Edwards, who played 21 games more]. We also went out to Sydney to win the Nissan World Sevens.

"Wigan dominated for so long, winning the eight cups in a row. They had Joe Lydon and Ellery earlier on, and Shaun spanned the eight years, but the team in 1994-95 with Henry Paul, Andy Farrell and that three-quarter line which also included Gary, Inga and Jason was probably the most talented Wigan team I played in. Andy was a force of nature and very skilful. Jason didn't even make the 1994 Wembley team, but he got back in 1995 and won the Lance Todd Trophy."

Offiah has two Lance Todds of his own, won in 1992 and 1994. While people still eulogise about his 1994 length-of-the-field try against Leeds, his two tries against Castleford two years earlier are now largely forgotten. Prime Minister John Major described Offiah as 'faster than a camera shutter', although he probably remembers the afternoon more for Billy McGinty's dressing-room antics. "The 1992 final was big for me because I had the pressure of the transfer fee at the time," said Offiah. "I scored two decent tries, especially the second one when I beat Mike Ford to the touch after Shaun's kick. John Major came into the dressing room and there's the well-known story of Billy going up to him naked with a pineapple ring dangling on his private parts!

"As for my try at Wembley in 1994, Alex Murphy had done a big story in the Daily Mirror, saying I was finished. It wasn't often Rugby League commanded the whole page in a red-top newspaper. That was big motivation that day, and it's the elephant in the room whenever I meet Alex now because I've never brought it up. I have no hard

feelings though because if he hadn't done that article, I may not have scored that try, and I may not be on the Wembley statue."

Offiah left Wigan midway through the 1996 Super League season, having scored 12 tries in 10 matches. He also scored six in the Rugby League challenge match against the rugby union champions Bath. He was still a class act, but with Wigan in a parlous fiscal position due to not making Wembley and some unwise spending, Offiah was offloaded. He was involved in a most unusual transfer - signing for London Broncos and Bedford's rugby union side at the same time.

"I was at an age when money was a factor and I wanted to play rugby union as well," said Offiah. "My agent spoke to Wigan who said they had money worries, and I was on a big contract. We signed a unique deal with London Broncos and Bedford Blues at the same time, but it didn't really work out, and I signed full-time for the London Broncos at the end of 1997. I got my MBE that year. It was on a Friday, and I got taken to our game that weekend in Richard Branson's helicopter as it was the only way I could play!" Alongside Shaun Edwards, Offiah helped the Broncos to Wembley in 1999 and scored the opening try against Leeds courtesy of another long-range effort.

Offiah's final club was Salford for whom he played in 2000 and 2001. He was past his best, but on 1st July 2001, he scored his 500th Rugby League try, a tally which includes those he scored in the Winfield Cup. "500 tries puts me in the same club as Billy Boston and Brian Bevan.

I think the try that did it was my second try for Salford against London. It was always nice to score against your old clubs. I can't remember much about the try, and I went out with a bit of a whimper to be honest. I was 35 - the oldest winger in Super League. The next year, I was the oldest winger in the rugby union Premiership. Recovery was tough at that age!"

Offiah still has a fond regard for Wigan. "It's only natural that I still look out for them," he said. "My try record was similar to what it was at Widnes, but I think I was a better player at Wigan. They still have a hold over the mind of Rugby League supporters. They'll always be the big name in Rugby League. They're the name that the public as a whole can identify and recognise. To go out at Twickenham like we did and attract a full crowd for the opening game of the Middlesex Sevens in 1996 - the first time Twickenham has ever been full for the opening game - was proof of that. Wigan remain a huge drawcard.

"I still follow the game. I'm part of Ellery Hanley's judging panel that awards points every game which decide the Man of Steel. I love watching Wigan and in particular Jai Field and Bevan French. To this day, I don't understand why Bevan came off after scoring seven tries in a game in 2022 with plenty of time to catch my [and Shaun Edwards'] record of ten in a match for Wigan. My phone was buzzing right through that game with people telling me he was going to do it. I love still being talked about all these years on!"

DOUG LAUGHTON

1967-1973

Doug Laughton is perhaps best known for his coaching exploits, but this outstanding back-rower starred for St Helens, Wigan and Widnes and captained Great Britain. He became player-coach of Widnes in the first of three stints in charge of his hometown club. In the late-1980s, they were twice champions of England and World Club Challenge winners. But he had less success at Headingley where he coached Leeds between 1991 and 1995.

If you could relive one day from your career, which would it be?
Winning the Ashes in Australia. We won the decider 21-17 with Roger Millward scoring a late try. I played second row. Malcolm Reilly was loose forward. I was usually a loose forward, so I could pass a ball, and I combined well with Roger and set up his late try. We'd talk about moves before the game, but Reilly didn't want to do them - he just wanted to knock people over. But moves between Roger and I came off.
Soon after, I presented awards to some kids. I watched them play and they had skills that I didn't develop until I was in my 20s. I said to someone that we might never win the Ashes again. And 50 years on, we haven't.

You played for St Helens between 1963 and 1966.
My hometown club Widnes made me an offer, but it wasn't quite what I wanted, so I went to St Helens. The A-team coach, Steve Llewelyn, said I was quick with good ability, but I wasn't big enough to play loose forward. He encouraged me to get into the weights, and I put on a stone in a few months.
It was fabulous to play alongside Tom van Vollenhoven and Alexander the Great. Murphy was incredible. John Warlow looked after me. You learn nothing by not being a cheeky little bugger. You have to listen, and I did. In those days, it was all about Wembley, and I didn't get to play there for Saints, which was a shame. I missed the 1966 final with injury.

Why did you join Wigan?
When I was injured, I'd just got married and I'd started my own business. One day I went for my pay packet. It was 19 quid less tax. I didn't look impressed, so they asked what was wrong and I said I'd like one of the envelopes they give Van Vollenhoven or Murphy. I didn't want to play for them again. You have to treat people properly.

Tell us about Wembley in 1970 and the following year's Championship Final.
Castleford's Keith Hepworth should have been sent off in 1970, no doubt. He was a hard little bugger, but there can be no room in the game for fracturing Colin Tyrer's jaw. Cas were a very good side and they beat us 7-2.
The 1971 Championship Final against Saints was agonising. They scored two late tries. The winner came in the final seconds as they hit the post with a drop goal, took the rebound and scored a try. You can't change yesterday, but you can make tomorrow. We knew we had to get our heads up and move on.

After winning the Ashes on Australian soil, why couldn't Great Britain back it up by winning the 1970 World Cup? And what do you recall of the multiple bouts of violence which marred the final?

I don't know. It was perhaps a case of after the Lord Mayor's show. Australia had Billy Smith back at scrum-half and he was excellent. Fighting was more common than you'd think - we had a few nutters in the pack! I think I was about the only forward who didn't want to fight. I do have one permanent reminder of that World Cup though - I still have a mark on my right arm where the French captain's tooth got stuck!

Do you regret turning down the captaincy of the 1974 Lions to take up a contract with Canterbury?
In the same set of circumstances, I'd do it again - I'm a strange character! I was captain against France. It was rare to do well in France because of the French refs, but I put Keith Fielding in for three tries. However there was a strong rumour that David Watkins would be tour captain because of Brian Snape's influence on the game. The RFL rang me up and said they'd heard the rumours I wasn't happy. We played France again at Wigan with me captain, but my mind was already made up.
It was a mistake, but the money was a factor as well. It was eight or ten grand for about 12 games, whereas many players were on £25 for a win or £5 for a loss in England. I didn't get on with the Canterbury coach Malcolm Clift. After one game, he read out the tackle counts, and I had only made 16. But I had played well. I'd poleaxed a couple of players and I'd made a try-saving tackle. But he told me to change my game. In the next game when a player was being tackled by someone else, I'd touch them on the head. Malcolm praised me after the game for making 71 tackles – an all-time record in Australia. But none of the tackles hurt anyone and there were no try savers.

You did captain the Lions in 1979, but you only played in the first Test.
I got injured at training. The performances in Australia were a disaster. We lost the first Test 35-0. They were just a lot better than us. Eric Ashton was coach, and he missed the first four weeks because his daughter had been in a car accident. We won five tour matches and then Eric flew in. He came in when we were having a drink, and he accused us of being a load of drinkers. He had us out at 6am running the legs off us. Half the squad were still pissed. He kept telling us Australia were better than us, which wasn't ideal. He had coached me at Wigan though, and he was good then.

Why did you move to Widnes from Wigan?
For some away games, we would stop for lunch. The players always got a mixed grill which was hardly ideal a couple of hours before a game. The chairman always had a turkey dinner. I was sick of mixed grills, so one day I intercepted his turkey and ate it. He put me on the transfer list!

You played in four more Challenge Cup Finals, winning two. What are your memories?
1975 was very special as it was the first for Widnes for so long. Vince Karalius, my idol, was coach, and I was captain. Lifting the cup was a dream come true, and that was the name of my book.

I was player-coach in the 1978-79 season, and it was a really memorable season. We beat the Australian tourists, and nobody has done that since. Then we beat Wakefield at Wembley. We came second in the BBC team-of-the-year award, and I won the Man of Steel.

How did you adapt to coaching?
When I was appointed player-coach, Reg Bowden said just because you were a great player doesn't mean you'll be a great coach. But I thought a good player had more to offer. I signed a young Andy Gregory - it was a mystery why Wigan didn't sign him. We got to Wembley in 1981 and beat Hull KR. I coached them until 1983 and then took over again in 1986.

Tell us about the signings of Martin Offiah and Jonathan Davies.
Ray French told me he'd seen a player who was as good as Van Vollenhoven, but a Saints scout had been pretty scathing about him. I then watched the Rosslyn Park Sevens on TV, and Offiah was outstanding. Rugby League had changed moneywise with signing-on fees and further annual fees, making the game much more attractive to people like Offiah.

Jonathan got 40 grand up front, but we got it straight back on his debut. I got into trouble for not putting him on until after half-time. The chairman and I argued about it, and he threatened to sack me, but I didn't want to risk losing the game by putting Jonathan on too early. I did put him on soon after half-time because we'd scored a couple of early tries and the game was won.

Was the highlight of your second spell the 1989 title decider with Widnes?
No, it was the World Club Challenge win against Canberra. The Wigan win was great of course. Maurice Lindsay phoned me before the game and wasn't happy that I was so confident in the press, but I was certain we would win.

Tim Sheens told me that Canberra's preparations were hit by Grand Final celebrations and players unable to travel.
Bollocks! They certainly did take it seriously – you could tell that by the way Laurie Daley tried to decapitate Jonathan. Look at their side – it was packed with talent. We were 12-0 down in no time and what we did to come back was magnificent. It was the first official World Club Challenge and I'm very proud of it.

Why did you move to Leeds in 1991?
Players were coming off contract and were worth so much more with everything we'd won. Other clubs had more money, so I knew things were going to get tough for Widnes.

Leeds offered me a good deal - 75 grand, a house, a car and a pension which I'm still getting money from. I said to myself if Leeds could match Wigan for spending, then no one would beat me. We were top at Christmas, so we started well, but Wigan came good again.

We didn't win a trophy, but I brought some good kids through. I signed Adrian Morley, Kevin Sinfield, Francis Cummins and Graham Holroyd – those last two were the youngest two players to play at Wembley.

Tell us about your relationship with Garry Schofield.
He didn't like it when I gave Ellery Hanley the captaincy, but not many people like the boss, so I was used to it. Ellery was the captain of Great Britain and he'd been a very successful captain of Wigan, so it was the right decision.

Schofield had been captain for a while and Leeds hadn't done much. Some of the things he did weren't going to endear me to him. The mentality of the side wasn't right. They looked like market traders getting off the bus, so I got them to dress properly.

Your departure from Headingley was very sudden. What happened?
I was in South Africa during the 1995 rugby union World Cup to look at Joost van der Westhuizen, the South African scrum-half, and Jonah Lomu. But rugby union went professional, so there was no point hanging around. Leeds then told me they'd agreed to get Dean Bell as assistant coach, but my contract said I could appoint the assistant coach. I didn't know Dean, so I left.

You went back to Widnes for a third spell.
Widnes were gone by then. I was cooking food and feeding them all on a Saturday morning. People weren't getting paid, including me. It was no good for team spirit. I tried my best, but it was never going to work.

JASON ROBINSON

1992-2000

Jason Robinson is one of Rugby League's great wingers, creating havoc for defences everywhere between 1992 and 2000, when he switched codes, leaving Wigan for Sale. He had won numerous trophies in the cherry and white. His great performances include winning the Lance Todd Trophy in 1995, scoring the crucial try in the inaugural Grand Final of 1998 and being the stand-out player in the final game at Central Park a year later. In a disappointing era for Great Britain, he was still a regular try scorer against Australia and New Zealand. Robinson was selected in Open Rugby's World XIII for four years in a row between 1995 and 1998.

IF I was picking an all-time British Rugby League XIII, my wingers would be Billy Boston and Martin Offiah, but in my Wigan XIII, Jason Robinson would edge out the latter. Both were capable of scoring the most extraordinary tries, but while Offiah had the edge numerically, Robinson spent nearly twice as long at Central Park. Both were world-class wingers for similar lengths of time, but Robinson was exclusively a Wigan player. He was at his peak right up to the end and still shone in mediocre teams like those of 1997 and 1999. He was, as Australian commentators would say, a freak of nature. Marking Robinson must have been one of the most onerous tasks to befall a Rugby League player in the 1990s.

Robinson, or Billy Whizz as he was nicknamed, broke the mould for Rugby League wingers. Hitherto, the great flankmen had tended to be prolific tryscorers like Brian Bevan, Tom van Vollenhoven, Boston and Offiah. Robinson may not have quite matched their scoring exploits, although he was no slouch in that department, but his all-round game was incredibly impressive. He did as much damage running from dummy-half deep in his own territory as he did plundering tries at the other end.

It was a crying shame for Rugby League when he switched codes after the Grand Final in 2000. He had signed a huge deal with the Australian Rugby League governing body in the mid-1990s, which was later bought out by Wigan. When it went into its last year, the club was slow to act, but with the game's new salary cap biting, perhaps they felt they couldn't offer him similar terms. Robinson instead plumped for pastures new and signed for Sale. Within a year, he had played not just for England in the Six Nations but also for the British Lions where he excelled in Australia.

One could potentially argue that with Brian Carney and Brett Dallas, Wigan didn't miss Robinson too much, but internationally, his absence left a void. Great Britain were much improved after Robinson's exit, but with him on the wing instead of David Hodgson in 2001 or Richard Horne in 2003, those two Ashes series could have been very different.

Robinson's story began in Leeds. Born to a Scottish mother in the summer of 1974, he endured a difficult childhood. His Jamaican father had left the family home before he was born. He didn't get to know him until his rugby union days. Robinson regularly witnessed his step-father beat his mother. He was the only person of colour in the household.

"My earliest memories are from school, when I didn't know anything about the game," he said. "I suddenly grew a love for it and even though I was tiny, I loved the physicality. I joined an amateur club, and I remember Garry Schofield doing a presentation, which was very

exciting. At 16, I knew I had some talent and wanted to play for Leeds, but they chose someone else. Wigan had a scout in Leeds and thankfully he saw some potential. I was disappointed because I was a ball boy at Leeds. Even throwing a ball back to your heroes was exciting! I had an offer from Hunslet, but that wasn't something I wanted. But Leeds ignoring me was a blessing because they didn't win anything back then."

Robinson was initially a scrum-half, and the player Leeds signed instead of him was Gareth Stephens who stayed at Headingley for three years before playing for a variety of other Yorkshire-based clubs. At Wigan, Robinson was eventually moved to the wing.

"Wigan had guys like Shaun Edwards and Frano Botica, so I was always going to be up against it," he admitted. "They saw my ability to beat defenders was better than my ball skills, so I moved to the wing. I wasn't bothered. The other winger was Martin Offiah, so I had a lot to live up to! I came in after an injury to David Myers and never looked back. I stayed there until 2000. It was such a competitive environment and if you didn't perform, someone would take your place. Winning is one thing but backing it up is another, and that's what we had to do at Wigan."

JUST a couple of months into his second season, Robinson was called up by Great Britain to play against the touring New Zealanders at Wembley. His debut was incredible as his two tries helped his side to a 17-0 win, but injury ruled him out of the rest of the series.

"It was unbelievable to play for Great Britain at Wembley and to score two tries," he said. "Everyone wants to play international rugby. I was up against Sean Hoppe, and I was named man of the match. It gave me a taste of international rugby and I wanted more, but I dislocated my elbow at Halifax and missed the last two Tests."

Later that season, there was more bad news for the winger when he was dropped by coach John Dorahy for the Challenge Cup Final against Leeds, although a month later he was back in the team and scoring a try as Wigan earned the tag of world champions in Brisbane.

"I do understand that you can't pick everybody - 30 into 17 doesn't go. But the issue was how it came about. I was told I was in contention if I played an A-Team game. I did, and I scored three tries. Then I had to play another and was man of the match. I just wanted to be told if I was going to be dropped. How much more did they want me to do? John Dorahy's problem was that he couldn't tell you. John Monie would just tell you. A few of us got bitter and twisted about it and didn't handle it in the right way, abusing a few people. I was a young, immature lad at the time. It's all part of growing up.

"The coach was sacked, and I was reinstated for the

World Club Challenge. We were on their turf, and we didn't have our strongest team. Billy McGinty was propping. Graeme West had taken over and he said we had a few days to enjoy ourselves - and boy did we enjoy ourselves! We had one hell of a party for a few days. Then reality kicked in and we knew we had to play well or be embarrassed, and we created one of the biggest upsets in the history of the sport. It was an amazing night. It's up there with my biggest ever wins in rugby."

In early 1995, Rugby League was turned upside down by the Super League War which was precipitated by an argument over pay-TV rights to the game in Australia. The result was both sides, the Australian Rugby League and Murdoch's Super League organisation, vying with each other to sign up as many players as they could. Salaries entered a new stratosphere overnight and leading English players like Robinson benefitted. Along with teammates Gary Connolly and Martin Hall, Robinson signed with the ARL, although the trio ended up remaining with Wigan.

"There was nothing set in stone, but I thought about playing for Manly," said Robinson. "Living on the beach would have been nice. The decision was down to finances. A lot of money had come into the game and when I was offered a million-pound contract, it was a case of 'Give me a pen!' It was a strange time. It happened overnight, and people were panicking. Every man and his dog were signing for someone. But after time, I wanted to stay in the UK and Wigan came to an agreement with the ARL."

VA'AIGA TUIGAMALA signed for Wigan after the All Blacks tour of the UK in the autumn of 1993. He made his debut the following February and took Robinson's place on the wing in the Challenge Cup Final. He then settled into the centres as Wigan fielded perhaps the greatest three-quarter line the British game has seen – Robinson, Tuigamala, Connolly and Offiah.

The signing of Tuigamala was important to Robinson for more than rugby reasons. Previously a big drinker and something of a wild child, despite the quality of his performances, Robinson was influenced by the Samoan. He became religious and stopped drinking.

"Everyone judges you on what happens on the field," Robinson stated. "If you're successful, then the perception is that life must be great. But some people do well at work and then go away and struggle. That's why the awareness of mental health now is great. People didn't understand I came from a real tough background. We were a very poor, one-parent family. Suddenly, I was shoved into an environment where everyone is obsessed with rugby and patting you on the back, and I didn't have the character to deal with it. People see you in new cars but don't have a clue what is really going on in your life. It would have been good to have been helped with that. The game teaches you to be hard and not show vulnerability, but sometimes you need to. You're not Superman. You have emotions.

"When you had a problem, you went for a beer, as if getting drunk would sort everything. I'd play in front of a huge crowd, then go home and feel lonely. Inga coming to Wigan was massive for me because I had someone to look up to. I realised it wasn't about having the best car or the most girls or the most money. He was the happiest man in the club. I knew I wanted that too. Faith was a big part of his life. I had a GBH charge over me. I was in the wrong place at the wrong time. I was really struggling - sometimes going out six nights a week. I looked after myself physically from 1995, so it was a key thing for my career. Mentally it helped too because you can be fit, but if your mind isn't right you will struggle."

Having won every trophy available in the final two winter seasons, including victory over Leeds at Wembley in 1995 when Robinson won the Lance Todd Trophy, Wigan's grip on the game's major prizes was finally loosened in 1996 as Rugby League's new era got underway. The first blow was at Salford where Wigan suffered their first Challenge Cup defeat since 1987. They ended the season having won the Premiership Trophy and rugby union's Middlesex Sevens, which was one of three cross-code forays they undertook in 1996.

"My memory of Salford was always complaining about the changing room," laughed Robinson. "It was always freezing. You come to realise over the years that sport is exciting for lots of different reasons and you can always get beaten if you're not at your best. It was hard to swallow because of our success, but days like that are good for the game. When Wigan didn't win, everyone else was happy. The bad memories I have are the best memories for others. I don't remember much about the game, but I'm sure Salford people will look back and recall plenty.

"The cross-code games with Bath in 1996 were great for the players. It felt like League v Union, working class v middle class. It gave us an understanding of how different the games were. They looked like fish out of water in our game, and we didn't have a clue in union. Only our natural skills made us competitive in that game. We tried to play union in the first half then at half-time, we decided to throw the ball around."

114

AFTER 25 seasons of the championship being decided on a first-past-the-post basis, Rugby League reverted to a play-off system that had last been used in 1973. This time the decider would be called the Grand Final instead of the Championship Final, and it was Robinson who starred in the first one. Wigan and Leeds had played two matches of State of Origin intensity during the regular season with the Rhinos prevailing in both. Wigan hit back to beat them in the play-offs. After Leeds beat St Helens, they met again in the Old Trafford rain.

After Richie Blackmore's try, Leeds led 4-0. Their captain Iestyn Harris had missed two kicks at goal. They had been the better team by some distance. And then Robinson struck. Kris Radlinski was tackled by Brad Godden on the 20 and nearly slid out of play. Robinson came into acting half, scooted to his left, shot through a gap between props Darren Fleary and Jamie Mathiou, and he escaped the clutches of Daryl Powell and Harris to score under the posts just before half-time. Andy Farrell's conversion gave Wigan a lead they would never surrender.

"Playing in the first Grand Final was huge," said Robinson. "There were only 43,000 there, and it was peeing it down. There was nothing in the game. I was always up for beating Leeds because they hadn't signed me. Richie Blackmore had scored for Leeds. There was

nothing on. Radders took it onto the 20, right on touch. I did what I always did and probed the line. Someone always wanted to smash you, but I could use my footwork to get between what was a very good defensive line. I skipped through, went round the fullback and scored under the posts. It was a great moment!"

Robinson had two more seasons at Wigan, but they failed to win silverware in that time. They came top in 2000 but there was no shield awarded back then, and they lost the Grand Final to St Helens with Robinson, in his final game of Rugby League, playing out of position at fullback. "It got to a point when I thought, 'I've won this several times, so what next?' If Wigan had offered me a contract earlier, I would have stayed. As a key player, you don't expect not to have your contract sorted out in your last season."

Three years later, Robinson scored England's only try in the 2003 rugby union World Cup Final, in which they beat Australia 20-17 after extra time. Less than 12 hours later, Great Britain were beaten for a third Saturday in a row by Australia in Rugby League's Ashes series, with only a cigarette paper between the sides in each game. Halfback Richard Horne played the entire series on the wing. The autumn of 2003 could have been very different for both codes had Wigan managed to keep Robinson in Rugby League.

COLIN TYRER

1967-1974

Colin Tyrer played just shy of 250 games for Wigan from the mid-1960s to the mid-1970s, having already made his mark at Leigh. He is perhaps best known for an incident at Wembley in 1970 when a late, high tackle from Castleford's Keith Hepworth broke his jaw, and without him, Wigan went on to lose. He also played for Barrow and Hull Kingston Rovers before becoming assistant coach at Widnes.

If you could relive one day from your career, which would it be?
Probably the 1970 Challenge Cup semi-final when Wigan beat Hull Kingston Rovers at Headingley. It was a great feeling, knowing we'd got to Wembley because a lot of great players never make it. Ray Ashby told me if I signed for Wigan, I'd play at Wembley, and he was right.

You played for Astley & Tyldesley Collieries. Were you a miner?
No, I was only 17 when I signed for Leigh. I played open age for Astley & Tyldesley. A few ex-pros played there, and they were really good. I learned a lot from them. Dicky Massey was one ex-pro, and it was great to play alongside him.

When did you realise it was something you could pursue professionally?
I didn't really think about it like that. I played at school and really enjoyed it. I actually played alongside the famous singer Georgie Fame at school. His name was Clive Powell then. He was captain of the team, but we knew he was a talented singer too, and he went on to have a couple of number ones. I also played with Frankie Parr, who was a great scrum-half for Wigan. He played in the 1965 Wembley final. As for me, I'd played a lot of stand-off when I was younger, and I always kicked goals. I played for the Great Britain Under-19s in Carcassonne. I had a trial at Wigan and played a couple of 'A' Team games, but they weren't interested, and Leigh came in for me.

You made your Leythers debut against Swinton on 18 August 1962. Were you nervous? And what were the highlights of your time there?
I wasn't nervous. I never was. I just enjoyed the occasion. I was very happy at Leigh. We won the Lancashire Cup Final with Bev Risman at fullback. I was on the wing. Bev was a big signing from rugby union. The best game was beating Wigan [18-9] at Hilton Park, and I scored all our points. I think that's when Wigan decided they wanted me.

Why did you leave Leigh?
Alex Murphy came to Leigh. He was just coach at first because of his contract situation with St Helens. Eventually he got permission to play, and he was our player-coach. Anyway, one day we conceded a try just before half-time. Murph was fuming, screaming his head off. "Who missed him?" he shouted in the dressing room. Well I was fullback, so I was one of the players who had missed him, and I owned up. He went mad. I thought he was going to have a heart attack. I took my boots off, threw them across the dressing-room at him and said that's my last game here. I signed for Wigan on the Wednesday. He thought it was a set up, but I hadn't spoken to Wigan before that.

You signed for Wigan as Ray Ashby's replacement. How did he take that?
Ray was brilliant. He'd played for Liverpool City and when Wigan took him in, he was made up to be there. He played at Wembley with them and was man of the match. He was so grateful for those opportunities and when I signed, he couldn't have been nicer to me.

You scored a try and three goals on your Wigan debut at Rochdale on 3 March 1967.
I don't remember the game, but I did settle in nicely at Wigan. Eric Ashton was the player-coach, and he was great with me. I played in a couple of 'A' Team games with Eric and all I can say is I wish I'd played with him at his peak. I broke the try-scoring record for a fullback two seasons in a row, and I received most of the try-scoring passes from him. I scored after two minutes in one game, and he said, "You'll get six tonight." I scored four, so he wasn't far off. Billy Boston was still playing, and he was magnificent too. But they were coming to the end of their careers, and I just wish I'd signed there as a 17-year-old.

You were playing when limited tackles was introduced in 1966. How did it affect you?
You had to keep your wits about you, but you soon learned to adapt. The game became more interesting because one team couldn't just keep the ball for ages. It could be boring, so I think limited tackles is the best thing to have happened to the game. Eric told me once about the great prop Brian McTigue. He scored a try in the first minute of a match, rubbed his hands and said, "That's it now!" because once a team took the lead, they could just keep the ball and win the game. McTigue used to hold up the ball, which he called the pill, and tell the players, "This is the boss. The pill is the boss." He knew the importance of keeping hold of it.

Wigan won the 1968-69 BBC 2 Floodlit Trophy with a 7-4 win over Saints.
That was at Saints I think. The Floodlit competition was exciting, and it gave us a rare chance to be on TV. Night games were great as well.

What do you remember of the build-up to the infamous Challenge Cup Final of 1970?
We were still over the moon to be at Wembley. At the press conference the day before, the media warned me to be careful about Castleford targeting me because they had played Salford the year before and had tried to do the same in that game.

What are your recollections of the Keith Hepworth incident and the rest of your day?
It was well into the game. It happened after 18 minutes. I brought the ball up and Hepworth hit me high and late after I'd passed it. I was disappointed with the referee. He was from Yorkshire and so were Castleford. Maybe him not

sending Hepworth off was down to it being the big Wembley final, but it was still a terrible decision. My jaw was broken, and I was concussed. I came back to the hotel in agony. I went to Wigan Hospital, where they stitched my teeth and jaw together. My food had to be mashed up for two months. My front tooth was missing and that turned out to be a good thing because they would have had to remove it for the straw to get into my mouth.

Did Hepworth apologise?

No, never. I cracked him a couple of times and even got sent off once by Billy Thompson. I couldn't believe it! "You can't send me off for that. It's not like I broke his jaw!" Billy was pretty apologetic about it and said it was down to the linesman.

Alan Hardisty told me the Wigan forwards had also targeted the Castleford fullback.

I don't think that happened. It was certainly never a tactic.

Did the incident affect your confidence?

No, I came back the same player.

What do you remember of the 1971 Championship Final defeat to Saints, who scored two late tries to win?

I don't remember that at all.

You were sometimes criticised for taking a long time to line up a kick at goal.

I just did what I always did! Eric Clay once said to me, "Come on! Hurry up!" He even threatened to penalise me, but I knew he couldn't do that. Imagine a ref hurrying up a footballer taking a penalty!

Why did you leave Wigan?

I'd done six years and wasn't going to get a testimonial, so the only other way to make money was to move. I went to Barrow. John Cunningham was at Barrow, and we won the second division when I was there. I knew they wouldn't be at first-division standard, so I said I was retiring. And I did.

Then Colin Hutton rang a few months later to ask me to play for Hull KR, and I made my debut on Boxing Day. John Cunningham had also gone there. Colin was a lovely fella and he treated me brilliantly. I retired as a player in 1978, and two years later they won the Challenge Cup at Wembley. It was a shame to miss that, but I was 36 by then.

You played with Roger Millward at Rovers. Was he better than Murphy?

Roger Millward was a brilliant player. There wasn't much of him, but by god he could play. But no one was better than Murphy.

Tell us about your coaching career.

I went to Widnes as assistant to Doug Laughton. We beat Hull KR at Wembley in 1981. That was when Andy Gregory needed some dental treatment in the morning, and he went on to have a blinder. Then we had the replay in 1982 after Mick Adams had scored the try off the crossbar to win the semi-final against Leeds. Doug then finished, and I took over for six matches with Harry Dawson at the end of the 1982-83 season, and we won them all. I stayed on as assistant when Doug came back, and the team we had in the late 1980s with Martin Offiah, Alan Tait, Jonathan Davies and Phil McKenzie is one of the greatest teams I've ever seen. Doug went to Leeds and wanted me to go with him, but I didn't fancy the travelling.

My sons Sean and Christian were starting to come through in the professional game - Sean with Wigan and Christian at Widnes. I decided to leave Widnes then because I didn't think it appropriate to be coaching there when he was playing. My grandsons now play the game. Three are at Wigan - Keiron and Josh who are Sean's sons, and Joseph who is Christian's son - and I'd love to know if Wigan have had three generations play for them before. John, David and Darryl Kay did it at Leigh, but I don't know about Wigan. It would be great to see them go on to have professional careers.

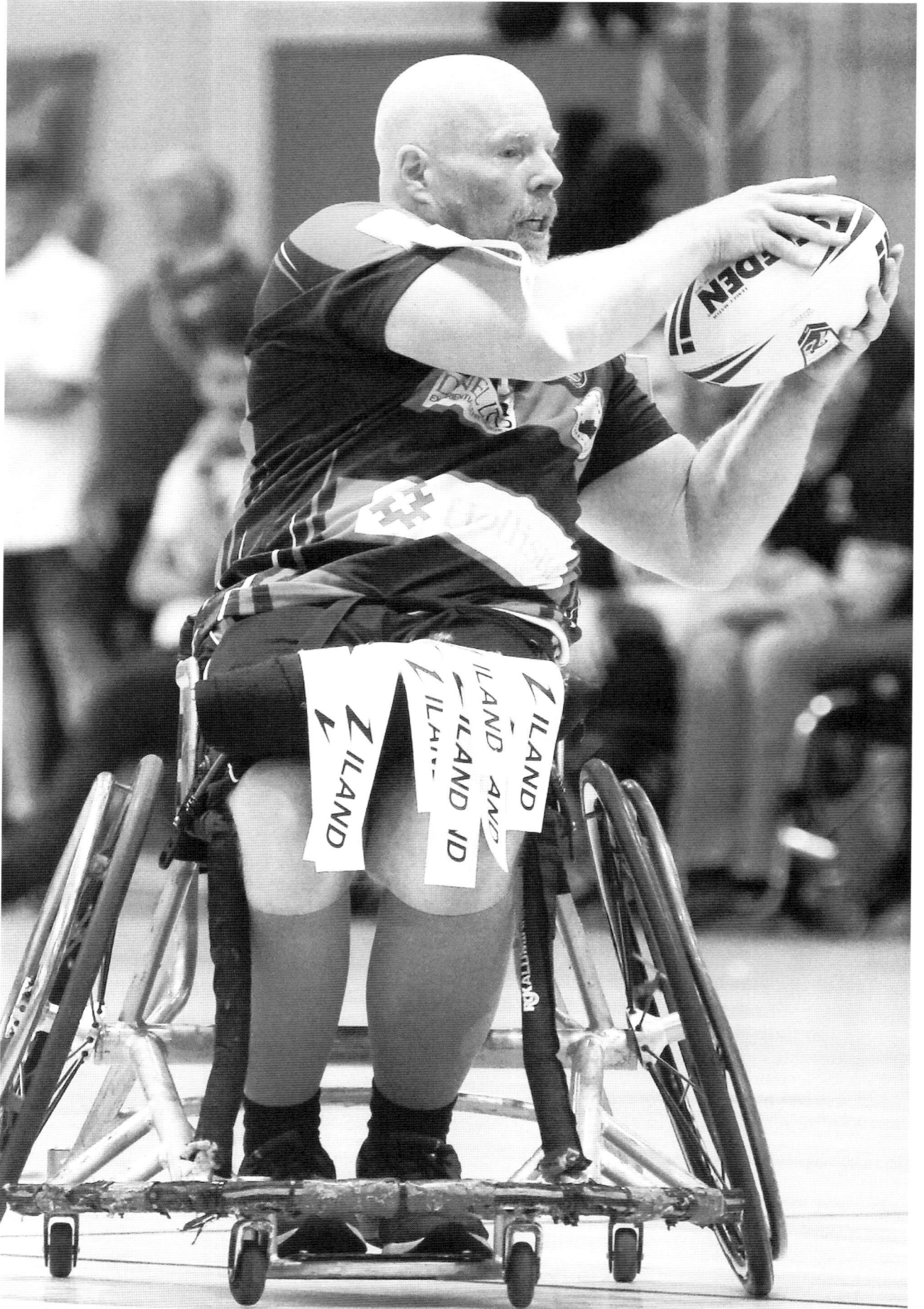

PHIL & DECLAN ROBERTS

2022-present

Over a million people watched the Wheelchair World Cup Final in the autumn of 2022 in which England beat France 28-24. As part of the squad, Declan Roberts picked up a World Cup winner's medal, as his father, Phil, had done in 2008 when England beat Australia. They both play for Wigan with Phil the player-coach.

VERY few Wigan players have won a World Cup.

The club wasn't represented in the successful Great Britain squads of 1954 and 1972. In 1960, there was Eric Ashton, Billy Boston, Brian McTigue and Mick Sullivan, all of whom played in the crucial win over Australia at Odsal. Thomas Leuluai won it in 2008 with New Zealand.

But in Phil and Declan Roberts, Wigan can boast a father and son who have each won the biggest prize of them all. It's hard to think of many father-and-son combinations in any sport who have each become a world champion. I think, as I enter their house in Orrell, that if it was up to me, there'd be one of those blue plaques on the wall proclaiming their successes.

Phil Roberts won Rugby League's Wheelchair World Cup in 2008 when his England team beat Australia 44-12 in the final. His son Declan was in the squad in 2022 when England beat France 28-24 in a match televised by the BBC, as the whole competition had been.

Both play for Wigan Warriors. Declan is the star player. Phil is player-coach and was named Wheelchair Coach of the Year in 2022. He's also player-coach of Ireland and an active referee.

Wheelchair Rugby League was developed in France in 2004. Both men and women play at the highest level, as do able-bodied competitors and those with disabilities.

The game has been devised to resemble the running version of the sport as much as possible. The same scoring system is in operation. There are six tackles in a set. The ball may only be passed backwards. The same offside law is used. Matches last for 80 minutes.

Differences include the wheelchair game being played on an indoor court. Kicks are executed with the fist. The court is less than half the size of an outdoor pitch. Players are strapped into chairs and have a tag upon each shoulder. When one of them is removed by an opponent, a tackle has been made. The play the ball is done by touching the ball on the floor before passing it to a teammate.

There are five players on each team, and at least three must have a physical disability which Phil does. Declan is able bodied.

"The French brought the sport over here and did some demonstrations," Phil said. "Malcolm Kielty, who is still involved at Halifax, brought it up north, and the only clubs were Wigan and Halifax. But it wasn't Wigan Warriors, it was Wigan and District Wheelchair Sports Club. Both clubs trained once a week and got together once a month to play for anything up to four hours with people rotating on and off.

"Things were a little more developed in France, and there was an annual game between the two countries. Things started to progress after the 2008 World Cup. Bury, Bradford Bulls and Mersey Storm started new clubs and by 2011, we very quickly had two leagues of four or five teams. Making it sustainable was the big challenge.

"There were some internationals between Great Britain and France in 2006 and 2007. I didn't play in those, but the first time the RFL got involved properly was in 2008, and that's when it became England. The first international was at Uxbridge against France. The tradition became that it would be played on Wembley weekend on the Friday evening, and then we'd all go to the final on the Saturday."

From humble beginnings, the game's popularity soared during the 2022 World Cup, which culminated in England's triumph over the French in Manchester watched by a peak TV audience of 1.3 million people.

WIGAN fan Phil Roberts was watching an episode of Boots 'n' All in 2007 when something caught his eye. It would change not just the life of the then 36-year-old, but also that of his nine-year-old son Declan. Phil's rugby story is fascinating. "I was a frustrated Rugby League player through school because I was born with dislocated hips," he told me. "I had operations to fix that, and I was walking by the time I went to school. I took part in all the normal activities, but I couldn't run quickly because my hips wouldn't move fast enough for me to sprint. I played rugby for my school, but it was never going to go anywhere. My hips started to get worse in my late teens, but I was still an avid fan, and I started to do some coaching.

"The problem with my hips doesn't bother me that much because I've got used to it. It's not like it was a traumatic injury that changed my life. It's something I've got used to. Things have deteriorated over time, and I'm pretty much a full-time wheelchair user now, although I can shuffle around on crutches indoors.

"I've never really been the victim of intentional discrimination other than some bullying at school because I walked with a significant limp. In terms of indirect discrimination, if you went looking for it, you could find it everywhere whether it's public transport or access to buildings or events, but society has changed a lot in the last ten years.

"In early 2007, I watched an episode of Boots 'n' All with Phil Clarke reporting on some wheelchair Rugby League at Robin Park. Wheelchair rugby was something I'd looked into, but it was Paralympic rugby played with a volleyball. It wasn't rugby in anything other than name. When I watched this programme and realised people were playing Rugby League in wheelchairs just a few miles away from me, I thought I had to give it a go, and that's what happened."

Phil and Declan are lifelong Wigan supporters. "I am," said Phil, "but with a slightly chequered history. My father's family were from Widnes and relatives were involved with the club. My mother's family were all from St Helens and were avid Saints fans. They moved to Wigan because I spent a lot of time in Wrightington Hospital as a child. I can vividly remember going to Central Park with my paper season ticket, queueing on Hilton Street, waiting to see what letter it was before you ripped your little ticket out of the booklet and handing it over. Declan also went to Central Park when he was just a few months old.

"I have many happy memories of being on the popular side by the halfway line. I went to the Wembley finals of the late-80s and the early-90s. I also enjoyed going to places that don't exist anymore like Watersheddings when it was freezing cold. One of my favourite games was the Challenge Cup game against Halifax when Joe Lydon kicked that famous drop goal at the old Thrum Hall stadium. Andy Platt was my favourite player. He was the archetypal professional. Over the course of his career, you could probably count on one hand how many tackles he missed. He played for 80 minutes every week. He was the first of the modern-day middle forwards.

"The atmosphere at Central Park was always electric, but I also used to love going on a Tuesday night when I'd park at the Griffin pub, have a pint with Billy Boston and then go and watch the 'A' team. Andy Farrell and Jason Robinson sometimes turned out as the halfbacks. Graeme West often pulled a shirt on when he was in his early 40s."

"My first stand-out memory is the 2010 Grand Final," said Declan. "It will always stick in my head. In terms of playing, I started at five at St Judes. I played up two years, but then there was a team at Shevington where I only had to play up one year. I played there for a couple of years then moved to Leyland and played there for the better part of 15 years. I started playing Wheelchair in 2013 with Bury's second team."

"When Declan played at Leyland Warriors," said Phil, "I went along as a parent, but I soon got talked into coaching, and I coached his teams from under-8s to open age. This was alongside coaching Wheelchair Rugby League, but I've always liked the variety. You coach the person, not the sport. That's always the message I've wanted to get across.

"On the back of the 2013 World Cup, there was some funding available to start new clubs up. We'd been involved at Leyland Warriors for years. I was on the committee and was coaching two or three different teams. We chatted about a wheelchair team, and that's how it started."

AT the time of publication, Phil Roberts was still playing Wheelchair Rugby League in his 50s and even scored the first try of the World Cup in 2022. Despite having won the competition with England 14 years earlier, he turned out for Ireland who lost the opener 55-32 to Spain.

Having only taken up the game in 2007, Roberts was the England player-coach in the 2008 World Cup. They beat Pacific Islands, Australia and France before beating the hosts again in the final by 44-12.

"It was a little bit surreal to say the least," said Phil. "What helped me significantly was the knowledge of the game in a tactical and technical sense. I just had to pick up the wheelchair side of things. There's no comparison between an everyday wheelchair and a sports chair. I was able to show some promise by being able to read some of the things happening on the court, and that got me onto the periphery of the squad. The first international I played in 2008, there was no expectation I would get on court, but the game was running away from us and with 25 minutes to go, I got shouted on. I must have played reasonably well because I stayed in the team.

"The people involved worked hard to make it a proper occasion. There were national anthems. The sports hall was full, although it wasn't big, so it was probably just a couple of hundred people. It was quite similar in the World Cup in Australia. The game had gone to Australia in about 2004, and obviously they're Rugby League mad, so we generally played in similar-sized venues to Robin Park. It was nothing like the scale of the 2022 World Cup where there were thousands of people at the Copper Box.

"Jack Brown, Martin Norris and Adam Rigby were involved in 2008, and they're still playing as we move into the 2023 season. Jack's younger brother Harry also played. We had a lot of hoops to jump through to get Harry in because he was only 14, but he was an incredible wheelchair athlete, and he's played basketball in several Paralympics now. Paul McCormick played, as did Andy Wharton who also featured in the 2013 World Cup, and Stuey Walker who had suffered a broken neck playing Rugby League in Featherstone. He was a stalwart from the early years in Halifax."

Their triumph in 2008 received scant media attention for which I'm as much to blame as anyone, having been editor of Rugby League World magazine at the time, but Roberts was philosophical about the situation.

"Compared to what we were used to, it seemed like quite a lot," he said. "We landed at Manchester Airport, and Nigel Wood was there, although there were no journalists. But Granada phoned, wanting me on TV that evening. We were all very conscious that what we were doing was new, so we weren't frustrated. We saw ourselves as pioneers, and there has been progression with every World Cup.

"We lost the 2013 World Cup Final 42-40 to France at Medway Park. Losing like that was indescribable, but we played well in that World Cup."

The Wigan team was launched in 2022, with the Robertses having reached the 2021 Grand Final with Leyland Warriors. In 2023, Wigan unveiled a second team. "We play across the road from the stadium at Robin Park Leisure Centre, or we try to when we can," said Declan. "It's a good size, not full size, but not many halls in this country are. We train and play most of the time there. Sometimes we have to go further afield if something else is booked in.

"A lot of people think we're new because Wigan haven't had a team for long, but a lot of us have played together for a long time. We've got some new additions from further afield like Wales and Hereford, but we have the same core team we had at Leyland. It's a nice variety of people coming together. We finished third in 2022, and we're hoping for a Grand Final in 2023."

"In 2022, there was clear distance between the top three - Halifax, Leeds and Wigan - and the rest," Phil added. "We had five players chosen for the World Cup – Declan and Adam Rigby for England, myself for Ireland, Matt Wooloff for USA and Mark Williams for Wales. We also have two female players at the club. We're very fortunate because we're part of Wigan Warriors. The Foundation set up a whole host of training sessions for beginners, and we can dip in and out of it, have a look at people, and ask some to come to our sessions on a Wednesday night. The club is very proactive. When Sean O'Loughlin runs a session on defence, coaches from all the teams attend.

"Our normal training session is once a week. That's the norm across the sport. It's a cost thing as much as anything because hiring the hall at Robin Park is £100 an hour."

Wigan made the news in 2022 when they staged a training session for players from all of their teams. "That was fantastic," said Phil. "That kind of thing has been driven by Matty Peet, and everyone in the senior

leadership at the club is of that mindset now. It wasn't a lip-service thing. It was a genuine investment from the senior leaders. All the groups were mixed, so each group, as we carouselled around the activities, comprised someone from the first team, the Academy, Women's, PDRL, Wheelchair etc."

"It was a pretty surreal experience, having travelled all over the country to watch these people play," said Declan, "and then I'm playing touch against them or doing passing drills with them. They were running rings around me, but it was an enjoyable experience, and it was great to feel part of a big club. You always get that feeling, but that event was overwhelming. To be accepted like that made a big difference to us personally."

THE Rugby League World Cup was due to be played in England in the autumn of 2021, but due to Australian and New Zealand fears over the Covid-19 pandemic, it was postponed for a year. The announcement, which was made in August 2021, was a blow to all the competitors.

"It was annoying because we'd worked so hard for so long," said Declan. "We'd been training since just before the outbreak of Covid. So instead of training, we did a lot of video analysis and created our game plan. We were doing gym sessions on Microsoft Teams and on Zoom from our bedrooms, just trying different things.

"It was frustrating, but the postponement was probably the best thing for us because we were a little bit undercooked at the end of 2021 when we lost a two-Test series to France when the World Cup would have been. That helped us as it made us realise what we needed to do.

"We beat them in the mid-season international in 2022. France didn't send a massively strong squad, but we took it as a chance to execute our game plan and iron out some wrinkles against what was still a strong team.

"Moving on to the World Cup, we played France in the final again. We had the three group games and the semi-final to get us to the right level to beat France. We put ourselves in a good position over the tournament to win the final.

"We knew Australia would be a real threat, but we talked about it being an England v France final. We were confident we'd beat Wales in the semi-final. We had a lot of support staff in the World Cup, so we left the analysis of the other teams to them. We just wanted to enjoy the experience and make the most of a once-in-a-lifetime opportunity.

"With every game televised, we watched them all because we love the sport. We didn't overanalyse, we just sat and enjoyed them. We went into camp at the end of October in Medway and then over to Belgium. We went to Ypres, looking at the battlefields of World War One. Then we came back and went into camp in London, just round the corner from the Copper Box. After the group stages, we came home for a night and then went back to camp in Sheffield for the semi-final and then Manchester for the final. It was four weeks in camp in total."

Phil and Declan came up against each other in the early stages of the World Cup when England thrashed Ireland. "When I stopped being involved with England," explained Phil, "Malcolm Kielty was aware I had Irish heritage through my mother, and he persuaded me to play a couple of games in 2015. That was the end of international rugby for me, or so I thought. I was 45 and I'd had a good innings. I was talking to a couple of the guys involved with Ireland at Christmas 2021 before they were going to be in the World Cup. Norway were originally in the eight, but I told them I was happy to be involved, and they ended up being included in the World Cup."

"So many people asked us about the game," said Declan. "It was just a normal game, but afterwards it was nice to think we'd played against each other in a World Cup game. We were inundated with social-media messages. It's probably never been done before."

"From an Ireland perspective, there was no way we were going to beat England," admitted Phil. "We had players who had come to us from other wheelchair sports whose first actual match was in the opening game against Spain. That's the level we were at. We set ourselves realistic goals like making sure we got to the end of our sets and make England kick on the last tackle. It's not about us or our family. It's that this is a sport where this can happen.

"I'm good friends with Robert Fassolette. When he first sat down to write the rules, it was that everything in Wheelchair Rugby League is divided by three. A court is 40 metres long and 20 metres wide. Because of the speed of the game, and you only have five players on court, if one player is retreating then the gaps are too big. Big scores aren't uncommon, and we just wanted to minimise it. A set of six tackles can take 20 seconds in the wheelchair game, and it's quite feasible to concede three back-to-back tries in five minutes."

England beat France 28-24 in the World Cup Final with a late try by Tom Halliwell breaking the deadlock in the 78th minute when extra-time had been looming. Halliwell was the skipper and was joined in the starting five by Rob Hawkins, Joe Coyd, Sebastien Bechara and Lewis King. Nathan Collins and Jack Brown came off the bench, while Declan Roberts, Wayne Boardman and James Simpson were unused subs.

Was Roberts disappointed not to play in the final? "Not particularly," he said, "I just wanted to be part of a squad that won a World Cup, and that's what happened. I wasn't disappointed. My main feeling was that we won a World Cup. We won it as a squad. The journey over the years and the culmination of work as a group that got us there."

"I was so proud as a parent," said Phil, "living in the same house, and knowing how much he has committed over the last two years to get to that point. I was over the moon."

There are no designated positions in Wheelchair Rugby League, and I was eager to learn how the teams line up, using England as an example. "The closest thing to positions are finishers who naturally gravitate to the wing," said Declan. "Lewis King and Rob Hawkins play on the wings with the other three floating around in the middle. In the middle, you tend to have more dominant players - certainly vocally - who are usually more technically and tactically adept. Nathan Collins is small but does all his work in the middle. People end up everywhere and need to do everything. The speed of the game makes fixed positions impossible. If you've just made a cover tackle on the right edge, you can't get back to the left wing because you'll cut everyone else off and guarantee a try to the opposition."

"I could crash the ball in on tackle one or three," said Phil, "and then in the next set I might do something more akin to a halfback's role. I can then park myself on an edge because I can see an opportunity coming. Experienced Rugby League coaches might get involved in the wheelchair game and struggle unless they adapt their mindset. It's probably more similar to touch in that it's about trying to create three on twos or two on ones."

On the eve of the 2023 season, Declan announced his England retirement. And, no, he doesn't qualify for Ireland. "It just felt like the right time," he said. "I've played internationals for the best part of ten years on and off. I can't commit to the hours anymore. I told the coach I couldn't give him 100%, and somebody else would be able to."

ONE of the big debates after the World Cup centred around the impact able-bodied players were having upon the sport. "I think we've got to be aware of the fact that there's been some very violent collisions," the French coach Sylvain Crismanovich told the Love Rugby League website before the final. "There's an element that we shouldn't be really utilising the same force when we've got disabled athletes taking part. My concern is that tomorrow night, if a disabled person - in particular a paraplegic wheelchair user - comes along, they might say it's not a sport for them given the violence and some of the collisions they will witness. We need to look back at some of the original rules of the game because when the game was founded, it was for disabled athletes, and able-bodied athletes were invited to join in. Now the sport is so popular, there are a lot more able-bodied athletes taking part, and it's obviously impacted on the way the game is played."

"It's an ongoing debate about the level of inclusivity the game is looking to host," said Declan. "Should it be inclusive to everybody or more for those who can play at the higher level? I think France were arguing that there needs to be a basketball-style classification which a lot of people would argue would make the game less inclusive. It's something that will go on for a while as the game moves towards professionalism."

"What makes the game unique is us playing together," said Phil, "someone with a disability and someone without. Internationally, that can't happen in basketball because the way their classification works. So a non-disabled player in basketball counts as five points, and they're not allowed five-point players internationally. There needs to be some kind of system in place to control this.

"There has been a huge influx of players into the game after the World Cup in 2022, but the majority of them are not disabled. We want to get as many included as possible because it's about protecting the inclusivity of the sport. There's a danger that in just having players without distinguishing between those with disabilities and those without, that would drive away the players with disabilities.

"If you have a couple of players with a high-level spinal-cord injury, they'll never compete against a team of players without disabilities. There's a rudimentary classification system in France, and I'm aware the international board has advertised for someone to come onto their steering group for wheelchair rugby. Part of that is about bringing in some kind of system.

"We're at a crossroad. We need to continue to grow the game and make it sustainable. Personally, I think if we go down the route of just having players, we'd start to lose some of the players Monsieur Fassolette would say the game was invented for.

"We've not seen a decline in new players with disabilities, but so many new players are coming along, most of them able-bodied, so we now have a lower percentage who have disabilities. You can have two non-disabled players on court, but if you get 50 new players and five have a disability, then the percentage of disabled players is going to fall, and that's what's happening.

"The French have taken this a lot further, and people in the game know they've been raising this for a while. Compare somebody with a spinal injury to Seb Bechara who is a single, below-the-knee amputee. Even when both players are strapped in a chair, Seb obviously has much more core control, he can turn his chair by throwing his bodyweight, and if he tips out of his chair, he can get up much easier.

"To keep the sport all-inclusive, have non-disabled players still playing, but find the right balance. What we don't want is people with a high level of disability saying, 'I can't play that because it's just non-disabled people flying around.'"

LOOKING ahead, how can Wheelchair Rugby League maximise its potential after the success of the World Cup? Will players be paid for their efforts one day?

"For sustainability reasons, we need to be involved with big clubs," said Declan. "One of the reasons Leyland ended up dissolving was finances because the wheelchairs are so expensive, as are court costs for training and playing.

"The sport has the potential to become professional, but not in the next few years. I don't believe it will be in the next 10 or maybe 20 years. We might be bordering semi-professional in the next ten years, depending on TV-rights deals etc. We would need a much bigger following, but that will be helped by the big clubs getting wheelchair teams. We've had people turn up to watch us who said they had never heard of it until we became Wigan Warriors, and they just want to support Wigan."

"There's evidence to support the positive impact it would have on performance," said Phil. "The nearest thing we've had to a professional wheelchair team is England before the World Cup in 2022. Declan is being quite modest with the level of sacrifice and time commitment involved for England. While they weren't getting paid for what they were doing in the training camps before the World Cup, there were sufficient resources available to enable them to train at a professional level."

"We did a full weekend every month," said Declan. "We had other day sessions and full weeks. There was video analysis, sports science, nutrition, conditioning. Training like that is only sustainable long term if it's your job, but we all have jobs outside the game. I'm an account manager at the Co-op Bank."

"I don't get paid for anything in Rugby League," said Phil." A lot of people think I work for Wigan, but I don't. I work as head of assurance in the safeguarding environment. My chair literally fell apart in a game against Halifax in 2022. I managed to find a chair to fit me and meet my requirements second hand for £2,500. I don't get anything back for that.

"Winning the World Cup was a huge boost," Phil continued. "It's something everyone in the sport is desperately proud of. I don't think anyone inside the game would have expected anything other than an England-France final. We all knew it would be really tight. The evidence to support professionalism is that England overcame a full-strength France team, and that was because of the way England were able to prepare. It shows the heights the game could go to if that sort of backing is there.

"There's definitely an argument to support professionalism as it will improve standards across the board, but we're a long way off that yet. We need to get consistently better with our standards at domestic level. Any team not aligned to a professional club is a hair's breadth away from disappearing."

"One of the problems that's holding us back at the moment is facilities," said Declan. "If you want to put a women's game on telly, you can do so easily, and they're normally part of a double header with a men's game. But with us, there aren't many full-sized courts available in the country - just a handful in the UK. A lot of halls can't accommodate all the TV cameras that are needed. Normally only the finals in the domestic game are televised, and that started in 2021."

"When Sky rock up at the DW Stadium on a Friday night," said Phil, "all the cabling is there, and they just need to plug into it. But at Medway Park, for example, they had loads of technicians running miles of cables all around the venue. They turned up on the Friday to do the game which was on the Sunday, and they were at it for two days. What has been good is various online platforms like The Sportsman and Our League who have had some games on. They can do it with one camera at each end and one on the gantry, whereas Sky really did justice to the 2021 and 2022 Grand Finals by having eight or ten cameras.

"It would be great to get more internationals at the Copper Box. Cost might be prohibitive, but it's a fantastic opportunity, and everyone who played there recognised that having such a large crowd adds to the experience."

The next World Cup is due to be staged in 2025. With Declan having retired, Phil may be the only family representative. He is hopeful it will be a bigger competition than in 2022.

"I'm aware of interest from other European countries, and I wouldn't be surprised if there were 12 countries competing in 2025, maybe even more," he said. "It's really good America came over and won a game which not many people expected because the majority of their players hadn't played before. Australia acquitted themselves well. It's all about ensuring the success is sustainable and the growth is managed. The last thing we need is a huge 2023 on the back of the World Cup and then things slow down. We need to maintain the momentum.

"I don't know if I'll still be playing in 2025. I've been saying for the last four or five seasons that it's time to give way to younger, faster people. We'll see in the next 12 months! I've just become the Ireland head coach, and I'll continue to play for them in 2023, but hopefully I won't need to play in 2025."

SHORTLY after I met Phil and Declan, I went to Robin Park to watch Wigan's opening match of the 2023 season in which they beat reigning champions Halifax, who boasted four World Cup finalists, 59-45. In an enthralling game, Declan was the outstanding player, scoring 25 points, and having a hand in many tries. I couldn't help concluding that it's a shame his international career is over. American international Matt Wooloff scored three. Jack Heggie crossed twice. World Cup winners Martin Norris (2008) and Adam Rigby (2008 and 2022) also had fine matches. Player-coach Phil was an unused sub but later in the day, he played in the second team's match against North Wales Crusaders which they lost 68-54.

Given it was the first game after the World Cup Final, it didn't have quite the crowd I thought it might attract. There were roughly 150 people there, and it was free entry. With the quality on offer, the competitors deserve much more recognition, and the leading players deserve to earn a living through the sport. Whether Wheelchair Rugby League achieves its potential or not is down to the clubs, but more so the governing body, which doesn't have a great track record in maximising the sport's potential. But the players are more than doing their bit.

ANDY PLATT

1988-1994

Andy Platt was one of the best British forwards of the 1980s and 1990s, representing St Helens, Wigan and Great Britain with distinction. He won numerous medals and was man of the match when the 1992 Lions hammered Australia in Melbourne. He later enjoyed stints at Auckland Warriors, Widnes, Salford and Workington, where he was player-coach. He is the brother of Duncan, who played for Widnes, Oldham and Leigh. After his career ended, he moved with his wife to Australia, where they still reside.

If you could relive one day from your career, which would it be?
Saints people will hate me even more, but I'll go for the 27-0 Wembley win in 1989. I'd left St Helens the previous summer, and their coach Alex Murphy really slagged me off, so it was a good feeling.

Who did you support as a youngster?
My dad and grandad were from St Helens, so I used to watch them. I remember Cliff Watson and Tony Karalius. The first team I played for was St Helens YMCA. I played union at West Park Grammar School. A couple of the boys played for the YMCA on Sundays, so I went along, and played there up to under-17s. I played one year with Wigan St Pats under-19s. With Joe Lydon and Mike Gregory, we had a hell of a team, and a heap of us signed pro after one year.

What were your early experiences of Saints?
Billy Benyon was the coach. He's still a good friend. He was old school. I played 27 games in the 1982-83 season which was way beyond what I expected. Saints had Harry Pinner, Neil Holding, Steve Peters, Chris Arkwright and Peter Gorley, so we were starting to get somewhere. My debut was against Leigh in August 1982. My first start was against the great Kangaroo side that went unbeaten. Saints picked a weakened side because they had the Lancashire Cup Final coming up. The Aussies picked their best team and beat us 32-0. I was devastated, but two weeks later they beat Great Britain 40-4, so we hadn't done too bad!

Mal Meninga joined Saints in 1984-85 which was something of a breakthrough season for you. What do you remember of him?
He and Phil Veivers were the two pieces of the jigsaw that were missing. We won the Lancashire Cup and the Premiership Trophy. I'd played against Mal in that tour match in 1982. He was incredible at St Helens. We'd never heard of Phil, but he was very good for us.

You mainly played in the second row for Saints, but also featured at prop and loose forward. Which did you prefer?
I also played a bit of centre in my first year. As I got bigger and stronger - and slower! - I gradually progressed to the front row. I wasn't bothered if I wore ten or three, I just wanted to play. I had good and bad games in each position.

Why did Saints come up short against Halifax at Wembley in 1987?
It was the biggest disappointment of my career. We should have won, but we lost sight of what we were going for. Alex Murphy was coach, but he took us down there on the Monday or Tuesday. We went to Royal Ascot, and here there and everywhere, and there were too many distractions. Halifax strangled us out of the first half. Mark Elia could have won it late on, but we should have had it won by then. It was my first time at Wembley, with nearly 100,000 people there - 70,000 from St Helens – and we felt like we'd let them down. The difference between Saints' preparation in 1987 and what I experienced in 1989 with Graham Lowe was chalk and cheese.

You debuted for Great Britain in 1985 against the French. Perhaps your first notable triumph was beating the Kiwis at Elland Road in 1989. How did you feel when Steve Hampson was sent off after two minutes?
We lost the first Test and then Steve got sent off right at the start of the second. Not the best start! But sometimes it can work with you. We had to tough it out. The sides were very evenly matched. Dean [Bell] was playing for them and many other great players. We went on to win, and then we won the third Test at Wigan. Malcolm [Reilly] was so passionate and instilled something that we hadn't had before.

You were so close to the Aussies in 1990 and 1992. Do you look back at that era with fondness or frustration?
Melbourne is the best memory. It was a great night. With Ellery and Andy Greg missing, Schoey was the captain, and I was vice-captain. I know I was man of the match, but Garry was absolutely magnificent. He had the ball on a string, and his kicks bamboozled them. You could say we were unlucky not to win an Ashes or World Cup, but they were too good for us. The World Cup Final hurt the most when Renouf scored in the corner at the end. If Gary Connolly had been on, Steve wouldn't have scored. There was nothing in the game apart from that. We were also close in 1995 at the end of my international career. I think Australia were really motivated by the Super League War, and they had too much for us in the final.

Back on the club scene, why did you leave Saints for Wigan in 1988?
I came back from the Lions Tour, and I'd been speaking to Maurice Lindsay and Graham Lowe. Saints still had Alex and after Wembley in 1987, I thought I had to leave in order to progress. It wasn't nice, and I regret some of that, but Wigan wanted me, and I wanted to go there. It wasn't amicable. I had to play the game everyone was playing when they wanted a move. I had six of the best years I ever had at Wigan. I rode on the back of a lot of good players and two good coaches.

How would you compare those coaches, Graham Lowe and John Monie?

Lowie was more emotive, although maybe not quite as astute as John. He was a great man manager who got the best out of people. John was ahead of his time, especially in England. He was very savvy and knew what he wanted out of his team. He'd move players on if needed, and he was maybe better tactically than Graham.

You played alongside a galaxy of megastars at Central Park, but can you pick out some of the underrated players?

There were a few, and that was a good thing that both coaches had. They got the best out of players other clubs might not have done. Billy McGinty came from Warrington where he'd been in and out, but he grew another arm and leg at Wigan. He was great for us. Ged Byrne came from Salford. He wasn't a regular, but when he came in, he played out of his skin. The team never suffered when they played, and they would often be the best players.

You and Dean Bell left Wigan nearly a year before Auckland's 1995 debut, in contrast to Denis Betts and Frano Botica. Why was that and why did you miss the Warriors' opening match?

I wasn't really supposed to go to Auckland. I wanted to stay, but [Wigan chairman] Jack Robinson said he couldn't match Auckland's offer, so off I went. I could have done the 1994-95 season at Wigan like Denis and Frano did, but I went early with Dean as we thought it would be better to have a rest from playing and then train the house down. I was flying, as fit as I'd ever been, training with Dean and Tea Ropati. I then went for a routine knee op in November 1994, to sort some floating cartilage, and the fella made a pig's ear of it. I didn't know if I'd play again. The Warriors

sent me to Sydney for a second opinion, and they got me playing again, but I missed a few games. I had the knee replaced a couple of years ago, and it all went back to that messed-up operation.

What were the highlights of your time there?

I enjoyed it, but we were very unlucky in 1995. We missed the play-offs because we lost two points for making one extra substitution when we beat Wests 46-12. The Super League War was a debacle which ruined the competition in 1996, but I was done and dusted by then. The knee and shoulder were no good, and I was just fighting to get through the year. I played in the 1995 World Cup and after that, the Warriors allowed me to sign a short-term deal with Widnes so I could have Christmas at home.

You came home to newly promoted Salford in 1997, and the team had a great year. What went wrong after that?

Joe Lydon wanted me back at Wigan, but only offered a year. I spoke to Andy Greg and with Salford also signing John Cartwright, I gave it a go, and we had a fantastic first year. We played Saints away in the Premiership and were unlucky not to win. In 1998, we endured the agony of that cup semi-final with Sheffield at Headingley, when they scored two late tries. I was off the pitch, but I can't claim it was down to that! Fair play to Sheffield for what they did at Wembley.

Did you fall out with Andy?

I didn't fall out with him, but I thought he lost his way a bit in the second year with some off-field issues. We played six years together at Wigan and we are still friends, but it was disappointing, and he tended to blame others. We've apologised to each other, and we're still friends. He's one of the best players I've ever played with, and he's one of the funniest blokes I've ever met.

Your next stop was Workington where you were player-coach in 1999. Did coaching suit you?

No, it didn't. I never thought I'd coach, but I gave it a shot. Some are made for coaching. I'm probably not. Workington didn't have much money, but we signed a couple of Australians in Evan Cochrane and Mick Jenkins. I told them if a Super League club came in for them, I wouldn't stand in their way. Sure enough, Jenkins went to Gateshead mid-season, and Cochrane fractured his skull at Keighley. We were having a good season, but without them we lost our way. I knew coaching wasn't for me. I didn't enjoy it. I was player-coach which was hard. I didn't see a long-term future, and the club understood. Cumbria is a great part of the world. I played in the Good Friday derby, and it was as intense as some of the Saints v Wigan derbies I played in. They hated each other! It's such a hotbed, and it needs some big investment.

What took you to Australia and are you in touch with any old rugby friends?

I knew I wasn't going to be involved in the game, so my partner and I looked long term and decided our future was going to be in Australia. I live in Townsville and play golf with a lot of ex-players. Neil Holding and I played an off-season at Wests in Brisbane in 1985, and I still see some of them. Andy Goodway lives at Tweed Heads, and I see him when I visit my mother-in-law. He's always at the same coffee shop at the same time because he's so set in his ways!

GEMMA WALSH

2018-2019

One of the all-time greats of the women's game, Gemma Walsh played for over 20 years with Golborne Girls, Hindley Ladies, Wakefield Panthers, Featherstone Rovers, Thatto Heath Crusaders and Wigan Warriors. She moved to St Helens, but due to Covid and injury, she didn't play for them, and announced her retirement in 2021. She debuted for Great Britain in the 2000 World Cup at just 16 and also played in the competition for England in 2008 and 2013.

THE LIST of great Wigan stand-offs is pretty impressive. From George Bennett, Cec Mountford and Dave Bolton several decades ago to Brett Kenny, Shaun Edwards, Frano Botica, Henry Paul, Trent Barrett and George Williams in more recent times, the club has nearly always had a world-class number 6 to open up the meanest of defences. And so, when Wigan entered a team in the brand-new Women's Super League in 2018, it was fitting that the experienced, multi-capped playmaker Gemma Walsh, a lifelong Wigan fan and daughter of former first-teamer David Walsh, should be the stand-off and captain. Sure enough, at the end of the year, she was lifting the Super League trophy after a nail-biting Grand Final victory over Leeds.

"From as early as I can remember, I supported Wigan," Walsh told me. "Like most Wiganers, I learned about Rugby League very early on. I loved the game from being able to walk. My brother Craig played too. I knocked about with him and other kids, and we always had a rugby ball with us. We always watched the Sky games, and my dad wouldn't let us talk! All these years later, being able to sign for them and captain them was a dream come true.

"Craig played for St Judes and Salford Academy, but he left the game. He was a good player, and we used to love watching him play. St Judes are such a family club, and my dad coached the first team for a while as well."

Gemma's father is David Walsh, a goalkicking stand-off or fullback who made his Wigan debut in April 1977 as a substitute in a 23-22 midweek defeat at Bradford, alongside the likes of Green Vigo, Keiron O'Loughlin, Bill Francis and Bill Ashcroft. After helping the team get back into Division One after their 1980 relegation, he left in October 1981. He had two seasons with Huddersfield and a short spell at Blackpool.

Daughter officially followed in father's footsteps in 2018 by pulling on the cherry and white. "There were no contracts or anything, nothing to sign," said Walsh. "I'd actually stopped playing. I'd played for Wakefield Panthers from 2002. They were the team everyone wanted to beat. We went about eight years unbeaten. It then became Featherstone Rovers, and I stopped playing in around 2016. I got to a point where I'd gone a bit stale and wasn't enjoying playing it as much as I used to.

"Then in 2017 there was talk of the Women's Super League starting up, and St Helens approached me first. I'd played for Thatto where Mark Brennan coached me, and he wanted me to play at Saints. This was before Wigan said they would be in the competition, and the minute I found out they were entering a team, it was a no-brainer. I missed the initial trials, but I got in touch with [Wigan coach] Amanda Wilkinson, and it went from there."

The club's first-ever women's match was on 15th April 2018 against Featherstone Rovers. Walsh helped her team to a 54-0 win. In front of nearly 400 spectators, Kate McMullen scored the club's maiden try. Nine further tries were added which included braces for Vanessa Temple, Sarah Harrison, Rachel Thompson and Georgia Wilson. Winger Michelle Davis kicked seven goals.

Walsh scored the first of her eight tries that season in the third game – a 14-all draw at Castleford. She scored four in a 50-0 shellacking of York. The team finished second in the table, a point behind the Rhinos. They entertained St Helens in the semi-final and beat them 10-6. Walsh's then-wife, Emily Rudge, was in the Saints' side, but Walsh was the best player on the field. "Wigan captain Gemma Walsh controlled things," reported Drew Darbyshire in League Express, explaining why he chose her as the fixture's gamestar. "She put in a couple of huge hits, and her kicking game ran the show." Wilkinson was even more complimentary: "Gemma Walsh was a true captain. When it got tough, she did the dirty stuff, and when she needed to calm the ship, she did that too. It was a fine performance from her."

"I loved the first season in 2018," Walsh recalled. "It was one of the most enjoyable seasons playing rugby I had. It was as professional as I'd ever experienced. The club was fantastic, offering us top-quality strength and conditioning, nutrition experts and great facilities. I didn't really expect to do that well because we had players who hadn't played before, but we also had some who had been around for a while - Cumbrians who had played internationally like the hooker Claire Hall and Amanda Sibbald. Our first game was against Featherstone who had recently been the benchmark. They still had international players, and we put 50 on them. I started to think we had a chance."

The final was against Leeds at Manchester's Regional Arena, just hours before the men's side kicked off against Warrington in the men's final at Old Trafford. "We didn't think we were underdogs in the Grand Final against Leeds," said Walsh. "We'd played them three times in league and cup, and it was two-one to them before the final. They beat us in the Challenge Cup semi-final, but we had beaten them at the South Leeds Stadium, and I kicked a last-minute drop goal to win. We certainly knew we could beat them. A lot of people had written us off within the game. That's what it felt like because they were on for the treble.

"It was a difficult week for me. Courtney Winfield-Hill and I did the press work at Old Trafford on the Monday - Wigan were also playing Warrington in the men's Grand Final. I felt poorly, went to bed and didn't get up till Thursday. I had hand, foot and mouth. It was like flu. I had blisters all over my mouth and tongue. I was on soup and milkshakes. I couldn't train and then got up on the Saturday to play the final."

The illness didn't seem to affect Walsh too much as she had a hand in all of Wigan's four tries. After an early Leeds try, she set up two tries for centre Rachel Thompson, as

Wigan led 8-6 at the break. Six minutes into the second half, Walsh found fullback Rebecca Greenfield who put Georgia Wilson in at the corner. The skipper then combined with hooker Claire Hall to create Thompson's hat-trick try to open up a 16-6 lead, but two Leeds tries levelled the scores at 16-all. With a minute to go, substitute Charlotte Foley stepped up to kick Wigan's first goal of the afternoon - the penalty goal that secured the inaugural Women's Super League title.

"I couldn't celebrate afterwards, but adrenaline got me through the game," Walsh recalled. "We went to Old Trafford after the game and walked around the pitch at half-time of the men's Grand Final, but I felt so rough that as soon as we were off the pitch, I had to get a lift home. It turned into shingles, and I couldn't go on the end-of-season trip to Dublin.

"We had some great players. Claire and Amanda didn't sign straightaway. They came in two or three games into the season. Claire was a hooker so was a massive part of what we were going to do. Amanda was an unreal second-rower. Rachel Thompson was excellent in 2018 and scored a hat-trick in the Grand Final. Joanie Aspin played prop and had played for a long time at Hillside in Rochdale. Scrum-half Sarah Harrison was another local girl from St Pats. Georgia Wilson was a centre then. It was her first season in the game, and she's gone from strength to strength.

"When I first came into Rugby League, I had a lot more pace about me than in 2018. My pace had gone by then. I used my knowledge to control the team. I could step back, scan what was going on and inject myself into the game. I'd like to think my experience helped the other girls. I could control a team without having to do the hard graft down the middle like the forwards. I made my Great Britain debut as a centre. I even played a bit of fullback. I played 13 at Wakefield. If I was 20 years younger, I'd love to be a 13 now, as they have more of the ball. I eventually moved into the halves."

But as defending champions, Wigan endured a torrid 2019, precipitating Walsh's departure. "We declined a bit in 2019," she said. "I felt a bit deflated because the club had been great in 2018, throwing everything at us that we needed. In 2019, we had no strength and conditioning coach. The men's Under-19s were running into our gym or field slots. We weren't as much as a priority as we had been in that first year. Amanda left halfway through the season. I felt a bit let down. There seemed to be a shift in the club's thinking. It felt like the women weren't as important as in 2018. It wasn't a nice way for me to end my time at Wigan.

"I signed for Saints at the end of the 2019 season. I'd picked up some injuries. Emily and I weren't seeing a lot of each other due to us being at different teams. I thought being at Saints would have been a nice way to end my career, but then Covid hit. Had it not done so, I would have played that 2020 season at Saints. Training was going well, but having a whole year without playing, my body struggled to get back up to the required intensity - Saints had such a good squad with so many England players. I hit a point when I realised my body wasn't going to get up to the standards needed. I picked up an injury in training, and I decided that was it. My body was in bits. I didn't want to play in that 2021 season and not do myself justice."

THE tributes flooded in when Walsh retired. After all, she had played internationally for 13 years, **captaining Great Britain and England along the way. She hadn't started playing Rugby League until she was 15 due to a lack of girls' teams. "I played for Golborne Girls Under-16s, and we just played a few friendlies," she said. "When I turned 16, I signed for Hindley Ladies. I had a season there and then signed for Wakefield Panthers, who are now Featherstone Rovers. Brenda Dobek was the player-coach, and she was a massive influence on me making that move. She is one of the best players I ever played with. I did one year of travelling, which involved my dad taking me to the train station, then getting two trains and a lift at the other end. I'd train twice a week, so it took its toll. I moved over for my next season, so I could commit properly.**

"Only Hindley and Hillside on this side of the Pennines had a team. I wanted to play for Great Britain, and with Wakefield and Bradford Thunderbirds the best teams at the time, it felt right to move on."

Walsh realised her international dreams at just 16, playing in the 2000 World Cup against Australia and New Zealand. Great Britain & Ireland, as the team was known, beat Australia twice to make the final but lost 26-4 to New Zealand at Wilderspool. Wearing number 21, Walsh was a substitute. Lining up for the home team that day were Brenda Dobek, Lisa McIntosh and Sally Milburn, the three inaugural inductees into the Women's Hall of Fame in 2022, an exclusive club that Walsh may well join one day.

"At the time, it was quite daunting," said Walsh. "I'd only had a few games in open age, so to earn a place in the squad and play against players I'd heard a lot about, was very exciting. I had a bit of cockiness about me and probably didn't realise how big an occasion it was."

Walsh then toured Australia in 2002 with Great Britain, who lost the three-match series by two games to one. Still a teenager, she captained the side in midweek wins over Queensland and Canberra and remembers only too well the sacrifices that had to be made as an amateur player.

"There was a lot of begging and pleading to get time off!" she said. "I had understanding bosses at the time, and they knew it meant a lot to me. We had to raise £1,000 each just to get on the plane. There was no support from the governing body. My club helped. We did bag packing in supermarkets, bucket collections at grounds like Castleford, and my dad had a few contacts who could sponsor me personally.

"I went into the tour with a knee injury. It didn't affect me all the time, but after one of the regional games, a local physio told me I'd snapped my ACL and I'd been playing without realising. The coach Jackie Sheldon thought it was wise to leave me out of the last two Tests. I only had my ACL operated on in 2009, so I played for six years with no ACL. I just strengthened the hamstring and quad muscles around it, and had an intense programme to make sure I got through the 2008 World Cup."

Walsh was the England captain in that World Cup which took place in Australia in November, just as their summer was beginning. The highlight of her trip was a hat-trick against France in a 54-4 win in Kawana on the Sunshine Coast.

"It was really tough," remembered Walsh. "The schedule was ridiculous - five games in eight days - and the cunning Australians scheduled our games in the midday sun! My mum and dad came out to support us, which was great. The games against New Zealand and Australia were so close, but silly little decisions let us down. It's still one of my biggest regrets that we didn't go all the way, and we

probably got even closer in the 2013 World Cup."

Despite the high profile of the Women's World Cup in the autumn of 2022, Walsh feels that it was in 2013 that England had the best chance of winning the World Cup. "My international career went from 2000 to 2013," she said. "I believed we had the best international squad I ever played with in 2013. The calibre of players across the squad was very good. A few decisions went against us, but I thought that was our chance to win the World Cup. I felt if we couldn't do it then, the game in Australia was growing massively and they would probably move to far away from us. I felt personally I'd rather retire then than go on."

Walsh is still a keen Rugby League supporter, and although she is concerned about an overemphasis on strength and conditioning rather than rugby skills, she believes the women's game is heading in the right direction. "With the introduction of Super League and RFL backing, the game has progressed massively," she said. "It's also moved forward at grassroots, with girls playing in schools and with junior clubs. On the field, things are different now in terms of style. There's more emphasis on strength and conditioning and nutrition, and there is now access to physios etc. At Wakefield, we just turned up, trained and played.

"I played with some exceptionally talented players in terms of skill levels and having a rugby brain, but now it's more a case of looking at athletes and turning them into rugby players. That's just my opinion, and others may disagree. I played with some of the best and I played against Australia and New Zealand in Tests. There was less emphasis on strength and conditioning back then, and more on the rugby itself.

"The top teams play a similar style to the men. The game plan isn't far away. There's a lot of emphasis on looking at what men are doing and implementing that into the women's game. And of course, male coaches will draw on their experiences as players.

"Since the creation of the Women's Super League, the game is moving in the right direction, but I still feel the English game is lacking the quality and support that the Australian and New Zealand players have. Women players in Australia are semi-professional and are contracted to the clubs. Over here, it's more of a struggle.

"The women just love playing the game. There are full-time workers, students and mothers playing the game. People who watch it are very positive. You'll always get comparisons with the men's game and there's sometimes a negative comment on social media. Garry Schofield tweeted about the standard of the 2019 Grand Final and got some backlash. What perhaps he didn't realise was that a lot of the players had worked a nightshift and then got on the bus to play in the game. If people come down and watch the game, they will generally like it."

FRANO BOTICA

1990-1995

One of the great goalkickers in the history of the game, the metronomic Frano Botica became the fastest player to score 1000 points as his 93 matches were 11 fewer than the great Lewis Jones had managed. A rugby union All Black, Botica initially played on the wing for Wigan and scored a try in every Challenge Cup round in 1991, the same year he made his debut for the Kiwis. He graduated to stand-off, forming a devastating halfback partnership with Shaun Edwards. He also played for Auckland Warriors and Castleford.

When did Wigan first approach you and how tough a decision was it to switch codes?
I was on an All Black tour of England and got a phone call from the Wigan chairman and met them in a KFC. It's not something the players discussed, but John Gallagher, Matthew Ridge and John Schuster all signed at a similar time. We'd all kept it a secret. I thought it would just be me, but I was the third to announce it in one weekend, so it took the heat off. It was a reasonably easy decision to make because we'd just had our second child and I was a courier driver, working 12 hours a day. I'd go for runs at lunch and then straight to training after work.

When did you realise Wigan coach John Monie hadn't wanted you?
I think I might have read it in the paper when I got there. He didn't sign me, Jack Robinson did. I was driving into Wigan and there were signs outside shops saying that Monie didn't like me. It hardly filled me with confidence! At my first training session in the gym, I came last in everything. So, not only did he not like me, he then discovered I was the weakest in the team!

How tough was the transition?
It wasn't as hard as I thought it might be and the main reason was I started on the wing, so I didn't do as much thinking or controlling as I would have done at stand-off. If I'd been thrown straight in at stand-off, it would have been a lot tougher. But we had Andy Gregory and Shaun Edwards, so I had no chance.

You were one of the great goalkickers. Is it true you weren't such a specialist before you switched codes?
I was a goalkicker in union, but not a very good one, and that's why I sat on the bench for the All Blacks. I decided I couldn't be as good as Grant Fox. When I got into League, I understood I was in trouble. I needed to make myself indispensable. I knew it would take time to develop my game in League, but I could see they didn't have a good goalkicker, so I focused on that. It was a mind shift, but it only took a few minutes to work it out. I decided to study videos of Grant Fox kicking and I tweaked a few things. There's no point in practising endlessly if you're not doing it right. When I got the technique right, it was then a case of practice, practice, practice. My two boys are good goalkickers because they've practiced.

Were you a target for rough play in your early days?
It's like anything in those days. There were fewer video cameras around! Plenty went on. I never wore a mouth guard because they made me choke, so I learned to duck and put my elbow up.

Your five seasons at Wigan yielded five league titles and five Challenge Cups. In hindsight, was their domination good or bad for the game?
I think it was a great thing. Some teams gave us a good run for our money, but it lifted standards and made other clubs more professional. It drove the other clubs. They had to change what they did. It took time, but other teams did eventually catch up and now you have a strong competition.

You scored all of Wigan's points on your debut, in a 24-8 defeat to Widnes in the Charity Shield. Every Widnes point came from union converts too. What do you remember of it?
It was pissing down with rain – I remember that! It was good to see union boys doing well because there was a school of thought that we were soft.

Wigan had to play their final eight league matches in 18 days in 1991. How did you cope?
I broke my scaphoid and had to play through those last eight games. The doctor said it wouldn't get any worse, so they strapped it up and told me to play on. That's just what you did back then. It was the same attitude with head injuries – they just gave you some smelling salts.

You scored tries in every Challenge Cup game in that first year.
Both of us wingers had outstanding centres, who did a fantastic job in creating - Kevin Iro and Dean Bell. Dean was the League equivalent to Wayne Shelford, the All Blacks captain. He was a massive figure in the game.

Less than a year after switching codes, you were called up to the Kiwi side and played in a 24-8 win over Australia in Melbourne.
It's always tough. You don't want to let your country down. The win over Australia was tough. They were the kings of Rugby League. Every now and then, New Zealand would be ok, but not all the time. Those sorts of games are a blur. But we knew they would come back at us and that's what happened.

Which of Wigan's Wembley finals brought you the most pleasure?
The games were fantastic and kicking goals at Wembley was amazing. But my fondest memories are of walking around with the trophy with my kids on my shoulders. They can still remember that, even though they were pretty young. They love looking at the photos and seeing how small their kits were!

We know all about the Wigan stars you played alongside. Which players did you think were

particularly underrated?

They were all superstars! When I first came into the team, I was the only non-international.

OK, who were the best?

I've already mentioned Dean and Kevin. The problem with Kevin was he was so good, he didn't try as hard as he could have. He could have been an absolute legend. Gene Miles was another amazing centre. Then there was Andy Farrell, who came in as a young fella and just got better with every game. He became a magnificent player.

You were still a Wigan player when you turned out for the Auckland Warriors. How did that part of your career pan out?

I'd gone to play for the Warriors during the English off-season, which was a common thing back then. While I was in New Zealand, I was negotiating a new deal with Wigan. We agreed a deal one Friday, and it was due to be signed on the Monday. But I broke my leg playing for the Warriors on the Sunday and then Wigan weren't interested anymore. Mark Geyer smashed me. It wasn't dirty, I just went back to collect the ball. I went to step him, my foot slipped and as he went to smash me, my foot got stuck in the ground and I broke a bone in my shin.

What was the highlight of your time at Castleford? I remember you playing well in a 26-23 win over Bradford.

I enjoyed playing for Castleford. They were the only ones who said they'd have me with a broken leg. It was a while before I could play after signing for them. There was no other choice, but I was glad they wanted me. I still lived in Wigan, but everyone made me feel welcome. It was a little tougher with the travelling. The crowd were really good to me which helped. My main goal was to get better again and to stick it to the doubters who thought I'd be finished. As for games, my memory isn't good enough – too many brain cells have been killed over the years!

How tough was it being at a club that didn't win everything?

It was strange - certainly a challenge. We had to work so much harder because we didn't have the superstars. I remember playing Wigan and so badly wanting to win. We were ahead late on, but they got a late penalty and Andy Farrell kicked it.

What were your thoughts on summer rugby?

I was 100% in favour, for sure. I still have memories of playing Oldham at Watersheddings with the sleety rain. I had a wet-suit top on underneath and still got hypothermia. I was shaking and thinking, "Why are we playing in this miserable weather?" I thought summer rugby was fantastic in England.

Have you had any connection with Rugby League since your Cas days ended in 1996?

Not really. As rugby union went professional, I decided I'd go back. My body was getting smacked and rugby union was easier on the body. The money was better as well, but I'd have gone even if it wasn't.

Do you still watch Rugby League?

I watch the New Zealand Warriors and I watch Wigan every now and again, but there's so much rugby of both codes on that you can't watch it all. There are five or six games a day if you want to watch everything.

Are you still in touch with old teammates from over here?

I bump into Dean Bell sometimes. He organises events for ex-Kiwis. I try and speak to Shaun Edwards and Andy Farrell when they're in New Zealand with rugby union. I stayed with Joe Lydon when I went to Europe last Christmas. I spoke to Inga last week [in 2019], but he lives in Samoa now, so I don't see much of him. I'd like to speak to more, but I'm pretty useless on Facebook!

FRANK PARR

1961-1972

Frank Parr was the Wigan scrum-half in the 1965, 1966 and 1970 Challenge Cup Finals, earning a winner's medal first time after a 20-16 victory over Hunslet. A Leigh lad, he played for 11 years at Wigan, clocking up 309 appearances and scoring 95 tries. Parr also helped Wigan to a Lancashire Cup, a league leaders' trophy and two Lancashire League Championships.

CHRISTENED Frankie by the fans, scrum-half Frank Parr was a firm favourite at Central Park in the 1960s. He didn't have an easy time at Wigan, having to see off competition from several other halfbacks, and he was treated poorly when he left, but Parr was a great player and a key cog in the team that triumphed at Wembley in 1965.

Parr hailed from Leigh and played at school with Colin Tyrer and Georgie Fame, the jazz musician who had three number-one hits in the 1960s. "Georgie's real name is Clive Powell," said Parr. "He lived a couple of streets away, and we used to deliver newspapers together. We played rugby with Colin at Windermere Road School. Colin was originally a scrum half. Tommy Sale was a teacher at my school, and he encouraged me.

"We knew Clive was likely to become famous. He was always musical. He was about 16 when his career began, and he moved to London. He used to come up and see us when he became famous. We'd be sat in the rugby club on a Saturday night, and he'd just turn up out of the blue, usually when he was fed up with London. You can take the lad out of the north, but you can't take the north out of the lad!

"I played for an amateur team called Leigh Spinners. They'd just started up when I left school. They were attached to a pub, the Spinners Arms. It was on Firs Lane, just around the corner from my house."

It wasn't long before Wigan came calling, and they beat Leigh to Parr's signature. "I was 15 when Wigan found out about me," said Parr, "but they couldn't sign me at that age. They asked a coach how old I was. He wouldn't tell them because he wanted to know why they wanted to know.

"Wigan came to my house a week before my 16th birthday. I'd just finished training, and I had my cherry and white shirt on. Two directors took my dad for a drink at the local. They left me at home! They came back the night before my 16th birthday. They got me up at a minute past midnight to sign the forms because they knew Leigh were after me.

"Someone had given Leigh the wrong birthdate, so they turned up a week later, but I always wanted Wigan. I signed in November 1959. I started in the 'B' Team where the trainer was Johnny Lawrenson who had played for Wigan, Workington and Great Britain. Then I moved into the 'A' Team. My first-team debut was at Salford in 1961. Eric Clay, the referee, penalised me three times for feeding the scrum. He called the captain over to say I'd be sent off if I did it again. I got moved to stand-off, and I scored a try from there.

"It was such a great side to come into. Fantastic players like Billy Boston, Brian McTigue, Frank Carlton and Bill Sayer played that day. There were other greats at the club like Fred Griffiths, Mick Sullivan, David Bolton and Eric Ashton. I used to be friends with Danny Gardiner and Stan McLeod. I was friends with Ray Ashby, and I still am."

Parr didn't hesitate when asked to name the best scrum-halves. He only named one, and it's not hard to guess who it is. Alex Murphy was arguably the best player in the world at various times in his illustrious career. "I liked him, and I admired him," said Parr. "I always held my own against him. He once listed me in his top-ten opponents. He couldn't come to my testimonial, but he sent a nice message, saying how good a player he thought I was. I was never intimidated by how good he was. I had a job to do, and I did it. In fact, one of my best memories involves a game against Saints in March 1965. I had a heavy cold, so someone in the dressing room gave me a drink of sherry before the game. It must have agreed with me because I scored two tries and had a great game against Alex!"

With competition from Murphy, Tommy Smales, Tommy Bishop and Keith Hepworth, Parr didn't win any Test caps. His representative record was two games for Lancashire in the 1965-66 season which yielded defeats against Cumberland and Yorkshire. Later that season he was told he had missed out by one vote for a place on the Lions Tour of the southern hemisphere. Carl Dooler of Featherstone Rovers went instead.

Parr also faced considerable competition for the scrum-half jersey at Wigan. Terry Entwhistle was the incumbent when he was breaking into the team. Brian Shillinglaw and Frank Pitchford also vied for the jersey. "I kept having to drop to the 'A' Team when a new player came in, then I'd fight my way back into the first team. It annoyed me at times. Terry Entwhistle went to Leigh, and we both got sent off for fighting when we played against each other. The game was at Leigh, so Terry was cheered off and I was booed off because it was my hometown!

"I played with some good stand-offs at Wigan too. I didn't play much with Dave Bolton because he left in 1964, but he was very good. Cliff Hill was exceptional as well."

PARR stood at just 5ft 5in, but claimed his height wasn't a hindrance. "It never bothered me," he laughed. "Players would swing their arms and I'd duck under them! When they had the ball, I could grab their arm and trip them up. We played Wakefield one day, and they had a big forward called Jack Wilkinson. He picked me up and drove me into the ground. Boston told him it was out of order and threatened him, so he went to acting-half for the rest of the game to keep out of Billy's way!"

The best day of Parr's career was, of course, the Challenge Cup Final in 1965 when Wigan beat Hunslet 20-16. South African winger Trevor Lake scored two tries. Ray Ashby, the Wigan fullback, was a joint recipient of the Lance Todd Trophy, along with the Hunslet stand-off, Brian Gabbitas.

"It was the best day of my career, bar none," Parr stated.

"But I don't actually remember any of the game. It passed me by a bit. I didn't even remember hearing any noise. You just blank it out. You go up the tunnel and you hear the shouts, but the noise is shut out when the whistle goes. I remember meeting Princess Alexandra and Harold Wilson, but that's about it. I do remember the evening celebrations though. Someone put me on the drinks trolley done up like a baby, and Martin Ryan, one of the directors, pushed me around!"

Parr was the only player to start in the 1965, 1966 and 1970 Challenge Cup Finals, although he had to accept defeat in the latter two, courtesy of a couple of controversies. "1966 was when we had no hooker," he remembered with a grimace. "Clarkey got suspended and we had no back-up, so Murphy kept straying offside, knowing a scrum would follow the kick to touch, and they'd win them all. They changed the rules after he did that.

"And then in 1970, Castleford's Keith Hepworth took out Colin Tyrer with a terrible challenge. He hit him with his fist then his elbow. He should have been the first person to be sent off at Wembley. It was upsetting for us all, and it made a right mess of Colin. He didn't want to come down in the evening, but I went to get him, and he had a drink through a straw. It was horrendous."

After 95 tries for Wigan in 309 appearances, Parr left Wigan and retired from the game, but the story of his departure doesn't paint the club in the best light. "I was named substitute for an away game at St Helens," Parr explained. "I worked for Ashton Coal Company. Our coach Eric Ashton told us afterwards he wanted to pick the same team for the next game which was on the Monday. I told

Eric I may not be able to get the time off. Two directors came down. I told them about my work situation. I suggested they ring the company at 8 o'clock on the Monday morning. If my company said I could play, then I could get home and catch the coach. But the directors didn't want to call them.

"My mother-in-law then saw the Daily Mail. The journalist Brian Batty had written that Eric had said I'd refused to play out of sour grapes because I was only a sub. I spoke to Eric, and he denied saying that, so my wife wrote to Brian Batty to complain. He wrote back to say Eric had said it, and that he'd said it in front of two directors. He also said he'd been told about a new signing, and that he'd be revealing it in the paper soon. Sure enough, Brian wrote a couple of days later that Wigan were signing Eddie Cunningham. When the club signed Eddie, we knew Eric had spoken to Brian.

"The club also signed Jimmy Nulty, a scrum-half. Jimmy came over to me one night after a few drinks and asked if he could sit with me. He asked me advice about playing and then said, 'Eric has signed me, and he's told me as long as he's the coach, I'll be in the first team.'

"I'd spent most of my Wigan career fighting people off, so it was disappointing to be treated like this. Barrow enquired about me, but a Wigan director told them I couldn't drive, which wasn't true - I could!

"When Eric left, I went back under Graham Starkey, who coached Wigan in the 1973-74 season, but it wasn't worthwhile. I have no problem with the club, it was just certain individuals at the time. I'm nearly 80 and I still go to home games now."

Frank Parr sits to the right of the Challenge Cup trophy in a 1965 Wigan team picture

GENE MILES

1991-1992

One of the great attacking centres of the last half century, Gene Miles was a major force in some of the best teams the sport has ever seen - the Queenslanders that dominated State of Origin in the 1980s, the undefeated 1986 Kangaroos when he kept Mal Meninga out of the side, and Wigan who, in 1991-92, swept all before them. Miles was one of the original Brisbane Broncos in 1988 and succeeded Wally Lewis as captain in 1990.

If you could relive one day from your career, which would it be?
I won grand finals with Wynnum Manly in the Brisbane competition, and I'd say 1986 was the stand-out, when we beat Brisbane Brothers. Wally had just taken over as captain-coach, and we had quite a bit of turmoil leading into that year with the previous coach being moved on. We had a young side, so to come out with the Premiership was very satisfying.

Why were Queensland so successful in the early days of Origin?
Right through the '80s, we had a team that had played so much football together in Brisbane and a lot of us were of a similar age. We didn't have a lot of stock to pick from, so the selectors stayed loyal, and we got some great combinations happening. We had great coaches like Artie and Wayne, and we played above ourselves. We played against superstars, but if you tackle them around the legs, they still fall over.

Can you pick one highlight of your Origin career?
I played in seven series, winning six, but I'm going to choose the one I lost as the highlight. We got whitewashed in 1986 but, looking back, it was the most competitive series I played in and there was never more than a converted try in each game. The Kangaroo Tour was largely made up of players from that series and it set me up for a great year with the grand final and that tour.

You didn't make the Test team in 1982, but what are your memories of that Kangaroos Tour?
I'd only been in Brisbane for two years, having moved from Townsville, so it was a great honour to be selected, but I knew I was going to be playing the midweek games because of Mal Meninga and Steve Rogers. There were 27 other guys, and the friendships made on that tour have stayed with me for life.

When you're a squad member, do you watch the Tests hoping for things not to go so well so you might get a crack?
Yeah obviously there might be a bit of that sometimes, but on that particular tour we were just marvelling at what the team was doing. They played some super football, but the camaraderie ensured we all had a role to play on match day.

What do you remember of playing for Oceania against Europe in France in 1984, a game you won 54-4?
I was proud to be involved and Wally, Mal and I often talk about it. We had Kiwis, Papua New Guineans and Aussies and we were up against Great Britain and France players. We had a great week, starting with a bonding session in Sydney. The Papua New Guinea lads loved it - they were starry eyed sitting on a plane with Wally and Mal! It was strange playing in Paris. There was no grass on the field. It was like a cow paddock, so not many of us wanted to hit the deck, and because of that, there were some unbelievable ball skills on show.

You toured again in 1986 and this time kept Mal Meninga out of the team.
We'd played a series with the Kiwis a couple of months before the tour and when we got to England, we played three club games before the Tests, so we had the miles in our legs for the Tests. Old Trafford hosted the first Test and I scored three tries. We had a handy lead, but the Brits fought back. The crowd was sensational, but they still applauded when we scored some great tries.

Were you lucky to win the third Test? There were rumours some of your team were the worse for wear. Was that true?
We certainly weren't the worse for wear, we wouldn't be so disrespectful, but mentally perhaps we just thought we could turn up and win again, but Great Britain were excellent. That was the most competitive Test we had. We were very lucky. Wally produced something special when he scored the try that clinched the match late in the game.

You mentioned the Kiwis. Did you come up against Olsen Filipaina much?
No, thank God! He always gave Wally such a tough test, but I was injured for 1985 and missed a very controversial tour which, in hindsight, was no bad thing.

You were one of the inaugural Broncos in 1988. What do you remember of the build-up and the first match?
There was so much happening in 1988 over here, and the build-up that the Broncos had was huge. We all came from different backgrounds in terms of the Winfield Cup, and it didn't sit well that the best players would be taken from the local competition. We had a squad of about 30 players, and they came from all over Queensland with a few from Sydney that Wayne picked up. We never started training as early as we did with the Broncos because going into the Sydney comp, as it was known then, was a step up. Manly were our first opponents and they were the 1987 Premiers. We couldn't have had a tougher start. I don't think we sold it out which was very strange because it was basically our Origin side that trotted out that day. We hammered Manly. Wally and Alf had great games, and Terry Matterson kicked a record amount of goals. We hit the ground running and won our next five games.

What happened when Wally was sacked as captain?
That was fun - not! Wayne was going to move Wally on as captain because he wasn't getting from him what he thought he could. Wally probably wasn't mixing with the

younger brigade of the team. He had a couple of injuries too. Wayne asked me to take the captaincy and I had to think about it because of my relationship with Wally. I figured if I accepted it, he'll accept it because it wouldn't be going to someone like Kevvie Walters or Alfie Langer who he might have thought hadn't quite earned it at that point. But I was totally wrong. He thought I shouldn't have accepted it. We're still great mates today, but we had a couple of rocky years. The players got behind me in 1990 and we tied for the Minor Premiership. I stayed at the Broncos for one more year and Wally went to the Seagulls.

Did Wigan approach you in the 1980s?
Maurice Lindsay was extremely keen to get me over there on a number of occasions, in particular after we toured in 1986. He'd had Brett Kenny and Greg Dowling, and they talked about what a great club it was. Maurice was the Great Britain manager, so it seemed like I had constant contact with him.
When I did eventually sign in 1992, Maurice was instrumental in getting me there. I remember him saying he wanted to see me run out at Wembley and I was so proud when I did that. I owe so much to him. When we arrived, we stayed at his house. Not with him - he moved out so we could move in! He moved heaven and earth to make us feel comfortable. Whatever he said, he did. We didn't want for anything. My son was born in England, and he even helped with things like baby seats.

How would you compare the Wigan team of 1991-92 to the best teams you played for in Australia?
They were unbelievable! That team would have been competitive in any competition. It was basically the Great Britain team and when they toured a few months later, they had a lot of Wigan players. They had so much depth and brilliance. We could have a couple of injuries and replace a quality player with another quality player.

Is Martin Offiah the best winger you've ever seen?
Yes, probably. All you had to do was put him in a gap and then turn around and wait for the kick-off. I remember refs trying to chase him down and they would give up too. I've never seen anyone go from zero to whatever speed he got to so quickly. He scored ten against Leeds in one semi-

final and five against Bradford in another. We also won the World Sevens in the rain in Sydney, and he left everyone in his wake in that too.

You were the Maroons chairman of selectors when Allan Langer was recalled to the side in 2001. How did it happen?
We'd just been beaten heavily in the second game and as we were leaving on the bus, Wayne leaned over and said, "What do you think about getting Alf back?" I agreed straight away. We spoke to powers to be, and we got to work on it straight away. We kept it under the radar and got the plans in place. It was a stroke of genius, and of course Alfie was magnificent. No one thought in their wildest dreams he could play that well. To go from Warrington to the level required at Origin was fantastic, and it wrapped up the series for us.

Tell us about FOGS and the Artie Academy that you are involved in.
FOGS stands for former Origin greats. Every player to have played Origin footy is a FOG. Every player has a number from one (Artie Beetson) to 221 (Tom Flegler). I'm number 28.
We're hands on with the Queensland team, the managers etc and supporting the team. The Artie side of that is using the profile of the FOGS to do government-funded programmes in schools with indigenous kids - better educated.
Arthur was a great man, and it was an honour to be coached by him and to name the Artie Academy after him. He was stoked to have his name used because he was passionate in helping his people. I made my debut for Queensland with Arthur in 1981 in the Interstate series. He coached me from 1982 in Origin. It's ten years since we lost him. I was a huge fan of his and just being on the bus to training was so much fun. All you wanted to do was play for him.

You told your daughter not to date a footballer, yet she married Corey Oates.
Ha - yes, that is absolutely true! I know footballers and there are a few rogues among us, so I wasn't keen on a footballer being brought home with her. Corey and I get on very well, but he knows the rules!

SHAUN WANE

1982-1990
2012-2018 (coach)

Shaun Wane signed for Wigan as a 17-year-old in 1981 and made his debut the following January. He remained at the club until the summer of 1990, in which time he won a league championship, three Regal Trophies, a Premiership, two Lancashire Cups, two Charity Shields and a World Club Challenge, the latter - against Manly in 1987 - being his finest moment in the cherry and white. After playing with Leeds and Workington, he returned to Wigan to work his way up the coaching ladder. He took over as head coach in 2012 and won three Super League titles in seven seasons. He coached England at the World Cup in 2022 and, all being well, will coach them again in the 2025 tournament.

EIGHT and a half years as the cornerstone of Wigan's pack and seven seasons as head coach, few can claim that they have given more to the club than Shaun Wane. As he played for and coached the club, I thought an obvious place to start the interview would be to ask how Wane the coach would have viewed Wane the player.

"I'd be pissed off with him," he said. "He could do more. He could play more, get more caps, play more games. On the plus side, I turned up on time with the right kit, but I stuck my head in places I shouldn't have, and I played a lot when I was injured. I had injections to play when I shouldn't have done, and I wouldn't tell a physio I was injured."

Wane was an old-school forward. As an all-action loose forward, he was one of the best players in the country as a youngster. He played most of his senior career in the front row, including twice for Great Britain. Both games were against France, and Wane failed to sample victory.

He was booted out of Wigan by John Monie and went to Leeds. "I first played against Shaun when Yorkshire and Lancashire Under-12s played each other," said Garry Schofield. "Waney was the best player in the country from 12 to 16. He could do literally anything as a loose forward. He even kicked goals, toe-ended, for fun. When he came to Leeds in 1990, he was brilliant. We signed a few players from Wigan, some of whom didn't bring their form with him. But Shaun did. He was fantastic for us."

In the summer of 1993, Wane signed for Workington Town where he would link up again with Ged Byrne. The Cumbrians got promoted to Division One at the end of the season, but Wane only played eight games, having ended his career in the November with a knee injury, but he did enough in that short stint to make an enduring impression on at least one of his teammates.

"We were playing title rivals Dewsbury," said Tony Kay, who had a spell at St Helens in the late-1980s. "Having studied footage, our coach Peter Walsh announced that Les Holliday was the only player they have, and if we stop him, we win the game. He'd previously identified Mike Kuiti for Rochdale in much the same way, and that worked. At training, we lined up as a team against Walshy, who still fancied himself as a halfback, along with a few second graders and most importantly, his secret weapon Buck Armstrong masquerading, of course, as Les Holliday. Buck was a tricky customer anyway, but when Walshy started to holler, 'Right arm, right arm, stop his right arm,' it became devilishly difficult to stop him offloading, and we weren't allowed to smash him much to Brad Hepi's annoyance!

"All week this continued. Come game day, Walshy was positively purring, content that his attention to detail would win the day. He stalked all us players one by one.

'Right arm boys, lock up that right arm!' Holliday's first foray almost spelt disaster. He slipped a ball as he hit the line and only a superb last-ditcher by Mully at the back saved a try. I turned around to see who was to blame for the lapse and saw Holliday flat out with bluebirds twittering around his head. As I watched their staff peel him from the turf onto a stretcher, Shaun Wane gave me that mischievous look of his, winked and muttered, 'Well, we won't have to worry about that fuckin' right arm again, pal!'

"At the video session next Tuesday, we saw Shaun bullocking his shoulder under Holliday's chin right at the moment he slipped the ball. That's what Shaun could do. He was old school and took care of business his way. That's how the danger men were sorted out back then!"

THE highlight of Wane's career came on 7th October 1987 as Wigan beat Manly 8-2 in a brutal, tryless World Club Challenge. Wane laughed when I read to him Joe Lydon's retelling of how the Wigan players goaded Wane into targeting Aussie hardman and boxer Ron Gibbs in every scrum to soften him up.

"Yep, that story is true." he said. "Ron Gibbs, the Golden Gloves champion of Australia! It was an absolutely brutal game because neither side backed down. I was sore for days after that. It was the toughest game I remember playing in. It was close as you can get to full-on combat, pure hatred between two teams. The first time I looked at the clock, there were only two minutes left. It went so quick. The game was on a Wednesday and then on the Sunday we were up against Warrington at St Helens in the Lancashire Cup, and we beat them. It showed a real mental toughness of the team to back up like that."

Wane made his Wigan debut on the third day of 1982, aged 17, against Barrow in a Division One match at Central Park. Barrow won 18-15. He played five times that season, scoring his first try against St Helens in the final match of the campaign - a 23-5 win in which Henderson Gill scored twice. Newly promoted Wigan finished eleventh on the league ladder, avoiding relegation by a mere five points.

"I started playing rugby at five, which I absolutely loved," he said. "Playing for Wigan schools was like State of Origin. It was the one thing that kept me in school. The talent from Wigan was immense. My debut against Barrow was the first time I played against men. I'd been running on as a fan asking the players for their tie-ups a few weeks earlier. Barrow had some tough players. They were a good team then, and they beat us. It was so physical.

"I could always play a bit, and I wouldn't back down. I was very competitive. I enjoyed my career. I started as a loose forward who could pass and kick. I woke up one morning two stone heavier, so I moved to prop! Rugby

League kept me on the straight and narrow.

"My first two coaches Maurice Bamford and Alex Murphy were very good to me. Alex was a great player and a great character."

Wigan's front row for much of the early- and mid-1980s was Wane and Brian Case at prop and Nicky Kiss at hooker. They comprised the front row for the victory over Manly, and all three would have played at Wembley in 1985, albeit with Wane in the second row, had skipper Graeme West not inadvertently injured one of his own players.

"I played in the semi-final against Hull KR when Graeme mistimed a tackle," said Wane. "He swung round, and his big, long legs snapped my medial ligament! I missed the final, having played in every round. It was devastating.

"Brian and Nicky were both fantastic. I learned a lot from them. I was a young kid coming through, learning behaviours, how to train, how to handle big games etc, and Brian and Nicky were great for me."

After 149 games for Wigan, Wane was released. His final match was a 24-8 defeat to Widnes in the 1990 Charity Shield at Swansea. "I remember the night Maurice Lindsay told me Leeds had come in, and he was heartbroken. He said they saw me as a catalyst for the change from the poor team to the dominant team in the late 'eighties. But I didn't want to stay where I was no longer wanted.

"I loved it at Leeds and made some really good friends there, but it was a shock for me, because there was a bit of softness in the club in that they were happy to play well and nearly get the win. At Wigan, it was win at all costs. We had a few big games at Leeds, playing ok, but not getting over the winning line, and some people seemed alright with that. I struggled with that attitude.

"But they were good people at the club, including the backroom staff. There was a real family feel, and me and my wife spent a lot of time there. My wife loved it. We were made to feel very welcome. I'm still good friends with Richard Gunn and Colin Maskill."

Wane played 43 matches for Leeds, scoring two tries. He then played just eight at Workington where he also scored twice. They both came against his old amateur club, Wigan St Pats, in a Regal Trophy match.

"I gave my all in Rugby League and had some shocking injuries," said Wane. "I'd never done anything else and to be told you were finished because of injury was devastating. I was at Workington at the time, and although I liked the place, and there are some great people up there, I probably should have known I was at the end. I'd play in a game. My knee would swell. I couldn't train. Then the next game would come about. I was getting whacked by people who weren't as good as me. I couldn't keep going. But I met some absolute characters up there, and I learned things I still use today.

"I still have issues with my knees, my back, my shoulders and my hip - just like every Rugby League player. We all walk the same! It's such a brutal game. It's not natural to do what we do, but we love it, and it's all we know. I owe the game everything. I met all my friends through Rugby League.

"I'd never done anything else. The best thing, though, for me after retiring was working and doing a proper job. That took my mind off things. I worked for many years in a job away from the game and learned more about life skills from that. I did my coaching badges as a player at 23, but I learned a lot about managing people from working in the tarmac business."

AGED 15, Shaun Wane left home covered in blood with just one shoe on. He had phoned the police, telling them there was a bomb scare. His school was evacuated. The police visited the Wane family home. When they left, his father beat him. It was a regular occurrence.

He went to the family home of his girlfriend, Lorraine, and asked if he could stay a night. He stayed for five years. They are now married with two daughters. Wane revealed his childhood trauma in interviews in 2019. His parents, who had six children, died when he coached Wigan, as did two of his siblings. Two other siblings had died in childhood before he was born.

"My dad's way of reacting [to my behaviour] was to lock me in a room for 20 minutes," Wane told the Out of Our League podcast. "You're in the corner being punched and kicked for 20 minutes nonstop, pissing your pants. Black eyes, lips and stuff. It started aged five, six or seven. I was badly behaved. I had a middle brother Tony and we got in quite a bit of trouble. We broke into places and pinched things. Where we lived, you had to stick up for yourselves. You couldn't let anyone take the piss out of you. That's how it was.

"Word would get back to my dad and he would lock me in a room and butcher me for 20 minutes. I thought it happened to everybody. My dad was bigger than me. It's the way he was brought up. It's what he thought was the norm [because] it had happened to him. My brothers and my mam would be banging on the door [to get him to stop]. Then I'd do something the next day, and it would happen again. I just remember feeling really bad many nights, in bed with my two brothers. It wasn't a nice place to be.

"When I was 14, I met a girl called Lorraine. She became my girlfriend. At 15, I rang in the bomb scare and that was the end. My dad nearly killed me. When I left, I only had one trainer on. I had no idea where to go. I had no relatives or anything. I went to the estate where Lorraine lived. I asked to stop for one night and stayed for five or six years. We got married at 21.

"When I was about 24 or 25, my uncle died suddenly. I thought I don't want this to happen to my dad with me not talking to him. We shook hands. There was no apology because he didn't think he'd done anything wrong, and that was the case till the day he died. It hasn't done me any harm though. Even now, I'm conscious not to let anyone take the piss out of me. I'm always on my guard. It made me a better dad because I didn't want them to feel how I did."

I asked Wane how it had felt to reveal such personal issues and whether the experience had shaped him as a coach. "I never meant for that to become public," he said, "but a reporter asked if I'd had a good childhood, and I hadn't. He asked outright, and I don't lie. If he hadn't asked, I wouldn't have mentioned it. That's how it all came about. It's hard to talk about. I don't know if it shaped me as a coach, but leaving home and going to my wife's was instrumental in shaping my life.

"The big influences on my coaching career were a couple of coaches I played under. Graham Lowe was one at Wigan. He was way in front of his time and changed people's philosophies. At Workington, the coach Peter Walsh was really big on quick play the balls and play-the-ball techniques. He taught me that the game was won on the floor. He was a great man manager, and I learned a lot from him.

"But you still have to be yourself as a coach. In my first year as Wigan head coach, I was trying to be everybody like Madge [Michael Maguire], Lowe and Walsh. Ian

Lenagan said, 'You've done ok.' I wasn't happy with ok. I went on holiday with my wife, and I said, 'I'm not going to get sacked not being myself,' so I had a massive change in how I spoke, brought in lots of standards, spoke to the players from my heart, and I was strict on non-rugby things."

Wane finished playing in 1993 but didn't become a head coach for 18 years. He combined working in the tarmac industry with coaching Wigan's lower grades, devising tactics and doing video reviews during his lunch breaks. He worked his way up the Wigan coaching ladder, earning just £2,000 a year at first, and took over from Michael Maguire when he returned to the NRL after the 2010 season.

"When I was 25, I was coaching in schools with Dean Bell," he said. "Then I coached amateur at St Pats and Wigan Schools, and I loved it. I was asked by Wigan to go and coach in schools, do some scouting and be around players. I got to look after the under-16s and under-17s. I did those two teams, and then I became assistant coach and moved up to the top job."

Even though Maguire had won the Super League trophy and Challenge Cup in his two seasons in charge, Wane was determined to make changes and instill his own methods. "I'm proud of our culture," he said. "We never set out with

Shaun Wane embraces Sam Tomkins after Wigan's 2018 Grand Final win

any particular idea. I just found it very comfortable being straightforward and honest. I wanted to be told straight. I wanted to be told the truth all the time. I coached that way, and it was very easy.

"Culture wasn't really spoken about before I became coach. For example, I wanted the bus to be left spotless after we'd got off it. I wanted the changing room to be clean. I wanted the players to say please and thank you. That hadn't been a big deal to Madge. He concentrated on rugby massively. I did that too, but these things were also important to me. Even now, I expect England players to turn up on time, respect people, train well and behave off the field. If a player's late to training, he'll get sent home."

"I'm also an avid writer. I make notes all the time. I went into my loft recently, and there were mountains of books from me making notes in late 1990s and early 2000s."

Sam Tomkins told a story, also on the Out of Our League podcast, about Wane's days as Academy coach. He told how Wane would issue every player with a filofax which they were to bring with them to each training session. One player kept forgetting, and Wane threw him out of the club. Wane chuckled when I reminded him of the story.

"There was nothing important in the filofaxes," he admitted. "I just wanted the lads to get prepared the night before and to not think of things at the last minute. One lad just couldn't remember it. He couldn't see the point. I just wanted them to get into good habits, and it worked. Things like that shaped Sam into the person and player he became."

DOZENS of Academy players made their first-team Wigan debut under Wane's tutelage. I found an article saying it was 41, but Wane corrected me. "Kris Radlinski told me it was 52," he said. "I've got a plaque at the stadium with every name on it. It says a lot about the strength of the Wigan Academy. I wanted to believe in the players. I wanted to play them, and I never got let down. Every Super League coach is under immense pressure, but that didn't matter to me. If my heart told me to put a kid in, I did."

One of the 52 is George Williams, who Wane appointed England captain in 2023. "George is a great kid and very easy to coach," said Wane. "He was fantastic in the World Cup. It's an easy choice with Sam unavailable. He's 28 now, and he's matured into a good man. He has a girlfriend and a baby. Watching him is very satisfying.

"I have great memories of so many great players. I saw Dom Manfredi last week, and he said some emotional things to me. It's good to see players like that."

Tomkins and Michael McIlorum debuted for Wigan before Wane became coach, but he is equally proud of them. When I asked him if any one individual's story brings him most pride, he plumped for the hooker. "Mickey Mac was a bit of a feral kid," Wane said, "but he's now living in France, he's in a fantastic relationship, he's just had a daughter, and he's living life to the full. Hopefully I've had a steadying influence.

"Sam joined our Under-18s and we played against Whitehaven's 20s. He was tiny, and I was concerned about his size, but I realised after a while how tough he was. He's taken some terrible stick in the time I've known him, but nothing fazes him. I look back at these guys, and I'm so happy with how he developed, and it's the same with Joel Tomkins, Paul Prescott, Dom Manfredi, Bob Beswick and many others."

SHAUN WANE's Wigan won the Super League title in 2013, 2016 and 2018, the League Leaders' Shield in 2012, the Challenge Cup in 2013 and the World Club Challenge in 2017. He can't match the trophy hauls of Graham Lowe or John Monie but, given how the talent is much more evenly spread in modern-day Rugby League, it is incredibly impressive.

After the disappointment of Wane's first season in 2012, Wigan hit back by winning the league-and-cup double after beating Hull 16-0 at Wembley and Warrington 30-16 at Old Trafford. "I was myself in 2013," he said. "I was Shaun Wane. The moment I remember is the fans counting down the last ten seconds of the Grand Final, knowing we'd won the double. Proving people wrong was a massive motivation for me. I remember thinking, 'This is why I coach - this feeling of winning.'"

Wane's feelings were at the other end of the scale a year later as he had to watch St Helens parade the trophy around Old Trafford. In the opening stages of the game, his prop Ben Flower floored Lance Hohaia with a right hook. He punched him again as he lay motionless. Red card. The image of Wane staring in disbelief at what had just happened became perhaps the defining image of the year. Former Great Britain coach Mal Reilly once told me he had been guilty on occasions of firing up his players too much with undesired consequences, but Wane denied this was the case in 2014.

"No, absolutely not," he said. "It was a totally normal build-up with a lot of detail on St Helens. We were ready to win, and if Ben had stayed on, we probably would have done. We still could have won without him. We'd trained with 11 and 12 men, but we just panicked. We were mentally weak, and we gave in. I was disappointed. As for the incident, Ben got elbowed in the face, he reacted, and the final punch on the floor was too much. I felt sorry for Ben, he was a good lad. I understand the reaction, but he shouldn't have done it.

"And then we lost to Leeds in 2015, and they did the treble. That was tough. They were a good team, but Danny McGuire knocked on at a crucial time. I was planning the next play, and they gave the try. We weren't great in the game though. We could have done better. Losing is a really bad feeling. To me, winning is the only thing. I'm not a gracious loser. I analyse everything - how I coached, how I verbalised messages etc."

Wane won two more Grand Finals and a World Club Challenge in his final three seasons before becoming the coach of England. The start of his new career was disrupted by the Covid-19 pandemic, and the 2021 World Cup was delayed by a year. When it took place, England annihilated Samoa 60-6 with an astonishing performance in the tournament opener at St James' Park. But sport is rarely predictable, and when the sides met again in the semi-final at Arsenal, the Samoans prevailed on golden point.

After several months of being kept in the dark, Wane's tenure was eventually extended, and he will lead them into the 2025 World Cup . "I don't think I'll ever get over that defeat," he said of the Samoa semi-final. "People will probably get bored of me saying that. A lot of hard work and detail went into it, and we came up short. It was torture because you don't get another chance when you lose a semi-final, but making up for it next time is a big motivator."

GARY CONNOLLY

1993-2002
2004

A world-class fullback and a world-class centre, Gary Connolly was magnificent for St Helens, Canterbury, Wigan, Leeds and Great Britain in a professional career that spanned 17 years. He was involved in a highly controversial transfer, he won numerous trophies at Central Park, and he picked up the coveted Lance Todd Trophy, despite his Leeds side losing the 2003 Challenge Cup Final.

If you could relive one day from your career, which would it be?
The World Club Challenge in 1994. I can't believe it's nearly 30 years ago! We'd had a long season, playing 50 or 60 games. We lost Andy Platt, Dean Bell and Kelvin Skerrett, so we were up against it. Graeme West was the coach, and he was brilliant because he said we could have a few days to enjoy ourselves and get our minds ready. We got back in training and were confident. The ball went our way, and we beat a very good Brisbane Broncos side.

If you could go back to the start of your career, would you identify as a fullback, a centre or someone happy to play both?
As an amateur, I never really played centre. I signed for Saints as a fullback, but it was only when Mike McClennan came over that I played centre. I'd never played there, and it was against Wigan who had the Iro brothers in the centre. We didn't win, but it went ok, and I stayed there. I did prefer fullback, but I played most of my career at centre. It was nice to swap as it keeps you fresh.

Your experience as a 17-year-old at Wembley in 1989 might have scarred other players. How much did it affect you?
It wasn't the best of days for myself and the team, but the biggest thing was just getting picked. I'd played every round but still didn't know if I'd play. Then Alex [Murphy] picked me and it was fantastic to know someone like him had faith in me. The experience didn't knock my confidence because anyone can have a bad game. Shaun Edwards came up to me after the game and told me to keep my head up which was nice of him. He'd had a similar experience at that age.

In the 1992-93 season, Saints thrashed Wigan at home, only lost the title on points difference and won the Premiership Final. Where does that side rank in those you played in?
It was an excellent team. We had some outstanding young players in Chris Joynt, Sonny Nickle and Alan Hunte, and we were building a good side. There was a good atmosphere. Everyone wanted to win. All I wanted to do was play for St Helens, my hometown club. I loved it there and I have some great memories. Then they sold me behind my back.

You were selected for the 1992 Lions. Weren't you the only player who could beat Malcolm Reilly in an arm wrestle?
Ha! Well, I never went to arm wrestle him. Steve Hampson lost to him then I beat Steve, so he went up to Malcolm and said, "I've found someone who can beat you." Malcolm laughed when Steve said my name. But I beat him easily! Getting picked for the tour changed my life because I was

a bricklayer getting up at 7am, but I packed the job in and became a full-time pro. I started in the second team on the tour and ended up in the Test team.

You made a good impression in a four-month stint at Canterbury Bankstown in 1993. What was going on back home?
I loved my time at Canterbury. We won the Minor Premiership and it's a big regret that we couldn't make the Grand Final, but we lost to St George and Brisbane. Canterbury wanted to sign me on a permanent deal and that's why I ended up at Wigan. I said yes to Canterbury but said I needed a week to tell my friends and family I was moving over. Saints would have got 60 or 80 grand for me, which was the most they could get from an Australian club. But they wanted more and sold me to Wigan without me knowing. I didn't have a clue Wigan were interested in me. Saints clearly didn't want me - or more to the point they wanted the money. So I went to Wigan and got all the Judas stuff from Saints fans for years.

Did that hurt?
I was shocked at first. I got back from Australia on a Wednesday and made my Wigan debut on the Friday against Widnes. Saints were playing at Castleford on the Sunday and my dad used to organise a bus for the speccies from his pub. Stupidly, I jumped on and went with him. When I got on the bus, it just went quiet. Word got round at the ground, and I got absolutely hammered. But what was I supposed to do? Saints had sold me to Wigan. I could hardly do an interview as a Wigan player and say I hadn't wanted to leave Saints.
But it proved to be the best move I ever made. I live in Wigan. I support Wigan. I wouldn't change anything. What St Helens did to me was a blessing in disguise.

You missed the first four games of the 1995 World Cup with pneumonia and made your comeback in the final. Were you ready to play?
I was fine. I declared myself fit for the semi-final with Wales, but Phil Larder said he'd keep me for the final. I felt ok in the final. It would have been good to have had the semi-final under my belt, but that's how the coach did it.

Were the cross-code games with Bath and the Middlesex Sevens a distraction you could have done without in 1996?
No, they were brilliant, and they broke up the season nicely. I loved both the Bath games – probably the union game more because it was such a challenge. We should have stuck to our own tactics, but we played Joe Lydon and Graeme West, who hadn't played for years. When they came off, we went back to what we knew in the second half, and we scored some great tries.
The Middlesex Sevens was fantastic. Every time we played,

the bars and car parks emptied, and there were 50 or 60 thousand in the ground wanting us to get beaten! When we got the ball, we were unstoppable.

Several of you played union in the 1996-97 off-season and Graeme West blamed that on you losing to Saints in the Cup. Was he right?
He might have had a point, but I snapped my cruciate in my last game for Harlequins, so I didn't play against Saints. I should have been out for a year with a cruciate knee replacement. But I said I'd play on without the operation and if it went wrong, I'd have the op and then miss the year. I came back a few weeks later and played the rest of my career with no cruciate. I had some needles to drain the fluid before every game. As the year went on, there was less and less fluid.

How did Wigan lose to Sheffield in 1998?
Look at the Sheffield team. Everyone underestimated them but they were a good side, and they didn't drop the ball until about the hour mark. You have to take your hats off to them. It was like Salford in 1996. We thought we'd win, but we also thought it would be tough. In the end, they were too good.

Did Wigan go through too many coaches in your time?
Yes, they did. They seemed to sack someone every year. But the biggest problem was losing players like Inga Tuigamala, Scott Quinnell, Martin Offiah, Henry Paul and Jason Robinson, and not replacing them.

What took you to Leeds?
My contract was up with Wigan, and I went to play rugby union for Orrell. Joe Lydon, the England Sevens coach, told me he'd discussed me with Clive Woodward for the England World Cup squad in 2003. But at the end of 2002, I ended up playing for Great Britain because Kris Radlinski and Paul Wellens were injured. Gary Hetherington approached me because he needed a fullback. I'd only played once for Orrell, but Gary convinced me to go to Leeds.

You're one of twelve Lance Todd Trophy winners to come from the beaten side, but you were criticised for your demeanour in collecting the award. What happened?
I was upset because I knew it was my last chance of a final and I knew what that Leeds team was going to go on to achieve. I wanted to win something with them. It was such a close game, and the atmosphere was unbelievable. They had just presented Bradford with the cup. They were all celebrating and spraying champagne, and I had to go up for the award in front of all my teammates who were also crying. I could hardly celebrate! It was very emotional, and I was so upset. I don't regret my reaction because there was no disrespect intended.

Why did you leave Leeds?
I signed for two years and wanted to stay. I'd had a good season and was picked in the Dream Team at fullback. I hadn't done a full season at fullback for ten years and was loving it. But Leeds changed their coach, and he [Tony Smith] wasn't keen on me for some reason. He said I wouldn't play first team. I asked if I could stay and help Richard Mathers develop. He said he didn't need any help. I said I could play centre. No again. "You're not needed," was the message, so I left.

I phoned Andy Farrell to tell him I was retiring. He put the phone down and quickly rang back. He'd spoken to Denis Betts, the coach, and although they couldn't pay me because of the salary cap, I was welcome to go back to Wigan. So I ended up playing for nothing in 2004.
I was going to retire again, but Terry O'Connor and Mick Cassidy moved to Widnes and talked me into joining them. I had an agreement with Frank Endacott that said I would play fullback, and that was what convinced me. I enjoyed the first three-quarters of the season, but it fell away after that, and it was a real struggle.

Was your nickname 'Gary Lager' a fair representation of your drinking abilities?
No! Believe it or not, I was never a big drinker. The name came about because I didn't like hanging around the dressing room after a game, so I'd be first out. I'd head to the bar and have a lager shandy. That's where the nickname came from, and I went along with it.

145

DEAN BELL

1986-1994

Dean Bell began his English career with Carlisle as a 20-year-old in 1982. He was unable to prevent them being relegated in his one season there, but he made his Test debut soon after his final game for the Cumbrians. After spells at Leeds and Eastern Suburbs, he signed for Wigan in 1986 where he enjoyed eight magnificent seasons. He left Wigan to captain Auckland Warriors in their maiden Winfield Cup campaign. He was on the winning side in three Test matches against Australia.

MEAN DEAN. The ultimate leader. Captain of New Zealand. Three times a Challenge Cup-winning skipper of Wigan. The first-ever captain of Auckland Warriors.

His Rugby League journey, in this country at least, began in the most unusual setting. Carlisle had just been promoted at the end of their first season. In the summer of 1982, preparing for life in Division One, the Cumbrians signed three New Zealanders, all from the same family. He made his Carlisle debut in the number-four jersey in a league match against a Wigan team that included David Stephenson, Henderson Gill and a 17-year-old Shaun Wane.

"Carlisle was great, and I signed for them with my uncle Ian Bell and cousin Clayton Friend," said Bell. "It was the catalyst for my career, and a great learning curve for me to play with such experienced players like Mick Morgan, Denis Boyd, Jimmy Birts, Wally Youngman and John Atkinson. I had just the one year there, because they ran out of money and couldn't pay us. To be fair to them, they still honoured our contracts."

Carlisle came last, but Bell had impressed the Kiwi Test selectors, and he flew home to play Australia with whom New Zealand shared the spoils in a two-Test series. He then toured England with the New Zealand Maoris before joining Leeds for the remainder of the 1983-84 season. The Winfield Cup was his next assignment as he moved to Eastern Suburbs where he played in the same three-quarter line as John Ferguson. In the summer of 1986, he was off to Central Park.

"My first year at Easts went really well, but I suffered a bad knee injury in the second year," said Bell. "Leeds got back in touch with me for another spell there, but Maurice Lindsay at Wigan phoned and said that the New Zealand coach, Graham Lowe, would be coaching them. I had a lot of respect for Graham, and after Maurice told me what sort of side they were putting together, I chose them. Leeds were offering more money, but I wanted to be winning more games."

Bell was an established international by the time he arrived in Wigan. He was still playing as much wing as centre, but he had made his mark on the Test stage in both positions. "Australia had enjoyed total domination of the international scene for a while, and we'd been beaten by 30 or 40 points on a regular basis," said Bell. "In my first Test at Carlaw Park, we lost by about ten points. It was daunting to mark Kerry Boustead because he was one of the quickest guys I've ever seen and one of the best wingers in the world. In the end, a runaway Eric Grothe try, the type of which only he could have scored, killed us off. That game was in Auckland, and no one gave us a chance in the second Test in Brisbane. We hadn't beaten Australia in years, but we put in one of the best performances seen in years and beat them in their own backyard.

"We took a lot of self-belief into that game, and it paid off. The night before the game, Graham Lowe showed us a video of the New Zealand Rowing Eight getting their gold medals presented at the Olympics, and he told us to look at their faces and to take in what it meant to them. Most of them were crying tears of joy. He said we could experience this too. The thing with tears of joy is you have to work for it, and we went out there and battered them. We dominated them physically and that hadn't happened to Australia for years.

"Our pack that day was the toughest I've ever been involved with. Players like Kurt Sorensen, Kevin Tamati and Mark Broadhurst had great presence. Graeme West was a great player and Gary Prohm was like an extra centre with the work rate to play in the pack. Australia were full of legendary figures too, and Lang Park generated an incredible atmosphere. It was an amazing feeling afterwards.

"There was also our 18-0 win in 1985 after we'd lost the second game, and the series, in the last seconds at Carlaw Park. I was carried off with a recurrence of my knee injury. I was in the changing room and the physio was updating me. With a minute to go, he came in, saying, 'We've got this one.' Then I heard all the groans. They'd scored. We'd lost the game and the series. I was just devastated.

"I was given no chance of making the third Test, but I was desperate to. I was on 24-hour physio with our alarm clocks set for every two hours during the night to try and get myself right. It was only when I passed a fitness test four hours before the game that I realised I had a chance. I played on one leg, but my cousin Clayton scored two tries, and we did it."

After playing in such an enthralling series, the Kiwis flew to England and immediately took part in another. New Zealand won a wonderful first Test at Headingley. Great Britain hit back at Wigan before the two sides played out a brutal 6-all draw in the third Test at Elland Road. "I never blame officials, but we didn't get the rub of the green [in the third Test], and the touch judge kept coming on after spotting things," Bell said. "It was a great kick from Lee Crooks to tie the series though. We'd won the first Test with a late try, and then there was the game at Wigan when Garry Schofield scored four tries. Only he could score tries like that. He was one of the best try poachers. It was a good series, but we should have won. But, with no disrespect to Great Britain intended, it was the games against Australia that stand out for me. I would never suggest that beating Australia in a one-off game makes you the world's best. Great Britain often struggled in the past. I don't know if it was their mental attitude or not, but one-off victories didn't get followed up. It's all about consistency, and winning over a period of time, which is something we had at Wigan. Staying there is the hard part."

BELL made his Wigan debut on 7th September 1986 in a league game at Leigh. Bell's try helped Wigan to a routine 35-0 win. It was a glorious campaign with Wigan winning the league at a canter, and also the Lancashire Cup and the John Player Special Trophy. Bell's eight seasons at Central Park saw him scoop six league titles, seven Challenge Cups, two Premierships, four John Players, four Lancashire Cups and two Charity Shields. He was named Man of Steel in 1992 and won the Lance Todd Trophy in 1993.

"When you're at the top you're there to be knocked down, and the longer you're there, the harder it is," reflected Bell on his Wigan triumphs. "We won plenty of games with the sort of flair that Ellery Hanley, Joe Lydon and Martin Offiah could offer, but also we had to grind games out. When you're 20 points down in the Cup at Hull, or 12 points down at Halifax going up the hill in the second half with the snow in your faces, you've got to dig deep. It inspired so much confidence to see guys like Offiah and Jason Robinson on the wings, Frano Botica inside you, Gene Miles in the other centre position, and either Joe Lydon or Steve Hampson at fullback. The list goes on and on. It was a very unique coming together of a lot of special individuals.

"My first Challenge Cup Final in 1988 against Halifax is an obvious highlight. It was a dream to get there. I was very humble, because I realised that so many great players didn't get the chance to play in a cup final. We had players like Andy Gregory and Joe who had played there before, and they spoke about staying focused and playing the game and not the occasion. When Halifax came onto the pitch, they were waving to their wives, but we were very focused and were there to get a job done. All the Wembley finals were special, and I always thought, 'This one could be the last,' as I did with the first one. The run of Wembleys was just a dream."

Bell was also quick to pay tribute to the coaches who were responsible for much of the silverware he won at Wigan. "Graham Lowe was the catalyst for my Test career," he said. "He got you looking deeper into the game and got the best out of players. I owe a lot to him. I was always very focused anyway, even as an amateur, so when I started working with him, it was a good partnership, and we had similar thoughts about the game. Then there was John Monie. People say that anyone could have coached Wigan back then, but history has proven that you can't just buy a championship-winning side, and that the coach has to mould the team and manage all the egos and the personalities."

Bell continued to play for New Zealand for two years after signing for Wigan, in which time he experienced a third victory over Australia in 1987 and led his team out in the 1988 World Cup Final. "I thought beating Australia would be a rarity, but to get three in a short space was great," he said. "The third win was also at Lang Park, and I picked up the man of the match, leading an inexperienced side against a high-quality Australian team. We won that one 13-6.

"I also remember our 12-10 win [against Great Britain] in Christchurch in 1988 that put us into the World Cup Final. The night before, Graham Lowe told us we had to win, not just for ourselves, but also for the players who had played at the start of the World Cup campaign like Kevin Tamati, Howie Tamati, Dane Sorensen, Fred Ah Kuoi, Gary Kemble, James Leuluai, Dane O'Hara, Olsen Filipaina and Gary Prohm. We were desperate to get to the World Cup Final, and I asked the guys to stand up

one by one and speak about what it meant to them. The tears were certainly flowing that night. The game was close. Great Britain had just had that famous 26-12 win in Sydney the week before, but Gary Freeman came off the bench to score twice, and we got through to the final 12-10."

The World Cup Final of 1988 turned out to be a crushing disappointment for Bell's men. Played at Eden Park in Auckland, the home of the All Blacks, in front of 47,363 spectators, they were regarded by many as favourites, and a potential victory, it was believed, would have been a turning point for Rugby League in the country. Instead, as they so often do, Australia spoiled the party, as they raced into a 21-0 half-time lead. The Iro brothers scored a try each in the second half as the game ended 25-12.

"To captain a side in a World Cup Final was a special moment," said Bell, "but it's certainly not an occasion fondly remembered in New Zealand. We underperformed on the day and got our priorities wrong. The New Zealand press built us up as favourites. Looking back, there are a few things we should have done differently that week. The Australians, with all their experience, were very quiet during the build-up.

"You've got to play the game and not the occasion. It's stage fright, and people let their emotions get carried away. You have to remember what your job is and what you're there to do, and we lost the plot that day. Looking back, you know there are things you'd do differently.

"Also, I wasn't happy with the way the New Zealand Rugby League dealt with the aftermath. They were looking for scapegoats and there was a lot of criticism flying around. That made up my mind to retire from international rugby. I must admit I was thinking about it anyway, as it was taking its toll on me at Wigan. I'd play a full winter season and then go back to play Test matches, so I was basically playing 12 months a year. I knew my career would be short lived if I continued to do that, so I decided to retire and devote myself to Wigan. It was a tough call to make and I wasn't entirely happy, but in life you have to make tough decisions. Playing for my country was the highlight of my career, but I ended up having a long career which I might not have had."

Bell did come out of international retirement for five games in 1989, but they were his last. He ended up with 26 Test caps. He struggled to pick out his best teammate: "Gee, that's a hard one! Different people stand out for different reasons like Kevin Tamati for his toughness, Kurt Sorensen for his explosiveness, James Leuluai for his finishing quality, Fred Ah Kuoi for his handling and Olsen Filipaina was a great stand-off who always played well for the Kiwis. There are a lot though."

BELL's final playing assignment was back home. Along with North Queensland Cowboys, South Queensland Crushers and Perth Western Reds, Auckland Warriors were one of the new clubs admitted into the Winfield Cup in 1995. Bell was their first captain and led the side out for their opening match against Brisbane Broncos - a heart-breaking 25-22 defeat.

"The lure to do that was too great, and I didn't want to regret not doing it later," he admitted. "If ever I could script the end to my playing career, it would be that. 1995 in Auckland was unbelievable. The build-up had been going on for three or four years to that opening game against Brisbane on March 10th, 1995, a date that I will always remember. The capacity was 32,000 at Mount Smart Stadium, but we could have sold it three or four

times over, and there were millions watching on TV. You had to be there to understand the pressure we were under in that one game. It was the opening game of the Winfield Cup season, and there had been a three-year build-up for the Warriors. The marketing people had done an amazing job and created this monster that was always going to be near impossible to live up to, so the pressure on us in that opening game was huge. I thought we could only fail. We were going into the unknown, and I didn't know how we'd perform as a team. We'd only had warm-up games and hadn't been tested in the big arena. A win would have been a bonus, but when I look back now, we should have won. We put ourselves in a winning position, but probably didn't bank on the genius of Alfie Langer bringing them back into the game.

"We aimed for credibility that year and had it not been for our infamous points deduction [for using five substitutes in a round-three win over Western Suburbs], we would have made the finals. History proves that a lot of new clubs struggle in their first year, like Canberra and Brisbane, so to come close to the finals was pretty good, especially as we were also entertainers. Like I said, the whole experience was fantastic.

"When I left New Zealand as a 20-year-old to go to Carlisle, it was just an amateur game, and we were lucky to get 1,500 fans. At Auckland we were getting 28,000 which is a huge turnaround. The game was getting the sort of recognition that had been longed for, for many years. I had reservations about going back because I didn't think I could top the Wigan years at that age, but it was a challenge I knew I had to attempt."

WITH his playing days now behind him, or so he thought, Bell flew to England to become assistant coach of his former club Leeds, but while the plane was in the air, coach Doug Laughton resigned in protest at Bell's appointment, meaning the 33-year-old went straight into the head-coach role. He did the job for three seasons with mixed success before deciding that his future lay in youth development.

"When I finished playing, I hadn't done much planning for my future," he said. "I had some connections with Leeds, having played there, and I was earmarked as an assistant to Dougie Laughton, but while I was coming over, he resigned! It was a bit difficult as I wasn't ready for it. I hadn't served my apprenticeship, but we did alright by finishing second in 1995-96.

"There were work-ethic problems, and I knew I'd have to sacrifice some quality players to develop the right work ethic. I signed Barrie McDermott, and I thought it would be great if I could carry on making signings like that. However, I quickly found out that the club's debt meant there was no money to spend for the rest of 1995 and 1996. We had so many injuries, that for a game against Paris in 1996, I even played myself. It was a relegation four-pointer, and I remember thinking, 'I could do a better job than that centre.'

"1996 wasn't good. I never really thought we were in a relegation battle, but I was determined not to get sucked into one and would have done anything to have steered clear of that. I'd never been so exhausted in my life because I hadn't done any quality training, but it was worth it.

"Looking back, I wouldn't change the fact that I coached Leeds, but I was very frustrated that some of the players didn't have my will to win and attitude. At the time, I couldn't comprehend that. I decided that I wanted to help instil that into players at a younger age, so I went to Gary Hetherington and told him I wanted to step down and work with the younger players. I also needed some stability. I'd seen quite a few coaches get the sack. My son was just starting high school, and I wasn't willing to take that risk.

"Sometimes you have to ask if what you're doing is what you want to do."

THOMAS LEULUAI

2007-2012
2017-2022

One of the hardest-hitting halfbacks in living memory, Thomas Leuluai made his NRL debut aged just 17. His international career yielded 40 Kiwi caps, and included World Cup and Four Nations triumphs. In 12 seasons at Wigan over two spells, he won two Super League Grand Finals, two Challenge Cups and a World Club Challenge. Leuluai's playing career went on for 20 years and even in his final season, he was instrumental in the club winning their 20th Challenge Cup. He is now an assistant coach at the club to Matty Peet.

If you could relive one day from your career, which would it be?
The World Cup Final in 2008 stands out. It was my first major trophy, and I was so young. No one expected us to win it. I was at an age when I was just happy to be in the team. We got beaten by Australia by about 40 points in the first game, and the coaches did a fantastic job to turn it around. We were a really close group that year. All Kiwi groups were close-knit, but that one stands out. Man for man, we weren't as talented as Australia, but we managed to win the trophy.

Two years after your World Cup win, you won the Four Nations Final against Australia.
That period of the Kiwis was class. It was a group that stuck together with Stephen Kearney in charge. We were young but experienced after the World Cup. In my first couple of years at international level, I felt I wasn't quite good enough, but by 2010, we were established and playing well with our clubs. We went into those camps very confident.

You said once you hadn't seen your dad's try from the 1985 cup final. Have you finally seen it? And how is he now?
Yes, I've seen highlights of the game, but not the whole thing. What I meant really was my dad was never the type to put on old tapes, and he didn't talk much about his career. He gave me good advice if I asked for it, but he was never a forceful person who tried to coach me. He didn't comment on my games, we just had fun. He has Alzheimer's now unfortunately.

Several other family members have played the game. Can you talk us through them?
Most of my family played. Kylie is my cousin and he played at Leeds obviously. MacGraff is my brother. He played for Widnes and Leigh among others. My Uncle Philip, my dad's brother, played for Salford and Cronulla. I have a little nephew who plays for the Canberra Raiders Under-20s. He's Siamani Leuluai.

You debuted for New Zealand Warriors at just 17 in 2003 and had a dream year. What do you remember of it and how had you got there?
I came through the ranks and got offered a contract at 15 or 16 and started training with the development squad. I was used to training against the first team. When I was 17, I got a call one day to say I was in the squad. Debuting at that age was pretty daunting. I wasn't at school, but I was doing a course with other young players. I came off the bench at stand-off, but we lost a close one to the Bulldogs in Wellington. A couple of months later, I came back into

the team when Lance Hohaia got injured, and we had a good run until the end of the season. I didn't do much - I just made my tackles and gave the ball to Ali Lauiti'iti! We lost to Penrith one game short of the Grand Final. I probably didn't understand the importance of it. You don't understand at that age. It all happened so quickly. I look back now and think it would have been great to have made the Grand Final. I played for the Junior Kiwis a week later, then I got a call to play for the top team the week after. I'm at school one minute, then I'm playing for New Zealand and beating Australia. That Kiwi team was great with so many fantastic players.

What was Stacey Jones like?
Awesome! He was such a natural, great leader, and he looked after me a lot. He did most of my work for me. He's an awesome bloke, and I loved learning off him. He's one of the best Kiwi players of all time. We're still good friends now. I was so young and all the players like Logan Swann, Monty Betham, Awen Guttenbeil and Francis Meli looked after me.

Why didn't you play as much in 2004?
There was more competition for places. Lance was back, and he was ahead of me and deservedly so. I was just back where I should have been. I'd signed a long-term deal, and they said if I had an offer I could go. I was going to go to Parramatta with Brian Smith, but they said I could only go to a Super League club. I was in the UK with the Kiwis for the Four Nations, and the London option was appealing, moreso than going back home and playing in the NZ Cup.

What are your memories of your time in London?
I really enjoyed London. There were some great people there. I grew up and learned about life being away from mum and dad. I had to look after myself! We made the play-offs in 2005, but we lost to Bradford at Odsal. Coming from the Warriors in New Zealand where everyone knows who you are, it was the total opposite in London. The club rebranded as Harlequins for 2006 which was quite exciting, and that's when I first met Ian Lenagan, but we weren't as good that season. I was actually looking to go back to the NRL, but Wigan came in and offered me a chance to go to a big club with so many fantastic players.

How do you look back at your early days at the club?
2007 was an up-and-down season, although they nearly got relegated in 2006, so we had done a lot better. I was still learning, and it was great to work next to Trent Barrett. I found out what the club was about in that first year. The big disappointment was losing to Catalans Dragons in the Challenge Cup semi-final. We were big favourites, but I don't think we thought we were such big

favourites because they had so many talented players like Stacey, Adam Mogg and Casey McGuire. It was a tough day.

I posted on WiganWarriorsFans.com, asking for supporters' memories of you. Most replies mentioned big hits, such as the one on Maurie Faasavalu in 2008. Where did that side of your game come from?
I don't really know. I never put much emphasis on it, but I did enjoy defending and getting stuck in. Big people running over me as a kid was good practice, and I got stronger as I got older. When someone is 30kg heavier than you, it's all in the timing.

What did Michael Maguire change when he joined Wigan for the 2010 and 2011 seasons?
He brought hard work, honesty, accountability, great structures and knowledge. The main thing was accountability, regardless of how many games you'd played. He started with a clean slate for everyone.

In his interview in this book, Sam Tomkins speaks of a pre-season training camp in 2010 when Mark Riddell refused to join in on the final day. What are your recollections?
It's true! Madge wasn't happy, and there were some hard words which we had to listen to. We did the rest of the day without Piggy. It was a weird time, but the best part of the story was Piggy and Madge are quite good mates now. As players, we loved Piggy, and we end up having a good year. He played well. He would have had to work hard after that camp, but he got the work done. He was always a fantastic player. I loved having Piggy. He's a champion guy.

You were superb in the 2010 Grand Final win. What did the win mean for the club?
It was huge because the club hadn't won the Grand Final for so long. Madge had come in and we lost in the Challenge Cup to Leeds at Headingley. We put all our eggs into Super League. There was a meeting before the captain's run before the semi-final. We'd lost too many semi-finals. That was a special meeting, quite emotional. We had to train after that, and I thought, "We've won it here." It was such a slick session, and we went out and beat Leeds in the semi-final, and we rolled into the final with Saints. We knew what we were doing and everything came together that night. We played how we practiced. Piggy missed a couple of kicks that would have made it easier, but I always felt comfortable. Martin Gleeson had a great game and to see Sean O'Loughlin lift the trophy was fantastic.

Why did you move to hooker midway through 2011?
It wasn't a difficult switch for me because I'd played lots of Kiwi games there. I'm not sure why we changed it up, but it was ok with me. I played in three positions, and I generally didn't mind where I played. I wasn't a traditional halfback later in my career, and I loved defending which helped at hooker.

Which players did you have the best combination with?
It's hard to pick just one. I had a great combination with Sam Tomkins, and I really enjoyed playing with him. I played straight and direct and he was a clever footballer, and also tough and competitive. When he was fullback, I

loved giving him opportunities. Trent Barrett helped me a lot with numbers and shape, things I hadn't really learned much about before I went to Wigan. He was fantastic. My favourite hooker was Issac Luke. He was destructive. And a great hooker too.

What was Shaun Wane like?

I loved playing for Shaun. We'd had a really structured and demanding programme, but when Shaun came in, he gave us a bit more freedom. As a team, we played our best rugby in 2012. We'd been together for a while, and we gelled really well.

Why did you return to New Zealand Warriors for four seasons?

I wanted to go home and see my family. I'd always wanted to go back. I'd established myself in England and thought it a good time to be near my family. The first year back was tough. I feel like I played some decent football there. We weren't successful, but I was really proud of my performances. I got a couple of bad injuries there, but I managed to come back from them. Sam came to New Zealand too. He copped some stick, but he was outstanding in his first season. He was in the top-three players, but he got a bad injury in his second year.

Why did you return to Wigan?

My wife and I had a kid, and she wanted to be closer to home. I was ready for a change too. I didn't want to go to another NRL club because I'd ticked that box. When Wigan were interested, I jumped at the chance because I had so many friends there.

What were the highlights of your six seasons in your second spell at Wigan?

My second game back was the World Club Challenge win over Cronulla, so that's obviously one. Then there's Waney's last year, when it was great to send him and Sam off with a Grand Final win. That was class. And then winning the Challenge Cup in 2022, my last season. My last year was a great experience.

On the flip side, how did you feel as the closing moments of the 2020 Grand Final unfolded?

That was awful. The good thing is we played as well as we could have done. If we'd not played well, it would have been hard to live with. Saints won it, but for long periods we were right in it. What happened will sting for a long time. We had a great group and we left everything out there.

You are currently one of Matty Peet's assistant coaches. Do you have head-coaching ambitions?

Not really. I'm certainly not at a stage to know yet. I just want to get a feel for it. I need to do this for a bit longer before I know how far I want to go with it. Now, I'd say no, I don't see myself being a head coach, but that might change.

What has Matty Peet brought to the club since he was appointed?

He's brought a different approach. He's freed us up. We're more player-led. He's very smart coaching wise. He has different philosophies. We speak a lot about culture, being good people first and getting back in touch with the community. They're the same values that the club's had for years, but he's put a fresh twist on them. He's been coaching for years, and he works really hard.

What is your role on gameday?

I go around the boys, making sure they understand their roles and that they're ok. I check out their feelings and the overall vibe and then pass on messages from Matty during the game. Matty likes to ask for the opinions of the assistant coaches. He's very open and we do what we need to do.

Do you miss playing?

No! I'd done 20 seasons. I don't miss it at all! There's no longing to put a jersey back on. The body still feels good, and I have a run around with the boys sometimes in training, but the desire to go out and play has gone now. I have some great memories, and I'll take those with me.

MARTIN DERMOTT

1985-1996

Seven league titles, five Challenge Cups, five Regal Trophies, three Lancashire Cups, two World Club Challenge titles, a Premiership Trophy and a Charity Shield is not a bad haul for an 11-year Wigan career. Martin Dermott is one of the greatest hookers the British game has ever produced and his timing in joining Wigan was exemplary as they were just about to embark on the most trophy-laden era British sport has ever seen.

AS Rugby League moved into an era of uncontested scrums, the role of the hooker began to change. There was less emphasis on striking for the ball and more on playmaking. And so when Martin Dermott replaced Nicky Kiss as Wigan's first-choice hooker, they were moving with the times. Dermott played for Wigan for 11 years and is the proud owner of an incredible haul of medals.

"It was 1984 and I signed from St Pats on my 17th birthday," Dermott recalled. "I played in the reserves and was called up to the first team for a game at Hull in March 1985. Nicky Kiss had a hamstring problem, and the back-up hooker Gary Owen had a bug. I was the youngest hooker ever to play for Wigan. The person whose record I broke was Colin Clarke who was the joint coach along with Alan McInnes. Colin actually asked if I wanted to play. 'I know you're only 17,' he said. 'Do you fancy it?' Absolutely! Peter Sterling was playing scrum-half for Hull, and they had a great team with players like Lee Crooks and Knocker Norton. I couldn't believe I was on the field with these guys. I was sat three places away from Brett Kenny in the changing room. We lost the game, but Wigan beat Hull just over a month later at Wembley."

The first of Dermott's 24 winner's medals came in the 1986-87 season when he picked up the Lancashire Cup, the John Player Trophy and the league title. It was a stunning season for the club. "I don't think you'll get so many internationals in one team - and not just internationals, but top internationals. We always had great centres, for example - Kevin Iro, Gene Miles, Joe Lydon and Dean Bell. We had so much quality.

"To sit in the same room as them was very humbling. It helped my game. I had to come up to their standard. I learned so much from these seasoned internationals. 'You either don't perform or you can come with us on this great journey,' they said. I did extra training and took my chance with both hands.

"We had a lot of Wiganers in the side as well. Playing Saints meant more because so many of us had grown up hating them. They had locals like Bernard Dwyer, Chris Arkwright and Graham Liptrot, but we had Shaun Edwards, Andy Gregory, Joe Lydon, Ged Byrne and me. Playing Saints meant more to us than the Kiwis and the Aussies. They couldn't understand what it meant to play in a proper derby. Everyone in the town wanted to beat Saints, and vice-versa. I watched the Easter derby in 2023, and it's great to see that sort of passion is still there."

Dermott became Wigan's first-choice hooker in 1989 when Kiss retired. In Neil Hanson's book, 'Blood, Mud and Glory', there was a suggestion that Kiss did not welcome competition for the number-nine jersey. "There was no problem with Nicky whatsoever," said Dermott. "I was a kid, and he was top class. I was more of a scrum-half type of hooker, a ballplayer, than a traditional hooker in the days of contested scrums. Nicky was a proper specialist

hooker going for the ball. To give Nicky his credit, he trained with me, he told me things I should or shouldn't be doing in the scrums. What he taught me in that first year, not just rugby wise, was so helpful. When I was an established player at Wigan, I always made a beeline for a new player to help them."

Hanson's book was a fly-on-the-wall account of the 1990-91 season which saw Wigan win the league title and the Challenge Cup but only after an incredible fixture pile-up which saw them play 14 games in seven weeks. They won 12, drew one and lost in the first round of the Premiership Trophy to Featherstone Rovers, having fielded a heavily weakened line-up. Hanson attended board meetings and sat in the changing room which, unsurprisingly, didn't go down well with Ellery Hanley.

"Ellery didn't like it," said Dermott. "He wanted everything to be just between the players. He was a very private person. I never had a problem with it, and we trusted Neil. He said that everything in the book would be rugby related and that he wouldn't reveal any juicy secrets from the dressing room. It was quite refreshing having someone outside looking in, but Ellery's opinion was understandable as well."

THERE are no hookers in the British Rugby League Hall of Fame, so I am keen to know which were the best that Dermott faced. He chose two, but neither were from these isles. The British hookers he praised were after Dermott's time. "The best was Royce Simmons, the Australia and Penrith number nine," said Dermott. "I had a lot of respect for him. I played against him at Anfield in the 1991 World Club Challenge. He came into the dressing room after the game, and we swapped shirts and had a beer together.

"Benny Elias was another, and he did the same after a game. Off the field, these guys were great, and I carried this on when I played internationals - and also in work outside rugby.

"The best hooker Wigan ever had was Terry Newton. He had everything - aggression, skill, a kicking game. I'd have loved to have played against him. And then there's James Roby. He will probably go down as the best British hooker of them all when he retires. His longevity is amazing. He keeps himself fit. He plays every week like it's his last-ever game. He's not a razzmatazz kind of player, but he's there all the time, and he's so consistent."

Another hooker Dermott went toe to toe with was Duane Mann. They were opposite numbers on Dermott's first visit to Wembley as a Wigan player. "It was a great game," he said. "I wasn't overawed because my teammates kept my feet on the ground. The build-up was fantastic. We trained well. I remember the wait in the tunnel. Going onto the pitch, the noise and atmosphere were incredible. I had a bit of a punch-up with Duane. You want to set your stall out and let him know he's in for a game, but we had a beer afterwards. I remember the heat and the pace of the game.

"If you ask me who the best player and the hardest player I ever played with or against, I'll say Shaun Edwards. He took so much stick, and he just carried on. Everyone wanted to knock his head off. He broke his cheekbone in that final, and he just carried on. He never took a backward step. He is my number-one player.

"Playing at Wembley was amazing. Your family and friends were all there. In fact, half of Wigan was. Everyone went down who I knew from the amateur game. It's something kids dream about. Not every great player gets to play there. Much better players than me never played there. I thought each one could have been my last. By the last one in 1994, I started to take it in a bit more."

I asked Dermott for his favourite Challenge Cup Final memory. His answer surprised me. "I'd have to say beating St Helens 27-0," he said. "As a Wiganer, that's the perfect result. Gary Connolly played for Saints at fullback that day. He was only 17. He lives three doors away from me now. Every time I see him, I shout over, "27 nil!" As Dermott told me this, I quickly checked the Wigan team. Nicky Kiss was the number nine. Denis Betts and Andy Goodway were the subs. Dermott's name isn't there.

"Really?" he said, puzzled. "Oh yeah, that rings a bell. I think I was first reserve. I remember being in all the photos, so I thought I must have played. So I only won five Challenge Cups? I thought it was six. Anyway, don't tell Gary!"

Dermott won the first of his 11 Great Britain caps soon after his first Challenge Cup Final. He was named on the 1990 Lions Tour of Papua New Guinea and New Zealand, sharing the dummy-half duties with Sheffield's Lee Jackson. Dermott played in the first and third Tests of the victorious series against the Kiwis.

"The organisation of that tour was brilliant," Dermott said. "To play with some of the top players in the country was great. They used to take two teams - the midweek team and the Test team, so there was plenty of competition for places. To be selected for a Lions Test is the ultimate. To get a Great Britain cap, you have to play three Tests against New Zealand or Australia. That is my most prized possession. I enjoyed the whole environment. The crack was great. We'd been arch enemies not long earlier, now we were best of friends. You always have that bond. The only dinner I get to is the Lions reunion every year. I love them. I always seek out my old Great Britain teammates and talk to them."

Dermott was back in Australia twice in 1992, firstly with Wigan as they won the World Sevens with Martin Offiah scoring four tries in the final against Brisbane Broncos. "One of the journalists asked Andy Greg, 'How did you beat the Broncos?' He just said, 'That fella in the corner won it for us,' and pointed at Martin. Sevens is lightning quick. It's a different game altogether with Andy throwing 50-yard passes to Martin."

Great Britain came agonisingly close to winning the Ashes for the first time in 22 years in June and July 1992. Dermott played in all three Tests and had a great game as the Lions won handsomely in Melbourne. With a bit of luck in the early stages, they could also have won the first Test in Sydney.

"Being coached by Mal Reilly was fantastic," said Dermott. "What a legend! He was fitter than all of us put together. He trained in the morning and then again in the afternoon with the midweek team. It was a pleasure to listen to him. The tour was great.

"We lined up in the tunnel before the first Test. Andy Gregory was in front of me. He's about five foot one. The Aussies came out. I turned around and there was Paul Sironen at six foot five, and they seemed to go up and up and up. Andy said to me, "Are we the curtain raiser here?" I laughed and my nervous energy just went.

"We did start that Test well, but we'd only had a few training sessions. You're not together long enough on tour, and the finishing touch isn't there. When I played for Wigan, I knew how each player wanted the ball. Andy wanted it as he was running away from me, so I had to pass it across his body. Shaun wanted it flat. Garry Schofield wanted it on the run. They were all different, but it's easier the more familiar you are with a player. That's always going to be your clubmates.

"We won the second Test 33-10, as everyone knows, but I remember it for fighting with Paul Harrogan. He had elbowed Ian Lucas in the neck in the first Test, and Ian never really recovered from that. So there was some needle going into the second Test, but I wasn't bothered about that sort of thing. Harrogan pulled my shirt back, and I just turned around and went for him, but it could have been anyone. When I saw it was him, I thought, 'Oh, shit!' I'm glad so many people ran in, and it broke up quite quickly!"

The first winner's medal Dermott won against an Australian side came in 1991 as Wigan beat Penrith Panthers 21-4 in the World Club Challenge at Anfield. "It was so fast, but we were well up for it," he said, "Kelvin Skerrett and Andy Platt were the enforcers, and they were always there when I turned around with the ball. Frano was a kicking machine. He always kicked the two points. What a great team. Everyone clicked. Credit to John Monie. He got us away for a week and prepared us so well. Not only did we have the best players, but we were the best drilled side in the world. We did everything in training to match the speed of a game. Everyone ran onto the ball at 100 miles an hour. If we dropped a ball in training, we were gutted. We trained how we played."

Dermott won so many medals, I was keen to know where he keeps them all. "They're not on display, they're in a Tesco bag in the attic," he laughed. "I lost a Lancashire Cup one and a John Player one in transit, moving house. I did have a display 15 or 20 years ago, but someone said if I got burgled, it's the first place they'd go to. Shaun has the most medals. I might be the second most and then Denis third."

DERMOTT's Rugby League career came to an end in 1997 after just three games for his new club, Warrington Wolves. He played just three for Wigan in their Grand Slam season of 1994-95 before figuring 13 times in 1995-96, with Martin Hall now first choice. His final game for the club was a 34-20 home win over Leeds in January 1996, and he bowed out with his seventh league title win. He had figured in eight title-winning seasons but didn't play enough games to get a medal in 1994-95.

"I broke a vertebrae in my neck," he said. "I should have finished playing when I had the op, but I carried on. I left Wigan and went to Warrington in 1997. I played just three games. It wasn't a happy place to be. They had signed quite a few players at the start of the year but had sacked some of them because they had money problems. We had to go to the players' union to get paid. Darryl Van De Velde was the coach, and it was a bizarre experience, especially coming from Wigan.

"Anyway, my neurosurgeon wanted me to go and see him in Southport. He asked if I was still playing. I said yes. 'Why?' he asked.

"He made me walk through the spinal unit. There were four beds. A young girl had fallen off a horse and was paralysed from the neck down. Two men were in there. One had had a wall fall on him and he was also paralysed from the neck down. The surgeon said, 'This could happen to you.' I knew he was right. He told me every time I played it was increasing my chances of becoming paralysed. It was a 'Come to Jesus' moment. I phoned Warrington and told them I was finishing. And that was it. My Rugby League career was over.

"My neighbour was a governor in Strangeways. He asked what I was going to do with myself. Even though I'd done all my coaching badges when I was at Wigan, I told him I didn't know. He suggested I get into the prison service. I listened to him, and I did it for 15 years. My only Rugby League involvement after my playing days ended was coaching the Great Britain Police squad.

"When I look back at my time at Wigan, I'm very proud. You'll get good teams, but not like ours."

JOHN GRAY

1973-1975

John Gray may well be the finest all-round sportsman the UK has ever produced. He was a proficient enough teenage soccer player to be offered a contract by Coventry City. He played first-class cricket for Warwickshire alongside the England captain, taking five wickets on his debut. He switched to rugby union, representing England in the 15- and seven-a-side versions of the game. After just five months in Rugby League with Wigan, he was selected for Great Britain. He was man of the match as the 1974 Lions beat Australia in Sydney, and he went on to excel in Australia with Norths and Manly.

If you could relive one day from your career, which would it be?
Winning the second Test at the Sydney Cricket Ground in 1974. It was my first start for Great Britain. We'd narrowly lost the first Test when I'd been on the bench. We didn't feel as though we were looked after by the ref, and we'd played in Brisbane which had been very warm. We knew we had to win the second Test not just to keep the Ashes alive, but because we got a percentage of every gate, some of which went to the players. If we'd lost, then the third Test would have flopped at the gate. I don't mean to sound mercenary, but it was a factor in those days.
We won the game 16-11 and I kicked three goals and a drop goal. I've never felt anything like it. The cricket ground was amazing. It was a whack-a-thon with people like Arthur Beetson, Jimmy Thompson and Jim Mills out there! I remember one scrum when I had my arms around Jimmy and Jim, and Arthur whacked me and split my eye. I needed 12 stitches and went back on. Different times! We went to New Zealand and the same thing happened there because we lost the first and then had to win the second to keep the series alive. We went home with about £1,500 each. I was a teacher and didn't make £1,000 a year.

Why did you turn down Coventry City?
I was offered a chance to go at 17, but I wanted to go through my sixth form and get some A Levels. I never believed I was good enough anyway. I was also getting too big for soccer. I was over 15 stone and doing weights.

In your first-class debut for Warwickshire, you took five wickets for two runs in ten overs. Why did you turn your back on cricket when you looked to have a big future?
The problem was you played for six months then you had to find a job for six months. You never earned enough to last you for the year. I just didn't see that as a career. I played with some fantastic blokes though, like Mike Smith the captain of England, Alan Smith, Lance Gibbs and Rohan Kanhai, who was a great West Indian batter. I got the England opener Mickey Stewart out in one match.

Did you benefit from rugby union's brown-envelope culture?
No, not a thing! I didn't see a future with the cricket, but I did with rugby, because I could pursue a career as a teacher as well. We won the RFU Cup in 1972 with Coventry, and we won a heap of Sevens tournaments. I went on tours with the Baa-Baas. The last game of rugby union I played was the Scottish Centenary Sevens in 1973. I was playing for England in a tournament with Australia, New Zealand, Wales, Scotland, Ireland and France. We won the tournament and because of that, I got an offer from Wigan. I was playing cricket at Leamington Spa and

three blokes with northern accents told our 12th man they wanted to speak to me urgently. "Holy shit, what have I done?" I thought. [Wigan accent] "Hey lad, we think you've got a real future with a team like Wigan."

What did they offer?
They offered me £5,500 and a job. It was too much to turn down. Again, I hope you don't get the wrong idea, but it was a huge consideration back then. I had tried to buy a house for £6,000 when I played for Coventry, but I was told I wasn't earning enough as a teacher to justify the loan. My salary was about £850. The signing-on fee didn't get taxed because you were relinquishing your amateur status. I bought a super house for about £4,000 in Standish. I was so lucky. Dad was a builder and mum was a magistrate. I didn't tell them I was going until I had packed my bags because I knew they would be upset at me moving away. I did enjoy union, but I was annoyed that I didn't get a cap for the internationals against Japan and Fiji because they weren't classed as Test-playing nations. And at Coventry, I wasn't allowed to be the goalkicker because I didn't play five-eighth or fullback, and only they kicked for goal. It was like some unwritten rule. Hookers didn't kick goals!

What were your first impressions of Wigan's team and the club itself?
I went up in July 1973. The first game was in the Wigan Sevens, and we won that too. I was used to Sevens. At half-time in my first full game, the Wigan coach Graham Starkey told me to slow down because I'd done 30 tackles by half-time. I didn't know what else to do, so I just tackled. To be honest, not many of the Wigan boys were particularly helpful at first maybe because I was a union player coming in on a big purse. I got a bit of the cold shoulder, but they eventually realised I wasn't that bad a bloke! Within five months I was playing for Great Britain. I was embarrassed, but maybe I was lucky that the officials wanted some new blood in the team.

When you taught in Wigan, did you teach any future rugby players of note?
I was at John Fisher, and it was a fabulous school, but I was only there for a year and a half before I went to Australia. I'm not aware of teaching any future Rugby League players. I did struggle with the Wigan accent though. I couldn't understand a word they said! But they were lovely kids.
My favourite pub was the Fox and Goose, a stone's throw from Central Park. I arrived at the same time as Green Vigo, and we stayed in the same hotel. The first time we went to the Fox and Goose, Green waited outside for us to bring him a beer. He didn't think he'd be allowed in because that's what he was used to in South Africa. He was a lovely fella and I'm still in touch with him.

Did you understand the significance of the Lancashire Cup?

I didn't realise how big it was at first. I knew Brian Snape had bought many of the best players for Salford, and we went in as massive underdogs. We went out there to smash them and run them off their feet. We won the game, and it was really tough. The boys were so elated because they'd beaten such a star-studded side. It was a hell of a pace. We had Colin Clarke, the Great Britain hooker, so I played prop most of the time. I used to throw myself into defence. I was a fairly good tackler. Defence is different in League with the ball-and-all tackle. I can't tell you the number of elbows I got because I hadn't been taught to protect myself. But it was a sensational feeling to win the Lancashire Cup.

You played in every forward position in your career. Which did you prefer?

I liked hooker. There was an advantage in being a big hooker than a slightly smaller prop. I could be more value and I had a bit of pace for my size.

Were you shocked to get a call-up for Great Britain against France in January 1974?

I had no idea that there were any GB matches coming up! Most of my teammates couldn't believe I'd been picked because I'd only played for a few months. I was puzzled too. I felt embarrassed because I still felt very naïve as a Rugby League player. I thought I was the best front-rower at Wigan, but there were still better players than me at the club. Being picked for Great Britain got me another £1,000. I didn't even know that was in my contract. That was more than a year's salary, and I didn't know it was coming until they gave me the money. I didn't really know who the other GB players were. All I knew was to go out and do what I'd been doing in every game. I ran the ball hard and threw myself into every tackle.

You also made the cut for the 1974 Lions.

It was on my mind towards the end of the season, and I knew I had to keep performing. I was still learning, and I was still asking the older players for advice. They taught me how to slip a short ball, but also how to protect myself so I didn't get creamed by an opponent. I was over the moon to find out I'd been selected. The first thing I had to do was tell the headmaster I needed some time off. I was ready to resign if necessary, but he couldn't have been nicer about it. It was the tour of a lifetime, with two months in Australia and one in New Zealand. I trained five nights a week because I wanted to be the fittest bloke going out there. All I could do was get on the weights and be as fit and strong as I could.

We won the first game in Darwin, but we were so tired. We drank and drank water and couldn't get to bed quickly enough. We then went across to Cairns, and the locals really looked after us - or so we thought! They took us to Green Island and told us to enjoy ourselves, have a swim and use the speedboats. They came back for us at 4pm but we hadn't realised how hot the sun was. We were all burned to a frazzle. We played two days later, and none of us wanted to tackle because our shoulders were burned. They had stitched us up beautifully! We did beat them, but it was a lesson learned. We then moved down the coast, winning four more games before we lost the first Test 12-6 in Brisbane.

You've told us how the Lions squared the series. What happened in the decider?

There were a lot of things that happened that you might not know. We were winning 16-10 at half-time and playing pretty well. Some of our boys who weren't playing saw Kevin Humphries, who ran the game in Australia, go into the changing room of referee Keith Page. He was in there for about three minutes. Suddenly we were getting nailed for penalties and the Australians weren't. They had all the possession and kicked a few penalties. We lost 22-18. Reg Parker, our manager, went ballistic when he found out. The home team always provided the ref, but that changed because of Reg's angry reaction. In 1975, we had neutral referees. And the first neutral ref we had was none other than Keith Page when England played France. In that game, I was lining up a goal when he suddenly put his arm on my shoulder. I asked him what he was doing, and he suddenly went down and was carried off. The touch judge took over, but they couldn't find the fourth official to do the line. We had to wait ten minutes while he was dragged out of the bar and onto the touchline!

What were the circumstances that saw you leave Wigan for North Sydney?

It could have been Easts because Jack Gibson and Arthur

Beetson flew over to sign me, which was very flattering. Jack really rated my goalkicking and the fact I won a lot of scrums, but I was still a bit embarrassed because I didn't think I was that good. Winning scrums was everything back then, as opposed to now when they are a frigging joke. The move didn't happen because Wigan put a £20,000 tag on me which was crazy. They eventually reduced it and North Sydney paid £12,000, which was still big money.

Why wouldn't I go? Again, money was a factor because it was huge compared to England. In Australia, I was on $8,000 as a teacher and $12,000 for playing rugby. It had been £1,000 for each at Wigan - the exchange rate was about 2:1. I loved it out there and stayed on with Manly, who doubled my Norths contract. And then after three years at Manly, I went back to Norths. I was 35 by then and had three kids and knew I wanted to stay here. We were settled.

You were named in the North Sydney team of the century. Was the highlight of your time there the 1976 AMCO Cup run?

Yes, that was a big thing for the club. The committee promised us a half share of the prize money which we could put towards an end-of-season trip. We got to the final, beating Easts and Canterbury. These were televised midweek matches. We only just got beaten by Balmain in the final, but we'd earned the club $100,000 in prize money. The committee had promised us half, but they wouldn't pay up. Eventually the ratbags coughed up when we threatened to go to the press. We got many reserve-graders and Under-23s, and about 40 of us went to Hawaii and absolutely loved it.

What happened when you met the Queen in 1977?

The Queen and Prince Phillip came to a pre-season cup game when they were on their Silver Jubilee tour. I shook their hands and told the Queen, "I'm from Coventry - I'm one of yours!" I told her my brother had been head chorister at the consecration of Coventry Cathedral which she had attended.

Did you get to know other British players who were in Australia in the 1970s?

We had meet-ups, a couple of times a year. The ones I got to know well were David Bolton, Cliffy Watson, Phil Jackson, Dave Eckersley, Charlie Renilson and Tommy Bishop. We would go to Chinatown and sit round a big table with our wives, and we had a nice time together.

What about Mal Reilly?

I got to know Malcolm, but he was quite withdrawn. He wasn't a big socialite, and he wasn't a big head. I liked him as a fella. He was calculating on the field. He used to nail people. He would follow people he didn't like, and he'd wait until he could get them. He wasn't a huge bloke, but he had fantastic timing. He hit people with every ounce he had. He was amazing. All the Australian players were wary of him.

How different was the NSWRL to the English game?

There were a lot more send offs in Australia. In England, refs didn't send many players off because they didn't want to have to drive to Leeds on the Monday night for the judiciary! The Lancashire-based refs, in particular, didn't seem keen on that, and they seemed to turn a blind eye to things. Fitness was higher in Australia, for sure.

We trained three nights a week, but many did their own training.

You are widely credited with introducing the round-the-corner goalkicking style to Australia, although Tim Sheens told me it was Bill Ashurst. Was it an English thing?

Yes, although some English kickers like Terry Clawson still used the straight-on style. The Aussies were all toe-pokers because they didn't play any soccer. On the 1974 tour, we went all over the country, and no one had seen that style. Only me and David Watkins that I can remember used the round-the-corner method and the Aussies would have seen me before David.

You were sent off in a semi-final replay for Manly against Parramatta in 1978 and were banned from the Grand Final and the replay. Peter Sterling made his full debut at fullback for Parra. Did you target him?

Yes, we wanted to nail Peter to put him off his game, but he still played very well. You could tell he would be a very talented player. Ray Price came in for a cheap shot. I retaliated and we both got sent off. The two-match ban ruled me out of the Grand Final and the replay which was a real bugger. They were the only games I missed all year. The club was really good and looked after me, and I was happy we won the Grand Final. Us both going off turned the game in Manly's favour.

You returned to the Bears in 1981 for a second spell.

We didn't have a bad side and we did fairly well. Mark Graham, captain of the Kiwis, was a fantastic player. We played Manly in a semi-final in 1982. I was the main playmaker at hooker for the Bears, and Terry Randall was in the Manly side. I tried to put a big shot on him, trying to get him out of the game, but he ducked, so I got him on the forehead, and it broke my arm! The lads fell apart a bit after that, and we were out.

Tell us about the accident you had in 2001.

I was 52 and still playing soccer. I'd snapped my Achilles tendon. I'd got it repaired. I ran up a set of stairs in my unit, and my Achilles gave way. I cannoned into the railing, went over it, and cartwheeled onto the next level. I landed on my neck. I was totally paralysed for about four hours before anyone found me. I couldn't even shout. There had been a massive trauma to my spinal cord. I was in hospital for two months and then had three months of rehab. I've never recovered totally, and I've never run since. My left side is stronger than my right, so my left pulls my right along. I've had six operations on my spinal column. I don't know where it goes from here. My age doesn't help, but all I can do is keep going and do what I can, or I'll be in a wheelchair.

What did you do career-wise after you finished playing?

I went into business with a couple of friends, selling the raw materials to people who manufactured pipes and cables for town supplies of water and gas, and also for mining. We were bringing in 300 containers a months - 70,000 tonnes of resin a year. We did really well. One of my partners is now 80, so we recently figured it was a good time to finish, although we still do some international trading. I had 40 years in the industry. People used to love talking to me about Rugby League, and that turned out to be a massive benefit to the business.

ANDY GREGORY

1986-1992

One of the most talented scrum halves Rugby League has produced, Andy Gregory was admired by English and Australian critics alike. He was magnificent for Widnes in the early-1980s and took that form to Wigan, via Warrington. He graced Central Park for six years, winning every possible medal. He played at Wembley nine times without losing. He played in six Ashes series. Gregory was one of the most iconic characters in an era of legends and was deservedly inducted into the Rugby League Hall of Fame in 2018.

I ONCE asked Wally Lewis who was the best British player he faced. "That little bastard!" he replied with a chuckle. It didn't take a genius to work out to whom he was referring. Andy Gregory tormented Australia in the third Ashes Test in Sydney in 1988 when Great Britain beat the green and golds for the first time in a decade. He was just as good in the 1989 National Panasonic Cup Final, producing a man-of-the-match display, when his unfancied Illawarra Steelers team, which also included Steve Hampson, came within a couple of points of upsetting Lewis's star-studded Brisbane Broncos. "I admired Andy Gregory as much, if not more, than any other player because of the creativity that he boasted and the determination to cause defeat for Australia," said Lewis. "He was also one of the toughest players that I ever played against."

Gregory played 26 times for Great Britain, from 1981 to 1992. He played in all six Ashes series during that time. Not surprisingly, that wonderful match at the Sydney Football Stadium in 1988, when Great Britain defeated Australia for the first time in ten years, is the highlight of Gregory's Test career. "I made a break and put Mike Gregory in for that try," he reminisced. "We were fantastic

that day. I remember all week Malcolm Reilly tried his best to get a team together because of injuries. There were a lot of changes, but it was still a Test match. We played some good rugby, and we surprised Australia. They just expected us to lie down, but we came up with a great victory and put some pride back into the Great Britain jersey. Henderson Gill's try was great, and I made a couple of breaks and put people through, but the outstanding try was Mike Gregory's.

"I played against Peter Sterling a few times, and what a player he was. You talk of great halfbacks and he's right up there. He's the best I faced on the international stage. We'd also played great in the first half in the first Test of 1988, but we didn't get much luck after half-time, and you need that in Test football, especially against Australia. Then they hammered us in Brisbane. We sat down and talked long and hard before the third game to turn things around. We knew we could play better and win. We certainly took them aback and were all over them. Being named man of the match in Sydney and being part of a winning side against Australia was one of the highlights of my career. You can't get much better than that."

As for his brief spell as an Illawarra Steeler, which saw him form a halfback partnership with the future England

coach Tony Smith, Gregory recalled: "They were good times. They weren't a fashionable club, finishing towards the bottom of the ladder quite often. But the year I was there, 1989, we did well in the Panasonic Cup. We beat Cronulla and carried on going all the way to the final. No one in Wollongong could believe we'd got there. We lost to a very good Brisbane Broncos team. I was man of the match in that game, and everyone was over the moon that we'd done so well. There was a lot of hostility towards Wally Lewis and his Broncos team that day from the Sydney crowd. He suffered in New South Wales with the crowds, even when he captained Australia. No one was more patriotic than Andy Greg when playing for Great Britain and Wally was the same with Australia. He was a good friend of mine and still is."

Lewis was missing the next time that Gregory faced the Australians – in the epic 1990 series when Great Britain came so close to winning the Ashes for the first time in 20 years. They beat Australia 19-12 at Wembley but were undone in the last minute at Old Trafford when Mal Meninga supported Ricky Stuart's break to score the clinching try as the Kangaroos won 14-10. Australia won the deciding Test 14-0 at Elland Road.

"The first Test was fantastic," said Gregory. "We all played well and came up with a great victory. 'Land of Hope and Glory' as we came out at Wembley was absolutely unbelievable with 60,000 people singing it, and that really lifted us. The end of the second game was terrible when Lee Jackson took the dummy off Ricky Stuart and Mal Meninga scored. That really destroyed our morale. In the third, they just cancelled out myself and Ellery. The end of the second game had finished us off. We lost something when that happened. That was the nearest we got to winning the Ashes. I sat in the changing rooms afterwards and just thought that sport was supposed to be enjoyable. It was the lowest I'd ever been in my life. But I'm proud of my international career, and I've lots of stories, good and bad, about tours. Too many to mention probably, but I loved them and when friends of mine go out there now, people ask them about me. 'What about that little Pommy halfback?' That's the highest sort of accolade you can get."

GREGORY's top-flight career actually began with Salford on 17th November 1978, which is something a lot of people don't realise. He played one trial game for them against Barrow at The Willows – a league match which the home side won 24-7. By all accounts, Gregory was the best player on the field, but Salford coach Alex Murphy refused to offer him the £2,000 his father wanted. Having been offered £1,500, Gregory walked away.

He signed for Widnes and never looked back. An incredible career was underway. Gregory played in eight Challenge Cup finals at Wembley, winning seven - five with Wigan. The other game, in 1982, was drawn before Widnes were beaten in the replay by Hull at Elland Road. Gregory struggled to choose a favourite final but had plenty of fond memories of winning at the Twin Towers for the first time, as a 19-year-old in 1981 with the Chemics.

"Obviously the first one, which was Widnes v Hull KR in 1981 [was a highlight]," he said. "I had to go to the dentist on the morning of that game to have a tooth out. It had bothered me for a few days. On the Friday night I was a bag of nerves and my roommate, Keith Elwell, probably thought I was a bit of a nuisance, keeping him awake. They took me in the next day to have it removed and we got on with the game. I came through it, scored a good try and we lifted the cup. I remember my younger brother, Bryn, asking what it was like walking out at Wembley, but I couldn't remember."

Gregory fell out with Widnes when they refused to improve his contract after the 1984 Lions Tour of Australia. He played just one more match for them and then refused to pull on the jersey again. The club listed him at £150,000, more than double the record at the time which was £72,500. It was halved on appeal. The Chemics were understandably reluctant to sell him to Wigan, so the scrum-half moved to Warrington in January 1985 in exchange for John Fieldhouse and an undisclosed sum of money. Gregory always intended to move to Wigan, and did so two years later, for a world record £130,000.

He formed a halfback partnership with Shaun Edwards that is perhaps rivalled only by Castleford's Hepworth-Hardisty pairing of the 1960s as the finest the British game has ever seen. According to Edwards, "Andy was the greatest exponent of the run-around and the short pass who ever played the game." With Ellery Hanley at loose forward, Wigan had a midfield triangle to die for.

"I also represented my hometown Wigan five times at Wembley and won the Lance Todd Trophy twice [in 1988 and 1990]," said Gregory of his most memorable Wigan moments. "Nilling Saints in 1989 was pretty good obviously."

After winning a bucketload of medals, the 5ft 4in Gregory left Wigan for Leeds in 1992, following the pathway Hanley had taken a year earlier. The other great playmaker in that team was Garry Schofield, but the trio were unable to inspire the Loiners to any silverware. The diminutive halfback left Headingley for Salford after just a season. He became coach at The Willows in 1995, and a year later he masterminded that famous Challenge Cup win over Wigan which ended his former club's incredible eight-year run of glory. You would think that would have been the highlight of his time at The Willows.

"No, that would be taking Salford out of the first division into the Super League," he said. "We'd finished top in the Centenary Season which was around the time we knocked Wigan out of the Cup, but there was no promotion. That made everyone determined to win it again in that first summer season and go up. In the 1997 Super League season, we did well, finishing mid-table.

"Then in 1998 we got to the Challenge Cup semi-finals. We'd been beaten at that stage by St Helens the year before. You talk about highs and lows as a coach, but that defeat to Sheffield at Headingley in the 1998 semi-final signalled the end of Andy Gregory's reign at Salford. To be perfectly honest, it took the heart out of me. I tried to put a brave face on it for the players though. Full credit to the board, who tried all they could to make things right, but it didn't happen, and I left. I couldn't watch Sheffield against Wigan in the final, but I look back on my time at Salford with a great deal of pleasure. I enjoyed a lot of great games, coached some great players and the supporters were great too."

Gregory has received numerous accolades since his time in the professional game ended. Perhaps the finest came in 2018 when he was inducted into the Rugby League Hall of Fame which comprises the best 32 players to have played the game in this country since 1895. Along with Jim Sullivan, Mick Sullivan, Billy Boston, Eric Ashton, Shaun Edwards, Ellery Hanley, Martin Offiah and Andy Farrell, he is one of nine ex-Wigan players to have received this honour. Nobody could argue with his inclusion.

MICK CASSIDY

1992-2004

Mick Cassidy could play anywhere in the forwards, although he spent most of his time in the second row. He caught the tail end of the Wigan glory years and never let his standards drop during the occasional struggles of the late 1990s and early 2000s. Cassidy played for Great Britain in the 1994 Ashes series and for England in the 1995 World Cup. He later played for Widnes and Barrow. He represented Ireland in the 2008 World Cup in Australia.

Like a lot of homegrown players, you started off in the second team. Tell us about those days.

I played with Mike Forshaw and Ian Gildart. Martin Dermott had just gone through into the first team. First-teamers would play in the Alliance if they were coming back from injury or if they were new, so it was great to play alongside Graeme West, Mark Preston, Martin Hall, Neil Cowie and Kelvin Skerrett. If you didn't get picked, you could play for your amateur club that weekend. One memory I do have is going to Halifax to play on a Sunday afternoon which wasn't the Alliance team's usual gameday. Halifax's first-team game got called off, so they sent their first team to play our Alliance team. We did pretty well, but we lost by a couple of points. I was 17 and I was up against Brendan Hill which was quite daunting!

Who were the big influences on you?

Two players stand out and they are Dean Bell and Andy Platt. I saw myself as a similar type of player to Andy, and Dean was the captain, so I looked up to both of them. They would chat to you, help you along and kick you up the backside if you needed it. If they had to play in the Alliance team, they'd take it on the chin. I'd like to think my mentality was similar to theirs.

As a teenager, were you intimidated by any first-teamers?

No, but I do remember one thing. One of my first experiences of Martin Dermott was at the old Central Park. There were two changing rooms - first team and Alliance. You had to get your boots from the bootroom in the first-teamers changing room, and you soon learned it was best to get there before they did. Their dressing room door would be locked at 5.45pm, just before training was about to start, and if you hadn't got your boots by then, you had to knock on the door to get them. Derms is a laugh, and he answered the door to me one night totally naked. What did I want and who was I, he asked!

What were your early first-team experiences?

I signed for the club in 1990 and made my first-team debut in 1992 in the Locker Cup game against Warrington. That was a pre-season game, but I think my competitive debut was also against Warrington. Playing for the first team was daunting because there were so many fantastic players. Everyone seemed so much bigger than what I was used to, and the games were so fast. But it was a real confidence boost to be getting games.

How good was it to play in the side that won everything?

We lost the first two finals I played in! They were against St Helens in the 1993 Premiership Trophy final and the 1994 Regal Trophy final when Castleford hammered us at Headingley. John Dorahy was coach that season, having taken over from John Monie. Dorahy was a good coach with some very unique ideas, shall we say, but his downfall was that he didn't get on with the senior players who had big influences. One of his strategies was to hand the players paper and tell them to fill in what they thought the team should be. That was such a strange thing for a coach to do, and we had no idea why he was doing it. Maybe he wanted some ideas on who to pick. But we still won the league and the Challenge Cup. I played in both Wembley finals against Leeds in the mid-'90s. In '94 I played about 20 minutes and set up Martin for his second try. A year later, I started the game but forgot to take my headguard with me. After nine minutes, I went into a tackle on Richie Eyres all wrong, got my head in the wrong place and woke up in the medical room wondering where I was!

What are your memories of the great comeback at Hull in the 1994 Challenge Cup?

Hull was never nice to go to, especially with the old stadium. We weren't prepared for Hull being as good as they were. There was a massive wind which we played into in the first half, and we managed to turn it round in the second half. The Threepenny Stand was intimidating and very vocal. The crowd got to us that day, but we were good enough to turn those situations around.

By this time you had made your Great Britain debut.

I couldn't have made my debut in a better game because it was when we beat the Aussies at Wembley with 12 men after Shaun Edwards was sent off. I didn't take it all in at the time, but it's a great achievement to look back on. They were so far ahead of us back then. Just look at their team, they had legends in every position. I remember the build-up more than the game itself. It was great to play for Ellery too. I hadn't played with him at Wigan but played against him when he went to Leeds. He was so professional as coach and taught us how important it was to win all the little battles on the pitch. I remember being worried that I might miss out when he named the 17, but I was on the bench. I was actually playing the ball when the hooter went. I threw it up in the air. It came down and hit Paul Harragon. He was a big fella and wasn't too happy, so I stayed out of the way and joined in the celebrations.

You also played for England in the 1995 World Cup.

I didn't play in the opening game but came into the side for a midweek game against Fiji at Central Park which, being a Wigan lad, was a great game to be involved in. I stayed in the side when we played South Africa at Headingley. It was strange to play against them because they weren't exactly a Rugby League nation at the time. We then beat Wales at Old Trafford in the semi-final and lost to the Aussies in the final at Wembley. The final's a bit of a blur to me. As usual they raised the bar when they had to, and it was devastating at the time. But the whole

competition was a fantastic experience because you get so much from meeting and befriending players you don't know. To be in camp for that long in such a full-on rugby environment is what you play the game for.

The end of the Wigan domination coincided with the start of Super League. What happened?
For a while it looked like Wigan should have gone back to playing in the winter! I don't think they forecasted that other teams would improve so quickly, but the cup tie at Salford in 1996, before Super League kicked off, had a big effect. I didn't play in that game due to a toe injury, but it was a terrible afternoon for the club - the first Challenge Cup defeat in nine years. I think that other teams quickly realised that Wigan weren't indestructible after that. There were still some real highlights in the first few Super League years. We only lost twice in 1996, and the 1997 World Club Challenge was a wonderful experience. Then in 1998 we won the first Grand Final against Leeds.

In that year you were banned for six matches for an infamous high shot on Adrian Morley at Central Park. What made you do it?
Everywhere I go, someone asks me that! The incident is there for everyone to see, and it doesn't look good does it? It was a brain explosion. I didn't mean to do what I did - I was just trying to put a good shot on him, and it went very wrong. People suggested that it was revenge for his shot

on our hooker, Robbie McCormack, in the first minute, but that wasn't the case at all. We had some great battles with Leeds that year - real tough battles, but we went on to win the one that mattered.

Why didn't you win it again in the rest of your time at Wigan?
We didn't replace the good players that we lost. We also let promising players go too quickly, not just in that period but also someone like Sean Long who would have still been with us. There were too many short-term fixes at the club from Australia and New Zealand, and while some of them were fantastic in the NRL, sometimes the best players don't settle in. But we managed to win the Challenge Cup in 2002 against Saints which was a huge thing for us. We weren't often underdogs in finals, but it probably helped us because we knew that if we were less than perfect, we wouldn't win.

Who was the best Wigan coach you played for?
John Monie, but Stuart Raper comes pretty close. They coached us at totally different times, and they had different styles. John gave me my first chances. He was very strict about how he wanted the game played. Stu came along later and helped me change my game. The game was changing to being a bit more skilful in the forwards, in terms of passing, linking with each other and playing on a particular side of the field. Stuart was a good coach, but he struggled to handle the personalities at Wigan. We had a lot of big personalities like Faz, Craig Smith and Denis Betts. That's where he struggled. Stu called a meeting with all the players in 2003 to say he was leaving at the end of the season. That is the norm now, but it was a bit strange then. Everything was fine in the meeting, but an hour later there was a meeting called with someone else to say Stuart was now leaving with immediate effect. Player power decided that. A select few.

Is that healthy?
The club should have been stronger and said, "He's the coach!" We were third in the table and doing pretty well. Within a couple of years, Ian Millward was the coach, and Wigan nearly went down. The club should have kept Stuart. It showed that the players ran the club.

Why did you leave Wigan?
Maurice Lindsay retired me! A mate of mine read in the paper that I was retiring according to Maurice which wasn't the case. So that was his way of saying I wouldn't be around the next year. Terry O'Connor was going to Widnes, so I went with him.

How do you look back on your time with the Vikings?
The highlight was winning the Northern Rail Cup in 2006. I was also their player of the year in 2005, but we got relegated, so it's not something I look back on with any fondness, and it hurt to be relegated to make way for Catalans. I loved my time there.

Do you still support Wigan?
Yes, but I don't watch them as much as I'd like to. I was a plumber before I started playing rugby, and I've set up my own business. Outside the game, you don't realise the sacrifices involved. I'll watch big games and I'll sometimes go down to Wigan if there's a big event, but I don't have the time to do it every week. They're my club though, and I'll always be a Wigan fan.

SEAN O'LOUGHLIN

2002-2020

One of the great loose forwards in Wigan's history, Sean O'Loughlin played 459 games for the club in a 19-year career. He captained them in 15 of those seasons, leading them to four Super League titles. He won the Harry Sunderland Trophy in 2018 and was named in the Dream Team on seven occasions, the same number as his brother-in-law, Andy Farrell. He is a member of the Wigan Hall of Fame. He won 36 Test caps for Great Britain and England and was made an OBE after his playing career ended.

IT was both the perfect cameo and a glimpse into the future.

Great Britain were 18-12 up against Australia in Wigan in the fifth game of the 2004 Tri-Nations as the game neared its hour mark. The Kangaroos had beaten Britain with late scores in their last four meetings, and every one of the 25,004 spectators expected another dose of late heartbreak, especially with Australia's substitute hooker Craig Wing running amok.

But the doubters reckoned without the home team's equivalent player. Terry Newton, who had enjoyed a great game, came off in the 57th minute. He was replaced by the 21-year-old debutant Sean O'Loughlin, who wasn't even a hooker, but his remarkably calm performance helped to ensure that the miserable run of close defeats would come to an end that night.

He made three tackles in his first defensive set. With Sean Long's kicking game having been criticised throughout the tournament, O'Loughlin, within two minutes of being on the field, took the ball from dummy-half on the halfway line and executed a perfect kick which bounced several times, turning the Australian fullback, Anthony Minichiello, around. After poor kicks from Andy Farrell and Danny McGuire, O'Loughlin turned the fullback round again.

He made 17 tackles in those 23 minutes. He made a crucial interception to prevent a try. And then he watched as Keith Senior snapped up a stray Scott Hill pass near the halfway line to score the try that sealed the match.

"My Test debut was obviously one of my career highlights," said O'Loughlin. "I was due to play in the first game against the Aussies in Manchester but got ill, and then I didn't get picked against New Zealand in Huddersfield. So the Wigan game was my first, and it was a real buzz, especially as we won the game. When you step up a level like from Academy to the reserves or when you make your first-team debut, you can feel out of your depth, but even though I was exhausted, I felt like I had an impact. The final wasn't so good though. I came off the bench at half-time and we were already 38-0 down!"

KEIRON O'LOUGHLIN was just over halfway through a great career when his son Sean was born in November 1982. O'Loughlin senior had given Wigan a decade's service in the 1970s before enjoying a trophy-laden four years at Widnes which included beating his former club at Wembley in 1984. He finished his career with a second stint at Workington in 1990.

Kevin, brother of Keiron, also enjoyed an excellent career in the professional game, playing for Wigan for 12 years. Sean's brother-in-law is Rugby League Hall of Famer Andy Farrell who married his sister Coleen, and Sean is uncle to their son Owen Farrell who has captained England in rugby union.

"I don't remember too much of my dad's career to be honest," said O'Loughlin. "I remember going to games but because I was so young, I didn't really take much in. But I've seen what he did on video, and I've seen his Wembley try a few times. He was a big influence on me taking up the game, of course, and a lot of my family played rugby. It was always on the cards that I'd play.

"I started playing when I was about nine. I played for St Pats throughout my amateur career, and they were a great club to be at, being such a hotbed of local talent. I signed for Wigan at 16 when I was coming to the end of my schooldays. Ged Byrne was the Academy coach at the time, and then I progressed to the Under-21s where I was coached by Billy McGinty. Frank Endacott was the first-team coach, and it was pretty intimidating for a young bloke to be at a club like Wigan because I'd grown up watching them and some of those players were still playing.

"Andy married my sister when I was young, so I've known him a long time. He was a role model, not just for me but the other Academy players too. I knew he was a talent from watching him at Orrell St James, and he established himself very quickly at 16 or 17. He was a big influence on me. He gave me pointers and taught me how to conduct myself. He never lectured me on anything. He just gave me real sound advice when I needed it.

"He was great for me coming through. In my opinion, he's the best number 13 Wigan have ever had. I played 13 growing up, and he was the player I tried to emulate. As a captain, Andrew was more emotional and vocal than I was. I learned from seeing him doing it. I was probably too young to have the captaincy, and I wasn't really confident enough to be a leader then, but I developed as I got older."

WEARING number 22, Sean O'Loughlin made his Super League debut in April 2002 in an 18-20 home defeat to Hull FC as a substitute for David Furner. A year earlier, he had been part of an England Academy team that had come close to beating Australia for the first time. With fellow future stars like Rob Burrow, Danny McGuire, Jon Wilkin, Gareth Hock and Kirk Yeaman, England pulverised the Junior Kiwis by 30-8 and 72-16, raising hopes they could land a historic victory over Australia. Alas, it was not to be. They were edged out by 18-12 in Brisbane before falling to a 44-22 defeat in Sydney.

"It was a great tour, and a lot of the players went on to play Super League," O'Loughlin recalled. "We were far too good for New Zealand, and that was the first time we'd turned them over in a long while. We also pushed the Aussies close in Brisbane. The following year's team then went on to beat them.

"I played a lot for Wigan in 2002, coming off the bench. We won the Challenge Cup, but I didn't play in that or any of the other cup games. I travelled up to Murrayfield as 18th or 19th man with Steve Wild, and there was a chance one of us could play because Kris [Radlinski] had a foot infection, but he played and won the Lance Todd. I wasn't that disappointed though because I hadn't played in those earlier rounds. I was pleased with how I went in Super League. We had a lot of injuries that year and myself, Steve [Wild] and Luke Robinson made debuts. I played in pre-season against Hull in Andrew's testimonial and then also played against them on my Super League debut off the bench. I can't remember too much about it apart from being absolutely knackered at the end. It was a lot faster than what I was used to.

"One of the things I remember from my debut year was Jamie Ainscough going for an x-ray on his arm, and they found Martin Gleeson's tooth in it! He'd had it strapped up, and he'd been playing with it in there. We thought that was funny, but it turned out to be really serious. He was in hospital on antibiotics, and he could have lost his arm."

O'Loughlin was back on the representative stage in 2003, playing in what turned out to be the last-ever Lancashire-Yorkshire fixture and for England 'A' against Australia. Even though O'Loughlin has no happy memories of the Roses match - his side lost 56-6 - he did see merit in the concept and is in favour of it returning.

"I was a big fan, and I'd bring it back," he said. "When I played in it, it had only been around for a couple of years, and it didn't get the buy-in it deserved. But it's played at Academy level, so lads coming through understand its importance, and it would have more substance now. From an international point of view, you get more quality than England playing France because you have 34 contenders playing for an England shirt. Playing France is important, but that should be an emerging England team. When I was young, it was called England 'A'.

"I have some great memories of playing for England 'A' against New Zealand and Australia. It was great preparation for me making the step up to full internationals. There's more mid-season activity now with England camps etc. At one point, we only met up at the end of the year when we had games. The game against Australia was great. We pushed them really close and only lost 26-22 with John Kear coaching us. It capped off a good year because I started most of the Super League games, and we got to Old Trafford after Greg took over as coach. I don't score many tries, but I got two against Leeds in the semi-final, a game best known for Brian Carney's tries. The final is a bit of a blur, and I don't remember too much about it. Danny Tickle put us ahead, but the Bulls were too good for us.

"Greg was a brilliant coach. He took us on the 2001 Academy tour, so I knew him from that, and I was made up when he took over at Wigan. He had the respect of everybody, and I'm sure that he'd have gone on to be one of the best coaches."

WIGAN lost several experienced players before the 2005 season. Midway through that season, Ian Millward became coach, soon after his sacking from St Helens for gross misconduct. He was Wigan's ninth coach in just ten seasons of summer rugby.

"Andrew, Adrian Lam, Terry O'Connor, Mick Cass and Craig Smith all went before the 2005 season, and they were all senior players," said O'Loughlin. "When so many leave together, it creates a huge void. The club saw me as being around for a long time. We massively missed them, and there was a void from a leadership point of view. The culture of the club was affected with so many senior players leaving. They were big characters and leaders. I wanted to emulate them, but your job is easier when you have a group of people around you who are equally invested in it. So yes, we struggled in 2005 as a result, but we also had a lot of injuries. I played seven games that

year and did my knee, which ruled me out of the season.

"I wasn't involved in the day-to-day side because I was recovering from my injury. Luckily, I'd done it early enough in 2005 that I had time to recover properly without being rushed back. There was no chance I could play at the end of 2005, so I could take my time and get it totally right so that by the time 2006 began, I had a lot more confidence in it. I was still nervous though and was relieved to get through the first few games."

Millward made O'Loughlin captain for the 2006 season, but after four months Wigan were rooted to the bottom of the table with just two wins in 17 league matches. Millward had been sacked at Easter and replaced by Brian Noble who eventually turned things around.

"Ian had a good crack at the job, but a lot of things didn't go his way," said O'Loughlin. "There were a lot of injuries, and we were in a big transitional period. He was a good bloke, and I was disappointed to see him go. You don't like to see coaches go like that because you tend to become friends with them. But Brian came in which was great for the club and, to be honest, it was a big kick up the backside for us all. We'd seen Ian sacked, and we realised we could follow him if we didn't shape up. Brian ripped into our defence and had us conceding less and less points. He definitely turned things round.

"2006 was a crazy year! I don't ever want to be involved in a year like that again. Even so, it was one of the most exciting years I've known. With the threat of relegation over us, every game was like a final. We made a shocking start, and it just went on and on. We were bottom for a long time, but I never felt we'd get relegated. We weren't playing well, but it never felt realistic that it would happen. Maybe we should have been more stressed than we were, but Nobby got a reaction from us, and we didn't look back. At the end, we were playing some great stuff."

O'Loughlin came off contract at the end of his first season as captain, but he soon re-signed, although not before talking to the NRL's newest club, Gold Coast Titans. "That was the first time I spoke to anyone over there," he admitted. "I met John Cartwright and chatted to him. I didn't really have a burning ambition to go to Australia. It was just a case of seeing what they had to offer, and it was less than I was on. I wasn't overly keen anyway because I was happy at Wigan and wanted to win things with Wigan. Later in my career, when the money was more of an incentive, but still not as good as it became, I spoke to Steve Price at St George, Trent Robinson at the Roosters and Nathan Brown at Newcastle, but the decision was always based on wanting to be at Wigan, and I didn't want to take my kids away from their grandparents."

In an action-packed year for O'Loughlin, he was also named in the Lions squad to play in the Tri-Nations. They won one of their four matches, failing to make the final, but the victory was memorable. It came against Australia at the Sydney Football Stadium.

"The Blackpool-Bondi tour!" laughed O'Loughlin. "It was my first experience of the publicity the game gets over there. Cameras followed all of us, even going for a coffee! It was a great experience from a rugby point of view, and we played against top players. We got the win in Sydney which was great. The experience of touring is pretty special, as is going with top English players. Over my representative career, the blokes that stood out that I played alongside were Scully, Longy, Gleeson and Keiron from Saints. They had a strong group of senior lads like Wigan did. There was Keith Senior, Kev Sinfield and Moz too. There are loads who I have a lot of respect for."

MICHAEL MAGUIRE replaced Noble as coach of Wigan ahead of the 2010 season and led the team to the Super League title at the first attempt. He stayed for two seasons, also winning the Challenge Cup in 2011. One of the changes he made was forming a leadership team of five players - O'Loughlin, Andy Coley, Phil Bailey, Thomas Leuluai and George Carmont – who shared the captaincy, although O'Loughlin wore the armband many more times than the others. Despite the success of 2010, the club scrapped the system, or so it seemed.

"When he told me about it before he came over, my first thought was the captaincy was being taken away from me," O'Loughlin reflected. "I did buy into it, but it still didn't feel great. The boys involved were supportive, and they made it known they weren't comfortable with it unless I was. They said they saw me as captain. I knew the value in it, and he sold it well to me. Having a strong group around me made my job as captain so much easier.

"It wasn't scrapped after 2010. We've always done it. We still have a leadership group, but we don't share the details. You're looking to develop more leaders than just one individual.

"The Grand Final in 2010 was a special time for the club. When you look back, it was a bit of a kickstart for the club to be involved in finals regularly. The game went our way. We knew we'd win with some time left, and that was a great feeling."

Back on the international scene, O'Loughlin was seconds away from appearing in a World Cup Final in 2013 when Shaun Johnson broke England's hearts at Wembley. Two years later, he was awarded the captaincy and led England to victory in a Test series against the Kiwis, earning the George Smith Medal as player of the series. In 2017, he was denied another World Cup Final, this time by injury.

"The atmosphere at the 2013 World Cup semi-final was unbelievable, and it was a great game," O'Loughlin said. "I'd love to go back and have another crack at that and get a different outcome. It was so disappointing. We were so close to winning it, and we could have done something special in the final if we'd got there.

"You want to play for England and the next honour is to captain them, so it was massive when it came. It was never an ambition to captain Wigan or England. It's just an acknowledgement you get, and it's a huge honour. 2015 was a great series to be part of.

"As for 2017, I tore my quad in the semi-final against Tonga. I did my stint, came off for 10 or 15 minutes, and then pulled my quad straightaway when I went back on. You can self-diagnose, and I knew it was a three-to-four-week injury straightaway, so I knew I was done for the final. It wasn't an injury I could have had a jab and played. I'd have done everyone an injustice if I'd played.

"Myself and Josh Hodgson missed the final. It was a kick in the teeth, but there's nothing you can do. Your job is to support the team. We felt as a team we were onto something and there was a lot of confidence in the camp. We were getting a lot of good press back home."

SHAUN WANE became the Wigan coach ahead of the 2012 season, helping O'Loughlin take his tally of Super League Grand Final wins to four. Victory over Warrington in 2013 was Wane's first success, and Wigan could have retained their crown had Ben Flower not been dismissed for his infamous punches on Lance Hohaia in the opening stages of the 2014 final, which Wigan lost 14-6 to St Helens. Earlier in

the season, O'Loughlin had produced one of the great derby moments when, having already scored a try, he broke through the St Helens defence and sent out an astonishing pass for Dan Sarginson to score in a 33-14 win.

"The incident with Ben was a brain explosion," said O'Loughlin. "I was confident of winning because we'd had a good year, and I felt like we had the better of Saints, but the gameplan went out of the window when he got sent off. I didn't see it live. Twelve men is tough at the best of times, but we had a crack at it, and we were close. There are a few little moments where if things had gone differently, we could have still got the win. You work so hard for a Grand Final, and you lose it like that. Saints probably felt like they'd jagged one.

"Ben had gone home by the time we got back to the dressing room. There was no bitterness from anyone. He knew he'd messed up. He apologised as much as he could. We just put an arm round him. It blew up massively on social media and in newspapers. When it goes past the sport, it becomes very different, and he had to deal with that. It was great for everyone when he made his comeback after his ban."

Another final, also against Saints, that got away was O'Loughlin's final match for the club. He was a substitute in the Grand Final of 2020 which was played in front of empty seats at Hull because of the Covid-19 pandemic. With the score 4-4 in the final seconds, Jack Welsby scored a freak try from a failed drop-goal attempt to win the title for Saints.

"Obviously, I'd have sooner won the game, but I was quite philosophical about it," said O'Loughlin. "There was me on one side and James Graham on the other, both playing our final matches. The defeat wasn't career defining though because I was quite content that we'd chucked everything at it. We lost with a piece of luck. It's not something to beat yourself up about. I was gutted because we'd lost as a team, not because it was my last game."

O'Loughlin, who was awarded an OBE in 2022, is now one of Matty Peet's assistant coaches and has no particular designs on becoming a head coach just yet.

"I got a letter telling me about the OBE two or three months before the news came out," he said. "I told my family but no one at the club. I was really surprised and chuffed to bits. I don't know if anyone nominated me. It was awesome to take the family to Windsor and see inside the castle.

"I don't particularly miss playing. I'd love to still have a game, but I don't miss the physical side. I played one game of rugby union. The press went mad, and about 2,000 people turned up! I'm involved in coaching. If I didn't have that, it might be different. I'd have missed the environment. I was 39 and when you get to that age, I knew I was ready to retire. If it had been snapped away from me in my 20s, I'd feel differently, but I was quite content with what I'd done.

"Being a head coach is a way off, and it's not something I want to fast track. I want to be a good assistant, developing and learning. I'm enjoying working with the group here, and I'm working with a great head coach. I have a lot of time for Matty, and I know how good he is. I know there's a lot more than just coaching in the role, and there are a lot of skills I need to learn. I'll see where it takes me. If you're involved with sport, you have to be ambitious. Somewhere down the line, I'd like to do it, but I won't chase it hard."

SHAUN EDWARDS

1983-1997

Shaun Edwards enjoyed an extraordinary Rugby League career, which saw him play for Wigan, Balmain Tigers, London Broncos, Bradford Bulls, Lancashire, England, Ireland and Great Britain. Edwards, who played in every position in the backs, is in the British Rugby League Hall of Fame. He captained Great Britain. He has been awarded the OBE. And he has won more medals than any other player in history. Edwards' playing days ended in 2000, after which he has coached in rugby union. After telling me in 2018 of his "burning desire" to coach a team to victory in a Super League Grand Final, it was announced he would take over at Wigan in 2020. It didn't happen. Nevertheless, Edwards is as big a Wigan legend as they come.

How would Shaun Edwards the coach deal with Shaun Edwards the player?
Good question! I think I'd have worked with him, not against him. But every now and again, I'd have said we're going to do this, not that. That's what good coaches do. There'll always be some friction in a top team because there's lots of big names and positive egos. People think egos are a bad thing, but they're not if they're positive. Everyone was competing. There's nothing wrong with some friction, and we had some of that at Wigan, but come the big games, it was always focused in the right way.

You captained England Schoolboys in both codes. How did that work?
My rugby master, Steve McLeod, was miles ahead of his time. He was into player welfare, and he'd hold you back. All the lads from St John Fisher talk very highly of him. He'd often send the Rugby League lads on a Lancashire rugby union trial. I was selected, and then also for North of England and then England. Me and Richard Gunn, who later played for Leeds and Featherstone, played in the centres. Although I was a Rugby League player, there was no animosity towards me. I was selected as captain and only knew half the rules, but I was always going to play Rugby League.

You signed for Wigan on your seventeenth birthday in 1983. What do you remember of your early days at the club?
I had a back injury, which caused my training to be interrupted. Fitness was a huge part of my game, but I wasn't as fit as I could have been. I gradually improved and hit form around Christmas. I was moved to the wing and then fullback, which was a great move by Alex Murphy. I did something similar with Danny Cipriani at Wasps. A good stand-off should know how to play fullback.

You are the most decorated man in the sport's history. Which of your achievements mean most to you?
The thing I'm most proud of is my international career. I didn't play against Australia as many times as I should have, but I started six and won three. I played ten against New Zealand and lost just two. I was man of the series in 1989, playing in just two of the games. And in 1993, we won the series 3-0. All I'd thought about was coming up against Gary Freeman again after our second game against them on the 1992 tour. I trained my arse off in preparation to meet him again, and he ended up getting dropped for the third Test, so I obviously did ok.

I'll come onto your Test career later. You played for a variety of coaches. Which have had an influence on your coaching career?
All of them from Alex Murphy to Allan McInnes and Colin Clarke. Graham Lowe was an unbelievable motivator. John Monie always looked so calm. Graeme West was a great coach. He had an unbelievable team in 1994-95 and won every trophy. He picked the right team for the right game. When I retired, I went to Australia to learn how to coach with Wayne Bennett. The RFL paid for me to go. He's someone I've kept in touch with, and he helped me so much.

Now you have been a coach, do you have some sympathy for John Dorahy after his season at Wigan?
Not really, no. I worked with Sir Ian McGeechan at Wasps. He had a knighthood, but he still realised he was at a well-oiled machine of a club and he never let his ego get in the way. He came in and saw the processes we had. John didn't do that. He tried to change it all and put his stamp on everything. I probably have even less sympathy for him now. Some of his tactics were good, but it was a nine-month slog, with us often playing twice a week. Our spare time was our family time, but he'd have us training on Sunday mornings at 8 o'clock, with lads like Kelvin Skerrett having to come over from Yorkshire.

What was your attitude to rugby union in 1996 when Wigan played Bath and then won the Middlesex Sevens?
I knew how hard it was to play union back then. There was no space. When people were saying we had a chance of beating them, I knew we didn't. I know Wigan scored a couple of tries at the end, but we went to uncontested scrums because it was getting dangerous. I respected the players, and it was one reason I never went to play rugby union. I thought it would be disrespectful to think I could learn it all in my 30s, having not played since I was 16.

Still on union, since Jason Robinson, many converts from League to union have returned to the 13-man code earlier than expected. Why is this and what is the future for cross-code transfers?
They have in a way. What you have to remember is everyone got compared to Jason, who is incomparable. He's the only player in the Northern Hemisphere to score a winning try in a World Cup Final. Lads have come over from League and got capped at union and been called a failure. That's ridiculous. You have to coach people differently. The Welsh lads are like the Wigan lads - working class and they miss home.

You were in great form in 1996 but were dropped for a while. Why was that?
I did what a lot of older players do. I lost my leg strength and a yard of pace. I lost my support game. And I got dropped. I went away and thought what am I good at? Scoring tries. So I worked hard in training and got my leg strength back and my pace. If you remember the Premiership semi-final, I beat Robbie Paul in a race to the ball for a try. Eight weeks earlier, I would have never beaten him to that ball.

You left Wigan for personal reasons as your son was in London. Were there rugby reasons too?
No. None. I lost nearly £100,000 over two years in that move. The move was about my son. I had two years left at Wigan on £125,000 and went to London for £85,000.

You had two spells at London Broncos, finishing second in Super League in 1997 and reaching Wembley in 1999. How did it compare to your time at Wigan?
Looking back, I have so much satisfaction over those achievements at the Broncos. Finishing above Wigan, Saints and Leeds in 1997 was fantastic and then getting to Wembley in 1999 was so emotional. I was close to some of the fans, and I remember one called John saying he cried as he walked up to the Twin Towers, as he never thought the Broncos would get there.

Robbie Paul once told me that you didn't fit into the working-class culture at Bradford Bulls. Is that true?
Everyone's entitled to an opinion, but no.

173

Was Graeme Bradley a reason you left Odsal?
It was nothing to do with the players. Bradford Bulls were such a professional club. The coaching and conditioning were excellent. But I was missing my son. I won't go into details, but I was having difficulty seeing him. It was nothing to do with Graeme Bradley. I can handle people like him. I've dealt with plenty of bullies down the years.

You spoke of a desire to coach London Broncos along with Peter Gill. What happened to that and were there other coaching opportunities for you in Rugby League?
We put in for it, but they turned us down. I had no offers I was interested in. Then one came in from Wasps. Geographically, I could be part of my son's life. Warrington then offered me a two-year deal on more money. Wasps was one year and less money, but I went for it.

What do you remember of your time as a Balmain player in 1989?
It was a disappointing period for me. I was man of the match in the first game, having just got off the plane. In the second game, I high tackled Peter Tunks - I always picked the big 'uns! I got suspended for a month. Then I tore my hamstring. I finally got fit but couldn't get back in the team. So I was on the bench. But I came back to England a 20-percent better player. I was determined to

make up for my time there. And that's when I was named player of the series against New Zealand. It was a very positive experience in learning what you needed to do to be a top-class player.

What do you know of your father's career?
I know a lot about it. He was the youngest-ever captain at Warrington at 16. Then he got a nasty injury. Friends of his say he was incredibly unfortunate not to play for Great Britain. He's in the Warrington Hall of Fame. He finished at 24, injured. He still played well over 200 games, having had a year out with injury. That's not bad!

How did you deal with your brother's passing? Is it something you have now come to terms with?
My advice to anybody who encounters something horrific like that is to keep yourself busy and try to do some good for others. My job at Wasps was a godsend. It kept me busy. I still struggle with it now. It'll never go away. There is no cure.

If you could have your time again, would you do anything differently?
It drives me mad that we lost the World Cup Final in 1992. It drives me insane. We had them, and then we made two mistakes and we'd lost.

Moving onto your international career, at 18 you became the youngest-ever Great Britain player in a young side in France 1985. What are your memories of that game and how much pressure did you feel stepping up at such a young age?

We won convincingly [50-4], and we had a strong team out as the score would suggest. I was quite tense before the game, but I didn't have many tackles to make at fullback in such a big win. I was an attacking fullback, so it was a dream game for me, being able to get into the back line a lot.

You faced the Kiwi tourists that autumn. What do you remember?

I think it was the dawn of good times for Great Britain. We got a drawn series against probably the best team in the world at the time as they'd just beaten the Australians 18-0. Tony Myler pulled out on the morning of the third Test, so I started in that, playing left centre against Dean Bell. It was probably the dirtiest game of rugby I've ever played in. It was very tight, and it was down to Lee Crooks to kick a last-minute goal to level the game and the series. Lee came off the bench and won man of the match, so that shows the impact he made. New Zealand had beaten Great Britain 3-0 in 1984, so the improvement was there to be seen, and I felt that I'd played in a real Test match which I was proud of.

What were the main things you learned by being involved in the GB set-up at that stage of your career?

Well in that game, I wanted to keep my head down as there were fists flying everywhere! It's very intimidating to be young playing at a level like that. You've got to give it everything and when you're hurting, hang in there.

After establishing yourself in the team over the next couple of years, you were an obvious selection for the 1988 tour of the Southern Hemisphere, but your knee injury against Papua New Guinea meant you played just seven minutes on that tour. How disappointing was that?

It was one, if not the biggest disappointment of my career. Me and Andy Gregory were all set to go to Australia and take on Lewis and Sterling, but after five minutes it was all over for me. It was probably the worst time of my career. I ended up in the television studio back home.

Were there mixed feelings when you watched the famous 26-12 third Test win?

Oh no. I was absolutely delighted the boys had won. There was no one more excited than me, and I wished I was there. Likewise, I was wishing I'd been in the other games. We could have won the first Test when we were winning at half-time.

In 1989, Great Britain defeated the Kiwi tourists in a series for the first time in 24 years and you were named man of the series. What are your memories?

I'd just come back from my spell with Balmain where I'd been suspended and injured my hamstring. I felt I'd come back a better player but had to prove it out on the pitch. Those first few months after I came back was some of my best form of my life. I came on as a substitute in Manchester in the first Test which we lost, and then we went on to win the series. After the disappointment of not showing my best form at Balmain, I was delighted to be announced as the man of the series. I felt I'd arrived as an international rugby player.

Steve Hampson was sent off after a minute of the second game. How did you win?

It was quite amazing and gets more amazing when you look back and consider we won after playing the whole game with 12 men. It was one of the most fired-up Great Britain dressing rooms with the captain Mike Gregory doing a great job. We wanted to redeem ourselves after the first Test, and we did. Andy Goodway was superb, scoring two tries, but we all dug in for each other, and it was one of the best games I ever played in.

With Hanley, Gregory and Schofield out, do you think you benefited from the added responsibility?

Possibly. I was at my best in Rugby League when there was pressure on me and with Andy Gregory out, I was the main playmaker. I always played well with David Hulme because I think our styles complemented each other.

Your fractured eye socket at Wembley in 1990 cost you a place on the tour of New Zealand.

Yes, I smashed my cheekbone in the Challenge Cup Final, and it was all over for me. I won 37 caps, but it could have been a lot more had it not been for the injuries.

You had further disappointment later that year when you only featured in the first test against the 1990 Kangaroo tourists.

I was on the bench at Wembley but missed out altogether for the next two. My form was poor at the start of the season, and I paid the penalty and missed a monumental series. I feel that I should have been on the bench though, and if I'd been on, I feel I'd have stopped Ricky Stuart when he made that break at Old Trafford. Malcolm Reilly made a big mistake by not putting a cover defender on late on.

In 1992 you finally made a full tour and were part of the famous 33-10 second Test win in Melbourne.
It was quite unbelievable. We lost the first Test then went to Parramatta and lost to them too. We were being portrayed as a laughing-stock over there. Even though we'd run them close in the first, they got away from us at the end. Before the second, we trained fantastically well and there was a real determination to redeem ourselves. It was a wet-weather night which suited us fine. They were trying to throw the ball around, and we really pressured them. It was my first start against Australia too. The rest is history. 33-10 in Australia is fantastic.

Yet again you came into the second Test starting line-up after Andy Gregory went home and after coming off the bench in the first Test. Did you think you had a point to prove?
It was my first start against them which is what you dream about all your life, so I wanted to give it everything I had for that reason. I'd been told about six days beforehand that I needed surgery on my shoulder and that I shouldn't have been playing but fortunately for me, I met a physiotherapist who told me how to strap it in a certain way. The shoulder had kept dislocating, and I thought that if I was to get injured, then it may as well be in a test match. I went out there and didn't really care what happened to my body. I just wanted to put my body on the line but, in the end, it was rewarding for me because I played with my shoulder strapped like that for another eight years.

How much did it help having an all-Wigan pack that night?
It didn't make that much difference although having Martin Dermott at hooker helped as the hooker and scrum-half relationship is important.

What was the mood like going into the decider?
We trained very well again and only lost 16-10. It was a very hot night, so it suited Australia, as they were used to the heat. It was wet the next night though. I felt that if it had rained like that when we'd played, we'd have won. But on the night we gave away too many penalties, and they got a mountain of field position. Their forwards were bigger, and we got a battering. I made 37 tackles that night, which is a lot for a halfback, but that had a knock-on effect when I had the ball.

How did it affect the side's confidence going into the World Cup Final later that year?
I think the problem was the team selection. Malcolm picked Deryck Fox and myself with Schoey in the centres which I felt was a mistake. He should have just picked two out of the three of us. But we were winning the game with eight minutes left. Unfortunately for us, Gary Connolly, a great defensive centre, had to go off injured, which was rare for him. Steve Renouf got on the outside of his replacement, John Devereux, and we lost the World Cup. Then Mal Meninga kicked the touchline goal to put them 10-6 ahead which was unfortunate because we got a late penalty which, if we were two down, we could have kicked. He seemed to kick them from everywhere against us but not in Australia.

What about 1993 against the Kiwis? That was a superb series for us.
That was the best Great Britain team I played in. We beat a strong New Zealand team. To win a series 3-0 against any Southern Hemisphere team is no mean feat. Malcolm had us trained to perfection and Schoey did a good job as captain. The understanding between the team was fantastic, and I remember John Devereux's incredible try at Wigan which was one of the best Test tries. He beat about six defenders and crashed over in true John Devereux style. It was also particularly rewarding for me because I'd played against Gary Freeman the year before when we drew the series 1-1. I've always looked at my performances critically, and in that drawn series, Freeman got the better of me. He was rated as the best scrum half in the world at that time. There was a burning desire on my part to have another crack at Gary. I'd got myself in the best shape of my life and I got my reward in that series by getting the better of him. Gary had been a real inspiration to me because I like the way he competed in games, and the crowds loved to hate him. I had a lot of respect for the way he played the game and thought he was a top-class halfback.

Did you pick up much from him when you played together at Balmain in 1989?
I picked up his competitiveness and also learned from his fitness levels. I really punished my body in the off-season before the Kiwis tour. I've never trained so hard in my life because I wanted to be as fit as him. He was super fit. I had to be in pristine condition to compete against such a great player which is why I trained so hard in that off-season.

Your most famous Test moment came at Wembley a year later when, as the newly installed captain, you lasted just 25 minutes after your shot on Bradley Clyde. Talk us through that incident.
Going into the game, I was thinking of the recent Wigan v Australia game. We'd played really badly, dropped lots of ball but still could have beaten them. We lost 30-20, so I really, really thought we would beat Australia. I was so pumped up for the game. We went into the game with a lot of confidence and were on top early on. Jonathan Davies missed a pretty easy penalty shot early on, but then I got sent off. They got an overlap and I over-chased trying to cover. Bradley Clyde stepped inside, and he was going to score. I aimed for his chest but mistimed it and hit him under his chin. It wasn't vicious. It was just a reaction.

How did you feel when you saw the red card go up?
I thought we'd lose, and I would be blamed. I remember the lads coming in at half-time, saying "Let's do it for Giz," and Ellery saying I'd saved a certain try. I was on the pitch for 23 minutes and was part of a great win.

What did you think about the decision?
Well I don't think an Australian halfback would have been sent off for that in Australia. If that had been Allan Langer on Ellery Hanley over there and he'd been sent off, there'd have been absolute uproar, but they're very patriotic and they stick together.

Was that the lowest moment in your career?
No, it was one of the proudest moments because we beat Australia. I'd been part of the preparations and had played although, of course, I wish I'd stayed on. The lads made me feel better by winning, and every time I see Jonathan I remind him that I owe him big time because he saved my bacon that day. I couldn't watch the game. I was sat outside Wembley smoking a cigarette, and I don't even

smoke! I'd got a cigarette off a steward, and I was a bag of nerves, but I was absolutely delighted the lads won.

How did the Australians react to the incident?
I don't really know. There was stuff in the media and Bob Fulton used to use the media to intimidate referees, but it was quite ironic because I got elbowed off the ball by Dean Pay in the third Test, and he didn't get sent off.

What changed for the second Test from Great Britain's point of view?
I wasn't with the team that much, but I sensed on the bus on the way to the ground that there wasn't the same intensity amongst the guys, and we paid the price by getting humiliated.

Ellery showed faith in you and restored you for the third Test in what proved to be your final Great Britain cap.
Yeah they did, and it was my last Test, but I'm proud of the fact that I started six times against Australia, including the World Cup opener for England in 1995, and won three of them. I was also voted my side's best player in two of the other three: the deciding tests in 1992 in Brisbane and 1994 at Elland Road. At Elland Road, we were incredibly unlucky. We got on top early on but suffered injuries and were down to our last 13 players. We were winning 4-0, and just before half time they scored one of the most fortuitous tries you'll ever see, with the ball bouncing off Paul Newlove's head. We were right in the game until about eight minutes to go, but I have to say that we came off the pitch having given absolutely everything.

You played in the opening game of the 1995 World Cup for England. Why were you subsequently ruled out of the rest of the tournament?
We won the first game, and I got a cut on my knee. I asked the doctor what to do. He said to just wash it in the bath, and that it'd be okay without stitches or cleaning out. So I did. He was the doctor after all. As the week went on, it was getting sore. I couldn't sleep on the Friday night and woke up with a fever. My knee was about three times the size it usually was. I got taken to hospital, and apparently if I'd left it any longer, I could have lost my leg. An infection had got into my bloodstream, and I was on a drip for a week, so the World Cup was over for me.
After that for me, there was the 1996 Lions Tour to New Zealand, but I needed surgery. International Rugby League suffered after the Super League War, and it wasn't the same for a few years. We'd missed great chances to nick the Ashes in 1990, 1992 and 1994, and it makes me laugh when people have said in recent years we're getting closer and closer to the Aussies because we were very close.

You have a lot of great memories to choose from, but if you could have one day of your Rugby League career again, which would it be?
That's a tough choice between starting against Australia for the first time in Melbourne when we won by a record margin in 1992 or going to Brisbane with Wigan and winning the World Club Challenge for the third time.

BRIAN NOBLE

2006-2009 (coach)

Brian Noble won the lot in five glorious seasons as coach of Bradford, including two Grand Final wins over Wigan. He had no silverware to show for his four seasons at Wigan, but he steered them away from relegation in 2006, got agonisingly close to the Grand Final on two occasions and built a foundation upon which Michael Maguire won the 2010 Super League title.

BRIAN NOBLE's curriculum vitae is more than impressive. Lions captain. Winfield Cup appearances. Eleven caps. Five times a title winner with Bradford as player and coach. Along the way, he rubbed shoulders with some of the greatest names in Rugby League, from the great Trevor Foster and a teenage Ellery Hanley at Odsal to the legendary coach Jack Gibson at Cronulla. And, more importantly to readers of this book, he steadied the Wigan ship when relegation loomed large in 2006.

"Trevor Foster took me to play for Bradford Police Boys' club when I was a kid," recalled Noble of his early days. "It was a youth club in Manningham, and I think most kids my age went down there just to stay out of trouble. I ended up in the Bradford schools' team and Gordon Jones, the chief scout at Bradford Northern, took me to Odsal in 1977. I signed the same day as Ellery Hanley and Henderson Gill.

"We were mates for a long time, training together and playing in the Colts. Ellery was destined for stardom. He ended up going to Wigan, and the rest is history. He'd be in my top-five players of all time. He had unbelievable self-confidence. You knew if you got him the ball, he'd do something. His record speaks for itself. He was an iconic Rugby League figure, and he conquered the Australian game as well. You have to be world class to do that. Mentally he was very tough, and physically he was very talented. He scored amazing tries but look at his defence too. His work ethic was terrific.

"Bradford might not have challenged for trophies in the mid-1980s, but we always had the ability to beat top teams. We were in transition after the championship teams of 1980 and 1981. I'd made my debut alongside the likes of Neil Fox, Len Casey, Keith Bridges, Jimmy Thompson and Colin Forsyth, but we were having to bring young players in a few years later."

I was interested to learn how the relationship between senior and junior players has changed in between Noble's time as a player and coach. "Modern psychologists might call it bullying, but younger players were treated a bit differently by the senior players compared to now," he said. "Hang your clothes on the wrong peg, and they'd end up in the bath. You'd have to do a lot of errands, but I think it's called a pecking order. There were some genuine silverbacks in that team, and you had to earn your stripes and prove your worth.

"We had a tough team at Bradford, and we were competing in the eighties with a Wigan team who bought up all the stars. They took Ellery Hanley and Kelvin Skerrett from us, but we always managed to compete. I've got Yorkshire Cup medals, John Player medals and Championship medals, so there were plenty of good times there. The biggest disappointment was losing three or four Challenge Cup semi-finals, including 1983 at Headingley, famous for Ellery's incredible try up the touchline, but Featherstone beat us and went on to win the cup."

Noble's efforts resulted in a Great Britain call-up for the third Test in 1982 with the Australian Invincibles. Within two years, the Northern hooker had played 11 times for Great Britain and had become the Lions' youngest captain in 1984.

"I'd captained the team before that tour against France earlier in the year," remembered Noble. "I made my GB debut in the last Test of 1982 at Headingley. There was no pressure because the series was gone, and we were looking to blood a few youngsters, so Mike O'Neill and I were brought in. It was close for 40 or 50 minutes, as it tended to be then, but the Kangaroos pulled away.

"1982 was the wake-up call. We had to improve after that, and we did. When the 1984 tour came around, Trevor Skerrett pulled out and then Len Casey pulled out. Frank Myler gave me the captaincy which was a great honour. It was a pretty young team that went out there. I was extremely proud of what we achieved. I remember the headline in Rugby League Week after the first Ashes Test. It said something like, "Bruising Battle - Test Matches are Back!", because it was on the back of the 1982 Ashes when they'd flogged us all over the place. We competed in 1984, although we didn't come away with a win. The disappointing thing was that we went to New Zealand and lost all three Tests which was a shock to us, but they were on a resurgence.

"Frank picked a team, the nucleus of which would be around for a long time. There was Joe Lydon, Ellery Hanley, Kevin Beardmore, David Hobbs, Andy Gregory, Tony Myler, Lee Crooks, Andy Goodway, Garry Schofield etc. They all went on to become iconic players and form the nucleus of the Great Britain side for a long time."

Great Britain's solitary win came against Papua New Guinea, where two tries from Des Drummond helped the side to a 38-20 win. "Going there was an experience I wouldn't have missed," said Noble. "It's an unbelievable place, and the people's enthusiasm for Rugby League is fantastic. The crowd scenes are hard to describe. The ground at Mount Hagen was packed and there were thousands of people outside and on rooftops and in trees."

Noble impressed many on the tour with his leadership qualities and off-field work. It led to the great coach Jack Gibson taking him to Cronulla in 1985. "When I got there, I didn't know what to expect," said Noble. "Jack was iconic in the Australian game, and I soon found out why. I remember walking around with Kurt and Dane Sorensen at one practice session. I hadn't had a first-team game at that stage because I was slightly injured when I got there. I heard this 'Fifty-six! Fifty-six!' I used to wear a New York Giants shirt with that number on it, but I had no idea he was talking to me until Kurt said, 'Hey Pommy, he wants you.'

"'I've got a job for you,' said Jack. And that job was playing for the first team! Cronulla had a tradition of Englishmen playing for them. They're all up there on the wall. It was a great club to be at. I enjoyed my time there. I remember my only try. It was against Eastern Suburbs. Big

Dean Carney gave me the ball and I got it down under the sticks. I played eight games with a few more in the reserve grade, and then I broke a bone in my back.

"It was quite sobering to be the Great Britain captain but realising that you still had to be playing to a certain standard to play in the Winfield Cup. The pleasing thing for me was that Jack wanted me to stay for a few years, but I decided to come back to Bradford."

YOU might think it was inevitable that Noble would end up a coach, but nothing was further from his mind as a player. "At 23, you don't think about it," he admitted. "On the tour, I had to do more than just play and captain. I had to do other things I shouldn't have had to do, but I did them and further down the track, I thought I might have a dig at this coaching business. I didn't think it could be that hard. How wrong can you be!"

The coaching journey began at Wakefield in the 1994-95 season, but a quirk of fate soon saw him back at Bradford. "I had a bad knee, but, at 35, I was creaking a bit on the birth-certificate too," he laughed. "I went to Wakefield as assistant coach to David Hobbs but ended up playing nine games really badly on one leg! I didn't want to play, but it was a difficult season, and they talked me into it. It didn't work out for Dave there, and he got the bullet. He was a friend of mine, so I left too.

"I'd agreed to go to Halifax with Steve Simms as one of his part-time assistants. Anyway, I went back to Bradford to get my old boots, believe it or not, and I bumped into Matthew Elliott who asked me what I was doing. I told him about Halifax, but he asked me to coach at Bradford, so I rang up Steve to apologise and tell him I wouldn't be coming. Matthew was in temporary charge until Brian Smith came over from St George.

"Chris Caisley, Brian and Peter Deakin were the driving forces behind the resurgence at the club. Matthew was great for me personally and as a mentor. He had the good grace to be patient with me and knock some edges off me. I had to put my ego in the back pocket and take five years to learn about coaching. In my first year, they gave me two teams to coach - the 21s and the 18s - and I nearly sank. I'm sure they were finding out whether I could sink or swim. In my last four years before I became head coach, I coached the 21s. I coached Leon Pryce, Jamie Peacock, Stuart Fielden, Warren Jowitt, Paul Deacon, Rob Parker, Stuart Reardon, Karl Pryce and Lee Radford in the Academies."

Smith coached the Bulls in 1996. Elliott took over until 2000. Noble was then appointed to his dream job. "I'm sure it was a big decision for Chris Caisley and the board to make," said Noble. "They made me sweat for a few weeks, but I'm told there was no-one else but me [in the frame]. I heard people saying I was the cheap option, and I was determined to prove them wrong. I was lucky that I had some good pros I could rely on. We had a talented team."

Noble led the team to two finals in 2001. Firstly, at Twickenham, in a Challenge Cup final defeat to St Helens, and then at Old Trafford, when the Bulls hammered Wigan 37-6 in the Grand Final with Michael Withers, who later joined Noble at Wigan, scoring a hat-trick of tries in a blistering first half.

"I thought we were going to blow Saints out of the water in the Challenge Cup Final, and I learned a huge lesson that day," admitted Noble. "Our preparation was great, everything was great, but they just weren't relaxed. I keep a picture at home of the players in the tunnel, and

they're all very tense, serious and determined, compared to Saints who were bouncing balls and smiling. They were mentally ready, and we weren't. We came close, losing 13-6. I fell out with a couple of players on the pitch. I remember Jimmy Lowes giving me a gesture, wanting to know why I was taking him off, and I had all sorts whizzing around my head.

"But we were ready for the Grand Final later that year. Nobody knew that we would win like that, but I knew for a fact that they were ready to play. I couldn't get them off the Old Trafford entertainment stage. They were playing cards an hour before kick-off when they should have been getting ready! We were 20-odd points up after 20 minutes and I was thinking, 'How good's this?'

"We had some great pros in that team. Henry Paul was outstanding in his last year, and he should have won the Man of Steel. Maybe it was a political decision that stopped him because he was going to rugby union. Then there was Brian McDermott, James Lowes, Tevita Vaikona on top of his game, Scott Naylor playing really well and Graham Mackay."

A year later, Sean Long's 80th minute drop goal broke the Bulls' hearts at Old Trafford. Noble described it as "emotionally crap", although they more than made up for it by winning the double in 2003. Two years later came perhaps his finest hour as a coach, as the Bulls recovered from a mid-season slump to become champions with 12 straight wins.

"The 2003 Challenge Cup Final was a great win for us," Noble reflected. "It was a tough game and a real arm-wrestle. I missed the final whistle because I was stuck in the stadium lift! The 2005 team was a special team. We were hammered by St Helens in June and there were calls for my head - I was going to the gallows! We still lost a few more, but the turning point was a defeat to Wakefield in July [after which] we had a clear-the-air meeting. Some of these meetings are more pivotal than others. Some of the players had been lacking some of the Bradford principles like never giving in and sticking together. We needed our better players back like Lesley Vainikolo and Shontayne Hape, but we had a great meeting that morning.

"There were a lot of players leaving the club and that can be a distraction, but we got it all out on the table. The salary cap was biting with young players deserving an upgrade, but Chris Caisley got it all sorted out and we committed to each other that we were going to win games. We got better and better, tougher and tougher. A couple of teams came close to beating us, but we had the momentum and we just kept winning. It was boot-at-the-throat mentality and we just performed magnificently. We knew the higher up the table we finished, we could shake it up even though it's a tough ask if you finish outside the top two.

"The club were magnificently supportive and it's a lesson for any administration. There are reasons why you have adversity and fans are allowed to whinge, but winning that Grand Final was the most satisfying. It's about the players. I conduct the orchestra, but they're the ones playing the music and writing the tunes."

BRIAN NOBLE coached Great Britain in the 2004, 2005 and 2006 Tri-Nations tournaments, having been understudy to David Waite between 2001 and 2003. It was an exciting six years for fans as the national team was much more competitive than it had been between 1996 and 2000.

With three wins out of four, Great Britain topped

the group standings in the 2004 Tri-Nations, but they were taken apart in the first half of the final by a Darren Lockyer-inspired Australia. Great Britain failed to make the 2005 and 2006 finals, but there was still one impressive win for them in each tournament. In all, Noble coached Great Britain to five Test wins including the first in Australia since 1992. To date, that win in 2006 is the last time Great Britain or England has beaten Australia.

"I'm extremely proud of what we achieved in three years," said Noble who coached several Wigan players in that time, including Andy Farrell, the skipper and Golden Boot winner in 2004 - his final year in Rugby League. "Andy was a world-class professional and an outstanding bloke. He was a good laugh too, and people don't always see that side of players. He was part of a great pack. Andy was iconic in that he ran the Wigan show as a player. He was a shoo-in for Great Britain. I always measured our players with Australia's, and there were no problems with Andy. He'd have killed the NRL."

Noble made Brian Carney vice-captain in 2005 and

clearly enjoyed working with the Irishman. "He had a shocker in one game against New Zealand, but I was never going to drop him. I went to sit next to him on the bus afterwards. He said, 'You'll be dropping me, won't you?' I said, 'I don't operate like that,' and he went on to have a great tournament. By the time we played the 2006 Tri-Nations, Brian was playing for Newcastle Knights. I wanted all the British players in the NRL to play for us."

Other Wigan players to play for Great Britain under Noble were Gareth Hock, Sean O'Loughlin and Terry Newton. "Gareth was outstanding," said Noble. "Internationally, he was very good. An Australian agent said to me that Australian players seemed scared of him. I said plenty more were as well over here! He was a very tough player. Sean O'Loughlin matured into a world-class player who would have hammered the NRL had he gone. As for Terry, what a world-class player he was. He was a leader, a motivator, he could change the game and he was aggressive in a time when you could probably get away with a bit more than now."

WITHIN six months of winning the 2005 Super League Grand Final, Noble had departed Bradford Bulls. Crisis club Wigan had sacked Ian Millward and links with Noble were initially dismissed, but Maurice Lindsay managed to entice the Great Britain coach to the JJB Stadium with the club staring the ghastly prospect of relegation in the face.

"It was a hugely difficult decision," said Noble. "I was granted permission to speak to Maurice Lindsay at Wigan. I knew they were in a bit of strife. People probably thought I was a bit stupid for taking the job because they couldn't win a game. The whole joint was in turmoil. There was lots of talent, but it needed someone to put some structures in place. I told Mr Lindsay there was a chance we'd go backwards before we went forwards, but he told me we couldn't do that! We won our first game, spanking Huddersfield, but then we lost the next six.

"We stripped things back to the bone, and I had the full support of Maurice Lindsay and Dave Whelan. We developed Orrell as a training ground. I knew if we won one or two games, we could get on a roll, and I knew Gareth Hock and Sean O'Loughlin were soon back from injury. It was tough but very enjoyable, and the fans were genuinely unbelievable. We signed Michael Dobson and Stuart Fielden who made a massive difference. The turning point came when we beat Catalans at the JJB. We kicked on from there and the confidence grew and grew. I even thought we'd make the top six, but we just missed out."

On the day of that Catalans game, 18th June 2006, the News of the World ran a story that should Wigan be relegated, they would offer the promoted team £1 million to remain in National League One, so they could stay in Super League. Whelan denied the story during Sky Sports' coverage of the match which Wigan won 24-18. Kris Radlinski played the first of six matches that season, having come out of retirement. Stuart Fielden signed from Bradford the following week and made his debut in a 30-12 home win over Warrington. Wigan were up and running at last. Over the next month, they steadily climbed away from the bottom.

"A lot of things went on behind the scenes I wasn't aware of, and I knew nothing of what the News of the World was reporting," said Noble. "But we did have some pretty lively Monday-morning meetings. 'Mate, I'm on your side,' Maurice would always say to me before meetings with Dave. I used to go in full barrels blazing because when you're new, you can demand things. But I wasn't really interested in the News of the World story because I believed we could do it, and we did it comfortably in the end. We nearly made the play-offs! I still have a Great Escape mug with my head on it instead of Steve McQueen's. We got great crowds that year. The element of adversity made it such an interesting season.

"Expectation is huge in the Wigan area because of the success in the eighties and nineties which is unparalleled in world sport. You can never guarantee success in the modern era, but the clubs who do well have a stable environment. Living your life in a soap-opera becomes difficult."

With the drama of 2006 behind them, Wigan signed Trent Barrett from St George-Illawarra on a two-year deal. Kiwi Thomas Leuluai was another incomer as Wigan's superb play-off performances, including a stunning comeback at Odsal, put them within one game of a remarkable Old Trafford appearance in 2007. But they were still inconsistent. In an occasionally difficult season, they were twice beaten at home by newly promoted Hull KR. They were embarrassed by Catalans Dragons in the Challenge Cup semi-final, and the club lost four Super League points for salary-cap indiscretions.

"If you look at the season as a whole, we had a terrific season," Noble said. "Without the salary cap penalty, we would have finished fourth, and we rattled some sides in the play-offs. I knew Catalans could beat us in that semi-final though. We'd had close games with them, and we certainly blew it that day. The start was shocking, and we just couldn't get back into it, although we almost did. There's no doubt that over-confidence set in that day.

"What a player Trent Barrett was! Maurice had great connections in Australia. Tony Myler was the best English stand-off. Then there's Wally Lewis, and Trent is in that realm. I had such a good relationship with him. At Hull, in a Friday night play-off game, he ripped the right side of their defence apart. He was magnificent.

"The comeback at Bradford was unbelievable. I was always uncomfortable going back to Odsal because I'd been there so long. I always kept a low profile. We were dead and buried in that game. I knew I'd have to cope with some comments afterwards, but we started coming back. I knew we'd win before Pat Richards dropped the goal because we had such momentum. It was a sensational win."

After reaching five consecutive Grand Finals with Bradford, Noble had a reputation as a coach whose teams came strong at the end of the season. 2008 was much the same, as they only came fourth but beat Bradford and Catalans to get within 80 minutes of Old Trafford. Their season ended with an 18-14 defeat at Leeds in Barrett's last game for the club. 2009 was remarkably similar. This time they came only sixth but wins over Castleford and Hull KR took them to the penultimate round of the play-offs where they lost 14-10 at St Helens.

"We lost Trent for the 2009 season, but we picked up Piggy Riddell, the St George hooker, and he was a big influence," said Noble. "That game at Saints proved to be my last. Joel Tomkins' try should have been allowed to stand, and it would have taken us to Old Trafford.

"The ownership changed after 20 months of my time there, and that was very difficult, especially with recruitment. In the period that it took for the club to sell, Maurice would tell me to speak to Ian Lenagan about recruitment, and Ian would say he couldn't talk about it because it was effectively sub-judice."

Noble's contract expired in 2009 and Wigan decided not to extend it. They recruited Michael Maguire from Melbourne Storm, and he led them to Grand Final success in his first season. "I still have a good relationship with Ian, but I think we saw things differently when I was coach," said Noble. "We came close, especially with that last play-off game. We were dudded with the Tomkins decision, but we played really well, and it was a measure of how far we'd come.

"People wondered if it was tough for me to see Wigan be successful after I'd gone, but that wasn't the case in the slightest. We'd turned them around and they were ready to win. I'm a big believer in someone gets to build the bridge and someone paints it. We built a considerable bridge at Wigan and Michael Maguire got to paint it. I don't mean that in an arrogant way, but I certainly left the joint in a much better place than I found it."

STEVE HAMPSON

1983-1993

One of the great modern fullbacks, Steve Hampson enjoyed a glut of success at Wigan. He missed three Wembley finals with injury, but he still finished up with five Challenge Cup winner's medals. He was a world club champion twice and played in the Great Britain team that came so close to winning the Ashes in 1990. He played for Salford in 1996 when Wigan's incredible run of Challenge Cup victories came to an end.

If you could relive one day from your career, which would it be?
I was playing for Vulcan in rugby union and decided to have a couple of trial games in League with Swinton reserves. I was down as A N Other on the teamsheet of course! They wanted to sign me, but Ian Mather, an ex-Warrington prop, knew Alex Murphy, the Wigan coach. He persuaded Alex to give me a go and after two reserve matches, Wigan signed me in November 1983. I didn't know much about Rugby League, and at 21 years old and only 10 and a half stone, it was pretty daunting. I made my first-team debut against York in the same game as Shaun Edwards and stayed in the team. I had a decent number of games that season, but I broke my leg three weeks before Wembley. Then I broke my arm the following season and missed Wembley again!

Do you have a favourite game?
I played in 25 finals in England, and I don't own a loser's medal, which is something I'm very proud of. There are so many highlights, but if I had to pick one it would be the World Club Challenge win over Manly in 1987. The atmosphere in Central Park was electrifying that night. The crowd was massive, but there weren't just Wigan fans there - there were people wearing Leeds shirts and others. It was a great game - very defensive. Our forwards were just so tough. Shaun Wane, Nicky Kiss, Brian Case and Ian Potter were all outstanding. That's where we won the game. Manly had a tough pack, but they weren't as tough as our lads. I saw the fighting from the back, but I didn't get involved. I left it to the experts! David Stephenson kept his cool with all his kicks, and we won 8-2.

You didn't play with him much because of your arm injury, but what was John Ferguson like?
He was so down to earth. I've never known a player fall asleep in the changing rooms before a game, but he'd sit in a corner and just nod off! That was his way of relaxing. He kept himself to himself. He socialised with us, but he was quiet - not rowdy like Nicky Kiss, Shaun Wane or Danny Campbell! John had incredible feet. I'd never seen anything like his footwork until Jason Robinson came along. He was so quick off the mark too. He could stand people up left, right and centre.

Having missed the 1984, 1985 and 1988 finals with injury, you won five Challenge Cups in a row between 1989 and 1993.
I wasn't too upset about missing out in 1984 because I was young and I didn't know too much about Wembley, but to miss out on two more was pretty hard to take, although I got the chance to make up for it. My first final in 1989 is the one I remember most fondly. We beat Saints 27-0. Joe Lydon could have scored himself, but he gave me the ball. He'd already been there and done it I suppose.

You prevented Joe from playing in his favourite position. Tell us about him.
Joe was such an all-round talent. He had the biggest kick I've ever seen. He had bags of pace. He'd been incredible for Widnes against Wigan in 1984. He could play anywhere in the backs. He was absolutely class.

One final you did lose was with Illawarra Steelers in 1989. Do you remember it?
It rained for all three months that I was there, and we barely won a game, but I'll always remember the Panasonic Cup final against Brisbane Broncos. Andy Gregory had a stormer for us, and we pushed them all the way. The Broncos had Wally Lewis, Gene Miles, Peter Jackson - guys like that - and they were world class. But the crowd got behind us and we almost pulled it off. The Steelers had an awful record in the competition before we got there, but we made the final, and I scored. Greg was awesome. Brisbane had a team of internationals, so for Andy to get man of the match shows how good he was. He was a freak of nature. He had everything. When we played against him when he was at Widnes, we tried to do him, get him out of the game, but he was a hard lad.

What do you remember about the match against Warrington in Milwaukee?
We were all on the beach together the day before and the day after the game, having a crack and laughing and joking, but the game was deadly serious. It was a very small pitch. Myself, Ellery, Andy Greg, Shaun Edwards and Joe Lydon travelled from Australia because we'd been playing in the Winfield Cup. The game was very physical - we really didn't like each other! I watched a clip recently, and John Holdsworth loved being miked up! That's the way John was. He was in your face, but in a good way. He was a good ref.

Tell us about the weekend in 1989 when you got sent off twice.
The first one was for Great Britain - in the first minute too! I still blame [coach] Malcolm Reilly for it because he was winding us up all week about [Kiwi halfback] Gary Freeman and how we should go for him if we could. So in the first minute, he grabbed hold of me. I wouldn't have kicked him, so I turned and headbutted him. I'd never even been spoken to by a referee in my career and I got sent off, although I still think I should only have been sin binned. Anyway, I played for Wigan against Castleford the next day. I tripped Steve Larder and got sent off again. Two red cards in one weekend!

Despite that red card, you were back in the Great Britain team for the 1990 Ashes series.
We pushed them so close. It was agony at Old Trafford when Mal Meninga scored that late try. But we had a

great team. I toured in 1992, but I only played against Papua New Guinea because Mal Reilly preferred Graham Steadman for the Test matches against Australia and New Zealand. I was in the midweek side - the Ham 'n' Eggers as everyone called us - and we had a great record. I played seven games on the tour, and we won them all, which I was very proud of.

You played in the cup game at Halifax when Joe rescued the side with a late drop goal. Did you think the cup run was going to end that day?
Ah, the snow, the rain, the drizzle and the sleet - all in one day. It was horrible! I later played at Halifax for two years, and it wasn't the best pitch. But we were so dominant back then, that we knew we could turn any situation around, and we did. We won 19-18. I think that was the game when Frano Botica and Sam Panapa got hypothermia. They had to spend about an hour in the showers to warm up again.

Why did you leave Wigan?
Because of Jack Robinson. I left under a cloud, and I was denied a testimonial that could have set me up for life. I'd done nine years and eight months, and I was still playing well, but the board felt that they wanted to give Paul Atcheson a shot at fullback, so Jack got rid of me. They did it in a poor way too. My wife went into hospital

on the Saturday to give birth while I was on an end-of-season trip with the boys. My wife came out of hospital and got a phone call from the club to say they were letting me go. I then got a message saying that a woman had been on the phone trying to get hold of me in tears, so I panicked thinking there must have been a problem with my daughter's birth. But with Salford in 1996, we beat Wigan in the Cup, and I stuck two fingers up to Jack after the game. Maurice Lindsay said, "Hampo, I saw that!" One of the reasons we won the game was we tired the Wigan forwards out. Our forwards weren't as big as theirs, but they were quicker. We scooted and tired the big fellas out.

What happened at the end of your time at Salford?
I fell out with Andy Gregory and that was the end for me at Salford. It was a real shame because he'd been my best mate for years. What happened was Salford lost a match at Hull by a couple of points. I stayed on the field after the game to tell the referee and the linesmen they didn't have a set of balls between them because they'd given Hull absolutely everything. Anyway, I got back to the dressing room and Andy was laying into the lads. I told him he was out of order and that we'd lost because of the officials. But he wasn't happy and when we met up a couple of days later he told me I was out of the club, so I missed out on the chance to play Super League for them.

TONY STEPHENS

1961-1967

Tony Stephens was a quick, powerful second rower who scored 17 tries in 88 matches for Wigan between 1961 and 1967. He won a Wembley winner's medal in 1965 before returning a year later with a less happy outcome. As Wigan's great team of the mid-1960s began to break up, Stephens had a spell at Swinton before retiring from the game at the end of the decade.

I DO most of my interviews by phone, but when Tony Stephens told me he had several boxes of newspaper cuttings, jerseys, medals and photographs that I could look at, I was at his Widnes home like a shot. The first contract he signed with Wigan in March 1961 was there, along with numerous match reports and stories that serve as a sobering reminder of how much coverage Rugby League used to be afforded by Fleet Street compared to the measly amount it gets today.

Stephens is the fourth player interviewed in this book who won the Challenge Cup with Wigan against Hunslet in 1965. It was the seventh time the club had won the famous trophy, the same as Leeds. It was a wonderful, free-flowing game that is rightfully regarded as one of the greatest finals ever played and, unsurprisingly, Stephens regards it as the highlight of his career.

"We stayed in Blackpool the week before and trained at Blackpool Borough and had Turkish baths," he told me. "It was a team-building thing and the club wanted to get us away. We travelled to London on the Thursday. We went to the London Palladium to watch Sammy Davis Jr.

"My memories of the game aren't the best, but I do remember the first five minutes because Brian McTigue put me clean through with 40 metres to go, but the ref blew - wrongly! - for a forward pass. Ray Ashby played well and shared the Lance Todd with Hunslet's Brian Gabbitas. Princess Alexandra was the guest of honour. We also met Harold Wilson. We went back to the hotel, had a few drinks and then there was a big dinner to celebrate. We each got a suit, a tie, a week's loss of work and £100 for winning the cup!"

Living next to Naughton Park, it was no surprise that Stephens supported Widnes, especially as family members had played for them. "I was 11 or 12," he said, "and they'd let you in at half-time for free. We stood under the old stand, and money would occasionally fall out of people's pockets down to where we were! I remember Billy Boston scoring six tries in one game. Never did I think I'd play alongside him. Widnes was a real Rugby League town. One player I remember is George Kemel, the hooker. My uncle, Frank Bradley, played fullback for Widnes at Wembley in 1950. Walter Bradley, played for them in the 1930s. They were uncles on my mother's side. Fred Newton was a mate who played for Widnes. I went to school with Frank Myler who was a fantastic player and a lovely fella. Bob Sherman, my brother-in-law, also played for Widnes. Tom Smith, Ray Owen and Jimmy Measures were other lads I knew who played for them.

"My amateur club was West Bank. I played under-19 when I was 17. Joe Williams was the club secretary, and we had meetings at the Angel Pub. Joe wrote to Wigan to recommend that one of their scouts come and watch me. They wrote back to Joe and said they weren't impressed. Joe replied that they'd obviously watched the wrong player, so they should come back and have another look. I think they must have done because I soon got an offer! I

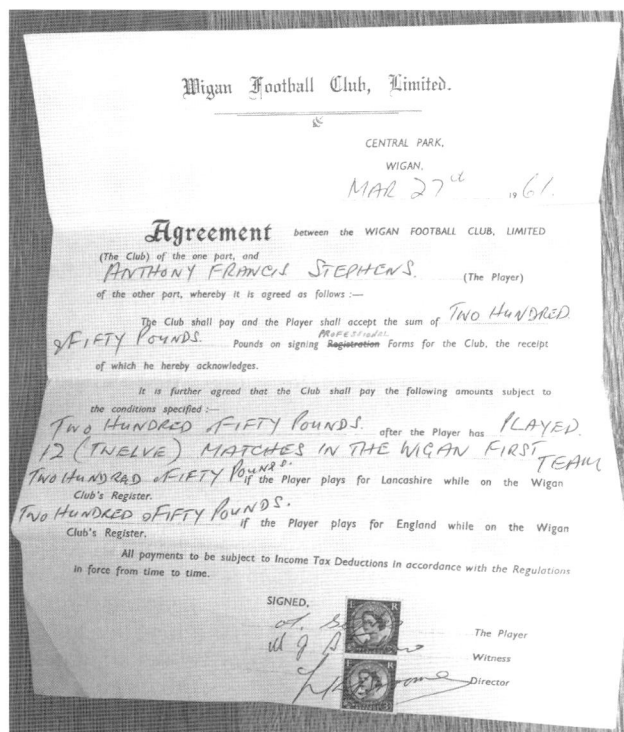

Tony Stephens' first Wigan contract

lived right next to Naughton Park, and Widnes only came down after they heard Wigan had come in for me. 'Sign for Wigan, and if you don't make it, you can always go somewhere else,' my father advised, 'but if you start at a lower club, you'll struggle to get to a higher club.'"

STEPHENS made his senior Rugby League debut for Wigan in December 1961 at loose forward in a 22-5 home win over Rochdale. "I don't remember the game," he said, "but I think I got knocked out, and that also happened in my first game with the 'A' Team. You'd draw a man and pass, and then you'd get hit after you released the ball. I signed for Wigan just before my 18th birthday, but they couldn't publish anything until I was 18 which was a month later in April 1961. I was a heating engineer in Liverpool. Rugby paid more than work if we won but not if we lost. I remember losing pay was £7 less tax.

"The 'A' team didn't train with the first team, but we'd cross paths, and we knew who they all were. I really enjoyed the 'A' team. We all started there. I played in it with Colin Clarke, Terry Cook and John Lindley. Sometimes the older players didn't give you the ball when you were young. Maybe they didn't have confidence in us, or maybe they were trying to protect us. After a while, when you had your feet under the table, then it was great.

"I was 14 stone 4, and I had pace. I could run outside or

take it short. I could come through the middle off a short ball. I had a good understanding with Danny Gardiner. If you didn't win a scrum, a second row was expected to get right across the field in a defensive role to cover whoever the ball went to. Eric Ashton used to say when we were in our 25, that he didn't want to see me or the other second row. But outside it, if a forward made a break, he wanted us either side of him. The game was rougher then. There were a lot of head tackles, but if you had a fight with someone, nothing carried on after the game, and we all ate together."

Stephens played with a myriad of legends at Central Park, and he told me about some of them. "Billy Boston was a nice fella," he said. "I didn't socialise much with the players because I'm from Widnes, and Billy was older, but you could really talk to him. He was one of the superstars, the most well-known. He was a firm favourite. He'd been there so long.

"Frankie Parr was a will-o-the-wisp scrum-half - very fast. Not big, but a good player. He was very important to us, especially after Frank Pitchford and Brian Shillinglaw had gone. Pitchford played in the 1963 final against Wakefield, and then Frankie took over.

"Brian McTigue was a great ball handler. Today's props are faster, but they don't have his hands. Brian was big and strong. He was a boxer in the army. He was my sprint partner in training, and he'd have a 20-metre start. I'd have 100 metres to catch him, and I'd usually do it. When I joined Wigan, Jack Gregory, the loose forward, told me I'd have a job to get into the team with international forwards like Brian, Bill Sayer, Roy Evans and John Barton at the club. I remember wondering if I'd made a mistake.

"Alan Davies was a great centre! I always remember him saying, 'Tony, do unto others what they'd do to you - but do it first! Let them know you're there.' He was a nice fella. He was always very smart when he came from work. Dave Bolton was a great stand-off and always very kind and friendly.

"Colin Clarke was a bugger for playing tricks. He would throw a bucket of cold water over those of us in the big communal bath. Then he'd walk past the bath a minute later, knowing everyone would get him back by drenching him, but he'd do it wearing someone else's coat, and that person would only realise once it was soaked!

"I remember a few other players that most people have probably forgotten now or had maybe never heard of. We signed a shot-putter called Arthur Rowe. I think he played one 'A' Team game, and that was it. Kia Bose was a Fijian playmaker who played one first-team game. Chook Wiseman was an American who fancied giving Rugby League a crack. He was a winger but never played first team, although he did for Blackpool. And Peter Davies joined us from Welsh rugby union and played one game. He was huge."

A year into Stephens' Wigan career, the British game ground to a halt with viciously cold weather playing havoc with the Rugby League programme. Stephens played 13 games in the 1962-63 season, but Wigan went two and a half months without a game between December and March. Wigan reached Wembley that season, where they lost to Wakefield Trinity, although Stephens wasn't selected.

"Widnes used a chemical called GL5 during the big freeze, but we didn't manage to get a game on," he said. "We hoped to play at Rochdale or Oldham, and they inspected the pitch, but it was called off. In training, we played soccer or tick and pass on the car park. We did some laps and other exercises, and we did some track work by the River Douglas. It was all about speed then.

"I didn't expect to play at Wembley. They'd done well that season, and there were no subs back then. The team was announced much earlier than it is now, so you knew when you were travelling down. In 1965, there was a bit of doubt because Geoff Lyon had been injured, and I'd played in some of the harder cup games, so I got the nod. But in 1963, I ended up getting tonsillitis in London, so it was just as well I wasn't down to play. We lost to Wakefield, so it was a miserable weekend."

After winning in 1965, Wigan were back at the Twin Towers in 1966 to take on St Helens, but some cunning gamesmanship from Alex Murphy, who played in the centres that day, was crucial in deciding the outcome.

"That was heartbreaking!" said Stephens. "The rivalry was fierce back then. We'd lost Colin Clarke to suspension after he'd been sent off against Leeds for striking for the ball too early in a scrum. Can you believe that? Bill Sayer had been sold to Saints, so we had no hooker. I filled in after Colin was sent off, but there was no chance I'd play there at Wembley, and Tom Woosey did the job. Alex Murphy knew we'd barely win a scrum without a recognised hooker, so he kept straying offside because a scrum followed a kick to touch back then. As a result, Saints dominated possession. I suppose you couldn't blame him. He did what he had to do to win. I remember 40,000 greeting us back at Wigan in 1965. There were about ten fans and 20 policemen in 1966!"

GREAT BRITAIN never came calling for Stephens, although he was in with a shout of making the Lions Tour in 1966. A year later, he left Wigan.

"There were a few reports that suggested I was close to playing for Great Britain," he said. "People were suggesting I had a chance of getting on the 1966 tour because the hard grounds in Australia would have been ideal for me. But it didn't happen. I got a few mentions when I was at Swinton too.

"I ended up on the transfer list at Wigan with six others in 1967. They were Laurie Gilfedder, Len McIntyre, Ray Ashby, Danny Gardiner, Keith Holden and Harry Major. It was soon after the 1966 cup final, but I don't know why I was listed. I wasn't happy with it and figured if they didn't want me, I should just leave. I could have stayed at Wigan I suppose, and maybe I should have done because I didn't enjoy Swinton.

"I should have gone to Leeds, but my father had just died, and I was living with my mother in the pub. I didn't fancy the travelling. Warrington and Swinton came in, and I chose Swinton. They were a good club, but I didn't enjoy it. There were often training sessions when you didn't see a rugby ball. They'd send us running round roads. I can't think of any other sport with a ball where that would happen.

"But they had some good players like the wingers Johnny Stopford and John Speed. Dave Robinson was a good back-rower, and so was the prop Barry Simpson. Ken Gowers was a nice fella and a good fullback. Derek Whitehead was another good fullback. I'd started working for myself by then in a plumbing business, so I had to put more time into that. My heart wasn't really in Swinton. After that, I never worked for anyone else, and I wasn't tempted by coaching."

Stephens lost touch with many of his Wigan teammates when he finished playing as he didn't live in the town but has recently engaged with the club's past players' association. "I love the events that they put on," he said. "When I last saw Bill Ashurst, he put his arms around me and said I'd been his hero. I was really touched because I didn't know him. He died six days later. When I left Wigan, I lost touch with everyone because I lived in Widnes. I always supported Wigan, but I didn't go to matches. There was always a past-players' set-up, but it's got much more serious since it's been run by Keith Sutch. There's a lot more players involved now. There were 70 at the heritage game in 2022 against Warrington. It's fantastic to see everybody."

Tony Stephens with his 1965 and 1966 Challenge Cup Final shirts

JOHN MONIE

1989-93 (coach)
1998-99 (coach)

One of the most successful coaches of all time, John Monie arrived in Wigan in 1989, having won the Australian Grand Final three years earlier with Parramatta. He built on Graham Lowe's great work at Central Park by winning four league-and-cup doubles in his four seasons at the club. He returned in 1998 to lead Wigan to glory in the inaugural Super League Grand Final.

How hard was Jack Gibson to follow when you succeeded him as Parramatta coach in 1984?
When you're young you work hard, and the hours don't mean much. You do whatever you've got to do to get the job done. I had three years working under Jack and Ron Massey which were very enjoyable - Massey was the co-ordinator who put everything together. It was a great learning time for me and when Jack walked away, he recommended I got the job. I inherited a very good football team with a tough mental attitude and plenty of football ability. You have to believe in yourself and keep your head down.

You lost a Grand Final in your first year by two points to Canterbury.
I had great self-belief and the players wanted me to do the job. At the time, I'd have probably rather not made the final than get beaten in it by such a narrow scoreline, but as the years go by, and you look back, it was all learning for me, and we rectified everything a couple of years later.

You coached some of the greatest players to have played the game in Australia. Who was the best?
I can't pick a best. They all have different qualities - same when I was at Wigan with Ellery Hanley, Andy Gregory and Shaun Edwards. They were three completely different individuals. It was the same at Parramatta with Peter Sterling, Brett Kenny, Mick Cronin, Steve Ella, Eric Grothe and Ray Price. They all had to be treated differently and ply their trade for the good of the team. The team comes first and the individuals have to do what they have to do.

How fondly do you remember 1986?
No-one's ever done what we did in 1986. We won the pre-season competition, we were the minor premiers, we won the Midweek Cup and we went on to win the Grand Final. We also had lots of players chosen in the representative teams. It was a fantastic year.

Why were the Eels never as good after 1986?
I think it had a bit to do with recruitment. The majority of the players who played in that era came through the local system. Ella and Kenny were Parramatta juniors, Sterling had played for the local high school and Price had grown up in Parramatta and played rugby union there. They held on to the belief that more would come through. I think they held on to that belief for too long and the recruitment wasn't what it should be.

How much did Maurice Lindsay have to persuade you to join Wigan?
Two or three phone calls per week for a month! By 1989 I wanted to have a year off from the game to do some surfing, but every couple of days the phone would ring, and a voice would say, 'I'm a little Englishman and I'm the chairman of a Rugby League club in Wigan'. He'd say, 'I think I'm talking to the next Wigan coach'. That went on for a few weeks - he was just persistent. He told me how great a club Wigan was and he came up with a famous line about how Wigan Pier was almost as good for surfing as Queensland! It was one of the best decisions I ever made.

How well did you get on with Lindsay?
I had a great working relationship with Maurice - he ran the business side, and I ran the football side. We had disagreements, but because we were friends we could understand where each other was coming from. We became very good friends [after I left Wigan] and we still saw a lot of each other.

You won four doubles in four seasons. Do you have a favourite year?
No. Those four years were a bit of a blur. We had a great captain in Ellery, who was an inspiration to everybody in training and in games. We had great players in many positions - Joe Lydon, Steve Hampson, Andy Gregory, Shaun Edwards, Dean Bell and many more. I remember not wanting Frano Botica when Jack Robinson bought him – I was after an Australian because I didn't want to take a risk with a guy who had never played the game before. But he turned out to be a great success story. All the players worked really hard, and there was a fear of failure. We broke a lot of new ground with things we did - things I introduced from Sydney - and we got a jump on the other clubs for a few years.

How tough was it to coach so many high-profile players? Were there personality clashes?
No because the players knew I was the coach and they had to do what they had to do. They all got on board with the philosophy of the club. We had many strong personalities like Andy Goodway who was fantastic - I was told he'd be

John Monie (right) with Maurice Lindsay

trouble, but he wasn't. I remember Andy Platt lining up to sprint against Martin Offiah, really believing he could win. There was so much determination in the players that it could only be a good thing. We trained really hard and did a lot of the hard work that other clubs weren't doing. People focused on the fact we had a lot of great players, but they busted a gut. They didn't take any shortcuts.

How big a decision was it to leave?
I went to Wigan for two years and left after four, so I thought that was long enough. When the Warriors got into the Winfield Cup, I thought the time was right to go there.

How do you look back on your time in New Zealand?
I enjoyed it up until the last year. We missed the play-offs in the first season by two points - two points that we were deducted for putting on an illegal substitute. Some mis-information came up to the coaches' box about how many we'd made, and I put Willie Poching or Joe Vagana – one of the two – on. I didn't need to put him on, I just did it so he'd get some experience in a game we'd already won, but we got docked the two points and missed the semi-finals which would have been a great achievement.

Were you disappointed with how things ended at the Warriors?
Yes, it's always disappointing when you get the sack, but there aren't many coaches around who haven't been given the sack. It was my first taste of that, and I didn't like it. The expectations were massive, and people thought once they had a team in the Winfield Cup, they'd be as good as the All Blacks. But it doesn't work like that - it takes time. People weren't patient enough and wanted success too quickly.

People say you should never go back, so how did you feel when Wigan approached you again?
I was very keen; still keen to coach and familiar with Wigan so I was delighted to go back.

You had a great year in 1998 but, famously, you lost the Challenge Cup Final to Sheffield.
By that stage in my career, I could accept the defeats as well as the victories. We didn't get off to a good start and probably lost the game early on. We didn't take our opportunities, and Sheffield got the momentum they needed. I probably wasn't as upset with that loss as some people would have thought. When you're coaching, you only want to win, but when it's over you have look at the scoreboard and accept what it says. I congratulated John Kear and the Sheffield players. It was gut-wrenching at the time - I'm not trying to make light of it - but when I look back at my Wembley experiences, it's been a pretty good ride.

You had some tremendous battles with Leeds in 1998, the last of them being the Grand Final, which you won.
Graham Murray coached Leeds and they set the pace that season. They had a very tough pack and were such a hard side to beat. I look back on that as one of my major achievements, winning that Grand Final. It took a lot of hard work and a lot of good players putting their shoulders to the wheel. Jason Robinson scored a great try for us that night. But I actually preferred the system where the team who finished top won the league, even though I'd come from a Grand Final system.

You lost some very good players at the end of the year and struggled in 1999. Were you aggrieved when the club pushed you out?
It certainly left a bitter taste in my mouth. I told the chairman that we'd struggle if we got some injuries and that's what happened. The start of the season wasn't as good as we'd have liked, and it wasn't pleasant to leave.

Do you regret going to coach London?
It was a mistake going there. There wasn't a lot of tradition down there nor much depth in the squad. I probably should have come back to Australia after Wigan because I don't have too many pleasant memories of 12 months in London. We moved across the city to a crappy little ground and lost a lot of young players we'd been developing. We did everything wrong.

And what about France?
I enjoyed coaching France and helping them move from European Cup level into the top league of countries who didn't have to qualify for the World Cup. We beat Wales in a final in Carcassonne. We pushed Great Britain close at Headingley in 2007 and were five minutes away from beating New Zealand in Paris. But we had to use too many players from the French Elite. They need another Super League club to choose players from; that would make a big difference. The 2008 World Cup was disappointing, but we won our first game and suffered injuries to players in key positions.

How did you feel when you finished coaching after the 2008 World Cup?
I think after the run that I'd had, I'd probably had enough! With any job in coaching, the emotional stuff you go through is pretty good. When you're a young coach, you get knocked down, but you get up again, and you're ready to go again on Monday. But as you get older, it takes a little bit longer to recover from the losses. You expect the wins, but you don't enjoy them as much as you used to. It gets harder on an emotional level I think. I loved my career in the game and I've got a lot of great memories to look back on.

HENRY PAUL

1994-1998

The wonderfully gifted Henry Paul was first introduced to English crowds as a member of the Junior Kiwis squad in 1993. On that tour, he signed a short-term deal to play with Wakefield before joining Wigan in the summer of 1994. He stayed for five seasons, winning two Challenge Cups, three league titles and three Premierships. He was allowed to join up with younger brother Robbie at Bradford Bulls in 1999 – a decision Wigan were left to rue.

HE didn't stay for as long as he might have done, but Henry Paul made a lasting impression at Central Park. He played fullback and stand-off in his first season, scoring a try in the 1995 Challenge Cup Final. He then took Frano Botica's number-six jersey and made it his own for four seasons. Paul was an audaciously talented player who could have had a great career with Auckland Warriors, but, at the age of 20, he was too impatient to start in reserve grade, and came to England, effectively in a swap deal with Andy Platt.

"Mum and Dad used to take me to my local club in New Zealand on a Saturday morning," said Paul, describing how his oval-ball obsession began. "I was three which basically involved me digging holes in the ground while the other kids ran around with a ball! I joined in when I was older, playing League in the winter and cricket or softball in the summer. I started playing organised games at six or seven.

"I was a big kid, bigger than most my age, so when I got the ball, I often scored. At 11 or 12, things even out and I had to develop some skills. I didn't play with my brother because he was two years younger and in a different age group.

"I really fell in love with League when I was 13 or 14. Our local video store used to get Winfield Cup games from Australia, and Robbie and I would watch them religiously all weekend, watching guys like a young Laurie Daley and some good Kiwi players. A few years later, they'd be on television in New Zealand, and I began to think that I'd like to do that. When I was 17, I made my local Premiership team and made a bit of money. I was going to uni, and the money I earned at the weekends supported me through that. Some of those games were even on TV. From there, I made the Junior Kiwis."

Paul's Junior Kiwis toured England in 1993 at the same time as the senior team, who lost all three of their Tests against Great Britain. "It was a great tour, and we had a good team," said Paul. "We stayed in pubs and a few university dorms all over the north and had a great time, finishing off in France. The games were tough, and we had guys like Joe Vagana and Bryan Henare. I wasn't the most talented player, but you have to take your chances, which I did. It was one of the best times of my life. We played a BARLA team, captained by Paul Sculthorpe, and we won quite easily, but you could see how good he was. I played against Iestyn [Harris] at Warrington in a physical game where there was a brawl, and we played at Wembley, which was fantastic, against the cream of the British youth."

Midway through the tour, relegation-threatened Wakefield approached the tourists about the prospect of Paul joining them on a short-term basis. "I was signed up to the Warriors on a two-year contract which would have paid my uni fees," said Paul. "There was such mad hype over there at the time, and I was the Under-21s captain. Frank Endacott advised me that it would be a great opportunity, so I went for it. The money wasn't great, but it was a chance to play against clubs like Wigan and Leeds before going back to the Warriors. I loved every second. Wakefield coach Dave Topliss was good for me. He just let me play my natural game. It looked like we'd get relegated, but we won some games and stayed up. I played against some big teams, and we won at Wigan which was amazing. Wakefield were keen to keep me, but I was contracted to the Warriors back home. I really wanted to play in the Winfield Cup, but I looked at their squad and couldn't see a way in. John Monie said I'd have to start in the reserve grade. I'd done well in England, so I didn't want that.

"I was still considering Wakefield, but they lost some players, and it wouldn't have been the same club that I'd been playing for. Wigan were massive of course and they'd just signed [Va'aiga] Tuigamala. He and Jason Robinson spoke to me and told me how big the club was. It wasn't a hard decision in the end, but John said they wouldn't release me. Wigan wanted me and instead of letting Andy Platt go to the Warriors for free as was planned, they slapped a fee on him so they could swap him for me.

"The first season [1994-95] when we won everything is right up there. I scored a try at Wembley against Leeds. We also won the Regal Trophy and the Championship with a couple of games to spare. Then we won the Premiership final at Old Trafford. That was an awesome team. We lost a few players like Clarkey, Denis and Frano, and a few young players came through. We always won a trophy though, winning the Centenary Season and the Premiership finals in 1996 and 1997, so we were proud of that, but we didn't win the league nor the Challenge Cup in those years.

"We'd lost guys like Shaun [Edwards] and Inga by then. Shaun was a real leader and, although there was still a hard-working and professional culture at the club, we missed him. He had been the heart and soul of the club for a long time. We struggled under Eric Hughes in 1997. He was a super-nice guy, and he knew his stuff, but he was having to rebuild, and he tried to make change and bring in his own ideas, but things didn't quite click. We could have sulked about 1997, but we picked up the Premiership Trophy over Saints and took that form into 1998 when we finished top and also won the Grand Final against a really good Leeds side."

1998 did produce one obvious blip - defeat by Sheffield Eagles at Wembley. "To be honest, Sheffield wasn't a real low for me - what I mean is, I didn't take it as badly as you'd assume," Paul said. "I'd just come back from beating Australia with New Zealand in the Anzac Day Test and had to prepare for the final feeling pretty pumped up. We'd worked our nuts off to get there but, to be fair, Sheffield had a good day. We were disappointed, but we knew the Super League Grand Final was being introduced that year, and we wanted to be the first team to win that. In the build-up to the Grand Final with Leeds, we reminded ourselves of losing at Wembley and it spurred us on to win at Old Trafford. Those games that season with Leeds were great. We got over them a couple of times late on, and I look back and wonder how. They probably wonder how they lost too. They had a great coach in Graham Murray. Adrian Morley was destroying people. Daryl Powell was organising them, and Iestyn was running the show, but we had a good team ourselves, and we won."

Looking back on his Wigan career, did he clash with Andy Farrell, another dominant second receiver? "No, he didn't hinder me at all," Paul said. "He'd want a lot of the ball, and I just copped it because he was a class player. I'd tell him to get out of the way and he'd tell me to get stuffed instead! It's good for a team to have different options, but I understand people thinking that stand-offs at Wigan after me might have suffered a bit with it. Faz and I had a good system though."

BY then, Paul was well and truly established on the international scene. His Test career began on the wing with New Zealand in a 3-0 series loss to Australia midway through 1995. The World Cup soon followed where the inconsistent Kiwis almost lost their opening game to a Duane Mann-inspired Tonga. Inspired by skipper Matthew Ridge, New Zealand grabbed a sensational 25-24 win with 13 late points.

The Kiwis came agonisingly close to beating Australia in a pulsating semi-final at Huddersfield. A late Kevin Iro try levelled the scores at 20-20, leaving Ridge, a kicker of renowned accuracy, with a touchline conversion to secure a place in the final. He fluffed his kick but almost redeemed himself with a 50-metre drop-goal attempt, off his weaker left foot, that sailed just wide. Unfortunately, extra-time saw Australia dominate, and they won 30-20.

"I was playing fullback in 1995 for Wigan, but Matthew Ridge was in that position for the Kiwis," said Paul. "We didn't get off to a good start, almost losing to Tonga, and everyone wrote us off after that. I ended up at hooker in that semi-final against Australia. This was something completely different for me, although I'd have played prop to have played in a World Cup. If only Ridgey's kick had gone over, we'd have been in the final, but I was buzzing having been given the chance to play in such a big game."

Three months later, Paul and his Wigan teammates were dumped out of the Challenge Cup by second-tier Salford. "I remember Scott Naylor having a great game," said Paul. "He was very fired up as an ex-Wiganer. It was heartbreaking to lose. Decisions went against us. We didn't have time to dwell with Super League starting. We had no excuses, we were a gun team. We couldn't get any flow in the game."

Wigan also failed to win the inaugural Super League trophy, losing out in a thrilling title race to St Helens by a point, but they won the Middlesex Sevens at Twickenham and played Bath in an intriguing two-legged cross-code challenge, winning on aggregate by 101 points to 50. "I rolled my ankle in the Sevens and missed the semi-final and the final," said Paul. "It was amazing to be in the changing rooms under Twickenham. It was an exciting time. Shaun made us realise how important it was. We had a great team and young stars like Kris Radlinski and Rob Smyth. We won the Rugby League game against Bath by 80-odd points, but Westy didn't want it to get to 100, so we put some young players on. Bath carried it strong and hard, but they were lost getting back the ten."

"In the return match, I was at centre. Joe Lydon came in at ten. Inga was outside me. They just marched us 50 metres with a driving maul. We couldn't stop it. They opened the game up a bit in the second half. It was a big crowd with lots of singing. There was a lot of respect between Wigan and Bath, and it was great fun. Jason Robinson and I went to Bath for a short stint at the end of the season, and Robbie went to Harlequins."

Back in Super League, Wigan lost just two and drew one of their 22 matches, but it wasn't enough to stop the title heading to St Helens. Wigan finished second ahead of a rejuvenated Bradford, whose star player was Henry's brother, Robbie. "It was a lot of fun playing against him because we thrashed them most times early on!" laughed Paul. "He was really nervous when he first came over. He was a small guy. He had a lot of energy and when he got regular games, he proved his worth. Bradford got a lot of value out of him. He used the pre-Super League season to find his footing. When Brian Smith took over, he was excellent. We had some real battles then. We had a lot of fun with each other with the odd dig to remind each other we were there. We did media work together. He did a lot of marketing work with Peter Deakin who transformed that club."

One particular teammate Paul has fond memories of is Tuigamala, the giant former All Black who died in 2022. "Inga was the best dude," said Paul. "He was so much fun. He was so optimistic, and he was a legend on the field. I followed him and reaped all the rewards from the opportunities he created. We worked together and he told me what I needed to improve. He and his family were amazing. He was always giving out life lessons. He was very spiritual and Christian. He tried to convert me, and I'd listen to his stories about scripture. He was awesome and I can't say enough about him. He was so nice and respectful to opposition. I hated losing, but Inga always played with a smile."

Paul's last season at Wigan was 1998, and he signed off with a 10-4 victory in the Grand Final at Old Trafford against Leeds. The two sides had built up a State of Origin-like rivalry that year, staging four wonderfully intense matches, but the Warriors won the one that counted courtesy of Jason Robinson's brilliant try just before half-time.

"That final was the toughest game I can remember," Paul admitted. "Jason's try was probably the only line break. We were just running into brick walls because both teams had great defences! It wasn't a fancy game. Jason scored and we held on. I knew it would be my last game for Wigan, so to go out with a ring on my fist was great."

ODSAL beckoned for Paul, giving him the opportunity to form a halfback partnership with his brother. Was there a breakdown in his relationship with Wigan? "There was a bit," he revealed. "John Monie came back in 1998. Maybe my relationship with him wasn't the best. I had left Auckland when he was there. I just didn't want to play reserve grade, and I was honest with him. Then he came back to Wigan. He was a super-good coach, professional - he'd been there and done it. I tried my best, but he wanted another stand-off. Maybe that's why the communication with Wigan was poor. They kept making me wait. Clarkey [Phil Clarke] was the Chief Executive, and he kept delaying me. I had to tell them I couldn't wait anymore. I told them I'd play my nuts off for them for the rest of the year and then leave, and that's what happened.

"It was because of Robbie that I went to Bradford. He was asking what was happening. I spoke to Canterbury Bulldogs, Auckland Warriors and Manly - but just the CEOs, not the coaches. One regret I have is not playing for Auckland Warriors. But when I spoke to Matthew Elliott about the Bulls, I knew he was bringing Joe Vagana over. I just looked at them and thought, 'Yes, these guys are going to be good.' I didn't speak to anyone from Wigan. It was weird."

After a disappointing fifth-place finish in 1998, Paul's arrival heralded a significant up-turn in performances for the Odsal club who finished top of the table. A 40-4 play-off win over St Helens, with Paul scoring twice, underlined their supremacy, but they were stunned by the same team in a wonderful Grand Final. A late Kevin Iro try won the game for Saints by 8-6 after Paul's long-range try had opened the scoring.

"I don't want to look back at that final," said Paul. "It angers me much more than Sheffield. Saints were a talented team who took their chances, and they got up over us a couple of times. Man for man, they weren't better than us, but they worked hard and beat us on a couple of big occasions. It certainly motivated us for the following season, and the great start we got to 2000 was probably down to that. We won the Cup at Murrayfield. It was great to win the Lance Todd, although there were a couple of other guys who could have got it. I kicked some high balls, and I was probably more of a steadying influence rather than a gamebreaker. We won it as a team, and the best moment was seeing Bernard Dwyer afterwards. He'd lost the other finals he'd played in, and he finally won one. He put in some big tackles late on when we were tired."

After looking invincible in the early stages of the season, the Bulls tailed off somewhat and bowed out of the play-offs with a 40-12 loss at Wigan but not before witnessing Super League's most famous moment - or infamous from Bradford's perspective. With just under ten minutes left, Paul kicked a field goal for an 11-10 Bradford lead only for Saints' Chris Joynt to score the Wide-to-West try after the final hooter.

"I thought that my field-goal was a winner," said Paul. "We gave everything and it was great to be involved in. It was heartbreaking to see some of the people around the club and that TV footage of Matt [Elliott] falling off his chair. You have to take it on the chin when it happens. After all I've been involved in plenty of last-minute wins. But, for a neutral, what a game!"

The Bulls made up for it in 2001 by thrashing hapless Wigan 37-6 in Manchester. "That was fantastic, and the boys were unstoppable," Paul remembered. "I felt sorry for Wigan - they just weren't in the game. We were a really good team and over the next few years, the hard work put in by Matthew Elliott and Brian Noble really began to pay off. We had a ton of respect for Wigan. A year before they had beaten us at the JJB in the play-offs which was heartbreaking. We knew their quality. We went into that game, confident in ourselves, but we didn't predict that. We were chilled out which is a good omen, but they had Faz and other great players. We had a bit of extra drive, and we took our chances. They lost Brian Carney which helped us. He tackled me and my stud cut his knee. He was so good out of dummy-half, making 15 or 20 metres a time. Jimmy Lowes came out of dummy-half to catch their big men going backwards. Little men scooted and big men followed them. We were patient. There was nothing risky. When we lost to Saints in 1999, we bombed so many chances. Any half breaks this time, guys weren't throwing it willy-nilly. Tactically, we got things right."

JUST as his last game for Wigan had been a Grand Final win, Paul signed off from Bradford with the Super League trophy. He spent four and a half years in rugby union before returning with Harlequins RL, a new and temporary identity for London Broncos. "At the time, switching codes was pretty unique," said Paul. "I wanted to lead my own life and do what was right for me. I'm pleased that I did. My Gloucester career was good. I played nearly every game in four years. They hadn't won anything for 20 years, but I was part of a successful team.

"Maybe I went a year or two too early, but I'd had five great years at Wigan and three at Bradford. I'd won everything. I couldn't have asked for anything more in terms of trophies and exciting rugby. I'd had a taste of union with Bath in 1996 and I'd grown up in New Zealand where the All Blacks are so huge. The timing seemed to be right, and I joined a good team in Gloucester. They reminded me of Bradford. They had a good young team on the rise, and we won trophies. I had five good years there. Maybe I could have stayed one more season at Bradford because they carried on getting to grand finals, but I don't have many regrets.

"But I wasn't enjoying my last season at Gloucester. I fell out with the coach, and he wasn't interested in playing me after a while. I went off to play Sevens for the season instead. Then I considered the NRL, but Ian Lenagan, at Harlequins, sold the club to me, and convinced me I didn't have to travel halfway around the world. I wanted the chance to live in London."

Paul played 61 Super League matches for Harlequins in three seasons. One highlight was a surprising 14-6 win at St Helens in round one of 2007. A different player now, Paul played at loose forward and made 40 tackles. "Harlequins was another great experience," he said. "I wish I'd been coached by Tony Rea for longer. Brian McDermott was great as well, but I really liked Tony. I loved that club. Ian Lenagan and David Hughes were both really passionate. I made a ton of good friends. Tommy Leuluai was there and other good players, but the infrastructure was tough - we were here for training and over there for runs. Other clubs are based in one place, but we were all over the place. I played a lot of loose forward which was tough to get used to. I made two or three tackles a game in the centres at Gloucester, then I was doing 40 at loose forward at Harlequins. Macca was a different kind of coach, and he had a great run at Leeds. I loved living in the Twickenham area, but the travelling was a pain, going north every two weeks."

Harlequins was Paul's final involvement in Rugby League. He returned to union for playing stints with Leeds Carnegie and Rotherham before moving into coaching.

When asked if he was happier at Wigan or Bradford, Paul responded: "They were very different clubs, but I loved my time at Wigan. I loved playing with the young guys. I was a senior player to them. Training was great. We were ultra-fit and ultra-professional. Things are instilled into you. I really enjoyed Westy because he'd been a Wigan legend. That squad in 1994-95 was amazing. We organised, set up, went out and executed. Westy didn't change too much, but he was a great man-manager with funny comments here and there. He was a massive presence with his height too! I loved the club and I'm proud of my time there."

BILL ASHURST

1963-1973
1977-1978

Bill Ashurst experienced an extraordinary playing career, establishing himself as a world-class second-rower at both Wigan and Penrith Panthers. A player of immense skill, he was always able to slip an impossible pass. He became something of a pantomime villain too, regularly sent off and often at the centre of controversial episodes. Ashurst led a most interesting life until his untimely death in 2022, at the age of 74. He was a born-again Christian, a father of seven and grandfather of 31.

Tell us about your early experiences of playing rugby and football.
We couldn't even afford a pigs' bladder, so we used a rolled-up newspaper and Sellotape! We played in the street. I started at 11 and always played with older guys, so I learned a lot. I played football too and had trials at Blackburn Rovers. The manager told me he was impressed but no money was mentioned. Sheila then announced we were having a baby, and I had to give everything up.

You were married at 17 and became a dad at 18.
My mum chased me with a poker when she found out we were expecting a baby! People may have thought we were too young, but we've been married 52 years. We have seven kids, 31 grandkids and six great grandkids! It was a bit scary getting married at 17, but I took it in my stride.

How did signing for Wigan come about?
Billy Cottam, my old centre partner, signed for them and at that point I'd given rugby up. When I read he'd signed, I knew I could make it too. I wasn't degrading Billy. He was actually an inspiration for me because I knew if he was good enough to sign for Wigan, I was too. And that's what happened. We were coached by Eric Ashton, whom I had idolised. We'd never had a telly until I was ten, and then my mum got a black-and-white TV so I could watch the 1958 Challenge Cup Final between Wigan and Working-ton. Eric was my hero from then and playing for him was wonderful.

Billy Boston finished at Wigan before you debuted but he asked you to play in his testimonial match.
That's right - it was a huge honour. I spoke at the Wigan Warriors dementia club [in 2018], and Billy was there. He was my absolute hero and he asked me to play in his testimonial as his centre, which was brilliant. I gave him my first pass and he chuffin' dropped it!

The background to your full debut against St Helens was quite unusual, wasn't it?
Yes. We were in the pub having a lock-in the night before because I hadn't been picked. Then [director] Martin Ryan turned up and said someone had dropped out, so I was in the first team. I'd had a bit to drink, but I did ok. I started on the wing with Bill Francis in the centre. At half-time I told Eric he had us the wrong way and he put me back at centre. We did a bit better after that!

What do you remember of losing to Castleford in the 1970 Challenge Cup Final?
Colin Tyrer was taken off after being hit by Keith Hepworth. He was a huge loss because he was the best attacking fullback around. I was the second choice goalkicker and when we got a penalty, our captain Doug Laughton gave it to Bill Francis instead, who missed. We

got several more penalties, but Doug decided to run them, and they proved to be costly decisions. He then made the same decisions which cost us the 1971 Championship Final when we lost late on against St Helens.

How do you look back on your Great Britain career?
It was very frustrating. I missed out on the 1970 Lions Tour, despite winning the equivalent of the Man of Steel, and 36 man-of-the-match awards that season. I was told I didn't have enough experience! I debuted against the Kiwis in 1971. I made a try, scored a try, had a great game and then got dropped for the next two Tests. I came back in the team and played twice against France in 1972. I was injured for the 1972 World Cup and then went to Australia, which meant I wasn't allowed to play for Great Britain.

Didn't you once punch a policeman at Odsal?
Ha! Yes - it was unbelievable! There had been a massive brawl, so tempers were frayed at the end. You had to walk up about a hundred steps through the crowd at Odsal to get to the sheds. I got hit, so turned around with a punch in retaliation and happened to hit a policeman! The directors smoothed things over fortunately.

Do you regret breaking Alan Bates's jaw in a Championship semi-final with Dewsbury in 1971?
I always regretted things like that. I've broken cheekbones and eye sockets. We knew we had to sort Alan out and I volunteered to do it. It was common in the game back then. I couldn't change what I did, but I was very apologetic.

How did you come to sign for Penrith?
I nearly signed for Cronulla. Two of their British players, Cliff Watson and Tommy Bishop, came to my house, and I agreed to join. Sheila and I wanted a fresh start, so we agreed to go, but then Penrith came in with a better offer, which included a car and a house with a swimming pool. I couldn't drive or swim, but it sounded a good offer, so I took it!

It was rumoured you and Stevo [Mick Stephenson] had a terrible relationship at Penrith, which reportedly split the club in two. How did you see it?
It was never that bad. He was a great hooker, and I'll never take that away from him. We didn't get on off the pitch, but we played the rivalry up for the press because it made us a few bob. We made it look worse than it was, so we'd get $500 each to open a shop.

Your first game as captain was pretty memorable wasn't it?
Yes, everyone was leaving with 20 minutes to go because we were 19-0 down to St George. I didn't get many passes from Mike that day, but then he got knocked out. I didn't

hit him, although I was accused! Then we scored 25 points in 15 minutes. No one could quite believe it.

You played with a young Phil Gould. What was he like?
I taught Phil how to kick a ball. He was in the Under-23s. When my autobiography came out, I was due to do a book signing in Penrith, but he wouldn't allow it because he said the way I'd lived my life wasn't a good example to people at Penrith. But my book was an honest story. For example, because I opened up about being sexually abused by my father, people told me that really helped them. It helps people deal with something like that.

Is that something that still affects you?
I still get triggers, but it's not as bad as it was.

You left Penrith under controversial circumstances - which is something of a theme in the Bill Ashurst story!
Well, yes, but I did nothing wrong. There was a huge polio scare in the UK where Sheila and the kids had gone back. It was a big story, but Penrith wouldn't let me go home for a few weeks. So, I jumped on a plane and left for good.

You re-joined Wigan but didn't get on with the coach Vince Karalius.
I knew he was a great player. I've never been as fit in my life because he was a fitness fanatic. But I didn't play his type of game. I was a footballer. I tried ambitious passes. I once pulled off an impossible pass to set up a try, but he still told me off. He said no one passes a ball like that in his team, so I handed him the jersey and told him I was leaving.

You joined Wakefield and last played at Wembley in 1979.
I hadn't played a round, coming back from an ACL injury. But the coach [Bill Kirkbride] said he'd rather have Bill Ashurst at 50 percent than someone else at 100 percent. I had needles, but I didn't perform.

You played with David Topliss at two clubs. What do you remember of him?
He was a magical player. We had a year at Penrith, but we had a terrible coach, and he never got a crack. He came in for me when he was at Wakefield. He said he rated me as the greatest footballing forward around, so I went to Trinity. We always got on and he was a great player. David died in 2008. He rang me one day in June at 1pm to arrange a meet-up later in the week. By 3pm, Trevor Skerrett phoned me up to say he'd died after a 5-a-side match. I didn't believe it, but Andy Kelly confirmed it. It was a huge shock.

You bowed out as a professional player in the most sensational way - sent off for Runcorn as a 40-year-old player-coach against Wigan!
We weren't the best team anyway and then the players were on strike. So we had to field an amateur team in a cup match at Wigan, and I put myself on the bench. So I went on. It was the only time I played for them. I had been long retired. Andy Gregory later said I could barely walk, but still opened them up three times with defence-splitting passes! I headbutted Andy Goodway and got sent off, which wasn't clever. I apologised. I loved coaching and I mentored at Ince Rose Bridge [in 2018]. I'd no mobility, but I could always use my mouth!

ELLERY HANLEY

1985-91

Who is the greatest Wigan player of them all?
That isn't a question I can answer definitively, nor can many I've asked, but Jim Sullivan, Billy Boston, Eric Ashton, Brian McTigue and Shaun Edwards get more mentions than most. Ellery Hanley would be in contention too, although given he spent six years at Central Park compared to Sullivan's 25, Boston's 15, McTigue's 15 and Edwards' 13, it's hard to argue with any certainty that he is Wigan's greatest individual.
But when you consider Hanley's exploits with Great Britain, Bradford, Leeds and Balmain, the whole package is so impressive that a case can be made for him being the greatest-ever British Rugby League player.

NO shortage of wonderful things have happened to Cuthwyn Ellery Hanley.

An MBE and the Golden Boot for a start.

Hanley was Rugby League's Man of Steel a record three times. He won the coveted Lance Todd Trophy. He has been named in a list of 100 Great Black Britons. He is a member of the British Rugby League Hall of Fame. He was voted Great Britain's finest-ever player by supporters.

Hanley's remarkable career saw him score 428 tries in 498 games. He won 36 Great Britain caps and 17 winner's medals during six glorious years at Wigan. Naturally, he is in the club's Hall of Fame. His extraordinary performances for Balmain Tigers in 1988 took them to their first Grand Final in 19 years. He was inducted into their Hall of Fame in 2012.

So when I asked Hanley in 2008 to tell me his greatest moment, I was pretty sure it would be contained in the above. Not so! "The greatest thing that has ever happened to me came very recently," he told me. "People ask me what was the greatest thing that happened to me. Was it a particular match or being honoured by the Queen or winning the Golden Boot or being inducted into the Hall of Fame? The greatest thing is the respect that you have from other players.

"Recently a journalist called me to tell me that Kris Radlinski wanted to send me a book. Telling you this story is giving me goose pimples by the way, even though I'm not an emotional person. Kris doesn't know me very well, but he wanted my address, and I just assumed he was going to send me a copy of his autobiography like many other people have done.

"But this book was in his own handwriting and was one of only three that he produced. He wanted to give me one of those three books. He told me that one was for his father, one was for himself, and the other was for me. I nearly died! I was speechless and struggled to explain to him how much his gesture meant to me. He told me that I'd been inspirational in his life and that, to me, was bigger than any award. It's the biggest honour I've ever received."

I MET Hanley in January 2008 when he had just been appointed the coach of Doncaster. I was immediately drawn to two signs on his office wall – 'Give your very best and no one can ask any questions' and 'Stay in control whether you're winning or losing'. "They are the key factors in being a champion and in moving on from being ordinary," he told me.

Hanley's appointment was met with not just surprise in the world of Rugby League, but also a degree of cynicism. 'How long will he last?' was a question on the lips of more than one journalist when his appointment was announced.

"They obviously don't know me, and that's the problem with journalists, people like yourself," he said. "You don't know me, and I don't know you. Unless you know someone, and you know them well enough, then you've got no idea.

"Can I tell you about journalists? I'm not interested in journalists. The reason I'm not interested in journalists is that 99% of them haven't played Rugby League and have no idea of what it's like to step over the whitewash and actually play. It doesn't matter what level you play at - amateur or professional - they have no idea. All they do is write a report and give their opinion. Any person from the public can do that so, for me, what they say holds no bearing on me whatsoever.

"I know how I operate and how my system works and how I like the players to go about their business. They'll continue to write things when I've left planet Earth because they have a job to do."

I ask Hanley if this is why he rarely spoke to journalists as a player: "I wouldn't say I didn't talk to journalists. How I conducted myself in the past has nothing to do with you or anybody."

HANLEY'S amateur club was the now defunct Corpus Christi in Leeds before he signed for Bradford Northern on 2nd June 1978. In fact, Rugby League was lucky that Hanley ever stumbled across it at all. According to a story Hanley told a journalist in 1985, a teacher had ordered him to play rugby to make up the numbers. "I'd never played before. I said, 'I'm not playing'. He said, 'you'll get the slipper', so I agreed! I found I had a natural ability. I got the ball, ran with it, and kept falling over the line."

That ability to get over the tryline was there on the occasion of his professional debut on 26th November 1978, aged 17, in a 30-18 win over Rochdale Hornets at Odsal. Hanley came off the bench to feature alongside the likes of Keith Mumby, David Barends, Nigel Stephenson, Tony Fisher and Neil Fox, who was in the final season of a wonderful 23-year professional career.

Hanley didn't play again for nearly three years, as Bradford won the league championship in consecutive seasons without the absent teenager. When he was back in the fold, he started at centre in the team's first game of the 1981-82 season, scoring another try in a 33-5 Yorkshire Cup win at Halifax. Hanley was finally up and running. He played in all but two of the side's 41 matches that season, scoring most tries with 15 and kicking 41 goals, although the campaign ended in controversy at Hull KR as Hanley and his teammates left the field in the 56th minute of a Premiership Trophy match in protest at referee Robin Whitfield who had sent off six players – four from Bradford.

"Corpus Christi is where I plied my trade when I was an amateur, acquiring my skills under a number of coaches," he said. "I gained a lot of experience getting time on the football paddock. The transition was never a problem for me because, in my mind, I was always a professional anyway, in terms of how I conducted myself on the football paddock and how I looked after myself off it.

"If you're a player who attracts a lot of attention on the football field, you've got to know how to handle yourself. The opposition hardened me both physically and mentally, as did some of the crowds. There was abuse and other things to endure as a player, and it toughened my resolve.

"Wherever I played in the world had no bearing on how I played. I knew what I had to do. I was focused and tunnel-visioned and sometimes that can be mixed up with arrogance. I was a total professional, and I am to this day as a coach or as a squash or tennis player. I'm still focused, and I know what I have to do.

"I can trace that attitude back to being much younger; to when I first understood sport and when I was first competing as a ten-year-old in cross-country running. I knew I had to win, and I knew what I had to do to understand the opposition. I always looked at their weaknesses and where I could be stronger and go beyond them.

"One of the hardest things in life is to be consistent as an individual and as a team - you'll gain massive respect. That's all I ever did. I turned up early to training and I prepared properly. I was focused on gameday."

Hanley admitted he received abuse, but how much of it was racist?

"Racism was always there, and it hardened my resolve," he said. "Let me explain this to you. Racism only applies in very small pockets. The majority of people in the game are the nicest you could meet anywhere. It's only a small minority who aren't. Racism has been cleaned up a lot since I first came into the game as a 17- or 18-year-old kid."

Hanley's greatest single moment as a Northern player came at Headingley, a ground he was to grace with such distinction later in his career. In the Challenge Cup semi-final of 1983 against the eventual cup winners, Featherstone Rovers, Hanley scorched up the North Stand sideline, beating player after player to score one of the most spectacular tries of the modern era.

"I don't remember it in too much detail because so many great things have happened to me since," said Hanley. "People remind me of it, but I haven't seen it for about 15 or 20 years. I may have the video somewhere though.

"But we lost that day and as a sportsman, you've got to be able to deal with losses and understand how you lost. That's something I do quite easily, and while nobody wants to be beaten, you've got to know how to handle it and turn the negative into a positive. I couldn't tell you now what my thoughts were after that particular game because it's just such a distant memory."

A GREAT BRITAIN call-up came along in January 1984 as Hanley made his Test debut in France as a half-time substitute for the injured Joe Lydon in a 12-0 win that also saw international debuts for Des Foy, Garry Clark, David Cairns, Keith Rayne, Mick Worrall, David Hobbs and David Hall. By the summer, Hanley was boarding a plane to the Southern Hemisphere to play for the Lions against Australia, New Zealand and Papua New Guinea.

Hanley's Bradford teammate Brian Noble captained a young side which restored pride to the British jersey after the hammerings handed out to them by the Australian Invincibles of 1982 as the Ashes Tests were much closer than two years earlier. The Bradford back played in all seven Test matches on the tour, scoring four tries, but coach Frank Myler was criticised for selecting several players out of position, including Hanley on the wing, in the three matches against Australia.

"It was the first time I'd played wing, which isn't as easy as people think," Hanley told a journalist the following year. "I felt let down that Frank Myler didn't take me to one side and explain."

"What I remember is that the Australians were way, way better than us," he said to me. "Individually and collectively, they were way too good for us. We were still lagging way behind the Australians, and it wasn't until years later that we got closer to them. But they're still the best Rugby League nation now. Anyone who does something so well for such a long period - decades and decades in this case - will still fall short from time to time, but overall, we have to recognise that they're the best on the planet.

"The reason that we're so far behind Australia is that their league is structured so they have a huge amount of players to choose from. They also play in a good climate on hard grounds so they can keep the ball alive and become more skilful.

"They had an enormous pool of players to choose from and still do. If somebody goes to Australia, they'll have a hell of a job getting into first grade because the competition is so strong. If you're not playing well, you'll go into the reserve-grade side, but in England if you're not playing well, you'll probably stay in the 17 because the competition is not so strong. So that competition brings the best out of the Australians because they know they have to perform at their best week in week out just to keep their first-grade spots.

"Don't get me wrong. We closed the gap to a degree a few years later, but we were still a long way from them. Great Britain could sustain pressure for only a small period of time, but Australia could do it for 80 minutes because of their competition. In our competition, the top sides beat the lower sides by 50 or 60 points, and that was no good for the Great Britain side."

BACK in the club game, Hanley won the Man of Steel award in 1985 after a season of scintillating performances at stand-off half. He scored 52 tries in 37 matches, registering nine hat-tricks along the way. One of his best performances came in the 7-6 Challenge Cup defeat by Wigan. By the end of the season, Hanley had scored 89 tries in 126 appearances for Northern, although his time at Odsal had failed to yield a winner's medal. It was inevitable that he would move on to pastures new.

On the eve of Northern's first game of the 1985-86 season, Hanley withdrew from the side over a financial dispute. A transfer request was subsequently turned down by the board who claimed the player was asking for a salary of £100,000. As he wasn't playing, he was ruled out of the Yorkshire team for the Roses match with Lancashire, but Wigan came in for the 24-year-old, offering £85,000 in cash along with Phil Ford and Steve Donlan in a world-record deal valued at £150,000. Northern agreed. It's hard

to conclude that Wigan's Maurice Lindsay hadn't got the bargain of the century.

Wigan had just beaten Hull FC in that classic Wembley cup final. They would soon sign Andy Goodway and Joe Lydon. With Lindsay's vision and a seemingly inexhaustible supply of cash, the Cherry and Whites were clearly going places. Hanley's six years at Central Park would see him net 17 winner's medals: four Challenge Cups, three league championships, a World Club Challenge, four John Player Trophies, a Premiership Trophy and four Lancashire Cups. Lindsay, unsurprisingly, regarded Hanley as Wigan's greatest signing.

His debut came in a 52-5 home shellacking of Widnes. His first try came three days later in the Lancashire Cup against Salford. He went on to score 35 in 40 matches in a 1985-86 campaign that yielded success in the John Player Trophy and the Lancashire Cup. Wigan also beat the New Zealand tourists 14-8 in the autumn, but they were denied the league title by Halifax – or to be precise, by the early blowing of the hooter in the final match at Thrum Hall.

Hanley enjoyed a remarkable second season, crossing the tryline 59 times in just 39 games. Five came in one match against former club Bradford. Other hat-tricks were notched against Whitehaven, Hull, Workington, Wakefield, Halifax, Featherstone and Oldham. He scored 30 tries in 13 matches in the spring after coach Graham Lowe switched him to the loose-forward position. Wigan retained the cups they had won the previous season and added the league championship and the Premiership Trophy.

The following season brought him a winner's medal in the World Club Challenge as Manly were invited to Central Park and beaten 8-2 in an enthralling tryless encounter. A third successive Lancashire Cup was landed, but the best was saved to last as Wigan returned to Wembley and beat Halifax 32-12 before a crowd of 94,273. Hanley scored an iconic try, supporting Joe Lydon's magnificent break, with a unique, crabbing run to the line which kept him from the clutches of the covering defender Martin Meredith. It was his 31st try of the season in 34 matches. It had seemed in February that Hanley was on his way out of the club after a dispute led to Hanley staying away, but a resolution was found much to the relief of Lindsay and Lowe.

If Hanley's stock was high in the spring of 1988, it would be in another stratosphere by the end of the summer.

ELLERY HANLEY's performances on the Lions tour of 1988 and then with Balmain Tigers in the latter stages of Australia's Winfield Cup competition saw him win Open Rugby magazine's Golden Boot as the world's best player. He captained Great Britain in the Ashes, scoring a superb try in the first Test, a game which saw Australia overturn a 6-0 half-time deficit to win 17-6. The tourists' assault on the Ashes was again unsuccessful, but the British did claim glory with their famous triumph in Sydney in the third Test, a game best remembered for Mike Gregory's long-range try.

Hanley then signed for mid-table Balmain Tigers in the Winfield Cup and hit a patch of such scintillating form that they made not just the semi-finals but the Grand Final. Balmain's team contained many a legend - Benny Elias, Steve Roach, Wayne Pearce, Paul Sironen, Garry Jack and Gary Freeman - but it was Hanley who sparked the club's best form in two decades.

Interviewing Hanley is not an easy task but mention of that eight-game Winfield Cup stint in 1988 brought a beaming smile to his face, and he was at his most relaxed in our time together. "You know you're doing well when the Australians say that they respect you," he said. "I had some great times in Australia, and when I go back they welcome me with open arms off the plane at the airport. That's something that I always treasure because it's such an honour."

Hanley's debut came against reigning premiers Manly at Brookvale Oval. Balmain lost 8-4. A week later came a must-win home clash with Penrith at Balmain's Leichhardt Oval. A 16-14 win meant the top five was still within reach. An equally important final-day win over Brisbane Broncos meant that the four teams occupying spots third, fourth, fifth and sixth ended up on 30 points. Nowadays, the Tigers would miss out due to their inferior points difference, but back then the two sides with the worst points difference would play off in a midweek fixture to take the fifth and last semi-final berth. Balmain beat Penrith 28-8 with their new number 3 scoring his first try for the club. Their season wasn't just still alive. They were becoming a force at exactly the right time.

Just four days later, Balmain were kicking off their semi-final campaign as rank outsiders. They faced Manly at the new Sydney Football Stadium, where Hanley had helped Great Britain conquer Australia six weeks earlier. The British captain was at the centre of another upset as his try was instrumental in a 19-6 win.

Hanley was earning rave reviews by now. Star-studded Canberra Raiders were next up at the same venue. The Tigers won 14-6 with Hanley crossing for another try which spelt the end of the season for Laurie Daley, Ricky Stuart and Wigan's 1985 hero John Ferguson.

Minor Premiers Cronulla were the opponents in the Preliminary Final, with the winners to play Canterbury Bankstown in the Grand Final. Again, Balmain were underdogs. Again, Hanley shone, scoring the only try of the match in a 9-2 win. Even the Australians were admitting that the best player in the world was now a Pom. The Tigers were in their first Grand Final since they had won the 1969 classic against South Sydney Rabbitohs when the great Wiganer Dave Bolton was man of the match.

Alas, the 1988 Grand Final turned into a nightmare for Hanley and Balmain. In the first half, Canterbury centre Andrew Farrar, who later played for Wigan, went in low on Hanley. Australia international Terry Lamb came in high with a hugely controversial hit. Hanley was concussed. He

staggered off. He returned very briefly on the wing but was clearly in no fit state to continue. Teammates told how when Hanley came to, he thought he was in the Wigan dressing-room. Canterbury went on to win 24-12.

Years later when Lamb was appointed coach of Wests Tigers (a merger of Balmain and Western Suburbs), fans with long memories protested the decision, still upset over the events at the Sydney Football Stadium in 1988. It remains one of the most infamous Grand Final incidents.

"I've forgotten about it because it's a distant memory," said Hanley. "Injuries are an occupational hazard in this sport. You're going to get injured, and you have to cope with that. It just so happened that on that particular day I got injured. I'm not really sure what happened, but I was unconscious for a little while and came to my senses later on. Like I say, it's an occupational hazard."

Hanley returned to the Winfield Cup in 1989 with Western Suburbs Magpies alongside Garry Schofield and Kelvin Skerrett, but there was no chance of any silverware with the Magpies miles off the pace when they joined. Ironically, had Hanley returned to Balmain, they would have probably won the competition. Without him, they were narrowly pipped by Canberra in one of the most exhilarating finals ever seen.

It was while in Australia with the Magpies that Hanley was presented with the Golden Boot as the world's best player for the year before, chosen by members of the Rugby League media in both hemispheres. This was the fifth time the Golden Boot had been awarded – the previous winners had been the Australian trio Wally Lewis, Brett Kenny and Garry Jack before New Zealand's Hugh McGahan and Australia's Peter Sterling shared the award for 1987. Hanley's was the first not to be awarded at a glamorous black-tie dinner – Jack's award had even been covered live on the evening news in New South Wales. As a tongue-in-cheek protest, Hanley accepted the Golden Boot, then sponsored by Adidas, at a low-key pitch-side presentation, dressed from head to foot in Puma gear.

AS Hanley spent that Sunday night in September 1988 sleeping off the effects of Lamb's high tackle, Wigan were losing 25-20 in a league match at Wakefield, having lost the Charity Shield to champions Widnes a fortnight earlier. They needed their captain back, and Hanley duly returned to the side at stand-off later in the month. He was soon back to his normal self, scoring four tries in the next three games.

Another Lancashire Cup was won in 1988-89. Likewise the John Player. The league title went down to the final match of the season in a winner-takes-all showdown at Naughton Park against Widnes the day after the Hillsborough Disaster. With Shaun Edwards and Andy Gregory injured, Hanley formed an unlikely halfback pairing with Ged Byrne, but they were unable to prevent Widnes from winning 32-18. In his second season in Rugby League, Martin Offiah scored a sizzling hat-trick for the Chemics. Wigan had finished top just once in Hanley's four seasons at the club.

They more than made up for it at Wembley. After losing 4-2 at home to St Helens in the first round of the Premiership Trophy, they played their derby rivals again under the twin towers six days later. The first-choice halves were back, as was Dean Bell, but nobody could have predicted the ease with which Wigan would win their tenth Challenge Cup. Hanley won the Lance Todd Trophy as the best player on the field and scored his 25th try in his 38th game of the season as Wigan beat St Helens 27-0. It was a scoreline their supporters would gloat over for a generation and more. As I put it to Hanley, it was another outstanding year for him on an individual basis.

"I would retract from that because I have to incorporate everybody that I played with and even everyone I played against because they propelled me to that position," he pointed out. "It's important to recognise those people. It's like someone who scores 30 or 40 tries in a season - they're assisted by other people.

"I always remember players like Ged Byrne, Ian Potter and Brian Case. They were the real workhorses, and their work was often unrecognised. They weren't flamboyant or stars, but these kind of guys epitomised the workmanship required to win games.

"Wigan had a mentality. One of the great catalysts in the game was Maurice Lindsay. He brought magnificent players together, but what he did that was so good was that he always asked the senior players whether a particular player would fit into the system well. Maurice always came to people like myself, Shaun Edwards and Dean Bell to ask our opinions.

"Once you create a winning habit, it's easier to keep on winning. When you're losing it's tough to break the habit. Added to all that, Maurice didn't just buy the best players or the mentally toughest players, he made sure we were dangerous in every position. There was a fear factor with every single team who came to Central Park. They knew that more than likely they would get beaten. Even if a couple of players were off their game on a particular day, there were other players who would step up."

Hanley missed the first 19 matches of the 1989-90 season with a pelvic injury sustained while playing for Western Suburbs. He went on play 20 matches, enduring his least prolific year in the cherry and white, not just in terms of total tries (10), but tries per game. Nevertheless, he collected his fourth John Player Trophy (now sponsored by Regal), his second league title and his third Challenge Cup with a try in the final against Warrington. Fourteen years later, he gave that cup-final medal to Mike Gregory,

the Wigan-born loose forward who was outstanding in primrose and blue that day. Gregory coached Wigan in 2003 and 2004, taking them to two finals. He passed away in 2007 after a long illness. Hanley's act of kindness on the day of the 2004 Challenge Cup Final, Gregory's last match as coach, was a classy tribute to a much-respected opponent.

The 1990-91 season turned out to be Hanley's last at Wigan. He won his fourth-straight Challenge Cup, but it was the way they retained the league championship that attracted praise. Wigan were fifth in the table after a 14-6 New Year's Day defeat at home to Warrington, but they won 13 and drew one of their last 14 matches to pip Widnes to the title by two points. The final eight league matches were played in just 19 days from March 26th to April 13th, a run that included a vital 26-6 home win over Widnes in front of a crowd of 29,763. Hanley played in seven of those games, scoring five tries. It was the ultimate test for the team, one which they passed in the most impressive manner to be crowned champions for the twelfth time. Hanley then needed a painkilling injection for a hamstring strain to get him through the Challenge Cup Final which an exhausted Wigan won 13-8 against St Helens.

WIGAN and Hanley eventually parted company in September 1991 after 189 tries in 204 games. The player claimed it wasn't a difficult decision to join Leeds in a playing-coaching role, assisting Doug Laughton. Hanley made his debut in the team's second fixture of the season, a 20-14 home win over Hull FC in the league, taking his place alongside Garry Schofield, Bobbie Goulding, Shaun Wane and Paul Dixon.

On one of the rare occasions that he fronted the Rugby League media in his playing days, Hanley said: "I have thought of moving into coaching for a couple of years, and although I was happy at Wigan, the offer to move to Leeds was too tempting. I have lived in the city all my life and as a youngster dreamed of playing here."

At the press conference Laughton claimed that Schofield would remain as captain, but within a week the former Widnes coach had handed the role to Hanley. Schofield was furious with Laughton and never forgave him. "It didn't create a problem with me and Garry," said Hanley. "We spoke about it, and we were ok. It didn't affect me or the team, and we just did what we had to do. Garry was a hugely noticed player who made a huge contribution to Rugby League, and we had a good, professional relationship."

It took Hanley four games to get off the mark. When he did score a try, at home to Swinton in the league, he ended up scoring three, but his first season was disrupted by a broken jaw sustained after a challenge with Hull's Andy Dannatt, who was left facing court action. Hanley missed 13 games which included a 24-0 Regal Trophy Final defeat to Widnes.

Hanley remained at Leeds for four years but failed to collect a winner's medal, as the Loiners finished fifth, fifth, seventh and second in the league. They did reach Wembley in 1994 and 1995, but they lost both finals to Wigan. The latter was Hanley's last game of Rugby League in this country. In four seasons at Leeds, he scored 106 tries in 114 matches.

"One of the things that happened at Wigan was that we had the strong mentality," said Hanley. "Even when I left, that mentality was still there. At Leeds, I wanted us

to adopt that mentality, but it was something that wasn't going to happen quickly. Remember, I was at Wigan a lot longer than I was at Leeds, but a lot of things got implemented there, and we got close."

During his last season at Leeds, Hanley was appointed Great Britain coach for the visit of the 1994 Kangaroos. He resisted calls for him to pick himself and coached the side to a barely believable first-Test win at Wembley, despite the sending-off of captain Shaun Edwards for a first-half high tackle on Bradley Clyde. Elsewhere in this book, Phil Clarke tells of Hanley's awe-inspiring half-time team talk which left him in no doubt that Great Britain could win without their skipper, and they did so by eight points to four. But such was the script back then, Australia came back to win the series by beating Great Britain at Old Trafford and Elland Road.

"The step-up to head coach was easy," said Hanley. "I'd coached all my life and knew how to get the best out of players and understood about the winning mentality. I was always coaching, even under John Monie at Wigan. Under John, there were three players who directed the football team, and they were Shaun Edwards, Andy Gregory and myself.

"When I look back to that Ashes series, Australia were the better side and, in terms of their competition, they were better prepared. Even at one-nil down in a series, they had the knowledge, the discipline and the mental toughness to overcome the handicap. Their playing environment gives them that."

Hanley scored 41 tries from loose forward in 1994/95 - a record for a forward - so was he tempted to lace the boots and take part in one more assault on the Australians? "Never. It didn't cross my mind at all. I thought that there were players who would fill the roles much better than I did and would give more to the team.

"My workload was enormous. I was working with the players, trying to get them to peak and to play consistently. I was managing the team and to then play would have been wrong. It wouldn't have worked."

AT the outbreak of Australia's Super League war, Hanley signed a lucrative two-year contract to finish his career with Balmain, the club that he had represented so memorably seven years earlier. They were briefly known as Sydney Tigers before reverting to their traditional name in 1997. He scored three tries and a drop goal in 26 matches in his two-season swansong.

Nineteen years after his professional career began on the bench at Odsal, the final game of Hanley's magnificent career was as a substitute in a 34-10 defeat at Newcastle Knights. In the opposition team that day was Matthew Johns, a future Wigan player, who had recently revealed to the media that he had named his dog Ellery in tribute to the former Great Britain captain.

"[Retiring] wasn't a difficult decision because I'd enjoyed my earlier spells in Australia so much," said Hanley. "The whole experience was fantastic, playing with guys like Benny Elias, Garry Jack, Paul Sironen and a host of other players. I knew I was coming to the end of my career. I played a game up in Newcastle, and I just knew that it was time to retire. I knew that my body didn't want to go through it anymore.

"I'd given everything that I could as a player. I knew that if I continued that I'd let myself down. I'd had a long career and I had to accept that it was time to leave gracefully - like a cricketer who's been bowled out. He has to take the applause and walk away. It was like a weight off my shoulders because I'd had to perform for nearly 20 years at that level. I'd had to be extremely disciplined throughout that time and you're forever scrutinised. After I finished, I could do what I wanted to do."

IT was now time for Hanley to move into full-time coaching. St Helens was his destination. Saints had won two Challenge Cups and a Super League title in 1996 and 1997, but they faded in 1998 and replaced Shaun McRae with Hanley for the start of the 1999 campaign.

It was a tempestuous but ultimately successful year. Saints won their first nine Super League games before losing three games in June. Hanley was sensationally suspended in July after accusing the Saints board of failing to strengthen the squad, claiming that he was having to blood young players who were not ready for the rigours of Super League. He referred to "the dinosaur-like thinking of the directors."

With fans and players pressing for his return, Hanley was reinstated and coached his team to a season-turning 28-12 win at Leeds. Sean Long later described Hanley's pre-game team talk: "We only arrived about 15 minutes before kick-off," the flamboyant playmaker told me. "We were offered a delayed start to help us get ready, but Ellery looked up at the official and just said, 'Don't bother. My players will be ready.' We only just had enough time to get strapped! He gave us the best team talk I've ever heard, and the hairs stood up on the back of my neck. He went through us one by one, telling us how good we were. 'Paul Atcheson, my champion fullback. Kevin Iro and Paul Newlove, the best centres in Super League'. That's how it went, and we went out onto that field that night, knowing we were going to win. And we did."

The win ignited Saints' season. They finished second and, although they were hammered in the play-offs at league leaders Bradford, they turned the tables on the Bulls in the Grand Final with a stunning 8-6 win, with Iro scoring a crucial late try from Atcheson's pass with Long converting. Three ex-Wigan players, four if you include Hanley, had combined to make St Helens champions. The two-week turnaround, masterminded by the 38-year-old coach, was extraordinary.

"I look back on my time at St Helens with an enormous amount of pride," said Hanley. "I had a great time there,

and the players were magnificent. They always gave everything, even when we lost.

"Midway through 1999, there was a dispute between me and the club, but the players rallied round me and told the club that they wanted me back. That told me everything about them. When I was reinstated, one of the things that I said to the players was that they knew how to win football games. And they went on to prove that."

The reunion was only temporary, however. After one Super League game in 2000, Hanley was sacked. Saints detailed three reasons for their decision in their letter to Hanley in March that year.

The letter claimed that Hanley was in 'fundamental breach' of his contract citing three reasons: "At a sponsors' dinner in the early part of this year, you made several comments which offended the reputation of the club. Prior to the Cup defeat to Leeds, you refused to give an interview to the BBC. You failed to attend the launch of Super League V despite request from the Rugby League."

Hanley denied the accuracy of the letter, but Saints quickly employed Ian Millward to replace him. Hanley was out of the game for eight years, apart from a brief spell in a consultancy role at Castleford, until he was unveiled as the coach of Doncaster in 2008. He stayed there for one season and got them promoted to the sport's middle tier after an 18-10 Grand Final win over Oldham.

Rugby League has seen only fleeting glimpses of Hanley in the ensuing years. He's rarely on television or in the papers. He's a lifetime teetotaller who doesn't attend Hall of Fame dinners or Lions reunions, and nobody expects him to. He has an aura of mystery and few in the game appear to be close to him.

What is certain is that Ellery Hanley was the most extraordinary player. Some of the best British players since Hanley's day have been loose forwards like Andy Farrell, Paul Sculthorpe, Kevin Sinfield, Sean O'Loughlin and Sam Burgess, but nobody would claim they were as good as Hanley. Those who watched him play every week for Wigan can count themselves lucky because they witnessed absolute greatness for six truly memorable years.